Interplaces

Interplaces

An Economic Geography of the Inter-urban
and International Economies

Nicholas A. Phelps

OXFORD
UNIVERSITY PRESS

OXFORD

UNIVERSITY PRESS

Great Clarendon Street, Oxford, OX2 6DP,
United Kingdom

Oxford University Press is a department of the University of Oxford.
It furthers the University's objective of excellence in research, scholarship,
and education by publishing worldwide. Oxford is a registered trade mark of
Oxford University Press in the UK and in certain other countries

Published in the United States of America by Oxford University Press
198 Madison Avenue, New York, NY 10016, United States of America

British Library Cataloguing in Publication Data
Data available

Library of Congress Control Number: 2016962082

ISBN 978–0–19–966822–9

Printed and bound by
CPI Group (UK) Ltd, Croydon, CR0 4YY

For 苗田, with all my love.

Preface

My favourite line in the documentary film spoof *This is Spinal Tap* comes when the hapless bass guitarist Derek Smalls of fictitious rock band Spinal Tap describes how 'we are very lucky, in a sense, that we've got two visionaries in the band. David and Nigel are both like poets, like Shelley or Byron or people like that. They are two totally distinct types of visionaries. It's like fire and ice, basically I feel my role in the band is to be kind of in the middle of that, kind of like luke warm water.' Despite the, by now, familiar trap of falling into dualisms or binaries in conceptual academic analysis, the middle ground hardly attracts much intellectual interest or excitement. The middle ground of analysis is often overlooked. Worse still, much like the character Derek Smalls in *This is Spinal Tap*, it can hardly be taken seriously.

I certainly hope that this book is not a tepid affair! I hope it is taken seriously although that is not the same thing as saying that I believe that everyone ought to be interested in it or follow the recipe. Instead the book displays some of my ambivalence as an academic: ambivalence towards some of the more aggressive displays of agenda-setting and self-promotion found in the academy; an ambivalence that sees me enjoy both abstract, macro-historical, or theoretical accounts as well as more micro, empirically-oriented research in economic and urban geography.

Inevitably, then, this book is something of a culmination of much of my interests and writing to this point. In particular it is a pragmatic and inelegant attempt to bring together what have emerged as three main partially connected strands of research on urban agglomeration, the politics and planning of (post)suburbanization, and the economic geography of the multinational enterprise and foreign direct investment. I am grateful to three referees for their comments on an initial proposal and I have done my best to respond to some of the suggestions made to fill gaps in the original coverage envisaged. However, it is also fair to say that the book reached a scope and size that I had not envisaged at the outset and it bears all the marks of my having tried to force it into some sort of shape. It is a curious book in some respects as the research interests on which it is based have existed independently of the teaching I have been responsible for during the past decade or so at the Bartlett School of Planning. It represents the only outlet I have had for many of my major research interests during this time and it has been all the harder to write for this disconnect with my teaching. I am not likely to write a book like this again. As a vent for some of my interests it is also a book into which I have poured quite a few pet frustrations with the present sensibilities of academic geography. Some may say that these are ill-directed or caricature others unfairly. That may be an unfortunate consequence of my own failings, though it was not the intention.

Much of this work has been produced without funding but much of it also does indeed draw on significant funding. In particular I am grateful to: the UK Economic and Social Research Council (grants R000222660, R000223067, RES062-23-0924); the British Academy (grants. SG35081, SG39277, SG100596); the National Geographic Exploration Fund (award GEFNE106-14); the UCL-Abbey Collaboration Fund; the Bartlett School of Planning at University College London; CONICYT (Project 80130003); the Great Britain Sasakawa Foundation (award 4865); and; the Social Science and Humanities Research Council of Canada (MCRI Global Suburbanisms: Governance Land, and Infrastructure in the 21st Century).

Over the years I have researched and written with a number of people and in its outlook this book, as well as many specific examples and some illustrations, it inevitably bears some of the marks of those collaborations. Doubtless, there are many people that I should be thanking by name but among the most notable collaborators to whom I really need to express a real debt of gratitude for intellectual interest and support are the following. Fulong Wu, Mark Tewdwr-Jones, Oleg Golubchikov, Andy Wood, and Dave Valler have been long-time friends and co-authors on topics that feature quite prominently in this book. As always I am grateful for their interest, support, critical comments, and for the solace measured in pints of beer. Several passages of this book draw on work influenced greatly by my involvement in a major international research network directed by Roger Keil at York University. I have benefitted here from attendance at events and conversations with people too numerous to list at this point but Roger's and Ute Lehrer's friendship is greatly appreciated. I have collaborated on and off over the years with Fulong Wu on the application of ideas to China. Miguel Atienza and Gianni Romano were fantastic hosts while I was based as visiting academic at the Universidad Catolica del Norte in Chile in 2014 and 2016 and Miguel, Martin Arias, and Marcelo Lufin and I continue to work on writing and research projects together. I have continued to write with Cris Fuller at Cardiff University on aspects of the economic geography of the multinational enterprise. Past and recent joint work features prominently in Chapter 8. Having dipped my toe into specific parts of the country in 2001, I began to research the cities and economy of Indonesia more seriously from 2007 onwards with Tim Bunnell and Michelle Miller, as well as with Delik Hudalah. Holi Wijaya became a collaborator on research examining small firm-based industry clusters including the batik industry in Central Java. Colleagues Neil Coe, James Sidaway, Lai Wa Wong, Henry and Godfrey Yeung among others at the Department of Geography at National University of Singapore have always made me feel welcome. Thanks go to Robert Kloosterman, Jan Nijman, Willem Salet, and Federico Savini at the University of Amsterdam for being great hosts while I was a Visiting Scholar in Urban Studies. Amparo Tarazona Vento and Sonia Roitman collaborated on work on the Spanish and Argentinian suburbs, some of which also features briefly here. Cristian Silva Lovera, Yingcheng Li, Hiroaki Ohashi, and Khairul Rizal have all helped in the preparation of materials for examples found in passages of particular chapters. I would like to thank Fransisco Ibanez Hantke, and Roseline Wanjiru for supplying their photographs as illustrations in this book.

Thanks are also due to a number of brave souls who volunteered to read draft chapters of the book. John Tomaney, Richard Harris, Andy Jonas, Danny MacKinnon all helped in this regard and are blameless for any errors that have crept in. Donald Hislop and Jamie Peck kindly shared their unpublished work as part of my reading towards the writing of this book.

Notable among those at Oxford University Press who must be thanked are David Musson, commissioning editor, and Clare Kennedy, Assistant Commissioning Editor, both of whom have been very patient with me over several failures to meet deadlines. I am grateful to three reviewers for their supportive comments on the initial book proposal and their constructive suggestions for its expansion. I am also grateful to Miles Irving at UCL for producing the maps and diagrams included in the book.

Finally, much of this book has been written between places. Parts have been written in Portsmouth, the place I call home. Other parts have been written in or travelling to Glasgow and the person that is home. In between is London, the place where I work. If my feelings towards this middle ground of my employer are distinctly ambivalent, my feelings towards the two poles of my life are anything but. Neither the book nor these travels have been easy but, for now at least, something of my intellectual interplace journeys have come to an end.

Nicholas A. Phelps
Portsmouth

Acknowledgements

A number of figures have been reproduced (in some cases redrawn) from previous publications. I am grateful to: Elsevier for permission to reproduce Figure 7.1 which appeared originally in the journal *Cities* in Phelps, Bunnell, Miller and Taylor (2014); Oxford University Press for permission to reproduce Figure 8.2 which originally appeared in the *Journal of Economic Geography* in Phelps and Fuller (2016); Taylor and Francis for permission to reproduce Figures 8.1 and 9.1 which originally appeared in articles published in the journal *Economic Geography* (Phelps and Fuller, 2000; Phelps, Atienza and Arias, 2015); Sage Publishers for permission for Figures 9.1 which originally appeared in Phelps and Tewdwr-Jones (1998) in the journal *Environment & Planning C*; the IDA Ireland for permission to reproduce the cover of their Horizon 2020 Strategy in Figure 11.2.

Contents

List of Figures   xv
List of Tables   xvii

Part I. Introduction

  1. Introduction   3

Part II. Theoretical Framework

  2. Human Geography and Interplaces   15
  3. An Economic Geography of Interplaces   41

Part III. The Inter-Urban Economy

  4. Suburbia   71
  5. The Mid-urban Realm   97
  6. Planes, Trains, and Automobiles   128
  7. Policy Mobility   150

Part IV. The International Economy

  8. The Multinational Enterprise   177
  9. Global Production Networks   202
  10. The Cognitive-cultural Economy   230
  11. The Non-territorial Realm of the International Economy   256

Contents

Part V. Conclusion

12. Conclusion   285

References   297
General Index   337
Name Index   350

List of Figures

3.1	The scope and delimitation of agglomerations, enclaves, networks, and arenas	65
4.1	The entrance and marketing suite of El Pueblo gated residential community, Pilar	82
4.2	The ZODUC developments of Colina	83
5.1	The settlement pattern of the Ruhr	101
5.2	The view west from the Landschaftspark Duisburg	102
5.3	The Yogyakarta–Surakarta corridor	104
5.4	The *desakota* mix of land-uses in Central Java	105
5.5	A new peripheral CBD for Nanjing in Hexi New Town	109
5.6	Signs of new economic activity in Khimki	110
5.7	Office meets residential in central Croydon	111
5.8	The central commercial area of Hachioji city	115
5.9	Motorola's campus in Schaumburg	120
5.10	Kendall Dadeland Downtown	123
6.1	Washington Dulles Airport	134
6.2	The exit ramp economy of Tysons Corner	138
7.1	A snapshot of Solo's travels	169
8.1	Scenarios of intra-corporate competition and local economic development	190
8.2	Processes of organizational change and the development of MNE subsidiary capabilities	191
8.3	The LG site in South Wales	197
9.1	The evolution of the mining town	221
9.2	The former mining town of Pedro de Valdivia	222
9.3	Athi River EPZ	228
11.1	The site selection 'industry'	266
11.2	The imagery of the IDA's Horizon 2020	270
11.3	Suzhou Industrial Park administration building	272

List of Tables

2.1 Continuity and change in the significance of agglomerations, networks, enclaves, and arenas   24

2.2 Alternative explanatory frameworks for four economic geographical formations   33

3.1 Four geographical formations and their logics   64

4.1 Trajectories of settlement change from a first to a second modernity   74

5.1 Employment change in the Yogyakarta–Surakarta corridor   106

6.1 Percentage of respondents engaging in work-related email and mobile phone use, 2008   140

6.2 Work-related tasks on business trips   143

9.1 Summary characteristics of different SEZ enclaves   227

10.1 Top ten investment brands 2014   245

11.1 The role of site selection consultants as bearers of information costs   268

Part I
Introduction

1

Introduction

The Inter-Urban and International Economies

A scan of several dictionaries suggests that 'between', when used adjectivally, describes: an interval, position or person that separates two things; a state of transit; as something joint, shared, or combined. These are just some of the properties that could be attached to what Casey (1993) refers to as *interplaces*. This is a term I take here as shorthand to depict what is (in the original title for this book) an economy in between. Each of these meanings has a relevance to the subject matter of this book. I am interested in the intervals or spaces between the nations and between the cities we have taken—and continue to take—somewhat for granted as the dominant containers of economic activity. I am interested in those individuals and groups of individuals who act as intermediaries between buyers and sellers in the active creation of new economic activities and new markets. I am interested in those economic activities that are only weakly attached to places by virtue of their being undertaken on the move or concerned principally with the movement of people, goods, and ideas. Finally, I am also interested in the notion of the combination of a number of different organizing principles or metaphors—namely the agglomeration, the enclave, the network, and the arena—that comprise the economy in between.

But why bother to study the economy between cities and between nations at all? Isn't it comprised of non-places, empty of economic meaning or value, or spaces that are rather too closely associated with 'the end of distance' (Cairncross, 2001) and 'borderless world' (Ohmae, 1999) theses? Undoubtedly a few of the spaces of the international economy such as the management practices of multinational enterprises (MNEs) or trade, investment, and intellectual property rights negotiations are charged with the sort of money, power, and sex displayed by the global finance industry (McDowell, 1988; Thrift, Leyshon, and Daniels, 1987)—the focus of much recent attention within economic geography. They at least present a story, perhaps, of 'MNEs and wannabes' (Lovering, 1993). However, many other interplaces seem a far cry from these most vigorous parts of the economy. Nor do they often embody the sorts of objects of study that conform to the self-image of many academics—in their banality, it seems, they have rarely been thought a laboratory fit for the *cognoscenti*. As Haruki Murakami puts it, 'There's a shadowy middle ground' in the hours *After Dark*. 'Recognizing and understanding the shadows is what a healthy intelligence does. And to acquire a healthy intelligence takes a certain amount of time and effort.' Interplaces require a bit of time and effort to appreciate. They are often not especially exciting or hospitable places for academic study. Often little or no adequate secondary data related to interplaces are collected and published.

This book will seek to demonstrate that the interplaces that make up an economy in between are important in both quantitative and qualitative terms. The majority of us in the world are now said to live in officially defined urban areas, though presumably the majority of us live in suburbs of one kind or another. This alone implies that a quantitatively significant part of the world economy takes place in the suburbs—the realm we understand to be somewhere between the city and the country. Some of us work in sizeable suburban employment centres or 'edge cities' like Tysons Corner—midway between Washington DC downtown and the Washington Dulles international airport.

An edge city like Tysons Corner is only one example—a very conspicuous and by now familiar example—of an economy, physically at least, in between cities and nations—the geographic 'containers' that we continue to use as reference points when accounting for stocks and flows of economic activity. Take, for example, the sorts of personal mobility—physical and virtual—which make many interplaces of the contemporary economy less conspicuous. Such personal mobility has not collapsed life, nor work-life, into a non-place urban realm—at least not yet. 'Spatial mobility is not an interstice, or a neutral liaison time between a point of origin and a destination. It is a structuring dimension of social life and social integration' (Kaufmann, 2002: 103, quoted in Kellerman, 2012: 51). Yet it is also true to see that 'our life experiences are . . . constantly embedded in all categories and forms of mobility and fixity and our complex personal needs structured into them simultaneously and interfolded. Specific balances among all the mobility and fixity categories are personal' (Kellerman, 2012: 30). The key word here is balance. By the same token, I might suggest that interplaces are important precisely as an outcome of the personal physical and virtual mobility that Kaufmann sees as so central to social life.

We seek and are able to find a measure of balance in our physical and virtual work-life on the move in a variety of places. Some of them we only perceive dimly as new realms of economic activity while others—such as coffee shops and motorway service stations have become familiar as 'new' sites of significant work. Increasingly, the home—for many of us in the suburbs of some description—has become a place to strike such a balance (or not!) between work, leisure, and familial care—an anchor point for all of our daily movements local and far flung. Before we arrive at, and after we leave, a place like Tysons Corner we traverse this middle landscape of residential suburbia whose outward appearance gives little or no clue as to the quantity or importance of economic activity contained within. A rather bald fact—such as 80 per cent of metropolitan population growth in the United States has been suburban (Kotkin, 2010: 131)—should be enough to tell us that the suburbs are important in economic terms, yet we have been slow to draw together the existing evidence which remains quite scattered across different disciplinary contributions.

The in between economy of interplaces is also important in *qualitative* terms as registered in the central position that intermediary industries and occupations play in the 'lash-ups' that help to produce, and speed up the production of, 'stuff' (Miller, 2010; Molotch, 2004) of all sorts in geographically extensive networks of production. Intermediaries as 'symbolic analysts' (Reich, 1991) add value in the cognitive-cultural economies (Scott, 2008, 2011) of the global north and even some part of the economies of the global south, though it is a value that is often quite hard to grasp empirically.

To some extent we take as read the power of MNEs as actors with an international reach to influence subnational and national conditions of work, remuneration, and even the regulation of economic activity. I would not want to deny this, not least because after something little short of an uncritical infatuation on the part of policy-makers and academics alike with the positive contributions of MNEs as bearers of scarce capital and technology, a whole host of 'old' complaints have resurfaced in the guise of tax avoidance, transfer pricing, exploitation of monopoly position, regulatory capture, and rent seeking by these same companies. The MNE itself, as perhaps *the* primary agent of international capitalism, embodies an economy in between. As a legal entity it is effectively a string of national companies (Kobrin, 2009). Yet a large part of international trade is by now intra-corporate—a reflection of the fact that as a strategic economic actor, the MNE seeks in the mobilization of resources and servicing of markets to transcend such national boundaries. The MNE might be considered a hybrid entity. Its network of facilities and operating units continues to touch down in distinctly territorial terms and it continues to take advantage of its peculiar differentiated legal basis to arbitrage on national differences or discontinuities (Beugelsdijk and Mudambi, 2013) while simultaneously seeking to exploit the managerial advantages of integrating and sequencing activities across national borders. In contrast to the tenor of much recent economic geography and international business literature, in Chapter 8 I seek to highlight the hybrid character of the MNE as embodying elements of network and hierarchical organization and its touching down internationally in often territorially circumscribed ways.

To be sure, much has changed in a very short time in ways that undermined received theory of the MNE. Businesses are now born global in a way they were not in the past with many of these apparent in the fashioning of ever more geographically extensive global production networks (GPNs). Here a range of other actors—such as trade unions, non-governmental organizations (NGOs) and the like can and have been woven into the picture. Moreover this picture of global production stretched across networks also presents a picture of the many intermediate stages of production and consequently the many intermediate places woven into the international economy in what Jacobs (1969) highlighted positively as one borne of the opportunities presented in a pattern of 'triangular trade'. It is these intermediate activities and locations that I highlight when discussing the rise of GPNs in Chapter 9.

Less familiar or immediately obvious than the MNE in accounting for the travels of commodities of all sorts in GPNs is the work in service of the international economy that is done by business service and other specialist intermediaries. These intermediaries help to make markets for these companies and bear some of the costs of operating in and across places. Some by contrast are at work in the endless rounds of trade, investment, and intellectual property rights negotiations and investment dispute tribunals and closed meetings between investment promotion agencies and potential investors. In contrast to the sorts of enclaves that continue to be part of the mode of operation of MNEs, this work takes place in rather different economic geographical formations. On the one hand, the people involved are often part of professional networks that are international in scope. On the other hand, they meet in particular places that yet could not be said to be of any place in particular. That is, they meet and make decisions that greatly affect international economic activity in specialized arenas. Lest we view the activities taking place in such *arenas* as simply regulatory or imposing costs on economic actors, it is as well to remember that there are huge economic gains to be had from them, and consequently much corporate and state lobbying that is focused on them.

These are all examples of places and spaces that speak to the fact that much of economic activity now somehow takes place between cities and nations—the containers of social, economic, cultural life that we take for granted. The examples I focus on in this book are interplaces of the inter-urban and international economies. Something of the banality of this economy in between the national is signified in the fact that the hyphen between inter and national has been missing for some time now. Inter- has ceased to be a prefix. It has been lost in the taken-for-granted coupling of nation and state that has invested analytical and popular discourse on the two and relations between them. Perhaps it has already seeped into our consciousness, so much so that it no longer needs exploration or examination? So seemingly commonplace are its places and spaces that we have lost interest in inventing new terms to explain or re-describe them—yet, ironically, we are, if anything, in greater need of rethinking the geographical basis of the international economy than ever before (Agnew, 2005).

Compare and contrast the terminological invention at the inter-urban scale as commentators struggle to name the explosion of the urban from its bounds of the city 'proper' with the quite modest and very recent deployment of terms such as 'glocal' to try to gain an analytical purchase on the inter-national economy. The inter-urban economy is something that we are still coming to terms with despite significant evidence of it. We are less comfortable with it, and as a consequence academic terminology has proliferated in an attempt to make some sense of its meaning. The implications of the emerging distributed pattern of work seem clear by now. Not only will economic activity increasingly be at places distributed outside what historically has been their primary container and our primary analytical reference point—the city—but also, logically, much of present and future economic activity will also take place on the move in interplaces as part of an increasingly distributed—inter-urban—economy.

Studying Interplaces

This book privileges the prefix inter- as an object of analysis for economic geography. At the risk of overusing this prefix it argues that an interdisciplinary perspective is needed on the notable interplaces of the inter-urban and international economies. In this book, then, I pull together insights from geography, urban sociology, international business and management, development studies, and international relations among other disciplines in order to understand the economy in between. I can be sure of one thing, I suppose, and that is that for some I will have failed overall with this cocktail. For many others I will doubtless have misrepresented important insights or findings of their respective disciplinary and preferred theoretical or conceptual camps. So be it.

It has become quite common in academic works for authors to call for a new lexicon to describe the world around us. Perhaps it remains an important part of the academic economy. In this book, beyond developing an explicit focus on what I refer to as interplaces or an economy in between, I have by and large wanted to resist the temptation to generate new terminology. I draw my general inspiration instead from what has been a long-standing duality ingrained deeply in our very being—that between place and space (Casey,

1993, 1997; Entrikin, 1991). The book opens in the next chapter by situating some of the specific economic geographical interests of this book in the wider field of inquiry within human geography. Space can only be overcome by the production of space—the contradictions of existing spatial fixes of capitalism can only be transcended by the production of new spaces of accumulation. This process has often been represented as one of the organization of human affairs at successively greater scales or the switching of capital into and out of territorial containers. However, the fuller annihilation of space by time implied in increased personal physical and virtual mobility has also brought forward an interest in non-territorial metaphors such as networks, rhizomes, flows, virtuality/simultaneity (Hess, 2004; Thrift and Olds, 1996), as well as terms such as 'glocalization' that do indeed in their own way offer a picture of the interplace economy. While such terminological innovation has been enormously popular with geographers there remain methodological questions over the tractability of these concepts in empirical research, whether they have real world analogues and whether they can be adequately verified in empirical research.[1]

My contention is that much, though by no means all, of this production of space does *not* result in such non-territorial forms of organization. Rather much of this production of space involves the coexistence of geographical formations or is manifest in formations that—as interplaces—lie somewhere in between. In more specific terms, as well as acknowledging the contemporary relevance and power of the *network* metaphor to understanding the organization of economic activities, I also draw on concepts that are by now well established in economic geography—such as the concepts of *agglomeration* and *enclave*. These I have continued to refer to—albeit with notable revision—to help chart the inter-urban economy. Yet, in this economic geography, I do mobilize one less familiar concept taken from the international political economy literature. Drawing upon Latham (2001) I distinguish the *arena* as a distinctly different trans-territorial formation. 'The network society has exploded limits, between human and non-human, between nation states, between the cultural and the material' (Lash, 1999: 344). Quite so; however the network is but one fully non-territorial or topological analytical metaphor and in this book I am concerned to place it alongside both traditional territorial metaphors (such as agglomeration) and concepts (such as deployments/enclaves and arenas) that lie in between these topological and territorial opposites. The terms deployment/enclave and arena are useful for my purposes in continuing to emphasize enduring if partial elements of fixity and place

---

[1] The term glocal/glocalization was later effectively lampooned in the film *Up in the Air*—presenting the unsettling thought of critical social theory unwittingly leading corporate management gobbledy-gook.

in a world it can be rather too easy to assume is entirely networked and mobile. The simple point I will reiterate at length in this book is that the geographic organization of the contemporary economy is neither purely one of agglomerations (place) or networks (space). Instead the geography of economic organization is one in between the major territorial containers we take for granted, is one in which some or all of these four concepts are seen to coexist and also one in which some economic geographical formations (notably the enclave and arena) could themselves be regarded as interplaces. Indeed, the concepts of deployments/enclaves and arenas may provide some of the very best examples of the genuinely relational character of economic activities, their being hybrid place/spaces—themselves somehow between the concepts of agglomeration and network.

In putting forward a theory of the geographically uneven nature of development in capitalism, Smith (1984: x) was able to observe how what a political economy approach 'gains in historical sensibility it lacks in geographical sensibility'. A lot has changed with respect to this geographical sensibility since then. The logic of urban economic agglomeration—seemingly a perennial topic in geography and economics in the preceding hundred years or so—has been advanced considerably by a number of geographers. There have been several incarnations of what—following Massey's (1984) own contribution on uneven development—has come to be termed, perhaps a little loosely, a relational approach. These relational approaches have culminated recently in an almost singular emphasis on the network as an organizing principle of economic activity. In arguing for an economic geography of the in-between, I try here to add to this geographical sensibility centred on agglomerations and networks by championing the concepts of the enclave—long apparent but rather neglected in comparison to the subject of agglomeration—and the arena.

My placing of enclave and arena alongside agglomeration and network as geographical organizing principles serves several purposes. The least important of these is that reference to a variety of coexisting principles of geographical organization of economic activity within capitalism can fulfil the objective of depicting a literal inter-urban and international middle ground of places and spaces that are important in economic terms. More importantly, taken together I believe they give a broader perspective on the production of space within capitalism implied in the dualities of differentiation and equalization, mobility and fixity, space and place, agglomerations and networks. These geographical antinomies can hardly be escaped for what they produce in terms of a dialectic to capitalism and necessitate in our academic method of analysis, but they have often had the inadvertent effect of precipitating lurches in academic endeavour between singular or overgeneralized accounts written from particular places and moments in time.

I suggest that enclave and arena when added to agglomeration and network contribute significantly to our vocabulary when seeking to understand contemporary economic geography.

The Structure of the Book

The book is organized into five parts, with this brief introduction forming a first part. A fifth part is composed of a conclusion which seeks to draw together some of the broader theoretical and policy implications of the perspective developed in this book.

In Part 2, I first set out the philosophical and methodological framework for the remaining substantive chapters of the book contained in Parts 3 and 4. I begin in Chapter 2 by setting a discussion of the economy of interplaces within the broader context of philosophical and methodological perspectives in human geography. Here, in Chapter 2, I seek to recover some of the original sentiments and thrust of what has been described as a relational human geography that has evolved through several incarnations (Yeung, 2005). I seek to recover some of Massey's (1984) and Entrikin's (1991) original emphasis in a relational perspective on the economy and society as one *between* an understanding of the uniqueness of place and the generality of relations stretched across space. In the following chapter, Chapter 3, I set out some possible ways of gaining an analytical purchase on the interplace economy—the places and spaces of the economy in between. The chapter is partial to my own views and preferences. I begin by noting the importance of intermediaries and intermediation to an economy in between. I go on to recover and rework the theory of agglomeration in ways that take account of the increasingly distanciated nature of economic relations and the collective economic benefits—external economies—that promote the concentration of economic activities in particular places. Less familiar to economic geographers here will be the work of Latham (2001) in international political economy, which I will draw upon. Latham distinguishes between deployments, arenas, and networks as transnational formations. Throughout this book I equate his term 'deployment' with the term 'enclave', partly in order to present the deployment as agglomeration's place-based 'other', as it were. Moreover, although Latham's use of these three terms is geared towards understating the international economy, I use these terms and the concept of agglomeration to highlight aspects of both the international and inter-urban economy. That is, all four key concepts—agglomeration, deployments/enclaves, arenas, and networks—are useful to greater or lesser extent and in different ways to grasp economic relations that transcend the familiar territorial containers of cities and nations.

In Part 3 I concentrate on elaborating the perspectives outlined in Part 2 with respect to some substantive concerns regarding the inter-urban economy. I begin by discussing the in between geography of suburbia in Chapter 4. Suburbs are diverse and deceptive in their appearance, housing a significant part of the economy of city-regions though to be sure their fortunes are varied. Nucleations or agglomerations of economic activity have been integral interplaces in the growth of industrial suburbs from the very start. More recent subtle transformations of residential suburbs into places of work of all sorts depend on the sorts of networks of relations facilitated by greater personal physical and virtual mobility. The home itself becomes a nodal point in inter-urban and international networks. To some extent the growth of the inter-urban economy has overtaken labels such as city and suburb, which have become 'zombie' categories (Lang and Knox, 2009). Instead, then, in Chapter 5 I describe how—following trends set in motion some time ago—the distinctly territorial or enclosed manifestations of shopping malls, corporate campuses as deployments or enclaves have become strung-out across sizeable metropolitan, megapolitan, corridors that compose a mid-urban realm. In Chapter 6 I go on to look at these inter-urban and international corridors formed from the specialized infrastructures that support mobility such as airports, railway lines and stations, and highways. While, as a result of some of the fixed infrastructures and the economic agglomerations they promote, much of this economic activity continues to produce distinct places, the mobility these infrastructures seek to promulgate is one involving liminal spaces of significant work done on the move in planes, trains, and automobiles. I attempt to tease out the economic significance of movement from the fragmentary evidence buried in bodies of literature that have focused, in the main, on the social and cultural meaning of these liminal spaces. Finally, in this section, I turn my attention in Chapter 7 to the subject of policy mobility which recently has become one of the most vibrant topics of discussion within human geography. Again much of this literature barely touches on questions of the economic as opposed to the political, social, and cultural significance of such policy exchange. I attempt to draw out some of the economic content and significance of such urban policy mobility when linking a discussion of it to processes to inter-urban competition and the elements of inertia that necessarily attend the urbanization of capital (Harvey, 1985).

In Part 4, I go on to discuss the in-betweenness of the international economy. I begin in Chapter 8 by considering the changing organizational form of, and coordination exercised by, the multinational enterprise (MNE) as simultaneously a transnational organization and yet one that often touches down in ways that remain highly territorial. I use the term MNE here precisely in order to emphasize the enduring territoriality of the MNE in contradistinction to the term transnational corporation (TNC) which tends to overemphasize the deterritorialized character of this key agent within the international economy. In Chapter 9, I underline the ambiguous or dual nature of the global production networks (GPNs) that are said to characterize modern-day international trade and production. Intermediaries are important to the functioning and stretching of these GPNs. Moreover, GPNs often touch down in the form of enclaves or industry agglomerations which are more familiarly regarded as territorialized forms of industry organization. In Chapter 10 I turn to the seemingly ubiquitous economy of signs and symbols as one centred on intermediation—a process in which value and markets are created. The discussion here includes consideration of the symbolic economy of territories—cities and nations—as brands. Finally, the international economy is supported by what could be regarded as a raft of policy and economic intermediaries such as lawyers, investment promotion professionals, and conference and trade show organisers which I discuss in Chapter 11. Doubtless they are partially organized as, and interpreted as being, professional networks. However, much of their business is done in distinct arenas that are in particular places but not of any particular place.

In a concluding chapter I begin by noting some of the omissions or silences in a book like this. I then go on to take a critical look at the how the role of intermediaries in the economy might need to be questioned and challenged. Likewise, it is important to consider the iniquities associated with the organization of economic activities in the four geographical formations considered here. While this book hopefully deploys the four concepts of agglomerations, deployments/enclaves, arenas and networks in ways which will be provocative, there are few if any easy recipes here for policy.

Part II
Theoretical Framework

2

Human Geography and Interplaces

Introduction

'What is place in this in-between world?' (Thrift, 1996: 212–13, quoted in Cresswell, 2004: 80). For Thrift and others, answering this question has entailed a marked move towards non-representational theory. In this chapter I argue for returning human geography to an ontological middle ground (Entrikin, 1991) between the two extremes of the sedentarist and nomad metaphysics that have been evident in human geography over the years (Cresswell, 2006); between, that is, an understanding of place and the spatial implications of processes. They are just that; extremes of perspective and the logical implication is that understanding in human geography is best promoted from dialectic thought that seeks to embrace both. Even within a sedentarist focus on places, the 'inside/outside attribute of place means that a relational perspective that is the heart of human geography demands the simultaneous involvement of more than one perspective' (Sack, 1992: 13). Moreover, even in a world of unprecedented virtual and physical mobility there remains a need to problematize 'both "sedenterist" approaches... that treat place, stability, and dwelling as a natural steady-state, and "deterritorialized" approaches that posit a new "grand narrative" of mobility, fluidity or liquidity as a pervasive condition of postmodernity or globalization' (Hannam, Sheller, and Urry, 2006: 5, quoted in McCann, 2011: 112).

This betweenness of human geographical affairs (Entrikin, 1991) is registered in other ways. In terms of theory building alone, the betweenness of our experiences suggests a renewed focus on meso-levels of abstraction as links between the particularities of place and the universalities of processes and their spatial ramifications. This might imply specific meso-level theories such as the mechanisms linking structure and agency in critical realistic approaches (Sayer, 1984), or structuration theory (Giddens, 1984), though economic geography might be better served in dialectic thought and method than the adoption of particular middle-range theories. Analysis of the interplace economy also implies human geographical inquiry striking a balance between theoretical abstraction and empirical description and verification. Arguably, perhaps the main strength of geography as a discipline has been its empirical content in comparison to the theoretical rigour of, say, economics. There is a reason for this and that is that the geographer is immediately confronted with an areal differentiation that cannot be assumed away. However, by today it is apparent that a premium has been placed on abstract theory building within human geography.

I argue that there is an enduring need in economic geography to generate a limited but adequate variety of geographical concepts with which to analyse contemporary phenomena. Recent tendencies for the place/space debate to collapse into oppositions between scale *or* networks have been unhelpful. My preference is for a limited set of concepts—some of which themselves lie somewhere between scalar or territorial metaphors on the one hand and network or topological metaphors on the other. To prefigure Chapter 3, the categories I suggest—the concepts of agglomeration, enclave, network, and arena—serve to highlight different but often coexisting principles of economic geographical organization in capitalist economies.

The value of deploying a limited conceptual arsenal in this way lies partly also in the fact that analysts locate themselves in a way such that the sorts of normative statements regarding the way the world could be (which follow from modernist theory-building) are reconciled as far as possible with the analytics of post-modernist critique of the multiple ways the world actually is. The process of objectification implied in such normative statements is an alienating one that has unintended and unanticipated consequences though it is as inescapable as the process of subject formation in our lives. It is this tension that often lies at the heart of questions of intervention flowing from economic geographical analysis.

The betweenness of being in modernity is an uneasy everyday experience. As Rabinow (1986: 258, quoted in Entrikin, 1991: 44–5) observes, 'What we share as a condition of existence . . . is a specificity of historical experience and place . . . and a worldwide macro-interdependency encompassing any local particularity . . . we seem to have trouble with the balancing act, preferring to reify local identities or construct universal ones. We live in-between.' In this respect, every individual mediates between some sense of place vital for a sense of self in a wider world and the loss of such a sense implied in the distanciated relations of space. Our living in between also provides a puzzle that is difficult for the academic geographer to solve definitively. To try to stand up straight in this middle ground and to absorb and reconcile extremes of experience in our own work implies no easy escape off into theoretical abstraction at the expense of empirical research and validation (the critique that might be levelled at some political economy or indeed regional science inspired work), nor a retreat into an endless often descriptive rendering of the particularities of places and people and differences among them revealed in detailed empirical research—the criticism that might be levelled at area studies and 'old style' regional geography. It is a rewarding, if somewhat presently overlooked, spot to stop and make a life of academic inquiry.

Between Nomothetic and Idiographic Perspectives

'To be at all—to exist in any way—is to be somewhere, and to be somewhere is to be in some kind of place' (Casey, 1997: ix). Despite its primordial properties, place has been overlooked in the long history philosophy. Indeed, 'At work... in the obscuration of place is the universalism inherent in Western culture from the beginning' (Casey, 1997: xii). This observation immediately sets the context for understanding more recent writings of geographers that have typically been understood as a divide between nomothetic and idiographic approaches; between, that is, theoretical approaches oriented to uncovering causal mechanisms or processes common to different places and approaches that concentrate on understanding and explaining the uniqueness of particular places. However, place-making and the making sense of place appear as processes in which 'concrete actions of primal place-instauration stand midway between the abstractions of cosmogonies/cosmologies and the existential predicament of place-bereft individuals' (Casey, 1997: 6).

It might be tempting to search for middling theories to capture these concrete actions of place-making that stand midway, and this is what Miller laments of many disciplines. Such middling theory is not necessarily what I have in mind in this book but rather the 'advantages to the simultaneous commitment to the extremes of particularity and generality' (Miller, 2010: 9) that the geography discipline seems well placed to exploit. Such a simultaneous commitment to nomothetic and idiographic perspectives in geography focuses attention on a series of tensions, paradoxes, and contradictions of human existence; tensions, paradoxes, and contradictions that arguably have become more pronounced within capitalism and with the more complex, hierarchical but also simultaneously more heterogeneous organization of society preceding the rise of capitalism (Dodgshon, 1987).

Entrikin (1991: 134) renders these thoughts in terms familiar to geographers when noting how:

> the divide between the existential and naturalistic conceptions of place appears to be an unbridgeable one... The closest that we can come to addressing both sides of this divide is from a point in between, a point that leads us into the vast realm of narrative forms.... we gain a sense of being 'in a place' and 'at a location', of being

at the center and being at a point in a centerless world. To ignore either aspect of this dualism is to misunderstand the modern experience of place.

The first instances of a relational approach within human geography were also ones with a substantive concern with economic activities. Massey (1984: 21) argued that 'the challenge is to...understand the general underlying causes while at the same time recognizing and appreciating the importance of the specific and the unique'. The approach in this book follows Massey's early work and that of Entrikin (1991: 3) in adopting a perspective that necessarily lies between centred and decentred views. The dualistic quality of place/space should remain at the heart of geographical analysis as 'the geographer's concept of specific place draws attention to the relation between particularizing and universalizing discourses and between subjective and objective practices' (Entrikin, 1991: 6). If this is a perspective somewhat neglected by geographers recently, it is one that anthropologist Miller appreciates when arguing that 'the term relationship refers to an inherent tension between the general category that a person inhabits and the specifics of that person' (Miller, 2010: 123).

Economic geographers Bathelt and Glückler (2011: 25) 'recognize a comprehensive transition in economic geography towards a relational conceptualisation' composed of a diverse set of trends and approaches in economic geography since the regional geography and regional science traditions that held sway until the 1980s. Yeung (2005) draws on much of this literature to depict several incarnations of a relational approach in economic geography.[1] Across these different incarnations I would suggest that something of the sentiments of the original relational approaches of Massey and Entrikin have been lost. In particular, some of the reasonableness of early incarnations of a relational approach—with its retaining an interest in the territoriality of human activity and non-territorial relations that potentially cut across place— has evaporated. The original sentiments of a relational approach appear to have been lost in developments that have been termed relational but which have focused seemingly ever more on relations that are to all intents and purposes not place-bound. There is little to disagree with in the desire to place action and interaction at the heart of a relational economic geography and to avoid treating space as a container of economic activities as Bathelt and Glückler (2011: 26) argue—indeed this book is premised largely on that thought. However, I part company with Bathelt and Glückler (2011: 26) in

---

[1] There have perhaps been three further incarnations of a relational approach during the 1990s and into the 2000s. Yeung (2005) distinguishes relational approaches which have focused on relational assets in local and regional development, those focused on relational embeddedness in networks and those focused on relational scales to note how some of the original theorists within the social relations of production version of relational geography have also moved their position and been active in these reincarnations.

elevating these concerns to the exclusion of 'space and spatial categories'. The generation of categories has long been an important part of a discipline whose strength is its attention to empirical variation. Spatial categories provide in an imperfect way for such empirical variation and should be thought of not as ends in themselves but as a valuable means of exposition for how economic relations produce economic geographic landscapes. Lost in all of this is also the connection between a relational economic geography and dialectical Marxian analysis as the former has evolved towards post-structuralism and a 'flat' ontology (Sheppard, 2008: 2608). To be sure, these losses are ones of degree rather than being absolute, though I believe they are ones that geographers should be wary of. Following Howitt (1998), Marston (2000) notes how the first two of scale's three facets of size, level, and relation are insufficient to unify a social constructionist view of scale, though it could equally be argued that flat ontologies (in which the latter is shorn of the former two) risk obscuring place again just when it seemed to have been rediscovered, since 'If space and place are both already relational, a sheer *order* of coexisting points, then they do not retain any of the inherent properties ascribed to them by ancient and early modern philosophers: properties of encompassing, holding, sustaining, gathering, situating' (Casey, 1997: 183).

Between the Past and the Future, Stasis and Change

Economic activities have never been as place-bound as past accounts in an economic geography of regional specialization and industrial agglomeration would have had us believe. However, nor are we and nor will they be, any time soon, as place-less as some of the recent critiques of this established metaphor found in contemporary economic geographical analysis would have us believe. Human beings and their relations are, as always, somewhere—even if on the move—in between.

Indeed, human societies have been on a very long journey somewhere between a nomadic and a progressively more geographically fixed existence (Dodgshon, 1987). Yet the contemporary sensibilities of human geography might be regarded as 'presentist'—often lacking much of an attention span and ignoring history (Peck, 2015: 18). If, then, from the vantage point of current sensibilities in human geography, theories have somehow appeared to reify places as containers, it is as well to remember that this undoubtedly reflects some of the limits of our finite minds to comprehend change over time and the constant flux of an infinite reality (Entrikin, 1991). As geographers we are perhaps rightly more fascinated with the complexity and flux apparent in the real world out there than some of our counterparts in economics or sociology, for example, whose theory-building tends towards the overly parsimonious. However, the limits of finite minds to contemplate an infinite reality also present real difficulties with what appears to be a drift in the direction of 'metatheorizing' in economic geography. Properly relational human and economy geography is not as all-encompassing or as linguistically fluid as such meta-theorizing seems to demand and consider possible.

Viewed in very long-term historical perspective, there is something of a paradox. Evolution in the organization of societies reveals both a greater complexity manifest in hierarchical organization and a greater fixity of civilization in place. 'Approached from an organizational perspective, societal systems can be seen as evolving through a succession of increasingly complex forms, moving from homogeneity to heterogeneity and uniformity to hierarchy' (Dodgshon, 1987: 5). Such societal processes of hierarchical ordering can be seen to have reached a high point in the 'organized capitalism' (Lash and Urry, 1991) of modernity which in turn can hardly be separated from the techniques used both to create states and then used by them in their literal production of territory and representations of it (Elden, 2011). The importance of an historical perspective even in relation more specifically to the rise of the modern nation state is vital since 'The national state ... whose existence is validated by the very concept of cross-national comparisons, is seen by historians as historically specific and as much a product of the processes they are investigating as an organiser or container of them' (Sutcliffe, 1986: 4). Commenting on the global reach of modernity, Bayly reminds us how the 'ambivalent relationship between the global and the local, the general and the specific had a long history before the present age' (Bayly, 2000: 2). The rise of what Jones (2005) describes as a second global economy of the present nevertheless 'depends on very particular places' (Moore, 2002: 481, cited in Carroll, 2010). What this alerts us to is how the very processes implicated in the production and reproduction of the scales of human organization that we take for granted—cities, nations, and the global—have also simultaneously produced alternative in between geographical formations (e.g. Jonas, 2006). If the city, nation, and the global have been the dominant scalar frames of reference for much economic geographical research, it is also the case that agglomeration, enclave, network, and arena highlighted in this book can be alternative and valuable frames of reference for analysis.

Recent writing highlights the disorganization of capitalism as a key feature of post-modernity.[2] Increasing personal mobility appears to imply dissolution of community including the anchoring of economic activities to place. What are we to make of this? In some respects the two perspectives—of organized places giving way to disorganized spatial relations—are not as incommensurable

---

[2] Rather than adopt a post-modern perspective on contemporary economic life, the term 'second modernity' used by Ulrich Beck underlines the fundamental continuities apparent in the unintended side effects of modern state interventions.

as one might at first think. After all, the new hypermobilities are also associated with significant socio-economic inequality characterized by 'spikes' (Iammarino and McCann, 2013) and 'stickiness' (Markusen, 1996). In this sense there are important continuities with the ranking and stratification that produced distinct geographical centres in societies long before the advent of capitalism as an economic system (Dodgshon, 1987: 88). Yet in other respects the basis of mobilities in 'network capital' (Elliott and Urry, 2010) implies a loosening of the hierarchy associated with the accumulation of capital over lifetimes or inter-generationally in favour of a less hierarchical set of social relations.

Even if the way we think about and represent territory have shaped theoretical approaches in economic geography, notably in favour of flat ontologies, the process of producing territory has not waned, let alone disappeared. Osterhammel's (2014: 110) history of the first (nineteenth-century) global economy reminds us that 'The rounding off of national spaces, where government control and emotional attachment centre on a single unambiguously defined territory, went hand in hand with the development of transnational spaces whose territorial moorings were weaker but by no means nonexistent' (Osterhammel, 2014: 110). What this points to is the need to retain a sense of the territorial alongside the non-territorial in economic affairs in the present moment—not least because of important continuities from modernity to a second modernity.

Recent calls for a topologically-oriented perspective on the organization of society (Allen, 2011) in lieu of outworn references to territory and scale have been exposed as somewhat ahistorical in their neglect of the continued significance of places as containers of social relations alongside the networks which are now seen to transcend them. 'Boundaries are an *outcome* of a concept of territory, rather than its condition' (Elden, 2011: 305) and, viewed in long-term history, the outcomes of human conceptions of territory have only comparatively recently been rendered in terms of territoriality.[3] Hunter-gatherer bands, for example, did not have a strong sense of territoriality though with the emergence of tribal forms of societal organization 'spatial order became structured around points and localities' (Dodgshon, 1987: 39 and 86 respectively). As Dodgshon (1987: 88) goes on to note, the subsequent emergence of ranking and stratification in chiefdoms represented a qualitative and systemic change in the organization of society. It marked the establishment of society in territory, though the establishment of territoriality in society came later (Dodgshon, 1987: 130) with the conscious and

---

[3] That is 'territory needs to be examined as a *historical* question ... It is *geographical*, not simply because it is one of the ways of ordering the world' but also because it 'signifies the emergence of a conception of space as ... something to be objectified, owned distributed, mapped, calculated, bordered and controlled' (Elden, 2010: 812 and 810).

active application of techniques to secure sovereign state power territorially with the rise of modernity. Seen in this light, the thought that 'the forging of networks represents a type of social and economic behavior that is timeless: it is an innovation neither of the nineteenth nor the twenty-first centuries' (Magee and Thompson, 2010: 59) may be overstating the case. It may be more accurate to suggest that 'The self-image of societies as networks...has its roots in the nineteenth century, even if the full range of meanings—up to today's "social networks"—appeared only much later' (Osterhammel, 2014: 711). In more specific terms 'the twenty-first century belatedly rediscovered empire' (Magee and Thompson, 2010: 22), with the networks of social, economic, and political relations of empires having been, to an extent, reactivated in contemporary global production networks (GPNs).

It may be that we are at a point of punctuation in long-term history where human conceptions of territory will prompt a decisive de-territorialization. Fundamentally, this is a question we cannot answer without the benefit of the sort of historical perspective that none of us will gain in our own lifetimes. However, what existing historical perspectives such as Dodgshon's (1987, 1998) ask us to do, I think, is to retain a sense of the *inertia* that characterizes society and to continue to entertain the significance of place and hierarchical forms of societal and economic organization in any rush to view a compressed, instantaneous world brought together exclusively or even primarily in topological, distanciated networks of relations.

To go further, it is important to pay attention to the history and geography of the way in which space—including interplaces—has been *produced* as a result of the overcoming of the contradictions of previous spatial 'fixes'. It is here that an appreciation of the production of space in modernity and second modernity must focus on the geography *between* scales and the potential variety found there (Jonas, 2006), not least because the key actor and scale inherited by the capitalist system—the nation state—is an active mediator of the accumulation process. Moreover, by now, much of this production is a *re*production of existing social space in the form of particular geographical formations. That is 'we produce only the reproducible, and hence we produce only by replacing or imitating past production. This is the ultimate contradiction: in as much as the capacity to produce space produces only reproductions, it can generate nothing but the repetitive, nothing but repetition. The production of space is thus transformed into its opposite' (Lefebvre, 1991: 377). There are a number of geographical formations—such as networks—but also agglomerations and enclaves—which have been visible historically and continue to be *re*produced alongside others—notably arenas—that ostensibly are recent *productions*.

Between Modernity and Post-modernity: The Production of Space in Second Modernity

If the preceding discussion highlighted an important sense of long-term continuity in the relevance of place to the organization of economic activities, then such continuities also remain in the present. They press for a perspective that seeks to understand and chart a world that exists somewhere between modernity and a second modernity. Figure 2.1 provides a suggestion of how the four different geographical formations have coexisted, have been (re)produced in the eras of modernity and second modernity, and how they have waxed and waned over this time-frame.

For Entrikin (1991) the betweenness of place means that an understanding of particular places is central to understanding modernity. Moreover, it could be argued that place has taken on a renewed significance in a second modernity (Beck, 1992; Beck, Bonss, and Lau, 2003). The first modernity had a counterpart-grounded critique based on local substantive practices of community (Lash, 1999). Indeed, for some, this critique and the internal inconsistencies of modernity have meant that we have never been modern (Latour, 1993). A second modernity is just as much grounded and place-based as it is groundless and placeless—though a thoroughly modern rather than traditional sense of place inheres within a second modernity according to Scott Lash. 'Only in modernity, and indeed after one or two centuries of high modernity, was it possible to achieve the sort of distance on tradition, on community, on place, to allow it to enter meaningfully into discourse' (Lash, 1999: 5). Thus as Lash elaborates,

> This ground which alternately takes the form of community, history, tradition, the symbolic, place, the material, language, life-world, the gift, *sittlichkeit*, the political, the religious, forms of life, memory, the monument, the path, fecundity, the tale, habitus, the body—is just as important a dimension of the second modernity as groundlessness (Lash, 1999: 5–6).

Even in an era of a second modernity, we remain confronted by both place *and* space as objects worthy of geographical inquiry and, moreover, ones that ought to be considered together.

In this connection it may be fruitful to think in terms of the inter-urban and international implications of a second modernity. Continuities have been apparent in the production of space—networks, agglomerations, enclaves—within capitalism and these extend to the unintended consequences of the production of these formations. Notably, it is the state interventions of modernity and unfolding responses to them (Scott and Roweis, 1977) that are the signature of capitalism in what Beck (1992) has termed a second modernity. Many of the spatial products of these interventions are to be found located

23

Table 2.1 Continuity and change in the significance of agglomerations, networks, enclaves, and arenas

	Modernity	Second modernity
Agglomeration	Very significant	Significant
Network	Significant	Very significant
Enclave	Significant	Significant
Arena	Insignificant	Significant

somehow in between cities and nations as the prime 'containers' of a first modernity (Table 2.1).

For some, the processes that have turned the city inside out are the product of a fundamentally different post-modern logic (Dear and Dahmann, 2008; Soja, 2000) in which time, space, and causality are changed (Dear and Dahmann, 2008). However, these forces and the interplaces they produced were set in train by modernist state interventions notably in the likes of orbital and inter-urban highway systems but also other less visible systems of incentivizing the development of an interplace economy—on land at newly accessible peripheries and elsewhere in the vast hinterlands of city-regions. If politics within a second modernity is distinctively one of addressing the side-effects of modernity, then much of the geography of that politics seems likely to alight on what could be regarded as interplaces. This might entail, for example, the sorts of reworking suburban land-use and morphologies envisaged in the retrofit or repair of the distinctly in between places of suburbia (Dunham-Jones and Williamson, 2009; Tachieva, 2010) touched on in Chapter 5.

The stalled development of many African nations is a powerful reminder of both the longevity of the *enclave* as an economic geographical formation and the historical and structural causes of a continued lack of economic development that belie the sorts of cultural explanations for persistent poverty that are commonly offered (Leonard and Strauss, 2003: 103). The unintended consequences of this very modern interventionary form can be seen at the international scale since nation states have actively reproduced territorial distortions of trade, investment and finance flows by way of the enclaves represented by EPZs and tax havens. Larger states in particular have become increasingly aware of some of the unintended effects of creating such enclaves while small, often island, states have been especially creative in the economic positioning of their jurisdictions. Networks of professionals of all sorts have grown out of the bureaucratic apparatus of nation states to become more or less internationalized epistemic communities or networks.

Yet new social space has been produced in the form of many specialized *arenas* which have grown out of and aid the articulation of nation states in the international political economy. Indeed, such specialized arenas have grown hand in hand with the gradual emergence of global governance and its bureaucratization (Boli and Thomas, 1999), which includes the production of numerous networks of professionals and experts. They exist as part of what Ruggie (1993) terms a non-territorial sphere of the international economy. These arenas often remain imbued with and entrench historic nation state centres of geopolitical and geoeconomic power. They are contested to an extent, but significant asymmetries of power remain between corporations and states and their citizens as a product of earlier developments in international law and some of their unintended side effects (Sornarajah, 2010). The death of the Westphallian system of nation states and international relations may have been greatly exaggerated. While MNEs are often able organize their activities transnationally as if in an actually existing borderless world, they are, as legal entities, a string of national corporations and continue to exploit this particular contradiction accordingly with respect to their business and ethical behaviour (Kobrin, 2009), not least given the fact that a genuinely cosmopolitan or post-Westphallian global regulatory architecture (Held, 1995) is a very long way off.

Significantly it is the geographical specificity associated with an economy of signs and symbols and of the identity transforming potential of new mobilities associated with the car, airplane, and information and communications technologies (ICT) that have come to the fore in this second modernity. Yet the rush to deploy non-territorial metaphors in human geography as a result of greatly increased personal physical and virtual mobility may be premature. Instead, 'mobility, like place, inhabits a middle ground. It is inconceivable to think of societies anywhere without either, and yet any particular way we have of thinking about them is self-evidently socially produced' (Cresswell, 2006: 22). Thus, in Chapter 3, I draw on the continuities embodied in distinctly territorial geographical formations such as agglomerations and enclaves on the one hand while seeking to embrace the deterritorialized formations of the network and the arena on the other.

Theory, Method, and Interplaces

What emerges from the preceding review is that what matters perhaps more than the adoption of a particular theory in an understanding of interplaces is a sensibility attuned to the human and economic geography of an in-between world.

Between Art and Science, Surface and Symbol: Place, Space, and Language

Methodologically, geographical inquiry has been considered to lie somewhere between an art and a science; presenting a form of understanding that is between description and explanation (Hart, 1982). Here we are confronted with the need to strike a balance between empirical description of surface events and explanation by way of theoretical abstraction. For Sack (1980), geography and history are placed on a continuum midway between artistic creation and scientific explanation.

The place and space duality has been refigured in economic geography, setting traditional concerns with place as bounded region against alternative metaphors of the spatial reach of processes in terms of networks, virtuality, flows (Thrift and Olds, 1996), and rhizomes (Hess, 2004). These have been a valuable part of an opening up of economic geography. However, it may also have come at a price in terms of an unfortunate and unnecessary parting of the ways in debate between those who work with and beyond the idea of territory and territoriality under the 'scale' label on the one hand and those who prefer non-territorial concepts and metaphors such as the network, virtuality, and flows. Indeed others have gone further to argue that 'hierarchical scale comes with a number of foundational weaknesses' that push in the direction of a 'flat ontology' (Marston, Jones, and Woodward, 2005: 417).

Such metaphorical profusion is revealing of human geography's temperament of 'eclecticism, skepticism, and impatience' and of progress being measured more by change than consolidation' (Peck, 2015: 14; Barnes et al., 2007; Sheppard et al., 2012). Such intellectual restlessness and theoretical churn may be harmless enough, though any conceit that human-geographical theory can really come close to grasping the restlessness of socio-economic processes may be more troubling.

It is surprising that the debate has played itself out in quite the stark way that it has given the, by now, familiar difficulties of transcending the place-space, idiographic-nomothetic duality that is human geography; but it has, and that is no doubt a reflection of some of the limits of language and a desire to transcend these limits in response to a changing world. As Jonas notes, 'the relationship between scale, process and explanation continues to pose enormous challenges for received conventions of narrative, theory and epistemology' and that 'a rejection of discussion of scale or territory as bounded place runs the risk of exposing the limits of our ability to use language effectively to account for the spatial organization of society' (Jonas, 2006: 400). In similar vein, (Kolb, 2008: 78) notes how 'There are no theoretical limits on how complex a place can be, but there are practical limits, for instance limits on memory and decision-making'—a telling point to which I return shortly.

For sure, 'the notion that things happen "in space" is not just a habit of thought but one of language too' (Smith, 1984: 85) and the accusation can be levelled that geographical inquiry rooted in such a territorial or scalar perspective typically has produced knowledge that 'wavers between description or dissection. Things in space, or pieces of space, are described. Part spaces are carved out for inspection from social space as a whole' and that 'what is always often overlooked is the fact this sort of fragmentation tallies not only with the tendency of language itself...but also with the goals of existing society' (Lefebvre, 1991: 91). Yet, Lefebvre himself does acknowledge the necessity of a measure of initial analytical reduction as a prelude to synthesis.

In the best and earliest of economic geographical work deploying the metaphor of the network and appealing to a relational geography (Bunnell and Coe, 2001), for example, it is clear that what is being sought is precisely something akin to a relational approach in the original sense in which Massey (1984) had used it. Thrift and Olds' (1996: 321) early preference for the term network was precisely because 'the network serves as an analytical compromise... between the fixities of the bounded region metaphor and the fluidities of the flows metaphor'. However, as discussed, there have been several incarnations of relational human geography (Yeung, 2005), not all of which retain these sentiments.

Thus, 'whilst the recent "relational turn" has some of its intellectual antecedents in the earlier debates of the 1980s (particularly the social relations of production framework), its substantive content has been broadened to include *social actors* and their *network relations* at different spatial scales' (Yeung, 2005: 38 original emphasis). The global production networks (GPN) framework might be regarded as part of this new relational turn and has itself been associated with considerable terminological development in little over a decade. In particular, much of this innovation appears to have emphasized the non-territorial metaphorical credentials of the framework. Yeung (2005: 38) argued in respect of earlier relational approaches that 'much of this large body of recent work is relational only in the thematic sense that relations among actors and structures are an important theme... the causal nature of relationality and power relations are under-theorized and underspecified'. Drawing on Allen's work, Yeung uses the idea of 'relational geometries' in a bid to add causal power to existing relational geographical approaches: 'Dynamic and heterogeneous relations among actors and structures are conceptualized as causal mechanisms of socio-spatial change in economic landscapes' in which 'the concept of relational geometries refers to the spatial configurations of heterogeneous relations among actors and structures through which power and identities are played out and become efficacious' (Yeung, 2005: 38). This is 'a relational approach to regional development [that] seeks to identify the complex relational geometry comprising *local* and *non-local* actors, *tangible* and *intangible* assets, *formal* and *informal* institutional strategies, and their interactive power relations. There is no a priori privileging of particular categories' (Yeung, 2005: 48). Not much, then, for our finite minds to conceive! As Yeung (2005: 48) is clever enough to pre-empt: 'how then do we apply this relational perspective in economic geography without being accused of creating greater fuzziness of concept and fragmentation in geographical research?' though this is a question those working with the GPN approach have yet to resolve adequately.

What Yeung and colleagues within the GPN approach are interested in here is not actors or structures themselves but 'configurations of relations between and among them' (Yeung, 2005: 38) since 'taking a relational orientation suggests that the real work of human organization occurs within the space of interaction between its members' (Bradbury and Lichtenstein, 200: 551 quoted Yeung, 2005: 44). There is little to disagree with here but I do question whether the binaries (or non-binary classifications)—in effect a meso-level of analysis—are not still useful as a point of entry to theory-building. Yeung (2005: 45) is explicitly critical of the work in the 1990s for focusing on mid-range analytical themes, though he does emphasize that generic concepts of relations and networks can be devoid of explanatory content (Yeung, 2005: 42) and that 'exclusiveness in binary thinking needs to be demonstrated in relation to the implied "inclusiveness" of relational thinking, not merely asserted' (Yeung, 2005: 44). Quite so!

Most recently Allen (2011) has questioned whether topographical metaphors (of territoriality and networks) have been subject to 'conceptual over-extension' and their explanatory power has become exhausted in the face of important changes in the contemporary world. Allen's (2011) elevation of topology as the prime metaphor—almost to the point of excluding any residual relevance of territoriality—derives from a focus, less on traditional concerns with the distances, surfaces, and boundaries associated with territoriality and even networks but on the *way* in which things are connected. Great weight is placed, in turn, on two key developments in an examination of the way things are connected in topologies of power. Namely, (a) the implications for simultaneity offered by new ICT and (b) the significance of 'quieter registers of power'. The latter have indeed come to the fore but are hardly absent in analysis based on concepts of territoriality and networks. To be sure the language of different types of power developed by Allen (2002) differs from that found in international relations and international political economy though these latter bodies of literature are also hardly silent on these issues.[4] This leaves an enormous explanatory weight placed on the role of ICT

---

[4] See, for example, the new emphasis in international relations on 'soft' power.

in accounting for differences in the way things are connected within topologies of power. While ICTs are already quite pervasive, and while we have long been familiar with their potential to produce a 'non-place urban realm' (Webber, 1964), we also know from the diffusion and impact of previous technologies that it can take a very long time indeed for their full effects to manifest themselves in the spatial organization of society. For this reason alone, but also because of what a longer-term historical perspective on societal inertia can offer, it seems important not to totally discard consideration of territory and territoriality in a contemporary world that seems to have sprung the bounds of place.

In this book then, I am interested in agglomerations or places that, on balance, are bounded as permeable organizing containers but in a way that is

> not writing about 'scales-as-fixed-structures' . . . [but] responding to the challenge of narrative and deploying scalar categories in ways that attempt to show how particular material structures and processes have become fixed at or around certain sites and scales, are in the process of becoming unfixed at a specific scale, or combine to differentiate the world in complex scalar and site-specific dimensions
> (Jonas, 2006: 404).

More importantly for the subject of this book, a focus on scale directs attention to the betweenness of human geographical organization, whereas the same cannot be said of an ontology based solely on processes that work through networks and topologies of actors and sites (Jonas, 2006: 402). These in between economic geographical landscapes are best captured not in single metaphors—of scale *or* networks, territory/topography *or* topologies but of several and their coexistence.

Between Theoretical Abstraction and Empirical Study

Lumping and splitting are both a vital part of the heterodox tradition of economic geography (Peck, 2015); nevertheless the subdiscipline's empirical orientation leads to cluttered modes of explication and a suspicion of highly parsimonious theoretical formulations. Economic geography 'attracts and produces small-scale lumpers, the manipulators and modifiers of (generally midlevel) theories, and more skeptical splitters, working between the deconstruction of coarse conceptual categories and the development of alternatives' (Peck, 2015: 13). In this connection, sociologist Urry (2003: 38) raises the thought that 'the enormously open character of global systems might mean that they are currently beyond systematic analysis. One might hypothesize that current phenomena have outrun the capacity of the social sciences to investigate'. One solution might be the deployment of new metaphors and with them ever more abstract analysis, though as Miller (2010: 79) warns 'dialectic theory must imply that just theory alone, like everything else humanity produces, will always tend to become destructive and follow its own interests, oppressing rather than serving humanity. Unless there is a counter-movement that . . . negates . . . abstraction and brings it back into the service of our interests and welfare'. It seems to me that Miller's concerns as an anthropologist, are every bit as relevant to human geographers. The current sensibilities prevalent across much of human geography have pushed in favour of progressively more abstract and meta-theoretical approaches. While appealing in their global breadth and ambition, such sensibilities also raise some uneasy questions regarding the purpose of theory-building and, ultimately, the possibilities for empirical validation.

Something of a premium has been placed on theoretical work within geography though in the case of some meta-theories it is extremely hard to see how they perform the function of a theory that can be verified or contradicted empirically (Saunders, 1981). An example here might be actor network theory (ANT), which is less of a theory and more thick empirical description (Murdoch, 1997). Miller (2010: 78) rejects ANT in favour of an approach to research done 'with feet on the ground'. What Miller (2010) is concerned with here is the sense in which ANT is often invoked purely for theory's sake.

A second example might be provided by a now large literature on GPNs which seemingly holds to the possibility of theory-building of vast geographical and temporal scope. It has been suggested that global commodity chains (GCCs) occupy a middle conceptual ground, lying above the level of economic relations within and between discrete national systems of production but below those operating at the level of the global economy (Gereffi, 1996, cited in Katzenstein, 2005: 109). The meso level of analysis is also one that has been claimed for the GPN approach. However, it is hard at times to escape the feeling that these approaches, in practice, are meta-theoretical—being largely synonymous with capitalism as a whole. Thompson (2004) notes the limits of an 'open systems methodology' associated with recourse to the network metaphor, not least because networks themselves do have boundaries and limits and are not entirely free-floating and self-organizing without some measure of external regulatory activity. In particular he emphasizes the need for 'operational procedures' in the social sciences in order for the network metaphor to be relevant, manageable, and useful in analysis.[5] Thompson's

---

[5] The procedures he describes are the need for: periodization; the identification of structure (such as levels of analysis); a theory of how change occurs; some teleology of where processes are heading, and; an understanding of where we are at any given point in time. The need or desirability of some of these can of course be debated but they point to some of the elements of parsimony that need to accompany an otherwise 'open systems method'. Indeed, the third of these procedures is one that has been taken up recently (Coe and Yeung, 2015; Yeung and Coe, 2015) precisely to add dynamism into the GPN approach.

(2004) warnings regarding the need for a measure of parsimony notwithstanding, others have gone further when attempting to weave time into a discussion of GPNs. Thus 'both territorial spaces and network spaces are relational products, not only of interactions between and within them (both past and future and now) but within and between the here and there. In this doubly—spatial and temporal—relational sense of path dependency, economic geographies are always becoming, always a product of interior and exterior influence' (Lee, 2006: 418). On the one hand, from an analytical perspective, there is little to disagree with here. On the other hand, from a normative perspective, the sense of infinite complexity implicit in such a view does raise the question 'as to whether the incorporation of values in this way into economic geography has the effect of making economic geography everything and nothing' (Lee, 2006: 428).[6] It is a problem that has also bedevilled the subject of planning (Reade, 1983; Wildavsky, 1973). The difference between geography and planning is that planning cannot duck the question of what should be done and as a result is pressed into more parsimonious renderings of real world phenomena (Phelps and Tewdwr-Jones, 2008). The same epistemological problem for economic geography will not be resolved by recourse either to a desire to embrace the totality of economic relations implied in the use of meta-theory, on the one hand, or overly parsimonious models, on the other hand.

A final example of meta-theoretical tendencies in economic geography might be that on neoliberalism and processes of neoliberalization. In many ways there is little to disagree with in critical human geographies of neoliberalism and neoliberalization. These ideas have intuitive appeal given many of our own life experiences over the past three or four decades and politically it is important to critique the often intentionally pernicious effects of policies devised in the name of libertarian philosophy. While, to some extent, work has sought to uncover the constituent processes of neoliberalization and varieties of actually existing neoliberalism, it continues to generate a sense of unease at the way it has inadvertently overemphasized their inevitability (Gibson-Graham, 1996; Larner, 2003) and the failure to specify the necessary causal connections between the universal nature of abstract theoretical claims and concrete empirical outcomes (Castree, 2006).[7]

---

[6] A similar criticism—of the difficulty of validating claims—has been levelled by Anttiroiko (2014: 24) at Doel and Hubbard's analysis of world city networks analysis which can be 'pointillist' or atomistic. As Anttiroiko (2014: 24) goes on to argue, 'At its extreme, in such a picture cities' positions and intercity relations are in a perpetual state of becoming. Whether such a hyperbolic conception matches reality is another matter.'

[7] In this connection Gibson-Graham (2008: 624) have emphasized the technique of 'reading for difference' and 'recognition of the always already diverse economic landscape in all geographical regions'.

My demurring somewhat from these examples of meta-theory is not the same thing as my saying that theory isn't important and that theoretical ambition isn't something that geographers ought to aim at—quite the opposite. However, for me at least, geography's better nature is found somewhere in between theoretical abstraction and empirical description.

A focus on the interplace economy is also a call for an economic geography that sees empirical validation of meso-level abstractions as key to understanding the possibilities for broader generalizations where they are relevant and the celebration of exceptions—of the uniqueness of place when these are not reducible to the dictates of metatheory. This is to acknowledge that 'the relativity of space is determined by the actual process of capital accumulation' (Smith, 1984: 83) and it is such actual processes that are in need of some form of adequate empirical investigation.

Some of my concerns here may be a product of the way the network metaphor has been overextended. Osterhammel (2014: 710) notes how 'Network analysis in the social sciences, useful as it is, always risks overlooking or underestimating hierarchies.' However, 'If everything is a network then nothing is' (Thompson, 2004: 413). Instead, it is possible to suggest that 'Network is too undifferentiated a term . . . We need a significant battery of other terms to characterize the dynamic and emergent relationships between such networks to develop the intense relationality of worldwide connections' (Urry, 2003: 15). For Urry, echoing three of the four metaphors mobilized by Thrift and Olds (1996), there are networks, regions and fluids. My point is that some of these metaphors or concepts are less tractable in empirical terms than might be desired and may be destined to remain as interesting but largely unverified academic abstractions—a point made more forcibly by Storper and Scott (2016: 1115) as 'a predeliction for . . . convoluted philosophical and epistemological abstractions that actually present barriers to . . . understanding'. In Chapter 3, then, I put forward my own suggestion of looking at inter-urban and international relations in terms of four formations or metaphors—agglomeration, enclave, network, and arena.

In deploying these four metaphors, I cannot claim to have any uniquely superior vantage point in terms of the specification of mechanisms to which causal properties can be attached. Each of these formations has been associated with significant conceptual development which I summarize in Table 2.2. My interest in these different geographical metaphors is as much for what they add to accurate empirical depiction of the world. Since this book is intended more as a panorama and a research agenda, I make no judgements among these different causal explanations here. It will be apparent also that I myself am willing to entertain an eclectic approach to an analysis which will frustrate some.

In sum 'the nomothetic and idiographic modes of concept formation both derive from cognitive interests. Both are modes of abstraction through which

Table 2.2 Alternative explanatory frameworks for four economic geographical formations

Agglomeration	Network	Enclave	Arena
Marshallian trinity (Marshall, 1932)	'Networks of relations' (Powell, 1990)	Social/class relations (Cardoso and Faletto, 1979)	'Arenas' (Latham, 2001)
Diversity (Jacobs, 1969)	GCC: Input-output structures, governance, territoriality (Gereffi and Korzeniewicz, 1993); hierarchical, captive, relational, modular and market based governance (Gereffi, Humphrey and Sturgeon, 2005)	Vertical integration and quasi-integration (Singer, 1950, Dietz, 1985)	'Nonterritorial realm of the international economy' (Ruggie, 1993)
Vertical and horizontal division of labour (Scott, 1983, 1986; Scott and Storper, 1987, 2012)			
'Structural coherence' (Harvey, 1985)		Logic of deployment (Latham, 2001)	'Cosmopolitan democracy' (Held, 1995)
Local dependence (Cox and Mair, 1989, 1991)	GVC: Process, product and functional upgrading; hierarchical, quasi-hierarchical, network and arm's length governance structures (Humphrey and Schmitz, 2002)	Legal/regulatory zones of exception (Baldacchino, 2013; Ong, 1999)	Global society (Boli and Thomas, 1997)
Structures and systems (Gough, 1991)		Composite framework (Phelps, Atienza and Arias, 2015)	'Regulatory capitalism' (Levi-Faur, 2005)
	GPN: power, value and embeddedness (Henderson et al., 2002); Power geometries (Yeung, 2005); strategic coupling (Coe and Hess, 2010; Yeung, 2016); optimizing cost-capability ratios, sustaining market development, and working with financial discipline (Coe and Yeung, 2015; Yeung and Coe, 2015)		'Tournaments of value' (Appadurai, 1986)
			'Temporary clusters' (Maskell, Bathelt, and Malmberg, 2006)
	Geometries of power (Allen, 2002)		'Field-configuring events' (Lampel and Meyer, 2008)

finite minds seek to create rational order out of an infinite reality' (Entrikin, 1991: 97). Here Entrikin neatly identifies the dangers of a conceit based on the possibility of infinite geographical minds—dangers that can produce the sort of 'referential mania' I allude to in Chapter 10. I believe it is something best avoided in our attempts as geographers to comprehend the world.

Dialectical Method and the Production of Space: The Betweenness of Interplaces

The task of constructing meso-level concepts and theory is an important one as, without such an intervening level of abstraction in conceptual thinking, all empirical evidence, all particular instances of phenomena and their manifestation in particular places, can be poured into a given meta-theory without the prospect of it being properly questioned in light of the evidence. That is not to say that the production of such meso-level analysis has always been entirely fruitful or without its own dead ends. Critical realism's aspirational ideals are hard to argue with but have perhaps been hard to live up to in empirical research (although see Morgan and Sayer, 1988). Structuration theory has likewise proved quite intractable as a basis for empirical research within human geography (although see Gregory, 1982). The localities research appeared to run into something of a cul-de-sac in its attempts to isolate local causal mechanisms (Duncan, 1989). Yet, what each of these approaches do in their different ways is to remind us of the effort required when trying to make sense of both the uniqueness and universality that pervade human affairs.

Miller, then, rejects middling theory in favour of a dialectical method to interpret the antimonies of existence. In particular he resurrects some of the idealism of Hegel's original dialectics. This approach is not without its drawbacks since Hegel's dialectical thought is considered overly restrictive in its recourse to binaries, its divide between object and subject and its teleology within a closed social system. If the collapse of distance implied in ICTs, for example, is 'an indeterminate relationship' of 'inside and outside, near and far, familiar and strange' (Bogard, 2000, cited in Urry, 2003), the question that arises is, is the language of Hegelian dialectical binaries enough? For some, the limitation of binary opposites is precisely the limit of dialectical method when set against context theoretical approaches (Jones, 1999). However, one danger in moving too far beyond the binaries so strongly connected to Hegelian dialectics is that dualisms remain apparent in economic affairs. The speed up and mobility of contemporary life for some rests on a stillness and relative fixity in particular places for others (Sharma, 2014). That is, the flow implied in some spatial metaphors cannot exist without a measure of place or, at the very least, site. As Cowen underlines in her discussion of the enormous importance of logistics to almost all areas of life, 'Ensuring flow and preventing disruption to commodity circulation seems to require containment' calling forth 'new forms of political geographic enclosure' (Cowen, 2014: 173)—a point I return to later in a discussion of GPNs in Chapter 9.

Another danger is what Miller (2010) identifies as the tyranny of theory when it is left unbalanced by empirics. Equally, without entertaining a human geography of interplaces there is a danger that dialectical method collapses back onto the antimonies of human life and experience as dualisms that provide its drive to analyse duality in the first instance. While the application of dialectical method in Miller's terms is precisely not about 'middling theory' it nevertheless could and should entertain a focus on the (re)production of distinctly in between places/spaces as a by-product of the antimonies of place and space.

A variety of dialectics (Bond, 2014) 'survives despite criticisms of its occasional idealism, teleologies, totalities binarisms, and, at times, its downright clunkiness' (Dixon, Woodward, and Jones, 2008: 2549). For Bhaskar, 'real negation embraces processes of *mediating*, distancing or absenting' (Bhaskar, 1993: 5, emphasis added) and provides a more fundamental negation from which transformative and radical negation can ensue in a critical realist rendering of dialectical logic. It is only in this way that the dialectic can be envisaged as 'the great "loosener", permitting... structural fluidity and interconnectedness' (Bhaskar, 1993: 44). For without effecting such a loosening 'how can such an immanent, totalistic, teleology be squared with the emergent, uncertain, and unpredictable nature of socionatural-spatial change, and our desire to imagine other possible worlds to that of neoliberalizing, globalizing, capitalism?' (Sheppard, 2008: 2605).

Interplaces provide one partial analytical glimpse of the processes of *mediating*, distancing or absenting that Bhaskar (1993) speaks of. Casey (1993: 275, emphasis added) has argued that 'a beginning-place and an end place may stand as the most conspicuous parts of a journey... but the inbetween places are just as interesting, and sometimes more so. Whereas the starting- and ending-places are often the same... the *interplaces* are intrinsically diverse'. The discipline of human geography and the subdiscipline of economic geography have expanded in ways which now embrace a greater sense of the diversity of space and place. Yet, arguably, such *interplaces* have rarely been a major focus of analytical or empirical attention let alone their diversity within the discipline or subdiscipline.

Some clues as to how one might begin to chart such interplaces of the contemporary economy are found by thinking not merely about the production of space (Lefebvre, 1991) in an abstract sense but adding to our repertoire by: (1) continuing to rethink existing metaphors that speak to the antinomies of economic relations (namely, the agglomeration and the network) in relational terms; (2) acknowledging the *coexistence* of these two formations, and; (3) adding greater consideration of geographical formations (namely, the enclave and the arena) that are in themselves interplaces—ambiguous manifestations, that is, of the place/space tension.

'By its actions, this society no longer accepts space as a container, but produces it' (Smith, 1984: 85). That is, 'The spatial immobilization of capital... as national capitals delimited by the boundaries of the nation state, is simultaneously the production of a differential geographical space. Insofar as this immobilization process is matched by the mobility of capital, these opposing tendencies throw up not a random but a patterned internal differentiation of world space' (Smith, 1984: 88). The question is, can this patterning be adequately captured in terms of scales? For, Smith, these scales and their internal differentiation were most definitely fixed (Smith, 1984: 147).

For others, reflecting developments since this time, there has been a rescaling of the state (Brenner, 1998). For me, one way of resolving this vexed issue of a need to entertain structural 'loosening'—in the present time—is to recognize that it is the production of places *between* such scales that is important not their fixity or their relativity even. While it may be the case, as Swyngedouw (1997: 169) has suggested, that scaled places—such as cities—operate as arenas for social relations, I want to define the arena more narrowly and distinguish it from the city as agglomeration. I distinguish the arena as a geographical formation in and of itself; one that, like the enclave, is based on a measure of exceptionalism though one, unlike the agglomeration, network, and enclave that has ostensibly been newly produced. The production of space is also important in relation to the nation state—a scale that in many respects is in between the urban and the global scales that Smith saw as being relatively fixed. Since the invention of the nation state preceded capitalism, this is one major immovable territorial-political obstacle that the capitalist system inherited but the state is not synonymous with the nation and Agnew (2005) would argue that, both historically and presently, there are important ways in which states mediate the accumulation process by helping to (re)produce space. States continue to do this in the form of designating enclaves as differentiated/exceptional places within and beyond their national territories. Such enclaves are also not easy to place in a scalar arrangement being at once transnational formations yet often present as part of (or within) the urban or national scales. Reflecting the drift of the greater rationalization of society regardless of the fate of nation states, states have also been co-authors of any number of arenas for the development of rules and regulations governing the international economy. Such arenas are important part-places in regulatory capitalism and an interstate system composed of regulatory states that is, in itself, increasingly regulatory in character (Levi-Faur, 2005).

Smith referred to the fixity of scales in order to account for uneven development since 'capital produces distinct spatial scales—absolute spaces—within which the drive toward equalization is concentrated' but also to the fact that 'it can do this only by an acute differentiation and continual redifferentiation of relative space, both *between* and *within* scales' (Smith, 1984: 147, emphasis added). This provides a way into a discussion regarding the differential space produced in response to the crises and spatial contradictions in the expansion of capitalism. 'Nor does the growth of the forces of production give rise in any direct causal fashion to a particular space or a particular time. Mediations, and mediators, have to be taken into consideration' (Lefebvre, 1991: 77). Recalling the earlier discussion, the production and *re*production of agglomerations, enclaves, networks and arenas as geographical formations elaborated in this book, reflect the continuities and discontinuities apparent in the modernity and second modernity of capitalism and the presence of intermediaries and processes of intermediation.

Inter-Disciplinary Relations

An examination of the interplace economy is one that entails an inter-disciplinary look at the subject at hand. There is nothing controversial in saying this. At least I hope not. Geography has always been relatively open to insights from other disciplines and long may this remain the case, though at times our own celebration of this openness belies the very limited way in which we as geographers really have been able to engage the interest of those outside the discipline. The geography discipline remains more inward looking than we might care to admit. I cannot claim to have had any special success in cross-disciplinary engagement let alone 'impact' but I believe inter-disciplinary perspectives are needed within human geographical analysis.

Of necessity, this particular geography of the interplace economy draws notably on literature from economics and, to an extent, from sociology in Part 2 when discussing some key manifestations of the inter-urban economy. Here the economic diversity of the suburbs is revealed as an in between territory that contains residential enclaves but is also crisscrossed by personal and corporate networks. Further out a mid-urban realm also contains signifi-cant enclaves in the form of corporate campuses, shopping malls, science parks, airports—many of which are intimately associated with the sorts of transportation infrastructures and networks I discuss in Chapter 6. I draw on literature from international business, international relations, international political economy in Part 3 when elaborating aspects of the international economy. The book also draws to a certain extent on the planning literature briefly at points in various chapters.

All of this places a strain on what human and economic geography can reasonably seek to do, not least when such interdisciplinary scope com-bines with some of the meta-theoretical approaches—such as neoliberali-zation, GPN, and ANT—briefly touched on above and elsewhere in the book. If the adoption of some of the new metaphors in economic geog-raphy might lead to a loss of focus (Martin and Sunley, 2001) then the problems are likely to be compounded when such meta-theorizing meets an appetite for inter-disciplinary scavenging. However, my point is that inter-disciplinary engagement is important not just in the wider promo-tion of geography but also for what it might usefully engender in terms of a greater measure of realism and modesty in theory-building within human geography.

It is for this reason that I have chosen to analyse the interplace economy with reference to a relatively parsimonious scheme that classifies economic relations into a limited number of different geographical formations. Inevitably, this meso-level conceptualization of different geographical formations reduces some of the complexity of the real world and entails a measure of closure of otherwise open economic systems. The different formations do not exhaust the range of possible realities but they are for me, for now, enough to begin to work with when attempting to analyse the complexity and change of the contemporary scene.

Between Analysis and Prescription

In addition to this question of analytical perspective, consideration of the economic significance the economy in between of interplaces demands that we consider not only 'why are things the way they are?' but also the normative question of 'what is to be done?' There is little to disagree with in the post-modernist critique and reconstruction in economic geography. It is a vantage point which adds much analytical value both as a perspective on the past of economic geographical inquiry and on the concerns that might motivate its future (see, for example, Barnes, 1996).

In human geography and, to an extent, in economic geography explicit adoption of post-modernist perspectives also appear to have come at a price—of a sort of paralysis, a fear of the reduction and simplification that inescapably accompanies normative questions in modernity and even second modernity. The view from in-between is one that I suggest can accept the critique of post-modernism and the complexity of different explanations of the world as it is. However, logically, recognition and acceptance of such complexity only negates modernist theory if it is believed that it is the intention of the theorist to produce a single best theory to the exclusion of others. I think this is to confuse the method of theory building and exposition with the motives of economists, sociologists, political scientists, and even some geographers with what these same analysts almost certainly understand at some level is the messiness of the sorts of economic, social, and political relationships they are seeking to analyse. That is, recognition and acceptance of the messiness of reality does not in and of itself negate theories and methods that are parsimonious. One of the key tools of the geographer has been inductive classification and comparison. While the comparative gesture has once again been advocated recently in urban geography, parsimony is important here too as contributions from outside of geography emphasise (Pierre, 2005; Wolman, 2008). Indeed, some measure of reduction perhaps through comparison and classification is, as we saw earlier in connection with Lefebvre (1991), even a valid element of the dialectical method associated with political economy approaches.

Neither does a recognition or acceptance of the messiness of reality logically negate the value of a measure of simplification in service of normative questions. At this point I hope I am not perceived as being insensitive. However, the sort of sensibility that I advocate here is one that does its best to grapple with the complex reality of the world as it actually is (though without retreat *ad infinitim* into ever more 'inclusive' meta-theorizing about such complexities) while at the same time having an eye on the positive sense of purpose of what is to be done entailed in modernist perspectives. After all, as Sack's (2003) emphasis on a search for the real and the good illustrates, relatively simple normative guidelines are not antithetical to the variety and complexity of human relations. To remain only at a critical distance from, or with a disdain for, the simplicity of 'impact' in the political and policy world would be for geographers to drift rudderless in the oceans of irrelevance (Phelps and Tewdwr-Jones, 2008). As Yeung notes 'what is the point... of giving multiple voices and representations to social actors if we cannot free tem from false consciousness and/or suppression by dominant hegemonies in organizations, institution, and localities?' (Yeung, 2003: 457). The reality of the normative world of policy and politics is one that does not care to admit to the messiness of the real world nor tolerate theories that mirror it to any great degree (Phelps and Tewdwr-Jones, 2008). If human geographers cannot be judiciously parsimonious in their theoretical and empirical analyses, they surely will be forced to be in political and policy processes if they genuinely wish to engage with them.

Conclusion

Historian Osterhammel punctures any conceit in the sense of hypermobility that we as academics might want to project onto the remainder of society: 'Even today, in the age of the Internet and boundless telecommunications, billions of people live in narrowly local conditions from which they can escape neither in reality nor in their imagination. Only privileged minorities think and act "globally"' (Osterhammel, 2014: xv). It is as good a starting point to begin in this conclusion and to re-emphasize the need to take both place and space seriously since 'traditional' references to nation, region, city, and place are far from outworn. They have a continued salience. Indeed the territoriality of the nation state continues to be redefined in ways that contribute significantly to the production of space in an economy that is ever more in-between in important respects.

My point in this book is not to argue for the complete undermining of the likes of nation or city as territorial conceptions, 'containers', or scales involved in some way in the organization of economic activities. Instead I want to suggest that they coexist with other geographical formations—agglomerations, enclaves, networks, and arenas—as a product of the tension between place and space apparent in the production of space within capitalism. Notwithstanding its long history in human thought and experience, this tension has become particularly intense within contemporary capitalism such that it becomes vitally important to identify and analyse intermediate geographical formations as prime foci for processes of differentiation (Smith, 1984) and as the differential space (Lefebvre, 1991) associated with geographically uneven development.

An economic geography of interplaces cannot escape the place/space duality that we have for some time been familiar with in human geography. That is, it cannot escape having to deal with and integrate an understanding of the uniqueness of places with the universality of processes across space, and it cannot escape the enduring importance of topography when set alongside that of topology. The ostensibly singular focus on networks or topological metaphors and conceptualizations within significant portions of economic geographical research and the, at times, quite stark use in opposition to conceptions such as that of scale is all the more surprising, then, for its rendering of economic geography as either one or the other, when it clearly has been and continues to be both. A flat ontology would reject 'hybrid both/and solutions' to theorizing (Marston, Jones, and Woodward, 2005: 417), but to my mind, interplaces embody an economy in between and as such are ones where there is, and has been, significant metaphorical overlap and coexistence of economic geographical formations.

If there is a line of critique directed at the network metaphor running throughout this book it is because I believe that this metaphor and associated conceptions of relations have been overplayed within economic geography. Network forms of organization are neither new nor can they offer anywhere near a complete depiction of the present economic geographical organization of economic activity. Other 'old' concepts such as agglomeration and enclave retain a salience and, alongside the network metaphor, can form part of a limited armory of concepts of geographical formations used to analyse the production of space in the contemporary economy. They are joined by a formation—the arena—that does indeed appear to be substantially new. It is to an elaboration of an analytical framework involving these four geographical formations that I turn in Chapter 3.

3

An Economic Geography of Interplaces

Introduction

The previous chapter introduced the broader philosophical context for this economic geography of the inter-urban and international economy with the caution that an historical perspective is particularly valuable if we are not to exaggerate the present significance of networks. The same historical perspective is important for understanding the role of intermediary individuals, organizations, and industries in an economy in between. We saw how Lefebvre (1991), for example, argued that the development of the forces of production has no causal connection to particular geographical forms at any particular time and that mediation activities were important in the production of space. In this chapter I begin by focusing on the role of intermediaries in the economy in between including their contribution to the production of interplaces. These groups of actors have ambiguous implications for the spatial organization of production. On the one hand, they and their activities often appear to reinforce city and national economies—the territorial 'containers' that have been the staples of economic and economic geographical analysis and precisely what this book is less concerned with. On the other hand, intermediation is closely involved with promoting the emergence of distinctly in-between places and in the between formations of arenas and enclaves.

In Chapter 2 I also argued for a measure of realism regarding the possibilities for empirical verification regarding the deployment of metaphors—and this extends, of course, to those deployed to make sense of the in-between economy of interplaces. With the exception of the concept of arenas, which is substantially new, in this chapter I work with extant and empirically tractable concepts to emphasize the in-between or relational geography of economic activities. I outline agglomerations, enclaves, arenas, and networks as four different but often coexisting geographical formations associated with economic activities. The network metaphor is recast as one that can hardly exist without reference to these other formations. Since absolute space might be considered to have the inadvertent effect of eliminating many differences (Lefebvre, 1991: 52), the absolute spaces associated with the nation state might be considered to have engendered the production of in-between or differential spaces in the form of enclaves or arenas.

Intermediaries

As the division of labour in society has grown, so the economy has become more 'roundabout' in nature (Young, 1928). This roundaboutness is registered in the raft of 'new' industries that have emerged in between primary industries producing raw material inputs and a set of industries oriented directly to final consumption. Research in economic geography has been devoted to explaining the relevance of producer, consumer and circulatory services to other parts of the economy (Allen, 1988). The complexity of the stuff we consume directly and indirectly has increased markedly even in the past few decades. As recently as 1970 the most valuable products in world trade were simple products made by simple methods but by 1995 only 14 per cent of the most valuable items were the same simple products (Rycroft and Kash, 1999: 56–7, cited in Urry, 2003: 15).

The rise of industries intermediate between resources and final consumption also raises broader questions regarding the economic contributions of intermediary activities. Notably these include: (a) the status, permanence, dynamics, and value added of intermediary activities viewed more broadly as occupational niches prior to consolidation as identifiable industries, and; (b) the spatial expression of these intermediate activities and their connection to the rise of intermediate locations or places. Perhaps more than anything, then, a concentration on intermediaries is revealing of the contemporary process of market making—a process of economization (Caliskan and Callon, 2009). Here, fragmented bodies of literature have a focus on intermediary actors and organizations, the functions performed by intermediaries, and, to some extent, the economic geography of intermediation.

For Caliskan and Callon (2009: 38), the economy is something that is achieved, not a starting point or pre-given reality. Instead it is something to be understood by way of the economic knowledges that are mobilized in market making. In turn, a focus on economization can usefully centre on the devices and techniques of actors when bringing together production and consumption. 'From analytical techniques to pricing models, from purchasing settings to merchandising tools, from trading protocols to aggregate indicators, the topic of market devices includes a wide array of devices' (Muniesa, Millo, and Callon, 2007: 2). Such techniques and devices may create markets but they also have their own unintended effects since 'they articulate actions;

they act or make others act' (Muniesa, Millo, and Callon, 2007: 2). Kitchin and Dodge (2011: 10) go further to underline the pervasive nature of software code in mediating our perception and engagement with place and space: 'taken together, coded objects, infrastructures, processes, and assemblages mediate, supplement, augment, monitor, regulate, facilitate, and ultimately produce collective life. They actively shape people's daily interactions and transactions, and mediate all manner of practices in entertainment, communication, and mobilities'.[1] The $8.34 billion spent by the US Federal Government and the $200–$600 billion estimated to have been spent by governments and businesses globally to mitigate risk associated with the Y2K millennium bug (Kitchin and Dodge, 2011: 11) provides one stark indication of the significance of code in mediating economic relations.

Instead of locating 'the economy' in either individuals or in society and economy as a whole, Caliskan and Callon (2009: 378) call for a 'focus on intermediary realities that can establish both a theoretical and practical a link between the two'. Here then the value attached to products and services at various points in their biographies is something which market intermediaries are important in shaping since 'valuation is no[t] . . . the effect of structures or regimes which affect the value through passive intermediaries, but it is a consequence of how competent and active people engage with specific things' (Caliskan and Callon, 2009: 388).

Although they argue that networks could be considered a timeless mode of organization, Magee and Thompson (2010) also emphasize the specific importance of co-ethnic business networks during a first global economy organized in large part around the British Empire. The question they pose is why did co-ethnic networks form in a world where market transactions were already extensive and quite internationalized? For them, 'the answer . . . lies in the uneven process of globalization. Barriers to integration frequently impact economic interaction by distorting or diverting certain types of economic behaviour' (Magee and Thompson, 2010: 6–7). As such, historically speaking, 'by improving the quantity and quality of information flows around the British world, by bridging relations between producers and consumers, and by facilitating the adoption of new technologies, imperial networks did indeed contribute powerfully to the growth in trade and to the convergence of income levels' among English speaking societies during the latter half of the 1800s into the early 1900s (Magee and Thompson, 2010: 20–1). That is, these

---

[1] Kitchin and Dodge (2011: 17) distinguish between coded space which can continue if the code fails and code/space which cannot exist without the dynamic relationship. They define code/space as a situation in which software and the spatiality of everyday life become mutually constituted, that is, produced through one another. Spatiality is the product of code, and the code exists primarily in order to produce a particular spatiality.

networks, or rather some of the key people and businesses who composed them, performed the role of market intermediaries.

Intermediaries have played a significant role historically in the orchestration of international trade and production as in the examples of British cotton merchants operating in the interstices between producers and consumers to integrate markets in the 1700s and in the role of *compradors* establishing trade with China (Jones, 2005). The numbers of the latter intermediaries were comparatively small though they grew to a not insignificant and qualitatively important minority in China from 700 in 1870 to around 20,000 by 1900 (Osterhammel, 2014: 769). Elsewhere, 'although European interest later intruded more actively in Java, the Chinese (comprising less than 1.5% of the population) remained indispensable to the colonial system and profited handsomely from it, acting as intermediaries' (Osterhammel, 2014: 770). Chinese enterprises continue to act today as intermediaries for Japanese investors across Asia (Katzenstein, 2005: 68). If anything, the importance of intermediary activities, occupations, and fledgling industries has grown in the increasingly roundabout nature of productive activity brought together over the geographically extensive production networks discussed in Chapter 9.

According to Magee and Thompson (2010), the individuals and companies that operated as intermediaries within the business networks of the first global economy proved adaptable in overcoming three types of barriers: informational; cultural, ethnic, or religious; and political. Taking my cue from these observations drawn from a first global economy I will now briefly consider each of these informational, cultural, ethnic and religious, and political drivers to the formation of networks of intermediaries in the contemporary second global economy.

Intermediaries and Informational Barriers

From a perspective rooted in information economics, much of the existing literature on the subject of intermediation has focused on the overcoming of missing, incomplete, or asymmetrical information in the formation of markets. Thus, for Casson (1997b: 155) 'intermediaries take responsibility for handling much of the information flow that is needed to make the economy work. They are specialized bearers of information costs.' The intriguing thing is that much economic theory would suggest that there is no valuable role for intermediaries and predicts their eventual demise as a result of markets working more effectively due to technological disintermediation and the greater availability and quality of information. For example, 'the supply chain concept, as it currently stands, is largely incapable of providing an explanation of this observed role for intermediation and may even be said to predict its progressive demise' (Popp, 2000; 151), given suspicions of the parasitical nature of intermediation. Yet, the economy represented by intermediaries of all sorts—for innovation, supply chain management, financial services—has continued to grow.

Casson (1997a) identifies five main tasks of market-making intermediaries: search, specification, negotiation, completion, and enforcement. It is easy to assume that intermediaries play their primary role in terms of reducing transaction (information) costs thereby improving the productivity and efficiency of business processes. Relaxation of the theoretical assumption of perfect information is one that implies a role for a host of intermediaries in reducing the impact of missing, incomplete, poor quality, or indeed an excess of information. From a geographical point of view, such a role can be particularly important where distance and culture impose barriers to communication (Popp, 2000: 154). However this potentially underestimates—from a corporate point of view—the value added by intermediaries. It is less appreciated that their role often extends into one of specification and thereby overall improvement of business strategy or entrepreneurship as I discuss in Chapter 11.

The literature on the innovation process typically has broader concerns with the geography of knowledge mobilized and the functions performed by intermediaries. Bathelt and Glückler (2011: 29) note how 'Production processes have become more complex over time, and depend on an increasing social division of labour that stretches over large distances.' Intermediaries are vital to such complex and geographically extensive production processes since they mobilize both bonding and bridging social capital where 'social capital is not attributed to the overall network of social relations but to individual brokers who are capable of establishing bridging relations' (Bathelt and Glückler, 2011: 79). Here they are concerned to recognize 'that knowledge is not exclusively produced in local networks. It results from the systematic circulation and exchange of ideas between local and non-local agents that are part of joint communities, or socially embedded producer-user networks' (Bathelt and Glückler, 2011: 12).

Cultural Intermediaries

The idea of a class of specifically *cultural* intermediaries is associated with Pierre Bourdieu (1984), who described how 'Because the appropriation of cultural products presupposes dispositions and competences which are not distributed universally...these products are subject to exclusive appropriation, material or symbolic, and, functioning as cultural capital...they yield a profit in distinction proportionate to the rarity of the means required to appropriate them' (Bourdieu, 1984: 228). The potential importance of the concept of cultural intermediaries to a relational economic geography of the in-between seems undeniable in the thought that 'One only has to bear in mind that goods are converted into distinctive signs . . . as soon as they are perceived relationally, to see that the representation which individuals and groups inevitably project through their practices and properties is an integral part of social reality' (Bourdieu, 1984: 483). Moreover, the concept appears to have a specific value to the subject matter of Chapter 10 of this book in that 'the new cultural intermediaries . . . have invented a whole series of genres half-way between legitimate culture and mass production' (Bourdieu, 1984: 325–6).

'Working at the intersection of culture and economy, they [intermediaries] perform cultural operations in the production and promotion of consumption, constructing legitimacy and adding value through the qualification of goods' (Matthews and Smith-Maguire, 2014: 1). That is, 'cultural intermediaries are market actors who construct value by mediating how goods (or services, practices, people) are perceived and engaged with by others' (Matthews and Smith Maguire, 2014: 2). Here, cultural intermediaries are subject to some of the same processes as other 'value adding' business services within global production networks (GPNs). For 'in the struggle to influence others' perceptions and attachments, cultural intermediaries are defined by their claims to professional expertise in taste and value within specific cultural fields . . . and they are differentiated by their locations within commodity chains . . . and by the autonomy, authority and arsenal of devices and resources that they deploy in negotiating structural and subjective constraints to accomplishing their agendas' (Matthews and Smith-Maguire, 2014: 2). For Bourdieu, a class of cultural intermediaries has reproduced itself and expanded despite some of the inherent difficulties attached to the work performed. 'Some of these new or renovated positions result from the recent changes in the economy (in particular, the increasing role of the symbolic work of producing needs . . .). Others have been in a sense "invented" and imposed upon their occupants, who, in order to be able to sell the symbolic products they have to offer, had to produce the need for them in potential consumers by a symbolic action . . . tending to impose norms and needs, particularly in the areas of life-style and material or cultural consumption' (Bourdieu, 1984: 345).

Nevertheless, the concept of cultural intermediaries has also been open to significant critique. Intermediaries of all sorts have a precarious, ephemeral or contingent position as part of the unfolding division of labour and indeed, at historical moments, its re-synthesis. The concept of intermediaries is one that is itself intermediate in this respect. The concept has proved influential despite Bourdieu's inclination to detach cultural intermediaries themselves and their work from processes of economization. As he emphasizes, 'economic power is first and foremost a power to keep economic necessity at arm's length' (Bourdieu, 1984: 55). Moreover, what he describes as a class of cultural intermediaries can appear as an unchanging ideal type since he argues that cultural intermediaries do not experience their own world as one of instrumental calculation (Smith-Maguire, 2014: 22–3). It is this that has led Molloy and Larner (2010: 375) to argue that 'where Bourdieu initially saw cultural intermediaries as...a remnant of the petit bourgeoisie desperate to claim cultural capital in the face of declining economic capital, we now see a new set of, and understandings of, cultural-economic businesses driven by global processes and changing gender relations'. In this way, then, 'the global political-economic mobilisation of culture...is premised on new forms of entrepreneurial labour in which the identities of producer, mediator and consumer are increasingly intertwined in the same actor. Moreover these actors are often multiply positioned in the complex cultural-economic networks that make up these new industries. Consequently the term "cultural intermediary" is now inadequate when it comes to capturing relationships between production, mediation and consumption' (Molloy and Larner, 2010: 366).

An array of occupations has been identified by Bourdieu as cultural intermediaries concerned with exercising a measure of authority and shaping consumer tastes. However, the definition such as it exists is probably too inclusive to be meaningful. Moreover, given my concerns in the previous chapter and in the book as a whole, it also overly stresses the newness of this body of intermediaries since some of the industries involved have existed since the early 1900s (Nixon and DuGay, 2002) if not before, given the discussion above regarding the rise of cultural intermediaries as part of networks of enterprise in a first global economy. Furthermore, while for Nixon and DuGay (2002: 498) the study of intermediaries nevertheless focuses attention on moments and spaces in between and 'away from the overemphasis on the moment of consumption', for others this can itself present a problem with the concept. For McFall (2014: 43), the concept of cultural intermediaries is ambiguous since 'production is only production when it is completed in consumption. This simultaneity makes the notion of intermediaries fraught because a process of intermediation inevitably introduces varieties of distance and time that are hard to reconcile with simultaneity and identity.'

Political and Policy Intermediaries in Regulatory Capitalism

Paradoxically, what can reasonably be regarded as a hegemonic neoliberal political economic project has been paralleled by the emergence of a more fully regulatory capitalism (Levi-Faur, 2005)—a situation that Vogel (1996) captured as *Freer Markets, More Rules*. As Levi-Faur, 2005: 14) explains, 'while at the ideological level neoliberalism promotes deregulation, at the practical level it promotes, or at least is accompanied by, regulation. The results are often contradictory and unintended, and the new global order may well be most aptly characterized as "regulatory capitalism"'. The outward signs of the emergence of regulatory capitalism are seen in the near exponential rise in the number of regulatory agencies across 16 sectors across 49 states during the period 1960–2002 (Levi-Faur, 2008).

However, regulatory capitalism is also registered at the international scale and in the workings of policy, law, and regulation of inter-state relations and the international economy. Some evidence of this is provided by the growth in international organizations (IOs) and international non-governmental organizations ((I)NGOs) from just 200 in 1900 to an estimated 4000 in 1980 (Boli and Thomas, 1999: 172). These now offer many new arenas in which much regulatory activity affecting economic activities is to be found and is part and parcel of an international order 'in which transnational networks of technocrats and professions have more influence than ever before' (Levi-Faur, 2005: 16)—more of which in Chapter 11.

Thus, intermediation might be recast more broadly as intermediation in, and emanating from, the public sphere of the economy. Politics, policy-making, implementation, service delivery, and monitoring have been subject to the division of labour. The political and policy-making process has itself become both more roundabout (Majone, 1989) and more particularistic and contested partly as a result of this and partly as a result of the politicization of the side effects of past state interventions within second modernity (Beck, 1992; Beck, Bonss, and Lau, 2003). Majone (1989) has challenged the assumption that policy-makers engage in a purely objective, rational, technical assessment of policy alternatives. In practice, policy-makers use theory, knowledge, and evidence selectively to justify policy choices which are heavily based on value judgements. It is persuasion (through rhetoric, argument, advocacy, and their institutionalization) that is the key to understanding the policy process. In this picture, 'Democratic governance is no longer about the delegation of authority to elected representatives but a form of second-level indirect representative democracy—citizens elect representatives who control and supervise "experts" who formulate and administer policies in an autonomous fashion from their regulatory bastions' (Levi-Faur, 2005: 13). The complexity of managing divisions of labour within the state also stem in no small measure from the fact that they are simultaneously territorial or scalar divisions of labour, producing distinctive politics of scale (Cox and Mair, 1991) and even new interplaces (as seen, for example, in the emergence of 'soft' planning spaces (Allmendinger and Haughton, 2012)).

However, within regulatory capitalism, the roundaboutness of the policy process is perhaps broader than this implies. 'One of the defining features of regulatory capitalism is that parts of the state are set up with independent capacities to regulate other parts of the state' (Braithwaite, 2008: 25). Braithwaite (2008) charts a series of successive transformations in the relationship of states to markets across the west from the seemingly ungovernable liberal economy, to the creation of the provider state, to regulation creating big business, to antitrust helping to globalize American mega-corporate capitalism and, finally, to mega-corporate capitalism evolving into regulatory capitalism. 'Across all these transitions, markets in fits and starts have tended to become progressively more vigorous, as has investment in the regulation of market externalities.... Both markets and the state become stronger, enlarged in scope and transaction density' (Braithwaite, 2008: 27). The market for regulation has expanded beyond simply the regulation of economic activity to the regulation of regulation itself. That is, 'regulatory capitalism involves heightened regulation of the state as well as growth in regulation by the state' (Braithwaite, 2008: 21).

All of this has important implications for the geographical organization of economic activity, since taxation, its collection, and organized disbursement through various centrally administered policies by national and supra-national states/organizations has itself become a focal point of the sorts of inter-locality competition I discuss in Chapter 7. The continued growth of the state and IO and (I)NGO organizations within capitalism and the increasing roundaboutness of bureaucratic and policy processes within regulatory capitalism means that significant flows of revenue have increasingly become detached from the economies of local jurisdictions in a way they were not previously. Economic development strategies have been positioned around such flows (as seen in Harvey's (1989) urban entrepreneurialism and Markusen's (1996) 'state anchored districts').

Moreover, some of the most internationalized and indeed cosmopolitan of experts—such as lawyers—play the role of double agent in the circulation of knowledge and prescriptive doctrines in a way that is 'reminiscent of the role of intermediary and mediator filled in the past by compradors working with merchants in colonial enclaves' (Dezalay and Garth, 2011: 280). The intriguing thought is that intermediaries are closely associated with the distinctly intermediate places that are enclaves. Reversing this connection we will also see how enclaves are interplaces bound up with rules-based experimentation and competition.

Intermediaries and Intermediate Places

We might imagine that since 'informational and mediative power is mobile, performed and unbounded' (Urry, 2003: 113) that we can dispense with metaphors and concepts that speak to the enduring territoriality of the economy. Thus, for McFall (2014: 49 and 50 respectively) commenting on cultural intermediaries specifically, 'the function of intermediation is spread across a network, not situated in the middle of a line connecting production and consumption' so that 'what emerges is a distributed, crowded network of intermediaries who, in different ways, contribute to the qualification of products'.

On the one hand, networks of intermediaries of various sorts appear to be permanently agglomerated—in a limited number of, typically, world cities. Historically speaking, it is here that the division of labour has reached its zenith to furnish a continual and early stream of lucrative market niches and opportunities for market creating.[2] This might be the case most notably with regard to Bourdieu's (1984) cultural intermediaries.

On the other hand, economic geographies of intermediaries are also at least partly associated with the production and reproduction of differential or in between space. Again, historically speaking, it seems fair to assume that intermediaries were important to the most open of economic enclaves, such as the overseas concessions of imperial powers. However, while intermediaries play a role in the establishment of some enclaves by and large they play a minor role in any subsequent development towards agglomerations. The conditions of the enclave are partly designed to limit such incursions by intermediaries. In a modest way and in the case of physical products and commodities, intermediation can result in possibilities for enclave-like economic formations in intermediate locations as we will see in Chapters 5 and 9 in the form of retail malls, intermodal distribution centres, export processing zones, and the like.

Commenting on the present, Urry (2003: 126) goes on to note how 'there are...specialized *periods* and *places* involving temporary rest, storage, infrastructural immobility, disposal and immobile zones. How, when and where these materialize are of immense systemic consequence, relating to the organization of time space'. Many of these periods and places constitute the emergent interplace economy of the present second global economy and they are rarely studied by economic geographers let alone further conceptualized. Urry's concern of course is with the offshore economy and although generally less concerned with its specific geographical manifestations he does provide one or two notable examples. He describes how '"temporary" tax havens are created in sporting "camps" in which major events such as the Olympic Games or World Cup are held' (Urry, 2014: 55). That is, the work of intermediaries is also to be found in specialized arenas. Some of these are squarely business-centred arenas in the form of temporary clusters. However, others have a more firmly regulatory complexion as Levi-Faur (2008: viii) describes in the new order of regulatory capitalism 'legal forms of domination are increasingly constituted by functional rather than territorial considerations...the distribution of power, and the corresponding form of interest intermediation in each of a number of arenas' (Levi-Faur, 2008: viii).

---

[2] Though of course this says nothing of the role of surplus extraction from hinterlands in the growth and development of cities (Walker, 2016).

Agglomeration: The Logic of Concentration

The theory of agglomeration might seem a curious place to start in an understanding of the in- between economy of interplaces. The *Shorter Oxford English Dictionary* defines agglomeration as a process of adding or joining 'together into a rounded mass' or 'cluster'. Alfred Marshall originated the term external economies to help explain how collectivities of businesses might benefit through the process of agglomeration. All this happens largely in the intense agglomerations of people and activity that we recognize as cities and which are taken as the primary evidence for the existence of external economies. Much of the voluminous literature on external economies and their relationship to the agglomeration of economic activity has emphasized the place-bound nature of economic processes in causal explanations that at times verge on the tautological (Phelps, 1992).

Rather than the theory of agglomeration and the concept of external economies being superseded by a relational approach (cf. Bathelt and Glückler, 2011: vii), the concept of external economies has continued to be elaborated in ways which reveal aspects of the underlying relational potential of the concept, as registered in ideas regarding the 'mobility' or reach of external economy effects or fields. This is a picture of what Casey (1997: 293) refers to as 'place as concentration'—bounded but not delimited. Here 'Places' inflow and outflow are such that to be fully *in* a place is never to be confined' (Casey, 1993: 29). It is these innovations that provide one means of grasping the production of space in the inter-urban economy as lying somewhere between strongly bounded processes of industrial agglomeration and dispersion (Phelps, 2004a). Indeed, recent work on the external economies so closely associated with agglomeration notes the complementarities between agglomeration and network externalities (Van Meeteren, Neal, and Derudder, 2016).

Marshall's definition of external economies involved three ingredients whose essence, while at that time seeming place-bound, nevertheless implied interaction whose range was not restricted. That is, 'geographical clusters can no longer be (if, indeed they ever could be) thought of simply as closed local systems' (Tracey and Clark, 2003: 11). Bearing in mind the transportation technology and the material nature of the products of that time, transactions tended to be predominantly local. The sorts of externality fields that mapped onto industrial districts, quarters of cities, or even whole towns and cities at the time were in principle mobile but in reality fixed to the extent that the majority of such interactions could be classed as contained within a particular place.

That the discussion of agglomeration became invested with a strong sense of the place-bounded nature of processes to the exclusion of their inherent relationality is perhaps understandable, though it persisted longer than it should have and prompted the sort of pendulum swing so apparent in human geographical thinking towards perspectives that stressed the un-doing of place. Walker, (1981: 385), for example, argued that agglomeration economies were a 'historically contingent feature whose force has gradually diminished to be replaced by the economies of internal organizational scale open to large companies'.

One starting point, then, for considering the emergence of the economy between cities—an inter-urban, interplace economy—is to consider the mobility or migration of externality fields or the scale over which external economy benefits are available. Interest in the subject of industry agglomeration was significantly rejuvenated after a brief pause by the work of Scott (1983, 1986) together with Storper (Scott and Storper, 1987; Storper, 1995). They recast and formalized an understanding of industrial agglomeration, though here again the focus was largely on place-bound processes of the vertical and horizontal disintegration of production. Doubtless this renewed interest in industrial agglomeration owed much to the emergence of new industrial spaces (Scott, 1988), though it was curious in the face of evidence of the lack of local linkages and indeed the dissolution of many industry agglomerations elsewhere. Indeed, as early as the 1930s Robinson described how 'Certain external economies, though by no means all, depend not on the size of that industry in one locality, but on the size of that industry in the world as a whole. . . . the proportion of all economies which are of this international mobile type is steadily increasing' (Robinson, 1931: 142). Something of this line of thought was apparent in economic geographical analysis. For example, Scott (1982: 118) noted how 'agglomeration effects in large industrial cities *cannot* be assumed to be geographically fixed' going on to describe how:

> in the early decades of the twentieth century, as firms were gradually liberated at the level of physical interlinkages from the imperative to cluster together, they could extricate themselves from the central metropolitan labor market with its high wages. . . . As firms assimilated new technologies they could also reduce their dependence on pools of specific labor skills that had been created and re-created within the core of the city   (Scott, 1982: 129).

Later contributions argued that the restructuring and associated decentralization of manufacturing activity have reflected the shifting locus of external economies from urban cores to peripheries (Suarez-Villa, 1989) and into the 'distant hinterland areas' of city regions (Scott, 1982: 129).

What we have here is a strand of work that points to the shifting locus of external economies facilitating industrial agglomeration and in particular their manifestation at progressively wider geographic scales from the industrial quarter, to the city as a whole, to the suburbs and peripheries of city-regions and further out into the hinterland. Terms such as 'polycentricity'

(Suarez-Villa, 1989), 'scatteration' (Gordon and Richardson, 1996), 'regional-ization' (Coe and Townsend, 1998), and 'meta-clustering' (Bennett et al., 1999) have been used to speak to this tendency, though they did not always distinguish between different types of external economy (Parr, 2002; Phelps, 2004a; Phelps and Ozawa, 2003).

From a political economy perspective Walker and Lewis (2001) argued that 'the process of urban industrial growth has another crucial dimension besides the outward flow and build-up of the city: the appearance of distinctive industrial districts within multinodal metropolitan area. *Classic agglomeration theory does not explain this phenomenon*' (Walker and Lewis, 1999: 7–8, emphasis added)—though it could equally be argued that recast classical agglomeration theory *does* seek to explain such multinodal patterns. The notion of there being a variety of 'scale dependencies' of different economic and indeed governmental activities which coincide to greater or lesser extent to underpin the coherence of local economies (Cox and Mair, 1988, 1991) appears to offer some purchase on the sorts of patterns that Walker and Lewis describe. I was able to observe how:

> These diffuse forms of agglomeration are notable for throwing up rather anonymous 'intermediate' locations...that are nevertheless important in economic terms....In comparison with the enormous weight of theoretical and empirical interest in industry clusters, we know very little about the economic basis of these seemingly banal locations   (Phelps 2004a: 972).

This remains something of a research agenda yet to be fully embraced. To an extent this has much to do with an over extension of the network metaphor in which the in-betweeness of economic geography of industrial agglomeration has been overlooked in favour of altogether more distanciated economic relations. To an extent it is also a product of the way in which an interest in evolution within economic geography has shifted attention to questions of the evolution and life-cycles of extant agglomerations (Potter and Watts, 2011).

A second development of the theory of agglomeration that has allowed for the latent relational properties of the concept of external economies to be elaborated effectively conjoins the network and agglomeration metaphors. A re-rendering of the concept of external economies in relational terms was implicit in Alonso's (1973) discussion of 'borrowed size'. Alonso described how 'The concept of a system of cities has many facets, but one of particular interest...is the concept of borrowed size, whereby a small city or metropolitan area exhibits some of the characteristics of a larger one if it is near other population centres' (Alonso, 1973: 200). He used this term to account for the manner in which people and businesses could retain the advantages of being in smaller settlements (for example, less congestion, lower rents) whilst also being able to reap the benefits on offer in larger nearby settlements (such as access to sizeable markets, business services, larger and more diverse labour markets and cultural amenities). Arguably this idea emphasizes the relational nature of urban agglomeration since it focuses attention on the way in which 'the greater availability of external-ities that can be found in smaller centers... is also the result of increased interaction between centers' (Senn and Gorla, 1999: 249). It is a line of thought that has slowly gathered momentum to be extended recently (Burger et al., 2015; Meijers and Burger, 2015) and is relevant to understand-ing the role of agglomeration as a distinct economic geographical formation as part of world cities. Here the advantages of agglomeration are predicated significantly on their international connectivity as much as their place-bound scale (Simmie, 2000).

Elsewhere, the term *desakota* (combining the Indonesian words for village and city) has been used in the context of East Asia to describe a distinctly 'rurban' landscape in which different land-uses are mingled together (McGee, 1991) and is one that also hints at the relational nature of urban economic agglomeration. In such spaces, residential, agricultural, and urban land-uses of all sorts including formal and informal business make up a patchwork that is somewhere between urban and rural—neither entirely agglomerated into a largely formal city-located economy, nor fully dispersed.

During an era of industrial capitalism, industry sought to capture external-ities in industry agglomerations that were contained within nation states. The economist Robinson had already questioned the applicability of this idea by the 1930s and political geographer Agnew echoes this line of thought to underline how, 'the technologies for providing public goods have had a built-in territorial bias, not least relating to the capture of positive external-ities. Increasingly, however, infrastructural power can be deployed across networks that, though located in discrete places, are not necessarily territorial in the externality fields that they produce' (Agnew, 2005: 443). The division of labour is, as Adam Smith noted long ago 'limited by the extent of the market' and today the market relevant to processes of the division of labour is no longer that of a single city or nation. Network externalities exist where the utility of consumers and the advantages to producers depend on the number of consumers using a product or service over time (Katz and Shapiro, 1985, 1986). If the ownership advantages of MNEs are derived from network exter-nalities, then 'competing effectively... requires that both firms and technical communities although locally embedded must have close ties to global tech-nology networks of innovation and learning' (O'Riain, 2005: 81). In the present era it is the network developmental states of Ireland and Singapore that have most successfully recognized and exploited the potential of network externalities as I discuss in Chapter 11.

The recasting of these concepts of agglomeration and external economies with reference to the metaphor of network compared to that of bounded region has been instructive for revealing how the particular perspective and scale of analysis are revealing of the limits of both metaphors (Van Meeteren, Neal, and Derudder, 2016). This recasting of the concept of agglomeration has also more fully revealed the latent relationality of the concept and produced a proliferation of terminology. Research has emphasized the non-local linkages or transactions of businesses located in industry agglomerations or the 'strength of weak ties' (Grabher, 1993). The strength of such weak ties has extended to the sorts of interactions associated with technological externalities thought to be most localized by virtue of their requiring face-to-face contact. Thus the 'new Argonaut' international reach of the non-traded interdependencies associated with labour markets and human capital formation has become apparent in the co-development of high-technology industry agglomerations (Saxenian, 2007). The place–space duality is visible in the characterizing of agglomerations as variations on the theme of 'sticky places in slippery space' (Markusen, 1996) and in the manner in which processes of agglomeration lie in the conjoining of interactions within individual places that form local 'buzz' with some of the diversity implied in global 'pipelines' of interactions between different agglomerations (Bathelt, Malmberg, and Maskell, 2004).

Deployments, Networks, and Arenas

Not only is the international economy infused with the enduring territoriality of the nation state but also transnational formations cannot be reduced simply to the non-territorial as one might assume. 'The key characteristic of the word international is that it proscribes international relations... International as interstate is a product of the success of state-centred politics legitimating itself as national politics' (Taylor, 1995: 1). Yet 'interstateness and transstateness have operated alongside one another through the whole history of the modern world system and continue to do so' (Taylor, 1995: 12). Moreover, the coupling of nation and state as the primary jurisdictional 'container' and regulator of economic activity since the Treaty of Westphalia *preceded* the rise of capitalism. As a consequence, 'competition in the world market is not directly between individual capitals, but is mediated by state boundaries... this enables the state to organise the external projection of national class interests through foreign policy, diplomacy and military force' (Lacher, 2005: 39). Thus the extra-territorial projection of economic interests by nation states has begun to generate a transnational or non-territorial space of the global economy and with it a geopolitics and geoeconomics that is not restricted to national borders.

Contemporary processes of globalization involve both interstateness and yet they also promote transstateness (Taylor, 1995: 14).

This brief interlude prior to the next sections of this chapter is by way of arguing that 'what is compelling about the opposition global/local is what lies silently between: the structures and relations that emerge through the intersection of social phenomena that vary in range, as well as form' (Latham et al., 2001: 6). It is to Latham's work that I turn to add to the concept of agglomeration and to help fashion a limited armoury of concepts to analyse the inter-urban and international economy. Before doing so it is worth remembering the same corrective put forward in the preceding chapter— that old social constructs die hard, have durability, and are associated with considerable inertia.

In order to understand this world in between, Latham (2001) distinguishes between three transnational formations with different logics. (1) Deployments—*enclaves* by another name—are represented by individual or groups of multinational enterprises (MNEs) and are defined in distinctly territorial terms surrounding their overseas operations. Superficially similar to agglomerations in their apparent territoriality, their economic logic is quite different. (2) *Networks* of actors are responsible for the transmission of capital (political, symbolic, information, finance) between nodes, under a logic of interaction. (3) The logic of convocation is found in the *arenas* which populate 'a sort of spaceless "international realm"' (Latham, 2001: 72). As Latham (2001) notes, the distinction between networks and arenas is not always clear. However, as Saunier (2002: 510–11) describes of this work, the focus is on how intersections are created between scales of territorial organization in ways which blur the distinctions between those levels and the sense of hierarchy between them.

Enclave: The Logic of Deployment

Latham likens the MNE and its overseas subsidiaries to a deployment comparable to the military camp of an invading army within a host territory. Here, and in what follows, I will use the term enclave interchangeably with this term. Doubtless some of this military imagery is derived from the history of colonial exploitation in Africa from which Latham's illustrations are drawn— though the enclave in this particular part of the world remains a potent formation in modern times (Ferguson, 2006; Leonard and Strauss, 2003). The colonial trading MNEs operated private armies in order to take by force that which they could not negotiate on the most favourable terms. Yet it is important to realize that there were important limits to the extent and depth of colonial control in Africa and elsewhere. Cooper (2001) depicts such control in terms of a series of special purpose zones that existed as islands in a shallow sea of imperial control. This may seem a somewhat quaint rendering of the MNE. It certainly jars a little with the global production networks (GPN) perspective discussed in Chapter 9. It seems hardly to intersect at all with a topological perspective under which 'the so-called far-reaching powers of trans-national corporations . . . are often best understood less as something extended across borders and networks and rather more as an arrangement which enables distant actors to make their presence felt, more or less directly, by dissolving, not traversing the gap between "here and there"' (Allen, 2011: 290).[3]

Nevertheless there are distinct, important and paradoxical insights to be gained by taking enclave forms of economic activity seriously whether they manifest in the overseas activities of MNEs or the gated residential communities, theme parks, airports, and other enclosures found in inter-urban locations. According to the *Shorter Oxford English Dictionary* to deploy means to 'unfold or display' while an enclave is 'a piece of territory entirely shut in by foreign dominions'. What the enclave as a formation indicates is a tightly, often formally, bounded territory occupied by an individual organization or a limited number of organizations. Although also place-bound like agglomerations, they are also distinctively strongly penetrated by non-local, often international, economic relations. Indeed, the curious thing about enclaves is that they are only part of a host nation economy in a physical sense while the main economic impacts pertain to the home economy of the organizations involved (Singer, 1950).

In those instances that are closer to an ideal form, enclaves are geographically defined but rarely concentrate economic activities in the way agglomerations do. In other instances of course the boundary between an agglomeration and an enclave can be less clear (Phelps, Atienza, and Arias, 2015). The definitional outline of the economic enclave that colleagues and I have offered (Phelps, Atienza, and Arias, 2015) doubtless does not cover all eventualities.[4] Nevertheless, the enclave stands as a counterpart to the agglomeration and one essential to understanding uneven economic development. As Sidaway (2007: 332) notes: 'intensified processes and patterns of uneven development are increasingly expressed in enclave spaces. These replicate features of the formal territorial enclaves . . . However, the variety of emergent enclaves considered here are wider, being governed by a range of legal norms and bounded in an array of formal and informal means.'

---

[3] The concept of the enclave is not itself without some confusions. The term is used in the ethnic enclave literature (Wilson and Portes, 1980) to refer to what here I regard as the advantages of agglomeration. Moreover some of the literature has reinterpreted ethnic enclaves in terms of networks of relations.

[4] Phelps, Atienza, and Arias (2015) discuss the enclave in terms of the dimensions of spatial delineation, pecuniary externalities (linkages), technological externalities, returns to scale, factor mobility, and social reproduction.

Latham elaborates how a transnational deployment 'is an installation in a local context of agents from outside that context' (Latham, 2001: 75). Such deployments are 'defined by limits. The more limited the deployment (the more narrow its scope and provisional its status), the more transterritorial it is' (Latham, 2001: 81). The picture of the territoriality of the MNE in its overseas deployments and the territoriality of collectivities of business in enclaves of activity this conjures is one around which there is no process of osmosis with the host environment and economy. Yet, for all the attempts of MNEs to internalize ownership advantages, it has been apparent that there are always environmental, political, and economic spillovers surrounding such deployments. Thus, as Latham (2001: 81) goes on to argue 'even the lightest of deployments can affect considerably life within the locale it enters... there is something uniquely powerful about the narrowness of deployments that works to their advantage in local contexts'. This is the power to abdicate responsibility—as seen for example in the Bhopal disaster in India, or the violations of human rights that surround the extraction of resources in Africa—and the possibility of not being constrained by the broader political and social environment of the host territory. In this way, 'self-contained forms of power abdicate to varying degrees responsibility for organizing and securing their external environment' (Latham, 2001: 83). Indeed, it is in the nature of the enclave as an interplace—an in-between economic geographical formation—that ensures that it does not need a functioning state or infrastructure to generate revenues (Leonard and Strauss, 2003: 16). The enclave involves what Latham describes as a tragedy of co-dependence that we will come across again later in the less than anticipated benefits of the foreign direct investment (FDI) of MNEs discussed in Chapter 8.

The ideal level of this power is perhaps only approached by MNEs in export processing and free trade zones (EPZs and FTZs) around the world. The deployment both in its individual corporate and collective state/firm-delimited form are worth reconsidering later in this book; not least because, in comparison to the notion of industrial agglomeration, the altogether less positive enclave counterpart strong version of territoriality enduring in economic relations has been seriously neglected in both empirical discussion and theoretical elaboration (Phelps, Atienza, and Arias, 2015). By the same token, 'when a deployment loses its narrowness, it loses latitude over its withdrawal. Since transnational deployments are narrow in scope and often temporary in status they are unlikely to be very good conduits as constitutions of order, even if they sought to be so' (Latham, 201: 85).[5]

---

[5] This is the case with the overseas manufacturing investments of MNEs where the bargain struck between an MNE and host state compared to extractive investments as Kobrin (1987) elaborated some time ago. For the extractive investor the huge sunk costs at the outset make the

If the enclave as an economic geographic formation has rightly been associated with questions of economic dependency and underdevelopment there is also in the above discussion enough to indicate that, despite the often poor results for communities, it has been a very important focus of private sector and government regulatory experimentation. Casey (1993: 122) describes the manner in which the process of 'implacement is an ongoing cultural process with an experimental edge' (Casey, 1993: 31) and how 'a truly transitional space is often a place for creative action, providing enough protection to encourage experimentation . . . without being overly confining' (Casey, 1993: 122). If enclaves in some instances are designed and, more importantly maintained and developed, as such transitional spaces, they are overlooked instances of such experimentation. In Asia such enclaves have been integral parts of regulatory experiments to create zones of graduated sovereignty (Ong, 1999).

Finally, following Latham's (2001) interests in the specifically transnational aspects of deployments/enclaves, much of the discussion to this point has focused on these geographical formations in connection with the international economy. Yet it is quite apparent that such formations are to be found at the inter-urban scale. The suburbs of many industrialized nations are pock-marked with specialized enclosures of one sort or another. The United States happens to provide perhaps the most extreme example of this pattern. These enclosures include the likes of airports, retail malls, science and office parks, corporate head office and research and development campuses, and, of course, gated residential communities. This pattern is not simply one involving a separation of land uses (including the nature of the economic activities taking place) but the delimited spaces that are distinct in various legal and regulatory terms. Moreover, these delimited spaces of the inter-urban economy fulfil the characteristics of the enclave in another important respect. Despite being firmly bounded as places of sorts the most important economic relations are non-local and frequently international in scope.

Network: The Logic of Interaction

Geographers have been propelled towards the network metaphor partly as a result of a broader explosion of interest in moving beyond the singular and rather limiting metaphor of territory or bounded places or regions (Thrift and Olds, 1996). It is the network that has been enthusiastically, if

---

investment vulnerable to expropriation. For the manufacturing investment as the indirect and induced multiplier effects increase over time the investor has a stronger bargaining position as a result of having lost some of the narrowness it had on arrival.

rather selectively, embraced at present as perhaps the dominant metaphor in human geography. The network as a metaphor is apparent in the widespread use of, for example, Actor Network Theory (ANT) in human geography—elements of which appear also to have influenced the global production network (GPN) approach in economic geography specifically.

The *Shorter Oxford English Dictionary* defines a network as 'work in which threads, wires or the like are arranged in the form of a net'. Powell (1990) notes the historical inaccuracy of viewing networks as intermediate between markets and hierarchies since they could be said to have preceded the emergence of the markets and hierarchies of modernity and second modernity. Moreover, echoing the discussion of intermediaries earlier in this chapter, he notes the homogeneity of groups organized into networks along ethnic, geographic, ideological, and professional lines (Powell, 1990: 326). The logic of interaction in networks is that of the transmission of various forms of capital (political, symbolic, information, finance) from one node to another. Powell (1990) (when contrasting networks with the prices associated with markets and routines associated with hierarchies) describes the means of communication as one of relations and the importance of remembering that the constituents of these nodes remain emplaced in various local contexts.

Perhaps the most obvious way in which scholars have alighted on the network form of transnationality has been with an elaboration of the MNE and its various external relationships as part of GPNs where these are 'dynamic topologies of production that link different places and territories' (Hess, 2004: 176).[6] 'GPNs do not only connect firms functionally and territorially but also they connect aspects of the social and spatial arrangements in which these firms are embedded and which influence their strategies and values, priorities and expectations of managers workers and communities alike. The ways in which the different agents establish and perform their connections to others and the specifics of embedding and disembedding processes are to a certain extent based upon the "heritage" and origin of these agents' (Henderson et al., 2002: 451). To the extent that the GPN approach attempts to 'elevate the tension between territorial relationships and transterritorial developments' (Hess, 2004: 178) it is a bold attempt to grasp the interplace economy that I am interested in. However, as I indicated in the previous chapter, it has been subject to some drift away from the concerns of an original relational approach. The GPN approach has itself been a source of further metaphorical innovation.[7]

---

[6] Curiously one of the main concerns within economic geography in the use of the network metaphor was to re-emphasize the agency of the firm (Yeung, 2004). I say curiously because to a large extent the firm and its agency have often disappeared from view in economic geographical writings mobilizing this metaphor.

[7] Hess has gone on to argue that 'Better than the mere network term, rhizome gives us a sense of how actors transmit their "genetic footprint" through relational processes, how actors are bundled

There is no doubting the huge and understandable interest generated by these metaphorical renderings of economic geography though in some extreme instances they take us into a distinctly 'flat' ontology in a world that is patently 'spiky' (Iammarino and McCann, 2013) or 'sticky' (Markusen, 1996). There are a number of potential problems associated with economic geographical accounts that rely largely or solely on the network metaphor—many of which were preempted at the time (Yeung, 2004) though may subsequently have receded from view. It can become a tautological or a chaotic concept (Yeung, 2004) in the sense that 'if everything is a network then nothing is' (Thompson, 2004: 413).The network metaphor also implies that 'the connections between places in our current global society are so complex that no broad spatial structures exist anymore' placing too much emphasis on the possibilities created by horizontal relations between places rather than persistent inequalities (Sheppard, 2002: 317 and 308 respectively). In this way, there is an enduring need within the likes of the GPN approach to reconcile individual instances of corporate and local upgrading to broader patterns of unequal development (Selwyn, 2015).

Notwithstanding these criticisms, network formations, and indeed the GPN approach, if I appear to have singled it out, constitute one indispensable way of understanding the contemporary transnationality of economic activities. Aside from the networks of purely economic activities orchestrated within MNEs or to a greater or lesser extent by MNEs as part of GPNs, it is a metaphor that speaks powerfully to the many intermediary actors and communities of interest, which also help to shape international trade and production and the regulatory environment in which it takes place.[8] Networks of intermediaries have played an important role in the creation of markets and industries in between the extraction of raw materials and final consumption in national economies and the geography of their organization and are present in many issue areas that are the subject of global business regulation (Braithwaite and Drahos, 2000).

Arena: The Logic of Convocation

The *Shorter Oxford English Dictionary* defines an arena as 'any sphere of public or energetic action' which admits to a wide range of possibilities. Latham

---

in particular, bounded places or territories, and how rhizome-networks develop and change in (topological) space' (Hess, 2004: 182). From botany, a rhizome is 'a subterranean stem that grows into a network and in places shoots into bulbs and tubers' (Hess, 2004: 179).

[8] The term 'epistemic community' is used in international relations to refer to 'a network of professionals with recognised expertise and competence in a particular domain and an authoritative claim to policy-relevant knowledge within that domain or issue-area' (Haas, 1992: 3).

(2001) provides fewer clues as to the geographical nature of arenas as transnational formations. However, the logic of relations in arenas is that of a convocation—a large gathering for a special purpose composed of standing and temporary committees and with special procedures. In these sites or arenas 'intangible social forms and practices such as international law or worldwide conventions share the characteristic of promulgating a sort of spaceless "international realm" which is everywhere and nowhere' (Latham, 2001: 72). To elaborate the geography of arenas a little more we can reorganize the observation that 'relativity also enables places to be the most revealing arenas in which to experience the dialectic of here-there, near-far, now-then . . . permanent-transitory' (Casey, 1993: 284) to suggest that arenas are interplaces or geographical formations in which these antinomies are present. Unlike agglomerations, enclaves, and networks, which have a long history, these specialized, temporary places of sorts are a substantially new phenomenon.

The logic of convocation would be represented by the numerous but periodic and partly nomadic rounds of trade, intellectual property, and FDI regulatory meetings and negotiations. These meetings take place for limited durations in particular locations such as Geneva, Davos, and Doha but are manifestly not of any particular place. Indeed, the often rather peculiar character and associations of these places as neutral 'retreats' of one sort or another doubtless plays a part in a carefully cultivated sense of the impartiality and *placelessness* of arenas. Meetings and their substantive work are also significantly characterized by issues of procedure. That is, they are concerned much of the time with deliberations that can be abstracted from the grounded realities and interests of territories and their states and populations. Moreover, while national and other interests are doubtless reflected and promoted in such negotiations as views from a particular places—ostensibly particular national territories—many of the key practitioners are likely to see themselves as promoting a global or transnational 'bird's eye view' from nowhere.

In contrast to deployments or enclaves, international arenas 'rest on the expansive possibilities of widely amplified discourses and practices' (Latham, 2001: 81). In this sense, arenas can be equated to what Held and McGrew (2002) have described as new sites of rule-making in the international economy. They note:

> The growing enmeshment of public and private agencies in the making of rules, the setting of codes and the establishment of standards. Many new sites of rule-making and law-making have emerged, creating a multitude of 'decentred law making processes' in various sectors of the global order. . . . many of these have come into existence through processes of self-validation in relating to technical standardisation, professional rule production and transnational regulation of multinational corporations, and through contracting, arbitration and other elements of *lex mercatoria* (Held and McGrew, 2002: 20–1).

These new arenas of law and rule-making in the international economy are the basis for what Held (1995) sees as the possibilities for cosmopolitan democracy in a 'post-Westphalian' era. However, it is also the case that numerous arenas represent unelected centres of power typified by the expansion of bureaucratic authority (Held, 1995: 13). What Held refers to as 'nautonomic structures' have created a variety of different sites of power, one set of which are concerned with the 'sphere of regulatory and legal institutions' (Held, 1995: 173).

Arenas might also be equated with what Braithwaite and Drahos (2000) speak of as the various forums in which much of global business regulation takes place. They underline how these arenas have emerged only comparatively recently but are now extremely important to economic organization and governance in both quantitative and qualitative terms when noting how 'international forum-shifting was not an important strategy prior to the second world war, when the number of international fora was so small as to afford little choice. It became an important strategy for the first time in the era of US hegemony' (Braithwaite and Drahos, 2000: 564).

The example that Latham (2001) provides of an arena are the different venues at which international investment disputes are settled (Mills, 2011) and it is one I return to later in Chapter 11. These arenas have undoubtedly proliferated as one belated product of the modernity of nation states and the inter-state system. Indeed, the unanticipated or unintended effects of decisions taken in arenas suggest the need for some form of post-Westphalian system of governance to reflect the realities of a multi-polar private-public sovereignty. However, 'it is extremely unlikely that these forms of global governance will materialize in the foreseeable future' (Kobrin, 2009: 361). Neither it would seem are they likely to represent cosmopolitan and inclusive arenas of global governance, given the predominance of private interests in their formation.

Bathelt and colleagues have put forward the notion of a temporary equivalent to agglomerations of economic activity. Temporary clusters or agglomerations might be taken as another example of the category of arenas since the likes of 'international trade fairs, conventions, and other professional gatherings have characteristics similar to those of permanent clusters, albeit in a temporary and periodic form' (Bathelt and Glückler, 2011: 181). 'Relatively little research has treated these events as *places* where international business networks are created and maintained' (Bathelt, Golfetto, and Rinallo, 2014: vii, emphasis added). Here then Bathelt, Golfetto, and Rinallo, 2014: 280) have usefully drawn attention to these often overlooked arenas of the international economy. While they have a long historical lineage in ancient commodity fairs found, notably, across Europe, they may be an increasingly important feature of the international organization of economic activities.

Finally, it should come as no surprise that since the concept of the arena suggested by Latham (2001) has been formulated with regard to the international economy, its relevance to an analysis of the urban and inter-urban arena is perhaps less established. I do not elaborate the relevance of arenas in the next section of the book on the inter-urban economy. Nevertheless it is conceivable that the concept offers some purchase on the role of the likes of private or shadow governments that now populate some of the fastest growing communities in the suburban and mid-urban realm of America, and to a lesser extent elsewhere.

The Agglomerations, Enclaves, Networks, and Arenas of the Inter-Urban and International Economy

As Iammarino and McCann (2013: 316) have noted with respect to the international economy 'Networks and agglomerations are in fact complements' (Iammarino and McCann, 2013: 316). By the same token, so are enclaves and networks. To a large degree agglomerations, networks and enclaves are partially related but different economic geographical formations that have coexisted historically and continue to do so presently. These three are not mutually exclusive concepts or metaphors. Seen as complementary parts of national and international economic systems and considered together, these three geographical formations have offered and continue to offer different perspectives on the geographical organization of economic activity. They are joined by one formation—the arena—that has not been significant historically, is a product of modernity, but which has come strongly to the fore in the era of a second modernity. As we have seen, these four are also complements by virtue of the fact that they draw attention to rather different trans-territorial economic logics summarized above and in Table 3.1.

In Figure 3.1 these four ideal types are arranged along two dimensions of place and space. The four formations are different combinations of territoriality on the one hand and non-territorial relations on the other. The first of these is the agglomeration which although most closely associated with the city as a prime container of economic activity is a formation that has a more ambiguous

Table 3.1 Four geographical formations and their logics

Formation	Agglomeration	Enclave	Network	Arena
Economic logic	Concentration	Deployment	Interaction	Convocation
Duration	Enduring/life cycle	Limited life	Continually (re)produced	Temporary/periodically reconstituted

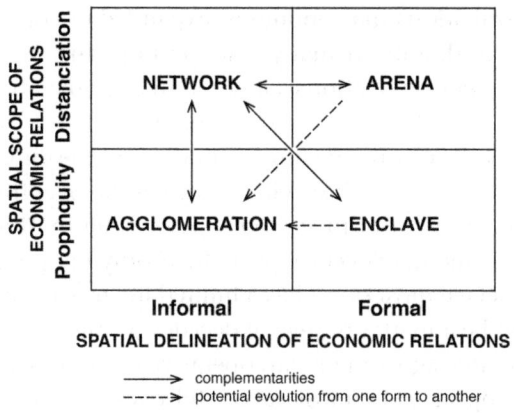

Figure 3.1 The scope and delimitation of agglomerations, enclaves, networks, and arenas

connection to urbanity than is usually assumed. This is an informally delimited territory or place in which erstwhile spatial relations have concentrated to become, on balance, place-bound. At the other end of the continuum I have placed the network which carries with it the most deterritorialized sense of economic relations as distanciated. The remaining two of these formations—the enclave and the arena—appear themselves to be interplaces—in-between in the sense of place that they embody. The territoriality of the enclave is different from that of the agglomeration—it is formally delimited but the most important spatial economic relations are, on balance, not geographically concentrated and indeed are frequently international in scope. The arena is essentially a non-territorial formation but yet is not completely placeless by virtue of the economic relations that come together at least temporarily in particular places.

The arrows that link some of the different formations in Figure 3.1 indicate some further outcomes that are in between these ideal types. Thus, the production complex type of industry agglomeration lies somewhere between an agglomeration and an enclave (Phelps, Atienza, and Arias, 2015). Mining camps might be considered as something of a 'dark side' outcome of GPNs—the product of MNEs organized as networks but touching down in extreme types of enclaves. Somewhere between networks and agglomerations lie the sorts of instances of industrial upgrading more often than not alighted on in GPN approaches. Arguably, the arena is perhaps a little unique in having fewer intersections with the other three formations—it is something that coexists or complements the other three formations rather than a form that lends itself to hybridity.

Almost by definition, agglomerations endure over the long run and indeed are subject to a measure of path dependency as well as life cycles. Curiously, some network formations may endure in expanded or contracted form over the long term too, despite in many respects implying the opposite to the sedentary or place-bound relations supposed in agglomerations. This is most notably the case with the family and ethnic bases of, for example, Chinese business networks. Arenas are the most temporary of the different formations, being essentially project or task-specific. They endure over the short term of a matter of days or weeks and may migrate over time to different regions or nations (though some may occur repeatedly if only temporarily at the same location). The enclave most often has a limited life too. In the case of mining towns this might be a matter of several decades. While some EPZs have been designated some time ago and remain operative it is also the case that for the most part they appear to be most successful over a matter of decades after designation as a source of new employment but rarely have evolved to amount to significant agglomerations or contribute more significantly to structural transformation of national economies.

Conclusion

The economy in-between is registered in any number of economic activities that have grown up to be intermediary between resource extraction and final consumption. Many of these are now firmly established as separate industries or professions with more or less distinct boundaries. However, it is the *process* of economization by which such new industries and occupations arise that retains a salience to understanding the rise of interplaces. As the 'lash-ups' needed to produce stuff in GPNs become more complex (Molotch, 2004), so it would appear that intermediaries are an important focus for an economic geography of the inter-urban and international economy. Moreover, inter-mediaries may also promote or be associated with a distinctly intermediate geography of economic activities—being organized, for example, in or through the likes of arenas at the international scale or inter-urban enclaves of various sorts. As the discussion in this chapter and Table 2.1 in the previous chapter indicated, intermediaries of various sorts have been important across the first and second global economies and therefore to the fashioning of economic activity contained in interplaces in the form of agglomerations, enclaves, networks, and arenas.

There was enough in the language and conceptual development associated with the theory of agglomeration to indicate its recasting as place-as-concen-tration (Casey, 1993), bounded but not especially firmly or formally delimited. The concept of agglomeration stands in some contrast to its place-centred counterpart, the deployment or enclave. The deployment or enclave is a place held together not by the intensity or concentration of economic relations but by the deliberate and selective corralling of some economic relations into firmly and formally delimited exceptional territories. Despite its territorial credentials, in other respects the enclave is the mirror opposite of agglomeration—at once firmly bounded and yet selectively porous to relations that are internationally dispersed. Arguably, because of this, it is a concept that sits somewhere between human geographical perspectives that emphasize place, on the one hand, and the spatial implications of economic processes, on the other. Also in a middle ground between agglomerations and networks is the concept of the arena—a temporary concentration of economic relations in place but not of any place in particular. This is a rather neglected formation but as Chapter 11 seeks to demonstrate it is undoubtedly a very important one to the functioning of the international economy. Geographical research on aspects of the international economy has perhaps been over-enthusiastic in its embrace of metaphors that dispense rather too readily with the legacy of the territorial organization of society and economy. Nevertheless the widespread embrace of the network metaphor in economic geography undoubtedly reflects some of the realities of transformations that are taking place in the geographical organization of economic activities such as the rise of GPNs and heterarchical business forms which I discuss in Chapters 8 and 9.

One purpose of this chapter has been to highlight how distinctly different territorial and non-territorial forms of economic organization have coexisted historically and continue to coexist today. Here I have drawn partially on some of the available concepts and metaphors identified in the extant literature (Thrift and Olds, 1996; Urry, 2003). Notably, I retain use of the network which appears to have become the metaphor of choice at present. However, I return to the older concepts of agglomeration and enclave and add a distinctly new concept of arena to offer a wider but yet limited conceptual armoury with which to begin to chart the interplaces of an economy in between. These different geographical formations crop up at various points across the remaining chapters of the book. In juxtaposing territorial and nonterritorial conceptions of economic relations in this way I have tried to remain true to an original version of relational human and economic geography that seems at times to me to have been rather lost sight of.

Part III
The Inter-Urban Economy

4

Suburbia

Introduction

'Sprawling on the fringes of the city. In geometric order. An insulating border. In between the bright lights. And the far unlit unknown'. So read the lyrics from the song 'Subdivisions' (by Rush). They capture perfectly the way in which suburbs have a 'geography...intermediate between town centre and the countryside' (Clapson, 2003: 2). Their in-between geography—including in economic terms—has a long history. As Fishman (1987: 27) reminds us 'suburbia can never be understood solely in its own terms. It must always be defined in relation to its rejected opposite: the metropolis.' Whether, in its original meaning pertaining to the expulsion of certain economic activities and populations, the later bourgeois escape from the Anglo-American city, or indeed the approach to the city found today in Mediterranean and Latin American cities, the suburbs occupy an ambiguous position.

On the one hand, suburbs have been a subject ripe for the sedentary metaphysics reserved for the understanding of place. Some residential suburbs have indeed changed very slowly, as a result of small-scale additions such as conservatories and lofts, to retain much of their original morphology and character (Whitehand and Carr, 2003). Yet, on the other hand, as Whyte argued, it was the *transience* of organization people that came together in the seemingly stolid suburbs. 'What suburbia best illustrates is "the need to revise our customary assumptions about rootedness"' (Whyte, 1967: 246). Not only could transient organizational men and women of post-war American suburbs never go home as a result of the 'intellectual breadth' they gained from moving away, but they were always on the move *between* places; mobility of segments of the population represents an important continuity between the settled and organized capitalism that produced the American suburbs and the contemporary transformation of residential suburbia. Moreover, 'the more people move about, the more similar the American environments become, and the more similar they become, the easier it is to move about' (Whyte,

1967: 255). Little wonder that much of the suburban landscape has been regarded as inauthentic. The newest of residential suburbs have been cast as placeless (Relph, 1976) or a geography of nowhere (Kunstler, 1993). Suburbs appear, then, to be both places and non-places. Perhaps as a result, the changing economy of the secondary and tertiary circuits of capitalism that residential suburbs embody has been analysed with reference to both territorial and non-territorial metaphors. Suburbs are in an in-between state of becoming: in the process of gaining a measure of authenticity, being made into places, or staving off the loss of a sense of place and economic vitality, when compared to established cities—it is important to subject them to longitudinal analysis (McManus and Ethington, 2007).

The economic activity taking place in the in-between geography of residential suburbia has tended to be overlooked. Yet evidence points to the increasing role of residential suburbs within national and metropolitan economies. Indeed, 'suburbia, originally situated as a distinct middle landscape between city and country has now become the armature and model of growth everywhere. Its original dependence on the commercial, social, and civic life of the city has dissipated. Today suburbia has become autonomous and pervasive, invading both traditionally urban and rural areas' (Dutton, 2000: 15). In this chapter I begin by defining suburbs and then outlining their role in the broader transformation of metropolitan and megapolitian areas. Ultimately, theoretically, it makes little sense to break up the unity of urbanization processes into those operative in different types of settlement. However, from a practical methodological standpoint, distinguishing different settlements with different socio-economic and other dynamics is a useful first step in understanding the unity in diversity that characterizes the (sub)urban scene.

Planetary Urbanism as a Suburban Revolution

It might seem strange to herald the revolution from the suburbs but if we have entered an age of planetary urbanization—a majority of the world's population now living in officially defined urban areas—then the bulk of that urban population will be in officially defined suburbs. Of course, Lefebvre was referring to the attendant qualitative transformation by which the experience and social relations of production had become fully urban and capitalist in character. Either way, what we regard as the suburbs are at the heart of this urban revolution.

The in-between geography of suburbia—including its economic content— was and remains a highly variegated one (Harris and Larkham, 1999). Suburbs have an ancient history as the location of economic activities and it is important not to overlook the distinctly industrial complexion of some suburbs or the fact that economic activity has often *preceded* residential development in suburbs old and new (Hise, 1999; Lewis, 1999). It is also clear in some national contexts that suburbs have increasingly taken on particular social class and ethnic complexions with important though underexplored connections to their economic fortunes.

Harris and Larkham (1999) offer a composite definition of a suburb drawn from a review of the extant literature as a settlement: (i) in a peripheral location relative to a dominant urban centre; (ii) partly or wholly residential in character; (iii) of low density of development; (iv) with a distinctive culture or way of life; and (v) a separate community identity often embodied in a local government. With the outward physical expansion of metropolitan regions, item (i) alone admits to an ever-increasing variety of suburbs to which the labels inner and outer suburbs and exurbs may not do full justice. The variety of the suburban landscape—including the economic complexion of suburbs—is also a product of the fact that items (ii) to (v) are subject to change over time. Notably, the historical employment contribution of (mostly industrial) inner suburbs has been obscured by processes of suburban annexation by established cities. The incorporation of affluent, purely residential, inner and outer suburbs as separate communities has often been motivated by a desire to *exclude* all but a narrow socio-economic and ethnic segment of the population. However, in other instances incorporation has also been the broadly *inclusionary* end-product as a sense of community and a way of life that has developed over time.

The residential-employment balance and building density of suburbs continues to change in ways that make it important to continue to try to find labels that adequately capture the complexion of different suburbs—including their economies. Thus, Table 4.1 presents a number of scenarios that capture crudely some of the contemporary changes in metropolitan regions. The scenarios were developed with differential land development pressures and state involvement in mind and not the diversity of economic activities taken as a whole. As a result, they do not exhaust the possibilities but they provide a starting point for the discussion in this chapter and Chapter 5.

Some of the ambiguities of the suburban economy have been highlighted in Walker's (1981: 409) classic treatment of American suburbs as a vast outlet for processes of capital accumulation: 'post-war suburbanization has served as a vast outlet for capital in all its forms; as direct investment in factories, infrastructure and housing production; as consumer buying; as credit creation. . . . It would be very hard indeed to imagine how American capitalism would have fared if it had had to make do with cities as they were in 1949.' This passage highlights a number of aspects of the suburban economy. First, some of the primary circuit of capital accumulation has long existed in the suburbs. Second, the production of suburban housing production has meant that a secondary circuit of capital has continued to grow in importance to the point that it

Table 4.1 Trajectories of settlement change from a first to a second modernity

---

MODERN CITY
    i. City->suburb
LATE MODERN CITY REGION
    ii. City->suburb->post—suburb
CITY REGION OF SECOND MODERNITY
    iii. Post-suburb->city
    iv. Growing suburb->post-suburb->city
    v. Stable affluent suburb->stable affluent suburb
    vi. Declining suburb->sub-suburb?
    vii. Declining city->suburb

Source: Phelps (2016).

represents a major if not *the* major focus of accumulation in some advanced economies. Third, the suburbs are important to a tertiary circuit of accumulation—to consumption of commodities of all sorts, a subject I return to in Chapter 10.

The Industrial Suburb and Capitalism's Primary Circuit

It has been argued that 'the place of industrial suburbs within the broader dynamics of urban growth has been lost in the historiography of the middle class suburb' (Lewis, 2004a: 3). Moreover, 'identifying the new with the suburbs and the old with the city fails to capture the complexity of urban form and development' (Lewis, 2004a: 13). Nevertheless, as scholarship devoted to the industrial suburb has grown, 'concern with the relationship between the rise of the industrial suburb and capitalist industrialization has pointed to the definite increase, in both absolute and relative terms, in the number of metropolitan manufacturing jobs found in the suburbs' (Lewis, 2004a: 7).

Manufacturing industries had begun to extract themselves from the labour and property market rigidities of American cities by the late 1800s and early 1900s (Scott, 1982). Indeed, echoing the very earliest connotations of the suburbs, Lewis notes how 'Indeed, many nineteenth- and twentieth-century industrial suburbs had longer histories than many areas within cities' (Lewis, 2004a: 12). Lachine, a working-class industrial suburb of Montreal in Canada, began life as a fur-trading entrepot with connections to London and Paris and declined before re-emerging around steel, metalworking, and glass. Lewis's (2004b: 81 and 86) data on the industrial suburbs of Montreal indicates that they grew from having a 13 per cent share of the stock of businesses in Montreal in 1861 to a 23 per cent share in 1890 to a 32 per cent share by 1929.

Manhattan's share of manufacturing employment fell from two-thirds to less than a third over the period 1869–1954 (Lewis, 1999) as industry moved to the suburbs. Indeed the resource channelling effects coupled with the scale of direct employment associated with the railways meant they had a profound draw on the relocation of manufacturing industries to the suburbs (Healey, 2015). The railways formed 'Metropolitan corridors' and at their height from the late 1800s to the 1930s within them 'suburban land was abundant, cheap, accessible by railroad, and lightly taxed; that insurance companies implicitly mandated it as the only safe manufacturing location made it even more attractive' (Stilgoe, 1983: 85).

From early on in the urban industrialization of America and, to a lesser extent, European nations, economic activities were moving to locations on the urban fringe or beyond. They may have been engulfed by the outward movement of the city to become suburbs but their initial location was also interpreted at this early time as a balance between centripetal and centrifugal economic forces (Taylor, 1970 [1915]: 6). As Taylor's account of satellite cities in the US describes: 'the big opportunity for escape from crowded cities is through the wholesale removal of work which city people do. Huge industrial plants are uprooting themselves bodily from the cities. With households, small stores, saloons, lodges, churches, schools clinging to them...they set themselves down ten miles away in the open' (Taylor, 1970 [1915]: 1). 'Although large integrated firms typically initiated suburbanization, the development of suburban agglomeration economies attracted firms of all sizes from a range of industries and produced a diversity of productive strategies on the metropolitan fringe' (Lewis, 2004a: 9). The satellite cities that Taylor described were only one format of the industrial suburb. Nevertheless they are a powerful reminder of a history of the in-between economy of interplaces well before contemporary times.

While the suburbanization process is often associated with the requirements of capital-intensive and land-extensive factories seeking economies of scale, smaller labour-intensive factories also decentralized to suburbs to create a 'highly differentiated and specialized industrial suburban landscape' in most US metropolitan areas in the hundred years or so from the late 1800s (Lewis, 1999). Indeed, Lewis goes on to identify four types of industrial suburb. These he describes as: the informally created industrial complexes often found at the fringe of existing cities; relatively self-contained satellite industrial towns that were nevertheless rapidly absorbed into the physical expansion of metropolitan areas; single-company suburban towns, and; the organized industrial districts adjacent to major infrastructure and often purposely developed by infrastructure-providing companies such as railway and utility companies. However they were produced and whichever form they took, industrial suburbs would have a mixture of industry and housing as in the Calumet River area in south Chicago, where 'industry hugged the lakeshore, the Calumet River, and the railroad lines, while working-class housing was sandwiched between industry, water and rail' (Lewis, 2004a: 1).

Agglomerations of industry were to be found at new inter-urban locations even if these were eventually absorbed into the larger urban fabric surrounding historic cities. For Walker and Lewis (2001), industry in the suburbs helped to build out the city in a way that the theory of agglomeration rarely acknowledged. Speaking of San Francisco, Walker notes how: 'suburbanization of industry appears to be the normal mode of urban growth.... In fact, the tendency for industry to seek spacious quarters at the fringe is so marked from the outset that it makes no sense to speak of an "old industrial core" that later suburbanized' (Walker, 2004: 122–3). The original core had been eclipsed as early as 1870 by other employment centres. More often than not with regard to the rise of industrial metropolises in the US but also elsewhere, important topographical constraints shaped something of the in-between geography of industrial suburbs. In Pittsburgh, as in San Francisco, the terrain prevented an orderly incremental and sequential outward industrialization process. 'While Pittsburgh formed a dense urban core for the region, industrial towns and residential suburbs stretched linearly away from this core along the major meandering river valleys and the main railroads that snaked through smaller tributary stream valleys. A series of satellite cities in the surrounding counties and the industrial settings at the clay and coal resources areas completed the metropolitan pattern' (Muller, 2004: 136–7).

The process of the relocation of industry to the suburbs of American cities continued to display considerable complexity as it gathered pace in the twentieth century. Erickson (1983) was able to identify three phases which he termed: 'spillover and specialization' (1920–40); 'dispersal and diversification' (1940–60); and 'infilling and multinucleation' (1960–). The result was that suburbs by the 1960s were as diverse as their respective metropolitan areas as a whole. Erickson went on to describe how 'the early postwar dispersed sprawl has increasingly given way to a structured, multinucleated pattern of economic activities referred to as urban subcenters, suburban nucleations, or minicities' with the resident firms benefitting 'both from the locations near suburban transportation nodes and from the external economies that arise from locational proximity' (Erickson, 1985: 19 and 20). Although these processes by which suburban nucleations or agglomerations had consolidated by the 1960s involved manufacturing industries, they also involved services, such as retailing. As early as 1929, roughly a third of all retail stores in metropolitan areas were in suburbs (Erickson, 1983: 98).

The historic dynamism of Europe and North Americas inner older suburbs typically has vanished.[1] The plight of these inner suburbs stands in marked contrast to the stable affluent residential suburbs and the post-suburbs and

---

[1] For some historic cities the loss of industry means that it may be no exaggeration to say that they have become suburbs in the sense of exporting labour to surrounding suburbs.

exurbs found elsewhere in the metropolitan economy. Given their manufacturing complexion and their reliance in some instances on a limited number of companies, these industrial inner suburbs have experienced population and employment decline. Moreover, industrial suburbs tended to have an associated working class residential market and a closer home–work connection than is associated with the generalized notion of residential suburbia as a bourgeois retreat from the city. As a result, employment decline in suburban industries has translated more immediately into problems of joblessness and poverty. As many as one in four or one in five of the suburbs of America's rustbelt metropolitan areas are those in which there is a close correspondence between manufacturing employment and poverty (Hanlon, Vicino, and Short, 2006).

The Residential Suburb, Intermediaries, and Capitalism's Secondary Circuit

For Harvey (1985: 11) 'The main thrust of the modern commitment to planning (whether at the state or corporate level) rests on the idea that certain forms of investment in the secondary and tertiary circuits are potentially productive.' That the suburbs as the key locale of the organized capitalism of the early post-war US were subject to both state and corporate planning is by now a familiar story. Less familiar is the accompanying story of the importance of the production and consumption of housing to the suburban economy.

Suburban Housing Production Networks

The ingredient central to the suburbs—housing—is itself a commodity produced from local, national and indeed international networks of activities to prefigure Chapter 9. Some measure of the importance of housing in this regard is given by the fact that as much as 70 per cent of personal wealth is accounted for by housing in Japan and 60 per cent in Australia falling to 20 per cent in the US (Badcock and Beer, 2000: 97, cited in Blunt and Dowling, 2006: 89). The recent sub-prime mortgage crisis affirms Lefebvre's (2003: 160) thought that 'it can even happen that real-estate speculation becomes the principal source for the formation of capital, that is, the realization of surplus value. As the percentage of overall surplus value formed and realized by industry begins to decline, the percentage created and realized by real-estate speculation and construction increases. The second circuit becomes the first, becomes essential' (Lefebvre, 2003: 160).

The inertia inherent in the built environment is one reason why the house building industry has often been overlooked as an important example of local industrial districts (Buzzelli and Harris, 2006). There is evidence to suggest that the networks of activity that compose suburban housing production (Buzzelli and Harris, 2006), and even, to an extent, commercial property development (Wood, 2004) have remained stubbornly local. Moreover, the production and consumption of housing while being open to interpretation with the metaphor of the network, remains stubbornly territorial, delimited or enclosed, in its appearance as increasingly specialized spaces of consumption at the urban scale.

Historically, the fact that the suburbs became centres for production of goods and services also had ramifications for the house-building industry itself. With regard to the Canadian case, while custom building for corporate clients was the ideal for builders, industrial suburbs 'offered builders the prospect of a boom in demand for modest, but standard houses' such that 'the concentration of new jobs in industrial suburbs offered builders a predictable, captive market. These were the conditions under which some builders ventured to operate on a large scale' (Harris, 2004: 101). These corporate suburbs of the modern era may have promoted the growth and consolidation of larger house building companies but the process was slow to unfold. Moreover, 'Arguably, the most important motives that built the corporate suburbs were not at all those of the consumers but those of the builder and financier. Mass housing was erected by the mass builder that had ridden in on the tide of corporate finance' (Harris, 2004: 144).

In early booms in suburb building in America such as in Boston, as many as 9,000 building companies took a share of the 22,500 homes built in the late 1800s (Warner, 1978: 37). The same was true historically of the construction of London suburbs with many builders being involved each accounting for small batches of buildings (Dennis, 2008). In the US, the mass market opportunities afforded with the post-war auto-centred suburban building boom meant that local builders for the first time branched out across the country to become modest-sized national builders. Even so, in neighbouring Canada for example, the scale of house-building companies remained modest and the organization of work rather fragmented. Harris (2004) notes that up until 1971 60 per cent of builders subcontracted as much as three-quarters of all construction work.

Curiously, at one and the same time, housing as *the* primary commodity of consumption in suburbia is even associated with particular forms such as the bungalow (King, 1984) whose travels internationally might be a prime example of the sort of interplace economy highlighted in Chapter 7. Despite being organized in distinctly local production systems until very recently in many national economies, housing designs, construction methods, and even associated plans for suburban subdivisions have also been widely mobilized in modern times. As King (1984: 7) describes of the bungalow 'it is a dwelling type—possibly the only one—which, both in form and name, can almost certainly be found in every continent of the world' (King, 1984: 2) but it is inextricably linked locationally with the suburbs. 'The most significant fact about the bungalow is that the term, the ideology it represents and the reality in which that ideology is expressed can be found in many quarters of the globe. It is a physical, but also an economic, social and cultural phenomenon.' Whilst interest has been on the social and cultural meanings of the bungalow there is no doubting its economic significance as a worldwide phenomenon since it must continue to make up a significant portion of all suburban housing built to date.

Intermediaries and the Selling of Suburbia

Speaking to the US, Knox (2008: 11) describes how 'the built environment of suburbia like many other components of material culture in romantic capitalism, has been the subject of successive and overlapping sequences of enchantment, disenchantment, and re-enchantment'. He goes on to describe how 'Demand and supply in this dialectical process of enchantment, disenchantment and re-enchantment is mediated by a wide range of "exchange professionals"', chief among which have been design professionals who 'by virtue of the prestige and mystique socially accorded to creativity...add exchange value to the built environment through their decisions' (Knox, 2008: 11). The fact that 'the real estate industry, homeowner associations, chambers of commerce, and banks are the most active managers of symbolic generalizations' (Gottdiener, 1986a: 207) indicates how central the urban image making of such intermediaries has been to the production and consumption of suburbia.

In the case of the US it seems clear that 'Successive phases of enchantment and re-enchantment have left contemporary suburbia a long way from the seers' and intellectuals' utopia and their vision of moral landscapes that would promote beauty, amenity, civility, restraint, decorum, privacy, status, and community. Only privacy and status have survived as attributes of the degenerate utopias at the leading edge of the New Metropolis. To the extent that community has survived, it is community commodified' (Knox, 2008: 172–3). The suburban housing market continues to develop increasingly as one segmented into several separate more or less lucrative markets. At the 'top end' is a clear demand for the 'McMansions' of 'Vulgaria' (Knox, 2008). The discussion here prefigures that in Chapter 10 where this particular product would be a prime case of how we express ourselves through consumption. The residential suburbs of the early post war years of organized American capitalism in particular were ones of 'inconspicuous consumption' (Whyte, 1967). By today they have become important locales of conspicuous consumption. In these new suburban residential landscapes the American Dream has been recalibrated in a way that 'means that home ownership in an arcadian setting now has to be packaged with a significant degree of suburban bling: bigness, spectacle, and affordable luxury have eclipsed mere residence. It is the American Dream Extreme' (Knox, 2008: 76–7). If 'Conspicuous construction has become an important precondition for conspicuous consumption, and suburban social space has become irradiated by bigness and bling' (Knox, 2008: 11), then some indication of the economy centred on the middle landscape of residential suburbia comes also from the increasing scale of the building industry itself. 'Metroburbia is largely a product of big developers whose firms are not only involved with land and building but also with many aspects of finance, insurance, marketing, and local politics' (Knox, 2008: 666) larger land parcels and land banks.

Ironically, New Urbanist developments have made up an important element of these lucrative new niche markets. As gated communities without the gates, these are communities in search of a self-selecting population. They are lifestyle developments in which any sense of community is entangled with financial and legal considerations. In this way New Urbanist developments are more of a political-economic phenomenon than previous efforts at community building (Passell, 2013: 117). 'New urbanism contributes to generating pedestrian-friendly environments and transportation options, but as long as people drive to work or shop, then new urbanists are generally producing more attractive suburbs' (Grant, 2006: 169). New urbanist developments take their place in the ongoing suburbanization of the United States. That is, as Kolb describes, 'New Urbanist developments combine spatial features of older towns with economic and cultural characteristics of today's linked and mixed places. The lists and the noncentric and the virtual penetrate the pretty villages, which cannot close on themselves. The strip waits just outside. Though the neighbourhoods have local centres, they remain nodes in the network' (Kolb, 2008: 165). As many as two-thirds of new urbanist projects have infilled the extant urban and suburban fabric rather than having been built on green fields. Nevertheless, the suspicion remains that 'The new suburbanism might be a truer label, because the *new* theme that links these projects is the redesign of that vast area in what most Americans now live, sprawled between the metropolitan center, which is emptying out, and the open countryside, which is rapidly becoming devoured' (Scully, 1994: 221, quoted in Trudeau and Malloy, 2011: 427).

'What New Urbanism has evidently got right, along with other kinds of master-planned developments, is its market appeal. As premium spaces designed to accommodate the secession of successful in enclaves ... they are perfectly suited to the shift in social, cultural, and political sensibilities that has occurred with the rise of neoliberalism' (Knox, 2008: 111). Seaside in Florida designed by architects Duany and Plater-Zyberk was the development that launched a collective effort to derive desirable urban qualities, while the Kentlands development in Gaithersburg, Maryland was integral to the New Urbanism movement's ability to reproduce itself (Passell, 2013: 37 and 71). However, house prices in Seaside and Kentlands are some way above the average for neighbouring suburban tracts and their respective metropolitan areas as a whole.

The development of new market niches has been bound up with the likes of the New Urbanist movement which has sought to highlight some of the ecological ramifications of distanciation in housing production networks as they have been orchestrated by larger corporations. At first sight, it might seem odd to regard the patchwork of more or less contiguous residential developments that have made up the urban fringe of metropolitan areas in the US as a distinctly territorial economic geographical formation. Yet Lerup (2005) echoes my use of the term deployment/enclave as one key analytical concept when regarding leapfrog suburban residential subdivisions as akin to a military mission. The case for conceiving the manner in which housing production networks touch down locally in formations that are highly territorialized is stronger still when one begins to recognize both the increasing degree of specialization emerging in housing production and consumption and the explicitly gated nature of some residential developments.

It is important to note that this dialectical movement that Knox speaks of has played itself out rather differently in different parts of the world. Ironically, it is the dominance of NIMBY and BANANA attitudes among existing rural and suburban interests in the planning system that has meant that large-scale housing developments have been resisted by communities across much of the United Kingdom.[2] A structural shortage of housing has developed as a result of new housing having come to be regarded as an externality. Although housing is regarded as a basic human need it is also clear that there is a distinct politics to this product that has had important effects on the structure and organization of the house-building industry and the extent to which suburban housing can be considered to have been re-enchanted in the way it has in the US. In the UK, suburban housing has often appeared as reluctantly planned and poorly served extensions to towns, an externality (Breheny, 2001) to be planned away by local governments (Phelps, 2012a).

---

[2] The by now well-known term NIMBY refers to 'not in my back yard' while the less well known term BANANA that has some currency in the UK refers to 'build absolutely nothing anywhere near anyone'.

In Latin America, gated suburban residential developments represent lucrative niches for developers and frequently have grown up among some of the otherwise poorest communities of the urban periphery. The municipality of Pilar at the outer reaches of Buenos Aires would be a case in point. Pilar is perhaps most famous locally as the most prominent location for such gated residential communities in the metropolitan area—there being over 100 of various types in this single outer metropolitan municipality. Here upscale residential sport resorts and other 'regular' gated residential complexes (such as El Pueblo in Figure 4.1) mingle with informal settlements. These residential enclaves are a source of employment for local populations and while contributing to infrastructure in their immediate environs have not contributed noticeably to that in the remainder of municipality. Moreover, they have also generated something of a new municipal centre—in the form of a new shopping mall—at a junction of the pan-Americana highway—well away from the old city plaza (Roitman and Phelps, 2011).

Santiago de Chile's suburban expansion has been extremely rapid in the past three to four decades and among the most lucrative niches have been a

Figure 4.1 The entrance and marketing suite of El Pueblo gated residential community, Pilar

Source: author's photograph.

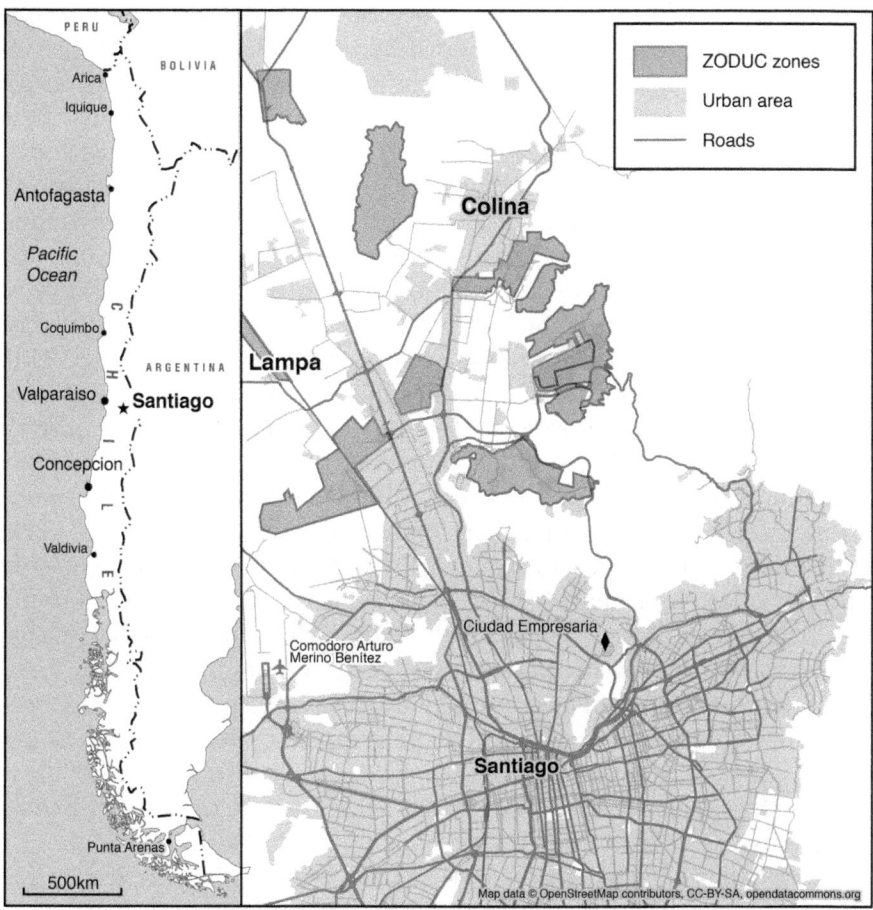

Figure 4.2 The ZODUC developments of Colina

series of new ZODUC (zones of conditional development) licensed by central government as a means of better organizing a haphazard and often poorly serviced pattern of development. Colina, a poor peri-urban municipality, is now also home to five separate master-planned residential communities. According to the Communal Development Plan (PLADECO, 2009) the commune of Colina encompasses a total land area of 985 km^2. Over the years it became settled informally by families employed in agriculture and other industries (PLADECO, 2009). These informal settlements often lack basic services and amenities but have also become attractive to the wealthy of Santiago since they offer sizeable plots on which to construct villas. While much of Colina remains agricultural, its population has risen to an estimated

116,410 in 2012.[3] At the end of the 1980s the predominance of the 'parcelas de agrado' (plots of pleasure) supported by law N° 3.516 (1980) fuelled an outward organic expansion of Santiago. In the face of pressure from real estate developers, the MINVU decided to regulate the expansion in the rural areas adjoining Santiago de Chile through new 'Conditioned Development Zones' (ZODUCs).[4] A minimum size for such ZODUC developments of 300 hectares was specified in order that they should develop as 'new cities separated from the metropolis, avoiding conurbations and extensive growth beyond the defined boundaries' (MINVU, 1998: 55). A 5 per cent target for land to be allocated for social housing projects was based on the idea of avoiding social segregation typically deployed in the rest of urban centres (MINVU, 1998). Five ZODUC zones established in Colina by the modification to the Metropolitan Regulator Plan (PRMS) in 1996/97. Ciudad Chicureo (commercial name 'Piedra Roja'); Chamisero (commercial name 'Valle Norte'); Pan de Azúcar (commercial name 'La Reserva'); Valle Santa Elena (commercial name 'Santa Elena'), and: Santa Filomena (commercial name 'Santa Filomena') are each under control of a real-estate firm with parcels of land often subsequently offered to other developers. They have helped to produce a polycentric outer suburban mosaic of income and infrastructure-rich residential developments amidst significant poverty and poorly developed municipal infrastructure.[5] However, these suburban mega projects are not as decoupled from the city as one might imagine. Indeed their proximity to other wealthy and business districts of Santiago forms part of their appeal while their cultural coding is close to the bourgeois retreat of classical Anglo-American residential suburbia (Heinrichs, Lukas, and Nuissl, 2011).

The selling of suburbia is also apparent in Indonesia where the 'enclaves of real estate housing appear as islands in a sea of kampong settlements' (Leaf, 1996: 1631), notably in the extended metropolitan area of Jakarta. Here gated residential communities can be seen as a mixture of societal needs, modern design ideas, and capitalist imperatives (Leisch, 2002: 341). Partial industrialization has nevertheless produced a new middle class and several major real-estate corporations such as Lippo, Salim, and Ciputra, catering to and shaping

[3] Biblioteca Nacional, 2012. Reportes estadísticos y comunales. Available at: http://reportes-comunales.bcn.cl/2012/index.php/Colina#Indicadores_demogr.C3.A1ficos. Accessed 15 September 2015.
[4] These areas aim to regulate new developments with a view to imposing impact fees for externalities related to transport and environment with further regulations stipulating a mix of land uses, specific densities of development and a percentage of land for social housing projects, though it is questionable whether they have achieved these goals.
[5] According to the National Survey of Socio-Economic Characterization (CASEN 2003–2009), the rate of poverty in 2003 for a total population of 81.454 inhabitants reached 21.6%. In 2009 the population had increased to 107,867 but the rate of poverty decrease (10.8%) was slower than the national average (15%) (Biblioteca Nacional, 2012).

the tastes of these new segments of society in developments such as Lippo Karawac and Bumi Serpong Datai in the Tangerang district to the west of Jakarta (Leisch, 2002). 'As the primary residential component of the landscape of modernity, these single-use, low-density, automobile dependent enclaves of single-family housing serve as a significant device for the introduction of "modern" lifestyles to Jakarta's consumer class' (Leaf, 1996: 1629). Land speculators and developers have been significant in generating the market for individual gated suburban residential areas as well as altogether larger new town or mini-city projects. As Leaf (1996: 1623) describes 'the major "visionary" behind changes in the city is Ciputra, an Indonesian-Chinese developer who business has been built on its ability to act as an intermediary between the wealthiest of Jakarta's capitalists and the regulators of urban development' (Leaf, 1996: 1623). Similar major real-estate developments in Cikerang to the east of Jakarta have produced new outer suburbs that are themselves polycentric as I describe in Chapter 5.

Enclosures, as Wu (2005) reminds us, have long been a familiar part of housing in China. Under socialist planning principles much housing was supplied alongside production under the *danwei* work unit concept which economized on the state's expenditure on collective consumption needs and in which, it is important to remember, real-estate intermediaries were absent. The scale of the urban transition in China since Deng's reforms ensures that much housing production involves dense, high-rise, mass residential suburbs. While these mass residential suburbs may not look anything like the American form of low-density, single family, detached home, they are nevertheless subject to intense marketing and image-making. Moreover, real-estate development itself is multiply mediated by the state since it is city governments who: help to make available new land for development via annexations; coordinate with developers around leasing arrangements; sometimes help to prepare land for development notably by facilitating or forcing the movement of populations; and are involved in the financing and actual development of land itself via municipal development corporations. Nevertheless, mass residential suburbs of the high-rise type are joined by low-rise residential developments catering to a new middle class. Luxury village developments such as Orange County outside Beijing are revealing not only of the market making by real-estate companies but the hybrid nature of the architectural and lifestyles being promulgated (Wu, 2004). The state is not absent in the process of taste making—licensing experiments with suburban real estate such as in the nine new towns designated surrounding Shanghai, each of which are designated to adopt distinct German, British, Dutch, Australian, French, Spanish, and not forgetting Chinese architectural and planning styles (Wu, 2014). The 'consultation fee' for Songjiang new town alone is reported as $US 6 million, providing some indication of how the designation of these new towns 'marked a new era in Chinese planning practices, which began to emphasize aesthetic landscapes and lifestyles' (Wu, 2014: 150–1). Indeed 'designating a very small pilot area to adopt the English style made it possible to achieve a brand' for the rest of the much larger new town of Songjiang developed in a more familiar Chinese planning and architectural format (Wu, 2014: 153). Wu (2005) has described these gated residential developments as 'commodity housing enclaves' which conform to the decidedly in-between logic of club goods (Webster, 2002).

Some of the same dynamics are found in the post-socialist context of central and eastern Europe where they are helping to fashion landscapes that appear similar in some respects to the mid-urban realm—of residential and employment enclaves of all sorts—that I describe in the next chapter. Hirt's (2012) account of the bourgeois retreat from the central city of Sofia in Bulgaria highlights the role of the state in licensing and endorsing gated residential suburbanization. The process began as a limited and ad hoc response to the conditions of the socialist and early post-socialist city by those with sufficient wealth. It involved the private construction of villas but is by now big business involving an element of selling 'holistic' lifestyles seemingly promised by gated residential communities and their attendant facilities. The task of selling suburbia is all the easier given the patent divergence between conditions inside and outside of these gated complexes.

The Transformation of Residence and Capitalism's Tertiary Circuit

The home is being reconstituted as an important economic site as a result of the dissolution of corporate contact systems, the mobilization of personal networks required to accomplish work, and as a result of changing patterns and processes of consumption. More than ever, it would appear, the home plays its anchoring role (Blunt and Dowling, 2006) with regard to economic relations, some of which I also touch on in Chapters 6 and 10—albeit that important inequalities endure in this anchoring of economic relations.

The Dissolution of Corporate Contact Systems

The geography of workplaces and corporate 'contact systems' (Thorngren, 1970) was a predictably hierarchical one, anchored on the strategic face-to-face contacts overwhelmingly concentrated in central city head-office-producer-service agglomerations for strategic decision-making (Goddard,

1975).[6] However, in the global north especially, the home is being reconstituted as a place of production with the dissolution of corporate contact
systems in an era of disorganized capitalism (Lash and Urry, 1994).
'Classic workplace geographies of the kind done on assembly lines or in
big offices...produced a certain picture of what "big" and "powerful"
meant and how much organizations succeeded or failed. Where work
was, who the workers were and how surpluses were being extracted' (Laurier,
2002: 5). In contrast, the implications of the distributed workplace for home life
begin to become clearer. The (re)organization of work on the move within key
sectors of disorganized capitalism is done at present largely by workers themselves (Harrison et al., 2004). In contrast to the fixed work places of factories and
offices of the mass of collective worker where individual workers remained
immobile as the company's world, or more likely its national or regional market
was brought to them, the nomadic workers of the distributed workplace working on trains, planes, and automobiles are left to connect up the company world
and its markets/regions (Laurier, 2002).

Much of the early interest in home work was forthcoming at a time of the
restructuring of the mass collective workplaces—factories and central business
district office blocks—of Fordism. This reflected the way in which 'the social
contract between business and labour, in which large companies provided
lifelong employment, steady pay increases with seniority, and generous
pensions in exchange for employee loyalty and commitment, started to
break down in the 1980s' (Mason et al., 2011; 627–8). In the global north,
home-working has continued to become both more prevalent across sections of the workforce and more embedded in suburban settings as a result of
new opportunities arising from the transformation of urban economies into
producer and consumer services (Glaeser, 2011). Figures for the UK put the
proportion of all businesses being operated from home at 50–60 per cent
(Mason et al., 2011).

The workplace now often includes an array of locations—such as the home,
cafés and restaurants, airports, and trains—away from a single factory or office.
In short, 'a redefinition of the term, "workplace" is needed' since 'knowledge
work in the future will no longer take place just at a single location...but at
multiple locations: in a network of places such as at company's headquarters,
at home, at a customer's locations or in a hotel, restaurants and train stations.'
(Harrison et al., 2004: 22). As major companies have restructured they have
engaged in the rationalization and automation of many activities and associated contacts to back-office locations, outsourcing many of these activities to

---

[6] Thorngren (1970) distinguished between the orientation, programming and routine contacts
that compose business organizations. The former are those of a strategic nature and which are vital
to the future survival and profitability of the organization.

third-party suppliers along the way, and developing a variety of means of employing their own staff more flexibly including a greater degree of home-working. In this way mobile work involves the 'accomplishment of the region', whereby workers in large measure 'put the region back together' on behalf of companies (Laurier, 2002), not least because of the relative lack of organizational thought given to how mobile workers will actually coordinate the tasks while being mobile.

The creative industries are more often than not associated exclusively with the buzz of central cities rather than suburbs. For Scott (2008), the suburbs within the contemporary cognitive-cultural economy seem to be largely addressed in the quite restricted terms of the important social problems for which they are containers:

> a new kind of balance and integration seems to be emerging at least in privileged sections of modern cities between economy and society, between production and consumption, between work and leisure, and between commerce and culture. A dark shadow is nonetheless cast over this gratifying picture both by the swelling underbelly of low-wage industrial and service functions that are invariably to be found in large metropolitan areas where cognitive-cultural economic functions are most highly developed, and by the often problem ridden residential areas ... that are the sources of the labour needed to maintain these functions   (Scott, 2008: 74).

Thus, literature on the cognitive-cultural economy (Scott, 2008) and creative industries (Florida, 2005) has been silent on some of the attendant intra- and inter-urban geographies. Where discussion is to be found it remains largely in terms of suburbs being part of an undifferentiated urban (city) whole or as adjuncts to cities. This may be a function of the scale and accessibility of the cities typically under consideration. Creative industries seemingly have a more multi-sited intra- and inter-urban contact system than the typical large manufacturing or service corporations of organized capitalism, as Brennan-Horley (2010) has illustrated graphically with respect to the economic role of the suburbs in Darwin, Australia, where nearly half of the creative linkages mapped are between suburban areas. In Darwin 'the magnitude of networked relationships that involve the suburbs implies that the role of the suburbs is vital to the functioning of the creative economy' and point to the likely signifi-cance of suburban economy in this respect in 'remote locations, places of low population or low density, where opportunities for networking or available facilities and infrastructure are scarce and distributed over larger areas'.

The Personal Networks of Autonomous Labour

The partial dissolution of corporate contact systems represents a de-synchronization of urban life—a de-synchronization that has occurred in those segments of the economy most exposed to the growth in personal mobility. The choice of how to use our time and the balance between paid work, unpaid work, and leisure becomes a problem of scheduling within temporal and geographical constraints where the solutions we adopt 'progressively redefine the problem' (Gershuny, 2000: 91). Capitalism has become more disorganized (Lash and Urry, 1991) such that 'organizing "co-presence" with key others (workmates, family, significant others, friends) within each day, week, year and so on becomes more demanding with the loss of *collective* coordination, "clusters" dissolve into personalized networks' (Sheller and Urry, 2006: 7) made possible by increased levels of physical and virtual mobility.

> The traditional 'office factory' of the nineteenth century and early twentieth century involved little face-to-face interaction or autonomy...the office of the future relies heavily on highly motivated individuals who are enabled by technology to have a high degree of autonomy and who use face-to-face interaction
> (Harrison et al., 2004: 10).

'At the scale of the individual, mobility and communications systems, like the automobile and the mobile telephone enable the manipulation of the spatial and temporal framework of everyday life...Activities drift across space and pile up in time, while being carried out at unexpected locations within the planned and engineered landscape of cities and regions' (Buliung, 2011: 1366). Thus, an important corollary to the dissolution of corporate contact systems is the mobilization of personal autonomy and networks by employers, employees, and the self-employed, which increasingly are centred on the home.

The literature on automobility, aeromobility, and the virtual mobility produced through ICT identify how home life is being transformed as the domestic sphere and home, leisure, and responsibilities of care are increasingly woven into the realm of employment and income generation. Automobility, for instance, 'is a system in which everyone is coerced into an intense *flexibility*...It forces people to juggle tiny fragments of time so as to deal with the temporal and spatial constraints that it itself generates' (Urry, 2008: 344 original emphasis). Thus,

> If *urbanization leads to the intensification of* human habitats, the concentration of places in space, and the unification of condensed temporal flows, then *automobilization, by contrast, leads to the extension of human* habitats, the dispersal of places across space, the opportunities to escape certain locales and to form new socialities, and the fragmentation of temporal flows, especially through suburbanization
> (Sheller and Urry, 2000: 742 original emphasis).

In similar vein, Cwerner (2009: 5) argues that 'The dispersal of organisations, networks and systems across space has drawn from, and then fed back into, evolving systems of mass air travel, which eventually led to the production of specific cognitive forms of space/time compression... which could be termed aeromobility *habitus'*. ICT has become a more important means of work in general as one US survey found that the mean time spent on line at work had risen from 4.6 hours in 2001 to 9.2 hours in 2010 (Rainie and Wellman, 2012: 177). However, ICT has also facilitated a more thoroughgoing dispersal of the workplace. Huws (2014: 58) describes how 'There has been an erosion of the clear boundaries of the workplace and the workday, with a spillover of many activities into the home or other locations, including an expectation that you should continue to be productive while travelling.' The significance of economic activities taking place on the move is discussed in Chapter 6 but for now it is enough to note that 'Boundaries between economic, political, and private life have pretty much dissolved. All conceivable time and space are raw materials for new products, for new commodities, for extended money relations' (Merrifield, 2010: 22). In one survey conducted in 2008, 60 per cent of all employed Americans did some work from home and 18 per cent worked from home almost every day (Rainie and Wellman, 2012: 185).

Modern mobilities can be 'revisioned as the ability of machines and people to *initiate* the movement of information, themselves, and goods between physical places, including fixed loci like home and work and mobile places like planes or trains or places within cyberspace' (Buliung, 2011: 1366, emphasis added). Networked individualism has been taken as the signature of this autonomy or self-discipline of company employees in the new cognitive-cultural economy whereby 'it is the person who is the focus: not the family, not the work unit, not the neighborhood, and not the social group' (Rainie and Wellman, 2012: 6). The principle of networked individualism is intriguing as it relates closely to the thought that it is personal and professional networks that are the primary institution governing contemporary patterns of agglomeration (Duranton, 1999), albeit that patterns of agglomeration have become more diffuse than in previous eras.[7] These personal and professional networks and associated self-regulation of work-life by an increasing number of individuals in various occupations appear crucially to rely on the deployment of 'network capital' (Elliott and Urry, 2010) or 'network sociality' (Lassen, 2010: 179). Elliott and Urry (2010) describe the virtual and physical mobility of select occupational segments as the vapour trails of network capital (Elliott and Urry, 2010). Whereas the cultural and economic capital previously prevalent and deployed in business had to be built up by

---

[7] Duranton (1999) suggests that it was guilds which constituted the key organizing institutions in the pre-industrial era. In contrast it was the land market and regulation of it through which economic activity was organized into more extensive cities with major residential suburbs. He suggests that it is personal and professional networks which are the organizing institutions of today's post-industrial age.

individuals, network capital is connections-driven and information-based. Such network capital is vital to the 'do-it-yourself scheduling and rescheduling' that has become necessary in an everyday, but increasingly complex, home–work life balancing act in many national economies. The self-actualizing work routines and the associated network capital deployed is at its greatest among what Elliott and Urry (2010) term 'globals'.

For globals, purpose-built forms of living can be at the centre of multi-sited work lives. 'An apparent paradox of residential life for urban elites is the way in which social and spatial seclusion in the neighbourhood persists alongside the advantages of these spaces due to their position as nodes in broader urban spaces of information, economic opportunity and leisure' (Atkinson, 2008: 43). The seclusion that Atkinson is referring to stems from the rise of gated residential communities that have emerged in many suburbs in many nations. Although they represent residential enclosures, with their superior communications infrastructures gated residential communities also present pockets of high connectivity and mobility in their respective contexts. Thus, 'Gated communities provide the central example of spaces that mediate between positions offering social refuge yet enabling contact via gates, electronic ports; and transportation appendages that enable seamless connectivity with other social and economic contexts and resources' (Atkinson, 2008: 43). They are a residential choice that forms an integral part of the sorts of network capital deployed by elite workers today: 'the social capital of the affluent now lies in extended networks and the latent resources inhering in relationships that can be mobilised when local contacts prove insufficient. Suburbia continues to "work" for the affluent even without proximate friends, family and associates because these contractual and reciprocal relationships can be invoked when they need to be' (Atkinson, 2008: 45).

The multilocational patterns of work into which residential suburbs are woven are also partly reliant on processes of 'circular migration' between residences. This is the case—albeit for contrasting reasons in the global north and the global south. In the global north, although not as yet quantitatively significant, multilocational living and working has become an emerging aspect of particular segments of the workforce in second modernity (Reuschke, 2010). Dick and Reuschke's (2012:178) figures suggest that in Germany by the mid-2000s over 350,000 workers had secondary residences. Although these are a select and well-qualified group of workers their total numbers are growing steadily. In the global south, the numbers of workers involved are much larger but it is 'urbanization without industrialization' that ensures a strong measure of circular migration between often informally developed suburbs and rural homes. In contrast to that in the global north, circular migration here reflects necessities of gaining sufficient income and of mitigating the risks associated with precarious livelihoods.

In some suburbs with significant concentrations of ethnic minorities, the worlds of global north and south are becoming bound together by long distance, transnational, circular migration. As Scott (2011: 305) describes, 'the social patchwork of American suburbs...is altogether more intricate today by reason of rapidly growing complements of racially and ethnically distinctive enclaves in the outer fringes of the city...Many of the residents of these enclaves are employed in the production worker jobs in the high technology firms and other industrial establishments that still occupy suburban locations in America.' Such 'ethnoburbs' are 'multi-ethnic communities in which one ethnic minority group has a significant concentration, but does not necessarily comprise a majority. Demographic composition can change rapidly, however, due to continuous and variable immigrant flows, and because the global outpost role of the ethnoburb creates certain peculiar population dynamics' (Li, 1998: 482). The enclave is a geographical formation evoked also by Li when describing how 'ethnoburbs thus function as settlement type that replicates some of the features of an enclave and some features of a suburb lacking a specific ethnic identity' (Li, 1998: 482).

Consumption in the Suburbs

The word 'economy' has its roots in the Greek word *oikos* (home/dwelling), though it is only recently that a body of work has begun to pay attention to the home as a place of work and the residential suburb as the locale of economic activities, paid and unpaid. In particular, the house represents a site upon which not only social reproduction but also production and consumption are centred. This is true today but also historically. Although the household economy is not something I dwell on greatly here, it can be regarded as a mediating place or site of 'small-scale social, physical, cultural and emotional infrastructure' (Marston, 2000: 233). More specifically, home can be considered 'a relation *between* material and imaginative realms and processes' (Blunt and Dowling, 2006: 22, emphasis added), the latter dealt with in Chapter 10. It is another distinct economic geographic formation to place alongside those of agglomeration, enclave, network, and arena.

An important part of bourgeois society—presumably in the suburbs—in England and France at the turn of the nineteenth century revolved around the use of consumption as a means of distinction (de Grazia, 1996, cited in Marston, 2000: 234). The politics and ideology associated with a bourgeois retreat to the suburbs in Victorian and Edwardian Britain were not antithetical to the cognitive-cultural industries. The search for higher amenity of residential living in London, for example, went hand in hand with the emergence of local demand for arts and crafts. Indeed, such was the scale of local suburban demand that it spilled over into the creation of new institutions underpinning education and training in these industries in particular London suburbs (Crowther, 2010). In this sense houses have long been the 'elephants of stuff' to use Miller's (2010) phrase.

By the mid to late twentieth century the use of consumption in a bourgeois retreat to the suburbs was also expressed in relation to the many services that were now produced and consumed collectively. Here again, the value of the suburbs to the tertiary circuit of capital accumulation in national economies continues to be underestimated. Tiebout's famous model of the market for local governments was centred on the exercise of consumption choices that extended well beyond housing. In this formal model, 'the consumer-voter may be viewed as picking that community which best satisfies his preference pattern for public goods.... Given these revenue and expenditure patterns, the consumer-voter moves to that community where local government best satisfies his set of preferences. The greater the number of communities and the greater the variation among them, the closer the consumer will come to fully realizing his preference position' (Tiebout, 1956: 418). For Tiebout, the suburbs were a realm in which something approximating a market mechanism of consumer-voter preferences was most visible, given the large number of such jurisdictions and the process of administrative fragmentation apparent in the US. The suburbs composed a landscape of consumption of the public services that went with houses. Indeed—and there's the rub—those key public services did not simply exist but had to be produced and supplied at some cost, prompting the almost immediate transformation of many residential suburbs into something post-suburban as I discuss in Chapter 5. Hence the growth of the suburbs has also involved the growth of employment in public services as rural counties have had to gain a more substantial bureaucracy and urban focus and as seceding communities have had to gain new service-providing capacities or contract for them.

In more recent times 'changing economic structures have opened up a "window of economic opportunity" for residential neighbourhoods' (Folmer and Risselada, 2013: 1891). Echoing some of the historic patterns described above in London's inner suburbs in the Victorian era, in the Netherlands those suburbs that have experienced significant gentrification are also those in which a suburban cognitive-cultural economy (Scott, 2008) has become apparent as a result of both local consumption and enterprise formation (Folmer, 2013). In this respect spatial planning institutions have been important mediators in the gradual transformation of residential suburbs. While in broad terms the built environment reflects the changing needs of capital, the process by which this comes to pass is far from a smooth or automatic one (Gospodini, 2006: 181). Inertia is inherent within the built environment of cities and suburbs (Dodgshon, 1998; Harvey, 1985). This includes the suburbs where Folmer and Risselada (2013) identify how different planning approaches have shaped the character of the formal suburban economy in different Dutch suburbs. In some of the city-regions investigated—including Amsterdam—residential suburbs account for the majority of businesses in the entire metropolitan area. The different planning approaches produce outcomes in residential areas that they typify in terms of 'markets' and 'mixed' character on the one hand where planning regulations permit or promote economic activities and 'deserts' and 'dormitories' where planning acts more commonly to restrict economic functions (including not just the amount of economic activity but the range of economic functions that might be present). Only the desert typology conforms to what we might think of as purely residential suburbs as the dormitory type may well contain a substantial number and range of home-based and informal business activities that remain out of the scope of their study.

For Kitchin and Dodge (2011) the home has become more porous to information flows which both enable monitoring and require regulation but simultaneously represent it as a site of expanded consumption and indeed 'prosumption' opportunities. It is the increasingly coded nature of the home that contributes to the distanciation of domestic practices primarily as a function of the supplementary capacity to solve micro-relational problems of coordinating all of the work, social, and care responsibilities that come together in the home. In particular the home has become an important site of e-commerce and through which online retailers access their customers though the picture is a highly geographically uneven one globally and within nations. In 2015, on line shopping was estimated to account for around 10 per cent of purchases in the US but less than 1 per cent in South East Asia (The Economist, 2015).

To prefigure discussion in Chapter 10, the self-actualized pattern of work described above is also closely related to the increasing autonomy and significance of consumption within the economy with work practices having shifted from discrete sites to society generally (Terranova, 2004: 74, cited in Lury, 2011: 103). This is registered in the idea of 'prosumers' (where the boundary between production and consumption activities is blurred) and where important amounts of unpaid labour are incorporated into the co-production of products and services. If 'In contemporary society, it is not uncommon to find cognitive-cultural workers who have carried networking to something like a fine art' (Scott, 2008: 69) they have done so increasingly from home(s). Some of the element of the networking and prosumption centred on the home has its lineage in the longer-term emergence of a self-service economy (Gershuny, 1978) and processes of social innovation whereby consumption emerges as the engine, rather than the product, of structural changes in economies: 'the material basis for a society's economic structure is the style of life, the pattern of daily activities, of its members. The mundane acts of eating and drinking and caring and learning and playing constitute the demand that maintains the economy, and thereby provides jobs in it' (Gershuny, 2000: 248).

New technologies frequently now deployed in the home have opened up important interstices for income generation. In some contexts these 'opportunities' may represent a new element in the geography of the informal economy borne of necessity; a curious mirror of some of the realities that have long been present in the global south. In other contexts they may represent an active choice—reflecting aspirations related to material well-being through the consumption of goods and services. These opportunities for supplementing household income may be registered in terms of the recycling of goods and services through the likes of car boot sales or on web-based 'C2C' retail tools such as 'eBay'.

Conclusion

Much of this chapter has been North America and to a lesser extent Europe-focused. In this respect, the US is *not* the norm regarding suburban development (Hirt, 2013) but it does represent a powerful and perhaps exceptional model, aspects of which have only just begun to be exported (Beauregard, 2006).

The contemporary picture that emerges from the partly exceptional American vantage point is an in-between one in which 'America's metropolitan areas are coalescing into vast, sprawling regions of "metroburbia" fragmented and multimodal mixtures of employment and residential settings with a fusion of suburban, exurban and central-city characteristics' (Knox, 2008: 2). It is in this sense of the mixing of different settlement types and the blurring of the boundaries between them—including assumptions regarding their economic content—that the exceptionalism of America may be indicative of trends elsewhere.

By now the suburban economy is old and expansive enough but with life left in it to offer more than a glimpse of each of the four economic geographical formations introduced in the preceding chapter. Historically speaking, the growth of industrial suburbs reveals a pattern involving important agglomerations and enclaves of economic activity. These twin logics of the concentration of economic activities and the enclosure of others remain in the present day as I also discuss in the next two chapters. The economic geographical formation of the network also appears to be important since 'community in the sprawling suburbs is based less on local enclosure and centering than on linkage and communication' (Kolb, 2008: 170).

The suburban economy is by now mature and expansive enough to represent an economy as broad and diverse as that usually reserved for the city proper. It continues to be an important location for agglomerations of industries that make up capitalism's primary circuit. However, if anything, it is the houses so synonymous with suburbia that have come to the fore as the secondary circuit of capitalism has continued to expand in importance. Since houses are the 'elephants of stuff', many of those activities implicated in the tertiary circuit of capital accumulation are also strongly present in suburbs.

If the state (national and local) was itself an important intermediary in the promotion of residential suburban development in post-war America, then in recent decades, private sector intermediaries of various sorts have come to play an important role in the re-enchantment of suburbia—the production and consumption of a more variegated suburbia. Their role appears set to increase in an era of unprecedented international economic integration in which housing and planning models and housing production networks stand to become considerably more internationalized. Yet, as we will see, the state and the political and policy processes associated with it remain important mediators in the emergence of mid urban realms around the globe.

5

The Mid-urban Realm

Introduction

In this chapter I continue with the contribution of the suburban matrix to the economies of many nations. The term 'suburb' is one that is imbued with the stasis associated with dwelling in a place and yet suburbs are charged with a greater sense of flux than this may suggest. As the architecture collective MVRDV argue: 'More and more regions have become more or less continuous urban fields . . . And as the population and its communications options continue to multiply, this metamorphosis seems far from finished. Not only has the process increased the number of these urban zones, it has also intensified the "in-betweens"' (MVRDV, 1999: 16). The networks of relations that come together in a mid-urban realm are the economic and social glue that binds together megapolitan and national economies.

Urbanization has continued to take place in a mid-urban realm despite a lack of attention to megapolitan forms since the 1970s. Megapolitan forms of urbanization are apparent in many national or continental contexts and signify an economy in between housing numerous interplaces. Within these regions, the suburban era has come to an end (Teaford, 1997) with the emergence of 'technoburbs' (Fishman, 1987) or 'boomburbs' (Lang and LeFurgy, 2007). The suburb has continued to evolve or be conceived differently in ways I began to allude to it in Chapter 4. As Osterhammel (2014: 249) suggests, 'Inner and outer boundaries are lacking in the present-day megalopolis of enclaves, diffuse, polycentric "conurbations" with middling degrees of compression.' The communities that compose much of the mid-urban realm are themselves fragmented into a series of enclaves including residential areas noted in the previous chapter but also places of employment such as industry and corporate campuses, retail malls and science parks. Finally, beyond the suburbs lie the interstitial spaces of the city's exurbs or rural hinterland.

As a space, the mid-urban realm is one that acts to organize and mediate the inter-urban and international economy, not least since Gottmann (1976) long ago recognized that megapolitan regions operate as economic hinges between national and international urban systems (Li and Phelps, 2017). Moreover, planning and politics have mediated the development of megapolitan regions across the world. In China national level strategic planning speaks to a number of megapolitan regions such as the Yangtze River Delta and Pearl River Delta regions (Wu, 2014). In some notable instances—such as Malaysia's Mulitimedia Supercorridor (Bunnell, 2004)—the mid-urban realm has been framed explicitly in order to promote and project aspirations to economic modernity internationally, though with mixed results (Lepawsky, 2009; Phelps and Dawood, 2014).

The mid-urban realm is also one increasingly serviced by premium infrastructure networks and woven together by the personal networks reliant on enhanced virtual and physical mobility. 'The landscapes of the extended, polynucleated city-region tend to transcend the possibility of rolling out singular or coherent urban infrastructures' and 'to eclipse geographically or even isolate the networked urban cores that were the legacies of the standardized infrastructure ideal' (Graham, 2004: 236 and 237). The nature of the mid-urban realm is therefore one that includes tightly bounded places in the form of various enclaves and yet also one that can be subject to any number of non-territorial metaphors such as flows and networks.

Megapolitan Regions as Hinges

The tendency for urbanization and industrialization to proceed at the scale of heavily urbanized corridors composed of linked settlements has been somewhat neglected in the economic geography literature. As one account describes 'the term corridor applies to a linear system of urban places together within the linking surface transport media. Corridors are very persistent historically, and they form the major types of urban systems in the New World' (Whebell, 1969: 1). Different urban economic corridors are therefore visible in the global south and north. Alongside Gottmann's megalopolis the terms *zwischenstadt* and *desakota* actually speak to the in-between character of contemporary urbanization in Europe and East Asia.

The morphology and functioning of economic corridors have been related to developments in transportation technologies such as water, rail, and road in the literature (Whebell, 1969) as I discuss in Chapter 6. For some, information and communication technologies (ICT) are associated with the emergence of 'intelligent corridors', which 'are more than linear areas that have been wired for ICT and thereby have information exchange capabilities. Intelligent corridors . . . also have multidimensional proximities that provide the specified development area with an identity and an integrated higher quality of work and living than occurs outside the designated space of the intelligent corridor' (Corey, 2004: 319). If the objective territoriality of such corridors is not always easy to perceive, then subjectively at least it is argued that they provide the material supports for globally mobile knowledge workers as they journey 'through a system of corridors... founded in the logic of a space of flows' (Lassen, 2010: 184).

For my purposes, there are several issues of interest that arise from a consideration of economic organization on this scale. First, the intelligence referred to immediately above relies on the manner in which technological networks weave together enclaves such as science parks, retail malls, and gated residential complexes. Second, economic corridors have formed as a result of the dispersal of economic activities and processes of invention. For Whebell (1969) the primary processes of economic, cultural, and social diffusion occur along the corridor with secondary processes of diffusion occurring laterally. Of significance is the fact that such processes of diffusion may lead to the establishment of secondary centres (Whebell, 1969: 4). In language that might, strangely enough, have come from Lefebvre, Whebell (1969: 7–8) argues how 'The real urban explosion, with the creation of urban–rural fringes and dormitory "exurbs"' occurs in such corridors. Third, a variety of economic processes might be viewed as operative at this spatial scale. The contribution of urban economic corridors to the overall economic performance of their respective nations is the subject of some debate but for (Whebell, 1969: 12) 'At the national level... these linear zones comprise the main, if not the exclusive loci of "net revenue production"—that is, areas which contribute more to national accounts than they receive.'

Megalopolis

Gottmann (1964) used the term megalopolis to describe the nationally and internationally significant urban economic corridor stretching along the Eastern seaboard of the US from Boston to Washington. At the time, and for a while afterwards, Gottmann's term spawned academic and policy interest but it has been overlooked until nearly fifty years later when there have been updates and a renewed and broader interest in the relevance and planning potential of megapolitan forms.

In contrast to the earliest and largely negative use of the term megalopolis in Britain to signal urbanization on a larger scale and undesirably disorganized way (Baigent, 2004), Gottmann emphasized the novelty of this spatial economic form and its relationship to unprecedented levels of affluence, mobility, and leisure time. Since the 1960s some of the main processes apparent in megalopolis have been the continued process of suburbanization, the extension of metropolitan commuting fields, and physical coalescence (Morrill, 2008).

Gottmann used a threshold of 25 million population to define a megapolitan region. Moreover, at this time megalopolis continued to be perceived morphologically in both academic and policy terms, yet he also emphasized the functional coherence as an urban economic system. In this latter regard, contemporary discussion of megapolitan forms has often overlooked the importance that Gottmann attached to the international connections of such corridors. He noted that 'all megalopolitan regions have been hinges in terms of trade, and cultural, technological and population exchanges between the countries they belonged to and the outside world they participated in' (Gottmann, 1976: 110).

The megalopolis concept has important connections to the regional planning tradition in America though the economic realities of such corridors have never really been matched by an academic or policy interest in economic activities organized at this scale. In America, recent interest has been driven by the realities of the ongoing dispersal of jobs across metropolitan areas. 'Most of America's economy, people, and connections to the globe will continue to be megapolitan based.... the rise of megapolitans as the dominant urban feature on the American urban landscape has already happened, and that position seems only likely to be strengthened in this century' (Lang and Nelson, 2011: 235).

Lang and Nelson (2011: 11) argue that 'What is needed...is a middle ground conceptualization that recognizes that America's emerging economic geography is far larger than cities or their metropolitan areas but smaller than broad-brush multi-state regions.' Some of this interest in megapolitan forms has preferred single 'big envelope' conceptions to the exclusion of a focus on the mid-urban realms of which they are composed (Schafran, 2014; Lang and Knox, 2008). However, it has also led on to the argument that the economic, social, ethnic, and political complexion of these inter-urban realms is not reducible to the spillovers from established historic cities. Instead it is the variegated character of the communities that make up this mid-urban realm that represent the physical, economic and social glue that binds megapolitan corridors—the example Schafran (2014) uses being northern California.

Europe's Zwischenstadt: *The Regional Scale City In-between*

Among the European muted and smaller-scale counterparts to megalopolis is the Randstad of the Netherlands celebrated for the polycentric economy based on a division of labour among the key cities that compose it (Kloosterman and Lambregts, 2001) and in some measure an inspiration for the mobilization of the term 'polycentricity' in planning circles more broadly across Europe. England's 'industrial coffin' stretching from London to incorporate the industrial midlands and northern cities remains a morphological feature even if some of its main city economies and its functionality are now much weakened. For Bennett et al. (1999) it continues to represent 'a cluster of clusters' or overlapping urban economies.

Industrial decline also figures prominently in the example of the Ruhr region in Germany where the settlement pattern is fragmented enough as a result of the environmental and infrastructural legacy of coal mining and iron and steel production to warrant the unique label of 'Ruhrbism'. Figure 5.1 shows the distinctive polycentric settlement pattern of the Ruhr which 'did not develop a single urban core throughout the nineteenth century. It was an early example of a "conurbation", a multipolar urban space, as radically new in its way as the concentrated industrial city of the Manchester type' (Osterhammel, 2014: 274). Industrial decline in the region has been accompanied by a declining and ageing population and a by-now-lengthy organized attempt to regenerate the region (Basten, 2017) with new industries including those based around industrial heritage tourism as partly depicted in Figure 5.2.

Indeed, patterns of urbanization in Germany were the inspirations for Sieverts' (2003, 2011) use of the term *zwischenstadt* or 'in-between' territory to describe a new urban landscape. As Young and Keil (2010: 5) describe it, 'the in-between city is a place of thoroughly interwoven functions of production and consumption. A place of both prime global capital accumulation and

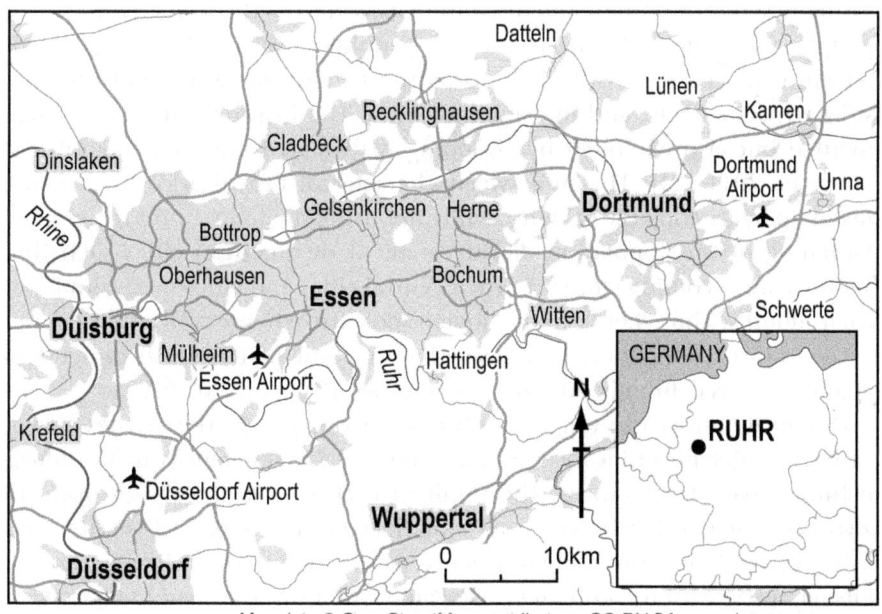

Map data © OpenStreetMap contributors, CC-BY-SA, opendatacommons.org

Figure 5.1 The settlement pattern of the Ruhr

Figure 5.2 The view west from the Landschaftspark Duisburg
Source: Photograph courtesy of Francisco Ibanez Hantke.

dispossession, the in-between city is a matrix on which the new urban dynamics of the twenty-first century is etched in its most visible forms.' One fundamental characteristic of the in-between, then, is the mixing of land uses: 'the old beloved hierarchy of meaning in the urban configuration between the formerly solely important and uncontested centre and the formerly irrelevant periphery is entirely dissolved: on the "periphery" we see the emergence of government centred institutions for entire regions, large hospitals, universities, hypermarkets, and massive industries. The historic centre is complemented but also exploited by shopping malls and large office complexes' (Sieverts, 2011: 24). The in-between character of urbanization is a theme taken up by De Jong (2014) who, while not using the term, notes the gradual flattening of the population density gradient of American cities such that suburbs are becoming similar to their central cities and cities more similar to their suburbs. Thus, 'between the obvious poles of extreme concentration and extreme dispersion, there is a vast range of form that is often difficult to characterize as definitely one thing or another' (De Jong, 2014: 15).

Despite its European and specifically German origin, Sieverts sees the concept as having global significance: 'despite the massive differences in the forces behind urban development, the result in each case is the diffuse form of *zwischenstadt*, which separates itself from the core city—if one still exists—and achieves a unique form of independence. These characteristics link the area of greater Tokyo with the Ruhr area, Sao Paulo with Boswash . . . and Mexico City with Bombay' (Sieverts, 2003: 6). For others 'the in between city is the overlooked sociospace between the glamour zones of the wealthy exurbs and the "creative" inner city' (Young and Keil, 2010: 4). It is then 'about time we concerned ourselves with the...transformation of the in-between cities, as regions have entered a more or less immediate worldwide competition with each other' (Sieverts, 2011: 24), not least because 'the in-between city is not just remnant space. Rather, it is constituted in the force fields of the most dynamic and active tendencies of the expanding global city' (Young and Keil, 2010: 4).

Discussion of the economy of such in-between territory has been muted in comparison to the interest generated among urban geographers, architectural and planning scholars. The evidence suggests that processes of economic dispersal have driven the formation of corridors in contemporary Europe, though it is less clear in a context of greater urban containment whether this mid-urban realm has a positive economic role to play. Speaking to the mainland European context, Witt et al. (2014: 5) note how 'Within urban regions, de-concentration from centres to wider regions may induce corridor development, as firms typically locate to accessible hotspots near or between larger urban cores.' These 'Corridors and urban regions are evidently not related to each other in a very clear cut way. Agglomeration externalities may become network externalities, differing over urban space in much more complex ways than (corridor) proximity suggests' (Witt et al., 2014: 21). However their examination of European urban economic corridors reveals that it is urban core and periphery rather than corridor effects driving productivity growth externalities (Witt et al., 2014: 20). Instead, then, they 'find little support for the hypothesis regarding the special function of corridors in economic growth due to agglomeration advantages. On the contrary, the results question the added value of corridors for growth and agglomeration' (Witt et al., 2014: 21).

East Asia: The In-between Landscapes of Desakota

'Sometimes the distinction between city and country seemed to lose all of its sharpness. The island of Java, for example, very densely populated in the nineteenth century, was not centralized in a few large cities, nor did it have the isolated, large autarkic villages that people liked to imagine in Asia: it was one large intermediate area of settlement between city and country, essentially neither the one nor the other' (Osterhammel, 2014: 252). The pattern that Osterhammel describes has been termed *desakota* by McGee (1991) in a joining of two Indonesian words *desa*, (village), and *kota* (city), to signify the mixed 'rurban' appearance (Figures 5.3 and 5.4) of many extended urban regions in East Asia. The pattern is one that is in between urban and rural but often in between in other important respects; being organized through a mixture of formal and informal employment and in between agrarian and industrial in its sectoral composition and land use (Phelps and Wijaya, 2016).

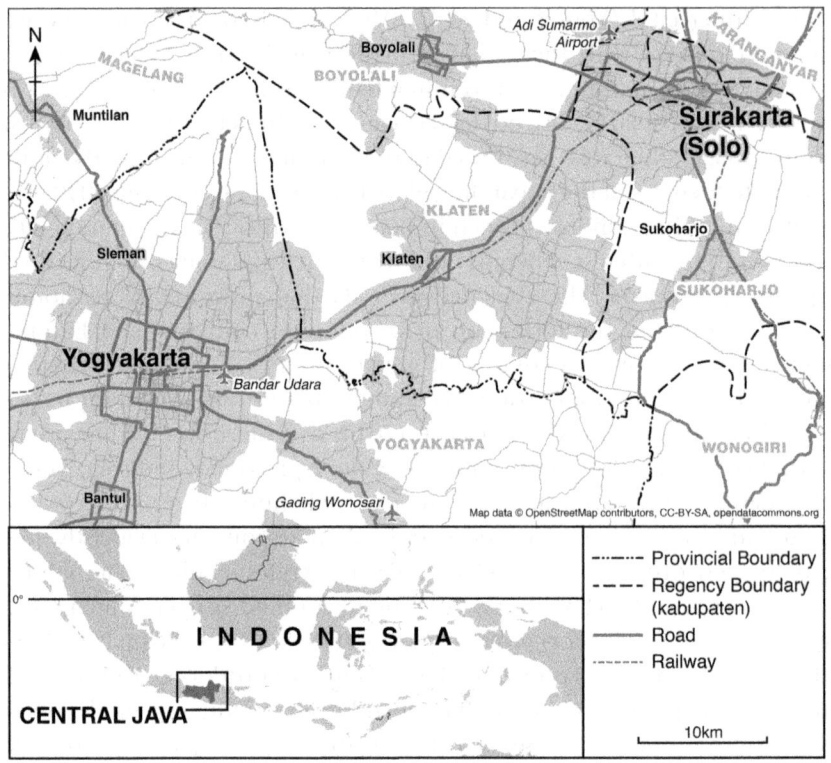

Figure 5.3 The Yogyakarta–Surakarta corridor

For McGee (1991), *desakota* extended metropolitan regions were similar to megalopolis in terms of their being 'highly integrated "transactive" environments' involving the movement of people and commodities but also different, being 'more intensely utilised than the American megalopolis' (McGee, 1991: 15 and 17 respectively).

McGee (1991) distinguished types 1, 2, and 3 *desakota* urban regions. Type 1 consisted of declining rural population and rapid urbanization and industrialization such as found in Japan. Type 2 involved rapid population and labour force growth adjacent to capital cities such as in the Jabotabek urban agglomeration centred on Jakarta, Indonesia. Type 3 *desakota* urban regions centred on secondary cities where labour absorption into formal urban industrial employment was less apparent. In a type 3 *desakota* context it is unclear whether the often informally organized companies and work patterns are able to draw upon or capture the sorts of external economy effects typically associated with urban industrial agglomeration in industrialized nations (Moreno-Monroy, 2012). For a start, the sorts of vertical disintegration of

Figure 5.4 The *desakota* mix of land-uses in Central Java
Source: author's photograph.

production that Scott (1983, 1986, 1988) has documented as an important aspect of urban industrial agglomeration have rarely developed.

The corridor between the two Indonesian cities of Yogjakarta and Surakarta provides a good example of the type 3 *desakota* pattern of industrialization and urbanization. Taken as a whole, this corridor comprising the two cities and three regencies has a present population of a little over 4 million. Figures for the most recent employment census in 2016 were not available but Table 5.1 indicates that the local authority areas that compose this 'rurban' corridor in between the two major cities of Yogyakarta and Solo are clearly very important in employment terms and have become more so. The share of the total population of this corridor accounted for the regencies lying between the two cities has continued to grow from 73.4 per cent in 1984 to 77.5 per cent in 2013.[1]

In this instance the *desakota* pattern of ribbon inter-urban development is part of a cohesive corridor that ensures a strong measure of both economic and administrative spillovers in the form of business competitiveness but also

---

[1] This last figure probably marginally over-represents the share as population figures for the two cities were for 2012 rather than 2013.

Table 5.1 Employment change in the Yogyakarta–Surakarta corridor

	1986 (per cent of total employment)	1996	2006	Percentage change 1986–2006
Cities (Surakarta, Yogyakarta)	208,305 (36%)	322609 (37%)	300815 (31%)	44.4%
Districts between (Klaten, Sukoharjo, Sleman)	370,148 (64%)	551088 (63%)	678738 (69%)	83.4%
Total	578453	873697	979553	69.3%

Source: BPS, Economic Census, 1996, 2006.

local government efficiency (Von Luebke et al., 2009). Nationally, important industries—such as batik—once clustered intensely in a city like Surakarta have by now decentralized significantly into the rurban corridor, partly due to environmental restrictions in the two cities but just as significantly due to labour cost and availability.

It was in Japan—in a context of type 1 *desakota* urban regions—that the term and full planning ramifications of megalopolis took on perhaps their strongest form.[2] Moreover, in the Japan case the mixed or rurban landscape is one in which there is now only extremely slow population growth. Japan's megapolitan urban forms are different from their North American counterpart in regards to the intensely populated in-between areas (Ginsburg, 1991). Notable in the Japanese case, then, has been population and associated economic declines in outer suburbs with their rather distinctive *desakota* appearance due to the ageing population—a process that has been exacerbated across metropolitan areas by the lack of any significant immigration and the tendency for planning policy to seek to concentrate additional employment at inner suburban nodal points. These outer suburbs remain in-between in physical form but can hardly be said to be a prime example of the economic buoyancy of the inter-urban economy emphasized in this chapter (Sorensen, 2011). Japan's experiences may yet be prescient regarding the policy dilemmas facing many developed nations where suburban shrinkage may become a more pronounced feature.

Post-Suburbia

Table 4.1 in the previous chapter introduced a number of possible trajectories regarding the evolution of different types of settlements in city-regions. One

---

[2] The megalopolis concept gained some traction in Japan, actively used to promote the national economy and identity, though it enjoyed a comparatively short life due to sensitivities regarding regional imbalances (Hanes, 1993).

purpose of the associated discussion was to draw attention to a class of settlements that could be said to be evolving from residential suburbs to post-suburbs. Table 4.1 and elaboration of it (Phelps, Valler, and Wood, 2010; Phelps and Wood, 2011; Phelps, 2012c, 2016 are very much rooted in the US context and there are real limits to how and in what way this scheme may apply beyond this context. Nevertheless, the scheme can be used loosely as a basis of discussion in what follows.

The scenarios visible across city-regions include cities that have shrunk to function as dormitory suburbs, declining industrial suburbs, and stable affluent and ostensibly residential suburbs. If, 'in the concrete reality of today's world places and non places intertwine and tangle together' then these scenarios also remind us that 'the possibility of non-places is never absent from any place' (Augé, 1995: 107). The possibilities also include subtle transformations to suburbs that remain stable wealthy residential suburbs albeit they become the hub in a network of work distributed on metropolitan, national, and international scales as discussed in Chapter 4.

However the two scenarios that I concentrate on in this chapter are those in which residential suburbs have acquired greater economic gravity to become post-suburban and those communities that are in the process of changing from post-suburbs to cities. As Dunham-Jones and Williamson (2009) note, 'The so-called "bedroom suburbs", peripheral to the core city when first built, now occupy polycentric locations in their vastly expanded regions. Jobs have migrated to locations throughout the metropolitan region and many suburban locations have become economic engines in their own right and now seek to distinguish themselves as destinations' (Dunham-Jones and Williamson, 2009: xii–xiii). For Fishman the era of the suburb came to an end with the emergence of the 'technoburb' in which a balance between jobs and residence is restored (Fishman, 1987). The emergence of the post-suburban economy is a product of a distinct post-suburban politics in which the economic (or rather fiscal) realities of service provision rub up against traditional suburban ideals (Phelps, 2016).

Some of this transformation of residential suburbs began some time ago (Teaford, 1997). This transformation was underlined as the accretion of economic functions of all sorts in the urbanization of suburbia (Masotti, 1973). Of significance in the US context here was the installation of what might be regarded as new (non)places in the form of office parks and research campuses in suburbia. Yet these enclosures were part of a new urbanity.

The process of high tech growth was actually a process of city building. The suburbanization of science in the late twentieth century helped to urbanize American suburbs making these places closer to the classic definitions of cities in terms of their economic diversity and self-sufficiency. No longer adjuncts to the central cities around which they grew up, the high tech suburbs of the early twenty-first century are a new and influential kind of urbanism   (O'Mara, 2005: 4).

To prefigure later discussion, this new kind of urbanism, is neither suburban nor urban.

Europe's suburban expanses do contain employment centres that have been likened to the edge cities of the US albeit with European characteristics (Bontje and Burdack, 2005; Phelps, 1998) while some settlements might be regarded as post-suburban (Phelps et al., 2006; Phelps and Parsons, 2003; Phelps, Tarazona Vento, and Roitman, 2015). The suburban employment nodes found in Europe are often significant enough to qualify as edge cities under the criteria suggested by Garreau (1991) but are found closer to historic cores, are more compact (Bontje and Burdack, 2005) and generally, less car-oriented than their US edge city counterparts.

Further afield, continued population growth in the likes of Indonesia and urban transitions of a massive scale (such as in China and India) have been associated with manufacturing and some office employment decentralization, often as part of deliberate efforts to fashion polycentric metropolises. Here and in Europe, then, major suburb-located employment nodes are more commonly the product of deliberate planning exercises than those found in the US, though care is needed not to overdraw contrasts in this regard.[3] Examples of this phenomena in China are too numerous to begin to recount but include, for example, the planned dispersal of manufacturing and offices in the Beijing metropolitan area (Boyang, Weidong, and Dunford, 2014) to places like Yizhuang New Town (Wu and Phelps, 2011) and the fashioning of a new central business district in Hexi New Town created in the Jiange and Gulou districts at the periphery of Nanjing (see Figure 5.5).

Suburb to Post-suburb

While, much of the vigour of population and employment decentralization found in US edge cities can also be found at the peripheries of the largest cities of post-socialist nations, it nevertheless cannot be understood as simply 'catching up' with suburbanization processes in the west, even if they have become more similar to them. In particular, pent-up demand for better housing conditions has seen residential suburbanization preceded or accompanied by that of economic activities such as retail malls and industry zones and office developments as part of redistributions of populations rather than overall growth in city region populations (Nuissl and Rink, 2005). In a pattern

---

[3] Planning can hardly be considered absent in the rise of many edge cities in the US, even in those instances where it seems to have been largely absent. Moreover some communities were born post-suburban (Phelps, 2016).

Figure 5.5 A new peripheral CBD for Nanjing in Hexi New Town
Source: author's photograph.

seen across post-socialist countries more generally, 'urban sprawl in post-socialist eastern Germany was mainly induced by a limited set of clearly defin-able parameters for the decisions of investors and households which stemmed from a peculiar mix of governmental "over-" and "under-regulation"' (Nuissl and Rink, 2005: 132). The state, alongside real-estate developers, has mediated in the production of outer suburban sprawl.

The municipality of Khimki (within Moscow Oblast but contiguous to Moscow itself) has become one of a number of preferred locations for major office, retail and residential development to the point that a 'new Khimki' has arisen next to the old closed military town (Golubchikov and Phelps, 2011) (see Figure 5.6). Yet the similarities to the sort of suburban growth machine logic that has driven growth at the metropolitan periphery in the US are super-ficial. The political economy of the post-socialist growth machine (Kulcsar and Domokos, 2005) revealed in a place like Khimki and at other parts of the Moscow periphery (Rudolph and Brade, 2005) is one in which a *political* rather than an economic logic that dominates. The potential for, and location of, residential and commercial developments and the 'allocation' of signature

Figure 5.6 Signs of new economic activity in Khimki
Source: author's photograph.

developments of government offices, sports stadia, and the like are determined by oligarchic political connections.

For Fishman (1987: 234), 'if there is a single basic principle in the structure
of the technoburb, it is the renewed linkage of work and residence'. It is this
post-suburban balance of employment and residence that adds an additional
layer of meaning to the betweenness of suburbia and has been brought to a
fuller expression in the term 'edge city' (Garreau, 1991) which has been used
to refer to employment dominated communities—some incorporated, some
not—that cluster around the peripheries of major city-regions. In comparison
to some of the subtle transformations that have occurred in the employment
complexion of residential suburbs, these represent discrete and highly visible
interplaces.

Croydon—today physically part of the built-up area of London—arguably
has never been a residential suburb. It was once a physically separate market
town. Even as it became more fully a dormitory for London with large-scale
housing development in the first decades of the 1900s, it also hosted London's
first commercial airport and significant manufacturing industries. It diversified into a major suburban employment complex in the 1960s and 1970s.
In terms of its office stock and associated employment it gained the economic

gravitas of a free-standing British provincial city (Phelps, 1998). This, as Saunders (1981) describes, was the product of the deliberate effort of a local political coalition, led significantly from within local government itself. These arrangements continued and formalized to make Croydon one of the very few instances in Britain where local government politics resembles that found in the US (Dowding et al., 1999) and where the council has long harboured claims to city status (Phelps et al., 2006). Nevertheless, the rather grim elevations of Croydon's central office complex are also testimony to the economic 'lock-in' that can be presented by the built environment. The office blocks designed for the paper-based back-office service economy have been left high and empty—unsuitable and unwanted as work environments for today's paperless service economy. Recent optimism regarding the possibilities for its re-development as an office location seem to have receded as Croydon's anchor office—Nestle's UK headquarters—has migrated to another in-between space—Gatwick airport. Instead, with its accessibility to central London, central Croydon is ripe for a new residential population it never had in the first place; office blocks stand ready to be refurbished into residential apartments.

Figure 5.7 Office meets residential in central Croydon
Source: author's photograph.

Croydon continues to evolve in ways that question whether it was ever a typical residential suburb at all.

In a few important instances some settlements were born post-suburban. This is the case with Schaumburg, Illinois, where the balanced nature of a city in function but not in form was envisaged by political leaders from the outset (Phelps, 2016). It is also the case in Europe. Commenting specifically on the development history of technopoles at Grenoble, Toulouse and Sophia Antipolis in France, Wakeham arrives at a similar conclusion noting how: 'In reality, technopolis was far more a suburban, or perhaps a post-suburban utopia rather than an urban one. It was a specialized, idyllic site in the constellation of specialized sites that often surrounded large cities in the late twentieth century-all of them linked by highways' (Wakeham, 2003: 266).

More common is the ongoing transformation of some European suburbs as in the case of Getafe. The suburban municipality of Getafe in Spain presents a story of transformation borne of socialist politics. Getafe grew from a small village in the 1960s as a belated drive towards the concentration of Fordist manufacturing activity around the capital Madrid was licensed through large scale releases of land for suburban residential and industrial expansion. Although Getafe was home to a handful of large industrial enterprises from the outset of its development in the 1960s, it nevertheless began life as a dormitory suburb to Madrid. However, the rapid speculative development of housing licensed under the Franco regime had left many basic facilities and amenities under-provided for (Phelps et al., 2006). Over time, basic amenities such as potable water, paved streets, schools, and health clinics have been fought for and won by the many *asociasiones de vecinos*. The grassroots politics of these residential associations formed the bedrock upon which socialist politics was formalized after the Franco dictatorship. Former mayor Pedro Castro's success in establishing Getafe as 'the capital of the south' (of Madrid) has drawn on and fed back into a process of place making. Over time a number of regional scale investments have been 'won' for Getafe including a dispro-portionate number of stations on the *Metro Sur* line, a campus of Carlos III University, a major hospital. Former mayor Pedro Castro's involvement in this transformation highlights the role played by political leadership in processes of suburban transformation but also the sense in which place making has been explicitly conceived in terms of breaking erstwhile relationships of economic dependence on established central cities (Phelps, Vento, and Roitman, 2015).

From Post-suburb to City?

The edge cities of the US identified by *Washington Post* journalist Joel Garreau are a specific instance of post-suburban communities. He identified nearly 200 existing or emerging new settlements on the basis of five key criteria.[4] Curiously, it is what is not explicit in this definition of edge cities that was their initial foundation—namely their ability to cater for rising demands for mobility (Kellerman, 2010). If the post-war American residential suburb was one that was promoted significantly by national and local state interventions and if private-sector developers have assumed a major role in re-enchanting suburbia, the history of edge cities points to the emerging significance of 'shadow governments' as important intermediaries in the building of mid-urban realms. Tysons Corner is presently one of the largest employment centres in the US yet it is suburban. It is effectively a second downtown of Washington DC housing many so-called 'beltway bandit' Pentagon defence contractors. Current land use plans envisage that office space there could double over the next 20 years or so as Tysons Corner is re-made into a proper downtown. The recent deliberations of the Tysons Corner Land Use Task Force resulted in a new comprehensive plan for the area and have entertained a quite staggering transformation of this out-of-town business node. Some of the scenarios envisage an increase in Tyson's small population of 18,000 to nearer 100,000. They also anticipate a doubling of commercial floor space in what is a suburban business centre that is already larger than many historic downtowns. What this means in terms of the sustainability or resilience of the Tysons Corner economy is as yet unclear. However, what is clear is that private or shadow governments—such as business and home-owner associations—have been important in the growth of the place and remain so (Peck, 2011; Phelps, 2012c, 2016).

Elsewhere in the US, Feagin (1987) reported some time ago how over half of all office stock of Houston existed in its suburban 'energy corridor'. The first office buildings in this elongated version of an edge city appeared in the 1950s. As oil prices go, so too it seems does office development. A first spike of office building occurred in the 1980s and a second had begun before the recent subprime mortgage crisis. These two booms have seen the office floorspace rise to around 22 million square feet by 2010, with corridor home to 77,000 jobs by that point. At 44,000, the population of this linear edge city is modest; nevertheless some of the same concerns regarding the sustainability of this format of development, as raised recently in the planning of Tysons Corner (Phelps, 2010), have figured in master planning for the energy corridor, albeit in more muted form. Only modest population increases are foreseen, though almost all of the growth will be in multifamily units rather than

---

[4] An edge city is defined as having at least 1 million square feet of office space, 600,000 square feet of retail space, more jobs than residences, as being recognized as a separate place but being nothing like it presently is as recently as 30 years ago.

single-family detached homes. The plan also calls for better use of and investment in transit as well as improvements in the public realm.[5]

'Ciudad Empresarial' was conceived in 1995 as the first 'office park' in Chile to be composed of a high standard of architecture, landscape and leisure spaces, residential spaces, and services to accommodate national and international businesses. It covers a development area of more than 340.000 m^2 and there are currently 680 companies (30 per cent of which are multinationals) and 30,000 workers. Plans foresee the enhancement of public venues and common spaces.[6] In the Chilean context places like Ciudad Empresarial have been the prime settings for free market conditions and provide a model of urban governance antithetical to that associated with city historically (Carrión, 2007). If the traditional city led by the state based its efficiency on the idea of an 'inclusive' environment supported by the importance of the public space and civil rights, Ciudad Empresarial offers a private mode of governance that appeals to the market as an engine for urban efficiency and the release of consumption power. Huechuraba commune in which Ciudad Empresarial is located (see Figure 4.1) was part of the unconsolidated urban periphery at the time but has now become an alternative urban nucleus to the city centre. Indeed, it has been fundamental to a broader reactivation of development activity centred on new middle-class neighbourhoods (Ducci, 2000). Ciudad Empresarial is one example of the ongoing metropolitan dispersion of Latin American cities, where commercial and entrepreneurial functions concentrated in suburban areas create new centralities integrated via motorways and private roads (Fuentes and Sierralta, 2004; Hidalgo, Borsdorf, and Sánchez, 2007). The various interests associated with these new centralities have sought increasingly to model them as 'cities' instead of mere 'business centres' (Carrión, 2005).

Elsewhere, the picture is more mixed. Urban development continued ever outward and apace and across a proposed but never enacted greenbelt around Tokyo and in its uniquely fine-grained morphology on typically small parcels of land under private ownership to reach the foothills in the outer suburbs during the boom years of the Japanese economy of the 1960s to 1980s. During this time, the pull of the suburbs for a still-expanding population was such that a 'core business cities' policy was instituted as a way of reinforcing the density of development and urban functions around a limited number of outer suburban centres such as Hachioji and Tachikawa. These two represent sizeable outer suburban centres of population and employment—Hachioji, an historic centre of the silk industry, had a population of 580,000 and 234,000 jobs by 2010 (see Figure 5.8). Tachikawa, ostensibly a new

---

[5] http://www.energycorridor.org/about/the-future/master-plan (accessed 16 May 2016).
[6] http://www.ciudadempresarial.cl/ciudad-empresarial/ (accessed 18 September 2015).

Figure 5.8 The central commercial area of Hachioji city
Source: author's photograph.

settlement, is smaller with a population of 180,000 but, with 118,600 jobs, has a higher jobs-to-residents ratio. A notable suburb-to-suburb monorail was developed partly in recognition of the increasing population and economic gravity of the likes of Tachikawa, Tama new town and Ome. For a while, growth prompted new spatial imaginaries—such as 'Tama Silicon Valley' for the outer suburban region as a whole.

However, as population growth rates have stagnated and turned negative due to ageing and decreasing fertility in a nation that has not been subject to significant immigration, these core business cities have been left exposed. Instead, the policy focus of Tokyo and national level government has been on the 23 wards that make up the inner suburban and central city core of Tokyo which has also benefitted strongly from a strong back to the city movement. With its built-out commercial core, a large historic city such as Hachioji that was designated as a core business city has struggled to acquire and retain government and private-sector office activities; the 'new town blues' of Tama are no longer those of the wait of pioneer population for the services and amenities to follow residences but those of problems of mobility and isolation among a population that has aged together in situ.

Tachikawa is fairing better due to its greater accessibility to central Tokyo and availability of land for development.

Despite their being quite numerous, Lang (2003) argues that edge cities were only briefly the preferred format of business real-estate development in America's outer suburban expanses. Instead, much of the current commercial real estate development in America's mid-urban realm takes the form of what he terms edgeless cities. Lang's data suggest that as much as 80 per cent of all businesses lie outside cities in edge cities and edgeless cities (Lang, 2003). The figures are supported by those of Angel and Blei (2016) who find that three-quarters of all jobs in the US are found outside CBDs and other employment subcentres. Here, then, it may be more appropriate to see Tysons' Corner as one edge city nodal point in a string of such nodes that form a longer 'internet alley' economic corridor running out from Washington DC to Dulles Airport (Ceruzzi, 2008).

Lang and LeFurgy have recently described America's fastest-growing communities as 'boomburbs'. Specifically they are speaking of places that have at least 100,000 population and grew at a rate faster than the national average. They are a complex bunch, being somewhere between suburban and urban, not least in terms of their governance arrangements. Partly as a result, they are also complex in terms of their morphology—being a conglomeration of separate master-planned communities loosely woven together or balkanized by road infrastructure. That is, 'Boomburbs occupy an in between niche in the suburban landscape—they are not typical inner ring suburbs nor are they exurban' (Lang and LeFurgy, 2007: 144). They are also in-between in a further sense of the bodies intermediating in their governance. They are described as 'inventive places' in which the gaps left by small local governments are filled by private governments, such as home-owners associations and various shadow governments, such as special improvement districts (Lang and LeFurgy, 2007: 121).

Irvine in Orange County would be an example of a boomburb as it consists of a series of private master-planned communities (Forsyth, 2002) and has been taken as something of the exemplar of the turning inside out of Los Angeles by an LA school (Dear, 2003). According to Lang and LeFurgy's (2007) figures, Irvine contained around 30 million square feet of office space in the 2000s and is reported to have a jobs to resident population ratio of 1.2. It may be exceptional but other such boomburbs are also nevertheless notable for their high ratios of employment to residence even if this balance is struck at the subregional scale.

The boomburbs that Lang and LeFurgy speak of might be thought to have their partial parallels further afield. One characteristic of these fast-growing sizeable new post-suburban communities is that they are often composed of separate privately master-planned developments and even effectively represent experiments with governance—being a mixture of public or municipal government and private governments in the form of residents associations and the like. The pattern is one that is visible in the clusters of new towns and industry parks developed around Jakarta (Rimmer and Dick, 2009). One example would be the regency of Cikerang outside Jakarta. Major developments were licensed by the Indonesian central government under the Suharto presidency well before the era of *reformasi* and government decentralization from the 2000s onwards. These new developments include master-planned new towns and two industrial parks occupied almost exclusively by multinational enterprises. Together they constitute a significant collection of internationally oriented industry and skilled working populations amidst an erstwhile rural, exurban, municipality. The private toll-road connections between the developments are poor to say the least. The rural municipality as yet does not have the planning capacity, powers, or resources to effect greater integration such that into the vacuum has stepped a new organization, ZONI, sponsored by developers and charged with attempting to resolve some of the urban contradictions of this polycentric outer suburb.

Johannesburg emerges as possibly the most extreme example of the emergence of new peripheral city-scale enclosures given that they have been added to 'an already distorted urban landscape divided along racial lines' (Murray, 2011: 2–3). The pattern is most visible to the north of the CBD where a polynucleated pattern of development has produced a northern growth corridor in which there was over 82 million square feet of office space by 2000. Here 'While suburban zoning used to ban non-residential land uses, this new urbanization of suburbia operates on a different principle: namely, blending mixed-use sites that combine residence, work, and leisure in a cocooned environment at a safe distance from the poor, the homeless, and the desperate' (Murray: 185–6). As yet, such peripheral centres account for only 10 per cent of total jobs in the metropolitan area compared to the 32.5 per cent still found in the CBD (Murray, 2011: 175). However, the newest privately master-planned post-suburban communities of Waterfall City and Lanseria Airport City (formerly known as Cradle City) might be regarded as composed of a series of single-use enclaves within an enclave. Retail projects planned for Waterfall City, for example, include the 1.25 million square foot Mall of Africa super-regional shopping centre (Herbert and Murray, 2015: 479).

Enclaves of the Post-Suburban Economy

The discussion of Cikerang in the previous section highlights a phenomenon of more general significance to understanding the in-between economic character of interplaces—namely the significant portions of that economy that exist in enclaves. Here the swathes of the mid-urban realm doubtless make a quantitatively significant contribution to the more general phenomenon of enclave urbanism (Angotti, 2013).

One element in the transformation of residential suburbia in many national contexts has been the appearance of office and research, science and high-tech parks and campuses. The product of processes of decentralization of economic activities from the city as the draw of place-bound external economies loosened, they were also deliberately constructed as enclosures for particular economic activities as a retreat from the city. Defined in distinctly territorial terms, their occupants have also become woven into a dense network of city-region wide contacts. Indeed, as the employment complexions of suburbs have evolved, the corporate and state network of interactions they have become woven into are markedly national and even international in scope (Gottdiener, 1977).

It is worth remembering that in western contexts from where much of the scholarly interpretation of suburbs emanates, and for at least a part of their lives, suburbs have represented relatively boundless tracts of separate residential developments. In the US they were often built on unincorporated land and only later enclosed with the creation of new municipal jurisdictions. Elsewhere, residential enclosures have been more familiar in general (as with the *danwei* in China) or else have formed a more distinct part of rapid suburbanization as in the new mini-cities (such as those outside Jakarta described above).[7]

Corporate Office and Research Campuses

'If innovation has become a business... then the creation of preconditions of that business becomes more and more important. These preconditions can be more easily sustained within the large multinational corporation and the state than by the small firm. And while spatial agglomeration of such preconditions... may be relevant, the spatial transfer of technology, albeit often under monopoly capital, is now so rapid as to render its specifically urban qualities moot' (Harvey, 1985: 157). Harvey may have prematurely banished the agglomeration as a distinct economic formation in this passage but he also drew attention to the fact that much of the business of creating these preconditions for innovation in large enterprises began to take place in the suburbs from the 1930s and 1940s onwards in the US and gathered pace after World War II to constitute what Mozingo (2011) has called 'pastoral capitalism'.

---

[7] The *danwei* is a quite widespread element within Chinese cities and is a workplace enclosure that includes dedicated housing and other facilities for employees.

As Mozingo elaborates, 'As companies had reinvented production facilities in the suburbs in the first half of the twentieth century to accommodate a new scale of manufacturing, so too would they reinvent management factories in the suburbs in the second half to accommodate the new "scale and scope" of management' (Mozingo, 2011: 5). Where Harvey (1985) and Walker (1981) saw monopoly capital conditions undermining external economies and agglomeration processes, these corporate enclaves also, in some instances, engendered suburban agglomerations of note.

In any case, by now, a certain momentum has been established in the movement out of cities to suburbs centred on these rather overlooked enclaves and it is unlikely to be completely reversed any time soon. Ultimately, 'how much this landscape of pastoral capitalism contributed to corporate success... is difficult to calibrate but pastoral capitalism's embrace across time, geography, and global cultures has to be indicative of a concordance with corporate impetus' (Mozingo, 2011: 221–2). They certainly compose important suburban located elements in the corporate contact systems mentioned in the previous chapter. While some corporate research and head-office campuses of major corporations have indeed remained as deployments in suburbia, they have also been important and substantial creators of direct employment, starting 'an avalanche of similar actions by a large number of small businesses in the professional, research editorial, design and related fields' (McKeever, 1970: 9). Here corporate culture and organization appears selectively to have driven significant new firm formation and innovation spillovers across city-regions (Glasmeier, 1988).

Pastoral capitalism was notable as an accommodation of significant employment facilities and land uses to the sensibilities of residential suburbia. 'Industrial parks could serve as vehicles for introducing industry into affluent residential suburbs: places populated by new homeowners concerned about property values; and community aesthetics, and keenly interested in keeping the perceived ills of the crowded industrial city at bay. The industrial park was designed to be the anti-factory, a place whose design standards aimed to blend industrial and commercial functions into the suburban landscape' (O'Mara, 2005: 65). In this way, the likes of research parks were an 'aesthetically pleasing disguise for revenue-producing commercial and manufacturing activities' in the suburbs. (O'Mara, 2005: 70). Little wonder, then, that Fishman (1987: 17) saw the widespread emergence of these campus developments as marking the rise of 'technoburbs' and the end of an era of traditional residential suburbs.

The fortunes of the companies that developed and occupied such extensive suburban spaces have changed significantly since many were created at the height of American industrial pre-eminence. These corporate office and research and development campuses projected the often monopoly power

Figure 5.9 Motorola's campus in Schaumburg
Source: author's photograph.

of, notably US, companies at their height. They represented a poor use of suburban space then but as suburban in-fill development has proceeded albeit slowly, they have assumed an altogether different value to the same corporations now struggling against more intense international competition. Instead they represent a new revenue stream from a real-estate perspective. The post-suburban community of Schaumburg described earlier grew significantly from the 1960s attracting several corporate campuses, including Pure Oil Corporation and Motorola. Pure Oil have already departed their former campus which is now the site for a university and IKEA. The local government has been in discussions with Motorola over marketing excess office capacity on its campus for rental to third parties. Motorola's large landscaped corporate headquarters in Schaumburg is now only 40 per cent occupied.

An increasing number of such campuses have now become entirely obsolete, though in truth they represent prime sites for residential or other employment-related development given their scale and single ownership. Moreover, as some become obsolete, the suburban campus model continues to have life in it as Apple's determination to house around 14,000 employees in a new single large four-storey campus in Cupertino city in California illustrates.[8] The sentiments behind its design are hardly any different from long-standing attempts to design-in creativity in expensively conceived new research campuses despite their questionable efficacy (Knowles and Leslie, 2001; Rankin, 2010).

The International Garden Suburb Campus Model

So pervasive have the enclosures of economic activity represented by science and technology parks become that they have been thought of as an international model of real estate development—the 'international-campus-garden-suburb' (Forsyth and Crewe, 2010: 179). This model of real estate development is sufficiently predictable and universal that it 'seems that they are now legion on the periphery of virtually every dynamic urban area in the world. They appear so physically similar . . . that the hapless traveller . . . would hardly guess the identity of the country, let alone the city' (Castells and Hall, 1994: 1) yet they have had impacts beyond their borders, though this has been recognised, in the most conspicuous success stories, after the event.

What of the future of such territorial manifestations of the campus economy of the mid-urban realm? There is some suggestion of a 'back to the city' movement by business. This is clearly the case with the evolution of science park policy in the UK (Charles, 2015). In fact, science spaces have diverse urban morphologies. Forsyth (2014) has decomposed these spaces into corridors, clumps, cores, campuses, technology subdivisions, and scattered sites pointing to the fact that their logic often remains tightly and narrowly tied to the economic and real estate realities of the day such that there are broader questions of the sustainability and evolution of these spaces as part of the ongoing process of urbanization and economic development.

In some instances the appearance of these enclaves reflects the secretive nature of the scientific work being done. The 'rural contradictions' of one of the UK's major science spaces—'Science Vale'—south of Oxford—party reflect the deliberate rural isolation among small villages of big science experiments (Valler, Phelps and Radford, 2014) such as Harwell—the home of Britain's wartime, and subsequently civilian, nuclear experimentation. Science Vale consists of three physically disconnected sites—Harwell, Culham Science Centre, and Milton Park—that existed for much of their time as closed and secretive *camps* rather than campuses. They nevertheless now have strong business and labour market connections to the rest of the Oxfordshire and the UK economy. The deliberate isolation of the three rural sites represent a particularly difficult challenge to land-use and infrastructure planners in terms of the area's longer term sustainability.

---

[8] http://www.cupertino.org/index.aspx?page=1107 (accessed 10 January 2015).

In other instances, science parks could hardly be considered as enclaves at all. In the case of China's 'optics valley' in Wuhan, the initial East Lake High-tech Park development has been followed by a number of other industry and science parks to form a model of 'many parks within a park'. In a pattern that is seen elsewhere in regards to technology development zones in China, successive extensions of East Lake High-tech Park have seen it expand from an area of 43 km squared in 1991 to 518 km squared by 2010. With this expansion has come a loss of focus on science and high-tech industry and an evolution towards lucrative residential and industrial real estate development as it now forms a major new town extension of Wuhan (Miao and Hall, 2014).

The Retail Mall

The distanciation of production, consumption, and circulation activities apparent in the organization of production into the global production networks (GPNs) discussed in Chapter 9 has the potential for particular spaces to become sharply delimited—presenting the paradox of the likes of substantial sites and fixed infrastructures associated with consumption of ever more globally sourced commodities. Retail malls are one signature of America's mid-urban realm but are increasingly visible in pretty much every other nation including in the global south.

Robert Sack describes how the distanciation of production within GPNs also aids the relative autonomy of consumption. Thus, for Sack, places of consumption attempt to sever themselves from the processes and other places that make up networks of production, circulation and consumption (Sack, 1992: 3). Here 'the place-creating and place-altering power of consumption extends beyond places of consumption to include commodity production, commodity distribution, and the pollution caused by both of these processes. But by severing its connection to these consequences and presenting itself as a world apart, the consumer's world magnifies and distorts this particular power of the consumer to create places' (Sack, 1992: 3–4). In this way the rise of consumption has led to something of 'a thinning out of meaning to produce common ground' (Sack, 1992: 88)—a thinning out of a sense of place. These spaces of consumption—such as shopping malls and theme parks—have been regarded as the embodiment of 'placelessness' (Relph, 1976) or 'non-places' (Augé, 1995). Indeed, so profound has been this severing process that more recent developments in the organization of the enclave space of malls and the stores within them have seen attempts to re-establish a measure of connection to production activities within GPNs. Thus, as Cochoy, 2007: 111) explains how 'Thanks to automobiles . . . big retail returned to the old site of medieval markets at the cities' outskirts . . . In doing so, contemporary supermarkets remind us of the extent to which markets, just like gardens, build bridges between cities and the open country between sites of consumption and spaces of rural production.'

The regional shopping mall has been an incredibly important feature of the mid-urban realm. Stuck out in splendid isolation for many years in some instances in green fields at the newly-built intersections of highways and beltways, these malls have often led housing development and set in train the decentralization of other forms of employment land-use. While some of them are now struggling as specialized centres of consumption, they have also been some of the most durable of land-uses and corporate interests in the mid-urban space.

Victor Gruen—the architect of many early malls in the US—envisaged them as new suburban downtowns: 'From the outset, Gruen's centres were designed...to serve the civic, cultural and social needs of new suburban communities and were intended to be developed alongside apartments, office buildings, theatres and so on' (Lowe, 2000: 264). This was the original vision, for example, for the Dadeland Mall in Miami-Dade County when it was conceived in the late 1950s. Ironically, it is only with a recent major planning initiative to fashion a new suburban downtown around the mall (see Figure 5.10) that it has belatedly fulfilled this original idea (Phelps, 2016).

Figure 5.10 Kendall Dadeland Downtown
Source: author's photograph.

The largest suburban retail mall in the US is the Mall of America in Bloomington Minneapolis which opened in 1992. According to the Mall of America's own figures, it covers an area of 4.2 million square feet and has 11,000 permanent employees rising to 13,000 at peak season. Moreover, it is more than a shopping mall as it also has nightclubs and an amusement park. Its role in this respect is set to expand further as a second phase of development will see mixed use development (including offices) on a further 5.6 million square feet of space. Its wider economic development impact is likely to be significant. The Mall of America operators claim that: it has more visitors than all of the state's other visitors attractions combined; 4 out of 10 of the current 40 million annual visitors are tourists; and that $2 billion dollars of economic impact are generated for the state.[9]

In and of themselves shopping malls provide significant direct employment— though, as the appellation 'regional' implies, while they attract significant non-local or export expenditures by shoppers from outside the suburban community concerned, there are also some leakages, since commuting workers are likely to spend their salaries in different suburban communities. The sum of their local economic impact is often rather less than the headline figures suggest due to diversion and displacement effects. Nevertheless, and for example, the presence of Woodfield regional shopping mall in Schaumburg has been the major factor in the community not having to levy a property tax and provides just one further indication of the economic significance of such malls (Phelps, 2016).

In Britain, central government relaxed planning restrictions during the late 1980s and into the early 1990s sufficiently for a large number of new retail centres to spring up often in 'non-traditional edge or out of town locations' (Lowe, 2000: 263). These now represent something of a latent framework for development across Britain—a framework that is distinctly edge of town and city. Thus, 'In spite of—and, indeed, perhaps because of—1990s government restrictions on future regional shopping centre developments, those that do exist are in the process . . . of fundamentally altering urban geographies and creating new urban forms' (Lowe, 2000: 263). Planning applications for expansions of existing retail facilities in these centres continue to be received while some centres have also attracted other land uses such as offices and housing.

The Interstitial Spaces of Exurbia

Some time ago Pahl (1966) noted the social implications of movements of wealthy and skilled incomers to commuter villages outside London and their

---

[9] http://www.mallofamerica.com/about/moa/facts (accessed 10 January 2015).

effects on rural community. From today's vantage point, and after evidence of a significant urban–rural shift in employment and enterprise formation in the UK (Keeble and Tyler, 1995) and the US (North and Smallbone, 2000), his observation of 'urbs in rure' is hardly of less significance for what it says about the interstitial or interplace economy of exurbia. Notwithstanding a recent movement back to the city, the ramifications of a long-running and substantial selective outmigration of skilled labour from cities has had important impacts on the mid-urban realm.

For Keeble and Tyler (1995) 'The theory of enterprising behaviour in relation to the urban–rural shift is two-fold. First the environment of rural areas attracts a higher proportion of decision-takers who are likely to be good at demonstrating enterprising behaviour wherever they locate. Secondly, rural areas, and especially accessible rural areas, have economic, physical and institutional characteristics which enable enterprising behaviour to occur more readily there than elsewhere.' However, what is perhaps most interesting about their findings is the rising importance of *accessible* rural areas. While the selective nature of counter-urbanization is not in doubt, it may be less the institutional characteristics of these interstitial spaces, as Scott (2012) has referred to them, than their accessibility such that they 'borrow size' (and the associated economies of diversity) from nearby major urban agglomerations (Phelps, Fallon, and Williams, 2001).[10]

The 'rural' economic scene is a complex one in and of itself in which some elements of urban external economies—as a result of borrowed size—may be important to economic performance in accessible rural/exurban areas while remaining largely unimportant in more remote rural areas. As Scott (2012: 159) explains 'Many of the economic and cultural features of the interstitial spaces... precede the rise of the cognitive-cultural economy as such, but have taken on renewed importance and intensity'. As he also goes on to note, 'while any sharp distinction between the urban and the rural has long been questionable, it is especially problematic at this moment in history.... the new capitalism of the 21st century is producing restructuring effects in many of the interstitial spaces between large cities that significantly redefine what it means to be rural' (Scott, 2012: xi). Here Scott sees 'non metropolitan areas comprising rural expanses and associated networks of small towns that participate in the new cognitive-cultural economy by means of their specialized forms of agricultural and craft production, their symbolic assets and traditions, and the appeal of their natural landscapes' (Scott, 2012: 145).

---

[10] Yet again, the innovative performance of small firms in remote rural areas cannot be entirely discounted (Oakey and Cooper, 1989), not least because some aspects of remoteness appear to have driven a measure of creativity regarding the development of new markets, while rurality itself is a resource in particular sectors such as tourism (North and Smallbone, 2000).

Processes of agglomeration may have some relevance to understanding these dynamics, as I explained in Chapter 3, but are less salient than in examples of suburban- and city-centred concentrations of economic activities. 'This is not simply a matter of the spatially widening influence of the city as a consequence of extended commuting fields, or the spread of second homes, or the near-universal intrusiveness of the media, but is more fundamentally related to the ways in which the new economy is penetrating into so many of the far recesses of the rural environment' (Scott, 2012: 149). Scott goes on to list a number of instances of this: (i) encounters with the natural world through the tourism industry; (ii) the heritage industry; (iii) locally specialized and ethically/organically produced agricultural produce; (iv) small towns have repositioned themselves around gastronomic specialities; (v) small villages and towns specialized in particular arts and crafts; (vi) towns with ethnic or other idiosyncrasies. The activities that Scott lists are evidence that 'while the new cognitive cultural economy is predominantly concentrated in major cities, it is far from being confined to large urban areas, and is, in fact, making its presence increasingly felt in a diversity of interstitial spaces' (Scott, 2012: 152).

As well as having become important containers of employment in quantitative terms, there is evidence to indicate that suburban jurisdictions have also become important in qualitative terms. One recent study indicated how suburban areas in the US performed especially well with regard to new firm formation, growth and longevity including in relation to urban cores thought traditionally to be incubators of new firms leading to the suggestion that 'more attention must be paid to the intermediate places in the rural–urban continuum.' Indeed, 'the entrepreneurial environment in these intermediate places is not well understood and deserves deeper investigation' (Renski, 2008: 71). Renski's study indicated how suburban areas in the US performed especially well with regard to new firm formation, growth and longevity including in relation to urban cores thought traditionally to be incubators of new firms. The suburban share of new entrant firms in high technology advanced services was 24 per cent higher than expected based on suburban population.

Conclusions

Much of the interest shown by human geographers in this mid-urban realm reflects its morphological complexity. However there is enough in the preceding review to suggest that this is also a complex landscape in functional or economic terms. Indeed, Bogart (2006) argues that metropolitan regions are now composed of specialized trading places, many of which are suburban or exurban in location. Lang and Knox (2008) and Shearmur et al. (2007) have depicted some of these specialized economic places and zones graphically.

While the city remains a triumph of human endeavour—not least in economic terms (Glaeser, 2011)—it has been joined and perhaps eclipsed in this urban economic triumph by a variety of settlements that make up a mid- or inter-urban realm—an economy increasingly housed in between the cities we take for granted as the primary containers of economic activity. This mid-urban realm has an economic dynamic that is often quite independent of historic city economies. Some of this independence is surely a product of the enclave nature of the key employment sites found there, since these often are the nexus of economic relations that are national and international in scope. As such, the appearance of such enclaves as part of GPNs is also driven significantly by the national and international accessibility and the infrastructures of physical and virtual mobility found in this mid-urban realm.

6

Planes, Trains, and Automobiles

Introduction

The mobilities of modernity—the liminal spaces of the train, the plane, and the automobile and their fixed infrastructures have produced a dizzying acceleration of life and a compression of time–space in our daily lives. Successively in a comparatively short period of the longer term history of human settlement they presage enormous changes in urban form and the inter-urban and international geography of economic activity. This might be true even of railways, which, although associated with their own distinct and time-marked effects upon cities across the world, took a very long time to shape urban life and may yet come to shape a measure of inter-urban life if rail infrastructures experience a revival for commuting in combination with cars, at high speed for longer inter-city and international travel, and as connectors to airports (Kasarda and Lindsay, 2011). The speed with which we have adapted as humans to the virtual mobility offered by information and communication technologies (ICT) such as the internet and mobile telephones is testimony to the way they have rapidly become an indispensable adjunct to our lives including our work lives. Moreover, not only do ICTs complement some forms of mobility (notably aeromobility) but also they work to a large extent with and within extant urban forms. Of all technologies of mobility, take-up of the Internet has been more rapid than any other. Kellerman (2012: 77) produces data from the US on the time taken for 50 per cent of the population to take up the telephone, the car, and the mobile phone. While it took a sluggish 68 years for half the population of the US to be making use of the fixed telephone service, it took just 17 years for half the population to be using cars and mobile telephones—but, and here's the thing, it took just 7 years for half the population to be making use of the Internet. Survey data pertaining to 17 (mainly developed country) economies reported by Rainie and Wellman (2012: 172) suggested that only 16 per cent of workforces overall used multiple devices and new communications applications. The global figure doubtless obscures wide variation, Rainie and Wellman's own survey data for the US indicated that around three-quarters of all workers were using Internet browsing, emailing, and mobile phones/texting (Rainie and Wellman, 2012: 15).

Since 'mobility involves a displacement—the act of moving between locations' (Cresswell, 2006: 2), the modern mobilities associated with the train, plane, and automobile have produced interplaces as never before. The terminals of railways are urban though the movement they encourage is inter-urban. Cars have helped to produce a new urbanity composed of suburbs and post-suburbs of various complexions, as discussed in Chapters 4 and 5, and have generally fuelled the inter-urban dispersal of population and employment. Airports are often to be found outside of city jurisdictions. Paradoxically, the promise of the international connectivity and all that this entails in terms of economic diversity is the subject of intense local inter-governmental squabbles.

Even this brief opening discussion makes it clear that 'defining space and place separately from technological networks soon becomes as impossible as defining technological networks separately from space and place' (Graham and Marvin, 2001: 216). Technological networks vary greatly in their take-up, and their effects in terms of time–space compression via physical and virtual mobility. Yet the mobility facilitated in technologies of rail, road and airplanes and ICT continues to call forth various forms of fixity in social relations.

To begin with, mobility requires often huge investments in geographically fixed infrastructures or else with ICT adapts itself to existing investments in existing urban areas. Chapters 4 and 5 considered the economy of suburbs and some of these inter-urban fixed infrastructure nodes indirectly. As we saw in Chapters 4 and 5, suburbs and post-suburbs are perhaps begrudgingly recognized as places in the making. Something of the same dilemmas face our interpretation of the liminal spaces of trains, planes, and automobiles and their associated fixed infrastructures or 'moorings' of stations, airports, and parking structures which are, however, often considered non-places. Unlike suburbs and post-suburbs, which are now being subjected to an exponentially increasing scholarship (Harris, 2010), the economy of these places has yet to be filled with much empirical content such that we know very little about them. Yet these 'non-places are the real measure of our time; one that could be quantified . . . by totaling all the air, rail and motorway routes, the mobile cabins called "means of transport"' (Augé, 1995: 79).

It might be unrealistic to suggest in the face of very profound technological change that places and a sense of place remain intact. Indeed, for Bonnett (2014: 283), 'what you see is that places are atrophying as routes and roads swell'—indicating an economy partly on the move in-between the containers or places—cities and nations—that we tend to take for granted. Life and labour are more than ever on the move rather than still. 'In the largest cities the transport becomes the place, its discontinuities practically cancel the sense of the city as a self-contained whole' (Harbison, 1989: 127).

The possibilities that trains, planes, and automobiles along with ICT now present for work on the move should not be underestimated. As Lash and Urry (1994: 252) point out, 'it is not the pedestrian flâneur who is emblematic of modernity but rather the train passenger, car driver and jet-plane passenger' (Lash and Urry, 1994: 252). That modernity has been associated with the limited intra-urban perspective of the pedestrian flâneur, they argue, has meant that the contribution of inter-urban transportation to modernity has been somewhat overlooked. Compared to the populated and sensory world of the flâneur, the heightened mobility of trains, planes and automobiles can appear 'to involve a number of absences—the absence of commitment and attachment and involvement—a lack of significance' (Cresswell, 2006: 31). This is certainly a view subscribed to by Relph some years ago in which 'roads, railways, airports, cutting across or imposed on the landscape rather than developing with it, are not only features of placelessness in their own right, but, by making possible the mass movement of people... have encouraged the spread of placelessness well beyond their immediate impacts' (Relph, 1976: 90). Perhaps as a result, despite the importance of mobility to both the world and our understanding of it, 'mobility itself, and what it means, remains unspecified. It is a kind of blank space that stands as an alternative to place, boundless, foundations and stability' (Cresswell, 2006: 2).

As we will see, these spaces have taken on increasing (economic) significance to the point that, while they may not yet be regarded as places, they are nevertheless no longer quite placeless. Indeed, 'If all relationality were mobile... then there would be no complexity' (Urry, 2003: 126) and it is some of that complexity of the relational geography of interplaces that I wish to retain in this book.

The Fixed Infrastructures of Mobility

In comparison to the extreme virtual mobility offered by ICT, the technologies of physical mobility—despite their profound historical and continuing effects on place and placelessness—seem clunky and unintegrated. Yet as Easterling (1999: 78) notes, 'redundancies among transport systems, like highways, rail and air... increase the possibilities of switching systems to produce a better fit between task and carrier'. Because of the way to date that these different technologies of physical mobility have been produced in isolation from each other, this potential for integration has barely begun to take shape—modestly in the likes of transit oriented development schemes—and it is one that is worth considering.

The Airport: Between Enclave and Agglomeration

If 'geographers have traditionally described the spatial patterns of air transport as a network, with flows of air traffic linking airports that stand as gateways to global city—regions' (Budd and Hubbard, 2010: 89), then airports are 'spaces of transition' (Gottdiener, 2001: 10–11). Their interplace character is captured in scathing terms in Douglas Coupland's *Generation X*: 'It's a pit stop, an in-between place, a "nowhere". A technicality . . . O'Hare is like what happens to you just after you die and before you get shipped off to wherever you're going, what happens to you while your destination is being determined. It is not judgment, it is transit distilled.' Yet they are also ostensibly *new* nodal points or interplaces. They are critical sites of inter-urban and international competition (O'Connor and Scott, 1992, cited in Freestone, 2011: 116). Indeed 'it is almost meaningless to analyze the dynamics and trends of work, business, family and personal relationships . . . and virtually all significant areas of contemporary social life, without talking into account the particular and distinctive time/spaces created by aeromobility' (Cwerner, 2009: 5). Airports—the fixed infrastructures associated with aeromobility—provide a gauge of the enormous scale and reach of employment-related geographical mobility. Commenting on the employment-related geographical mobility associated with the oil sands economy of Alberta, Canada, Cresswell, Dorow, and Roseman (2016) note how during a decade when the population of the city of Fort McMurray doubled, its airport traffic increased ten times—largely as a result of the sorts of fly-in-fly-out mode of work associated with the extractive industries that I also discuss later in Chapter 9.

Airports provide good examples of the code/spaces described by Kitchin and Dodge (2011) and as such 'are neither monuments to immobility, nor instruments of the mobile society, but instead, the improbable conjunction of both' (Pascoe, 2001: 14). This is particularly the case with regard to the regulatory complexities in which airports are enmeshed as places. 'Airports coalesced as more permanent constellations of the state and regional authority, holding together the idea of national airspace, but doing so on the ground. They were the nodes around, over and through which nationalist sentiments or even more regional and localized identities were formed' (Adey, 2010: 67). However, this process of bordering became ever more uncertain to the point of being regularly and continuously undone (Adey, 2010: 70). Thus national airspace has been undone in several ways: 'airports have become associated with a post-national terrain of flexible citizenship and personal mobility' and the 'disintegration of national airspace into a patchwork quilt of uneven authorities and overlapping sovereignty'. The 'upstreaming of international borders' implies that states extrude into one another (Adey, 2010: 76–7). Airports are therefore special places that to some extent negate the places or containers that we take for granted—cities and nations. They are places which act as projectors but are also associated with an airport politics which is anti-city and to some extent anti-nation.

The fixed infrastructure of airport terminals displays an architecture of anticipation—a place to wait somewhere between here and now and there and then (Fuller, 2009) as the exerpt from *Generation X* reminds us. In economic terms, airports are crucial sites in and through which inter-urban and international competition and indeed policy mobility (Bock, 2015) are played out. Not least because it has been argued that 'the aerotropolis represents the logic of globalization made fresh in the form of cities' (Kasarda and Lindsay, 2011: 6) and has travelled as something of an economic development/planning model. In this respect—of their being an object implicated in inter-city competition—they are not only places in-between in the literal sense of their physical location but also 'they remain an in-between space whose development paths are ultimately governed by the alternating roll-out and roll-back of government neoliberal policy reforms' (Freestone (2011: 116).

The economic activities contained within the architectures are significant in and of themselves. Doubtless, a good portion of this centres on serving a key element of the mobile labour force. As Sharma (2014: 30) notes 'the airport is a particularly vital node for the reproduction and maintenance of global capital's most valuable subject: the frequent business traveler' (Sharma, 2014: 30) and 'as subjects of value within global capital, the time of the frequent business traveler is an important object of biopolitical regulation'. The evidence on the local or regional economic development contributions of airports is rather mixed. However, for Florida et al. (2015) there is indeed an important role for airports within their urban regional economies, not merely in terms of flows of materials and goods but more particularly the human capital contribution that airports make to local economies. Discourses that surround the application of code applied to air travel emphasize the rationality and efficiency of code/space for 'globals' but also in facilitating global trade and investment and expanded opportunities for consumption (Kitchin and Dodge, 2011).

The full scale of the economies centred on airports as fixed infrastructures and places go well beyond those immediately associated with the activity and subsidiary industries of air travel themselves to include any number of economic activities to be found in a typical city. That is, 'in the global "space of flows", airports are critical nodes and have latterly assumed major economic significance extending beyond core aviation functions' (Freestone, Williams and Borden, 2006: 491). 'They may develop into small-scale global cities in their own right, places to meet and do business, to sustain family life and friendships, and to act as a site for liminal consumption less constrained by prescribed household income and expenditure patterns' (Urry, 2009: 27). For the mass of travellers these inter-urban enclosed spaces ensnare a captive market of consumers of all sorts since 'the eighty-six minutes of time that passengers average between clearing security and waiting for takeoff is an unaccounted for time, open to investment by retailers and other machinations of global capital' (Sharma, 2014: 51–2). 'Airport master plans and development plans have targeted uncommitted land assets for non-aeronautical business developments such as hotels, business parks, regular and discount retail malls, and bulky goods and fast food outlets...such developments are transforming airports into major activity nodes with implications for spatial structure, transportation, commercial property markets, the environment and the efficacy of planning systems' (Freestone, Williams, and Borden, 2006: 492). In this way, airports and the numerous other specialized facilities agglomerated around them have become new inter-urban places in part of the more distributed pattern of work and corporate contact systems described in Chapter 4.

Debate surrounds the real economic significance of airports as new inter-places. Some measure of the sorts of the potential economic importance (notably sales tax revenues) of airports is provided by the intense local and city-regional jurisdictional politics surrounding them, as seen, for example, in the cases of Moscow's Sheremtyvo Airport, which was annexed to the rapidly expanding Khimki (Golubchikov and Phelps, 2010) and the case of O'Hare, which was annexed from the suburbs by the city of Chicago by a narrow strip of land along the I-90 interstate. With over 290,000 jobs within a 2.5 mile radius of the airport, O'Hare is large in comparison to other suburban magnets such as the regional shopping malls described above (Cidell, 2015). O'Hare may also prove to be the exception rather than the rule as in the same study of 25 US airports only half proved to be regionally significant employment centres of their own accord while a quarter were unimportant. Indeed, some airports, such as Washington Dulles (Figure 6.1), have stood in splendid isolation with little ancillary development until recently. On other measures and based again on a study of major airports in the US, 80 per cent of airports anchored employment agglomerations of some note—being, on average, one-third of one-half of the size of the central business district of their respective downtowns (Appold, 2016).

Schiphol airport close to Amsterdam in the Netherlands has become a major hub of office activity to the point that rental prices are on a par with those in the centre of Amsterdam. It forms part of Amsterdam's south axis which has grown significantly after the decision of ABN-AMRO bank to move its headquarters there. A master plan of 1998 foresaw it developing into a US edge city size concentration of economic activity with up to 1 million square metres of office space and 8,500 apartments (Bontje and Burdack, 2005: 328).

Figure 6.1 Washington Dulles Airport
Source: author's photograph.

The planning regime in which Schiphol has developed might be described as a hybrid of restrictive and development-oriented approaches and instruments in which the 'airport lobby' has nevertheless tended to win the day on most planning debates surrounding expansions and intensification of land use. Airport boundaries and criteria for airport-relatedness of economic activities have changed over time, and policies have become more institutionalized and legalized. Yet planning restrictions have helped ensure that the vast majority of companies attracted to surrounding business parks were airport-related (Van Wijk, Brattinga, and Bontje, 2011). One study estimated that for every direct job associated with the airport itself a further two jobs were supported indirectly or were induced through local expenditures (Hakfoort, Poot, and Rietveld, 2001).

As products of an economy located somewhere between mobility and fixity airports provide a glimpse of a world that is somewhere between two of the economic geographical formations introduced in Chapter 3. Their boundaries are secured like an enclave. However, in the case of the largest among them no one could deny their power to attract and concentrate a diverse range of economic activities to produce some of the best contemporary examples of economic agglomeration.

Rail Corridors and the Mid-urban Realm

By the end of the nineteenth century, that is 'by the end of the urban railroad transformation, railroad companies possessed between 5 percent (London) and 9 percent (Liverpool) of the land in British cities and indirectly influenced the use of another 10 percent' (Osterhammel, 2014: 301). These figures give some idea of the quantity of urban land-uses turned over to railway-related economic activities in Britain and doubtless in the cities of other European nations as a well as the United States. Little wonder then that Cooley (1894, cited in Fleming and Hayuth, 1994) identified what he referred to as the 'channelling effects' of transport routes and attraction of other allied functions and industries. It was these channelling effects that Healey argues meant that the railways themselves had important generative effects on the emergence of the American Manufacturing Belt (AMB) rather than playing a role subsequent and subordinate to the scale economies of manufacturing which have been said to produce urban agglomeration at the macro scale. The generative effects of a transportation infrastructure such as railroads was in terms of their 'factor channelling' such that 'flows of raw materials were directed to chosen locations in a planned and managed fashion, sometimes contrary to the economic logic of transportation and cost minimization' (Healey, 2015: 502). There were several stages to such effects. 'First, close inter-relationship between natural resource exploitation and then expansion of the railroad network... focused natural resource streams on specific locations, with only limited regard for transport cost considerations. Second, the first major phase of these developments during the 1850s provided a key direct employment stimulus at the time... Third, both railroad shops and natural resource processing industries encourages by factor channeling, stimulated secondary manufacturing' (Healey, 2015: 531).

By the late 1800s these dynamics produced a railroad industrial complex in the US which Stilgoe characterizes as the metropolitan corridor. 'Metropolitan corridor designates the portion of the American built environment that evolved along railroad rights-of-way in the years between 1880 and 1935. No traditional spatial term, not *urban*, *suburban*, or *rural*, not *cityscape* or *landscape* adequately identifies the space that perplexed so many turn-of-the-century observers' (Stilgoe, 1983: 3, original emphasis). The fact that no traditional spatial term seemed to capture this urban economic corridor, it could be argued, implies that this was one historic incarnation of an economy in between in turn composed of distinct interplaces. 'In its heyday, form about 1880 to 1930, the metropolitan corridor objectified the ordered life, the life of the engineered future... For one half century moment the nation created a new sort of environment characterized by technically controlled order' (Stilgoe, 1983: 339). That is 'the corridor announced modernity, planning and systems engineering' (p. 13) and was vital to ushering in a the sorts of suburban decentralization of manufacturing that began in the early 1900s and had proceeded far enough by the 1960s for Gottmann (1964) to depict it as specifically inter-urban. Here, then, 'suburban land was abundant, cheap, accessible by railroad, and lightly taxed; that insurance companies implicitly mandated it as the only safe manufacturing location made it even more attractive' (Stilgoe, 1983: 85).

The rail corridor is one that retains some latent potential. It is a feature that can emerge if and when the limits of the automobile are reached (Stilgoe, 1983: 344). And there is some sense of this in the reintroduction of trams and suburban rail lines in Europe and even one or two instances of the extension of metropolitan rail lines out to the likes of edge cities and airports as we saw in the case of Tysons Corner in Chapter 3. For others, however, 'trains won't replace planes, but they will make it easier than ever to fly' (Kasarda and Lindsay, 2011: 351). In this respect, although rail density contributes to the enduring attractions of the city, it also plays into an economy that extends beyond the city per se, to important inter-urban nodes of economic activity when providing for high local and global accessibility at the metropolitan if not megapolitan scale (Niedzielski and Malecki, 2012).

In this connection, large fixed and seemingly specialized infrastructures such as airports and rail freight terminals are locations of co-presence that actually perform roles which represent city-regions as a whole as multimodal passenger and freight terminals within the international economy. As a result of technological, management, and communications innovations 'cities and regions have become units within a larger system of logistics rather than self-contained distribution systems of their own' (Cidell, 2011: 832). These distribution-related workplaces of cities as units are very much at the suburban or urban fringe or even inter-urban in location. Paradoxically, developments such as containerization have meant that movement rather than storage has become a more important part of logistics industries and have pushed towards inter-urban locations. Yet these large, clunky, fixed infrastructures hardly seem to personify the mobility of goods with which they are associated. Indeed, 'the spatial imaginary of land use planners remains largely bounded within their own municipal territories, contra the global talk that characterizes most discussions of logistics and distribution' (Cidell, 2011: 845).

A case in point would be Chicago. As Cidell explains 'Chicago's history as a transport center is fundamental to its identity... there are the rail tracks laid down starting in the 1840s, followed by the interstate highways from the 1950s that still act to physically concentrate US freight traffic through this metropolitan area... While the city itself is modernizing its rail infrastructure... shippers and distributors are taking advantage of agricultural land on the fringe of the metropolitan area to build distribution centers and intermodal yards on a scale not previously seen' (Cidell, 2011: 833). These now have a centrality of sorts but it is one that is very much a centrality that balances the forces of centripetal and centrifugal forces. 'With little room to expand within the central city, new intermodal facilities must be built on the far edge of the metropolitan area to attain the elusive balance between sufficient infrastructure and labor on the one hand, and large parcels of land and lack of congestion on the other' (Cidell, 2011: 836).

The Exit Ramp Economy

The 'borders of interstate highways are regularized, perhaps an epitome of what all roads strive for—to be nowhere only to be going' (Harbison, 1989: 127). As such, 'it is increasingly accurate to talk of transport networks being fed by places, the classic instance being roadside sprawl, those non-place urban realms that provide a complete support system for, yet are subsidiary to, the demands of travel' (Bonnett, 2014: 281). The intriguing thought that accompanies this observation, then, is that it is the infrastructure between historic places, the traditional containers of economic activity, which now governs the location and orientation of much of the contemporary economy. That is 'the non-places created by this restless movement feed the traffic and keep the wheels turning. Yet they are so subsidiary to mobility that they also resemble parasitic growths, latched onto an indifferent host' (Bonnett, 2014: 286).

In the early 1900s Benton MacKay spoke of fixed infrastructure networks as America's new 'industrial wilderness'. That is, in displacing one nature, humankind had created another nature or wilderness as yet little discovered or utilized very efficiently. 'This "industrial wilderness" ... lay as the undiscovered territory within the successive flows of population and development' (Easterling, 1999: 42). However, by today, the fixed infrastructures of America's interstate highways, beltways, and state parkways could hardly be said to remain an industrial wilderness since they have been well and truly found by businesses of all sorts. To be sure, 'the interstate highway system was conceived as a frozen shape that neutralized interplay among various species of network carrier. It was a dumb network with dumb switches' (Easterling, 1999: 7) which tends to indicate either that its economic potential will remain limited or else may become more fully realized in the future.

Commenting on Los Angeles, Banham (1971: 213) was able to note how 'coming off the freeway is coming in from outdoors. A domestic or sociable journey in Los Angeles does not end so much at the door of one's destination as at the off-ramp of the freeway, the mile or two of ground-level streets counts as no more than the front drive to the house.' If this is the effect of the exit ramp on social interaction, it is an effect multiplied in relation to economic interactions. Little wonder that Harbison described the world of US retail mall developer Eddie Bartolo as one in which 'his jet plane makes actual his mental speed and his jumps from place to place prove that "downtown is dead". He sees expressways acting as lines of force on the landscape and builds his giant toy villages at their intersections, points which to pastbound people look like nowhere' (Harbison, 1989: 54). Somewhat later, then, the importance of roads or highways to local economies in the US led Bruce Katz (2001) to speak of the 'exit ramp economy'. What Katz is referring to here is the tendency for inter-state highway junctions to be the focal points for the location of much new business activity and correspondingly for economic development strategies. The development of 'edge city' Tysons Corner (see Figure 6.2) initially followed this sort of logic since for much of its early growth a lack of further interchange improvements to the limited access Dulles Toll Road meant that: 'Tysons Corner, almost exactly halfway between the airport and the White House, was not only the first but also the last practical place for commercial activities between Dulles and the District' (Ceruzzi, 2008: 55). 'Business-oriented hotels have expanded their locations to outlying, suburban and even exurban business centres or "edge cities"' (Kellerman, 2010: 172). Indeed, such exist-ramp based economies have filled out minimally to include

Figure 6.2 The exit ramp economy of Tysons Corner
Source: author's photograph.

the triumvirate of offices, hotels and conference centres, with economic development strategies emphasizing the local multiplier effects of business tourism.

As we also saw in Chapter 5, Lang (2003) and Lang and LeFurgy (2007) have argued that edge cities such as Tysons Corner have by now been super-seded in the US. Lang and LeFurgy (2007) use the term boomburb to speak to some of America's fastest growing—ostensibly suburban communities. These 'boomburbs typically develop along interstate freeways that ring large U.S. metropolitan areas. The commercial elements of the new suburban metropolis—office parks, big box retail stores, and most characteristically, strip malls—gather at highway exit ramps and major intersections' (Lang and LeFurgy, 2007: 10–11). As they go on to describe 'the first word of advice for anyone looking to see a boomburb business district is to forget about downtown and head out for the highways. You may not find much of a "there" in a traditional sense, but boomburbs, freeways often anchor some of their region's biggest economic engines and recreational attractions' (Lang and LeFurgy, 2007: 80). Major road infrastructure can, in important instances, physically mark out an economy of interplaces found between historic urban cores or downtowns and the mass of business now emerging in the new suburban or exurban expanses of American metropolitan or megapolitan regions. Route 128 in Boston would be an example since 'it created a geo-graphical corridor that demarcated the boundary between the metropolitan Boston of the early twentieth century and the suburbia that developed after world war II' (O'Connell, 2013: 149).

Britain's major road infrastructure has promoted an altogether more modest set of interplaces given the strong tradition of urban containment within the planning system for all but a brief period in the 1990s. Nevertheless the relaxation of planning controls on out-of-town retail and office developments that occurred briefly in the 1990s might be said to have ushered in a latent framework for development given the land holdings and business interests that were developed at edge of city locations in this period. Motorway Service Areas (MSAs) were not as large as regional shopping centres or new towns (covering just 50–100 acres) but between 1992 and 2000 there were 120 proposals for new MSAs in England and Wales (Walton and Dixon, 2000: 334). The inter-urban nature of motorways made planning decisions regard-ing these nodal points particularly difficult in a context of urban containment (Walton and Dixon, 2000: 335). Yet, 'the strengths of the MSA market (under-pinned by rising levels of car ownership, car usage and leisure-related expend-iture will ensure that planning authorities will continue to be confronted by applications for proposals on new sites in stand-alone and infill locations in the years ahead' (Walton and Dixon, 2000: 352). There is very little informa-tion about the economic significance of these interplaces. Casual observation reveals that business meetings take place at these inter-urban watering holes and some have deliberately developed office space as a consequence but it is unclear just how much of a typical day's work might take place at such spots or what type of work and decisions take place there. Hislop and Axtell's (2015: 7) recent survey data reported in Table 6.2 tends to underline the significance of these banal spaces since at near 45 per cent, service station car parks recorded the highest proportion of respondents conducting work tasks—more than on train carriages or at airports or on planes. Indeed, the same survey data revealed that the service station car park was actually nearly twice as important as the MSA buildings as a place of work.

The Fast and Slow Subjects of Globalization

'The nature of the contemporary globalizing firm, characterized by geographical dispersion, global production divisions and complex sub-contracting/supplier networks, provides the impetus and need for physical travel' (Beaverstock et al., 2010: 1). If the dissolution of corporate contact systems (described in Chapter 4) has provided something of the impetus for physical travel as part of the mobility of business activities more generally, then that impetus has only gathered real strength since the advent of ICTs. 'ICTs, especially mobile phones and the internet or world wide web, have facilitated a more mobile corporeal relationship with space, including micro-coordination and rescheduling on the move . . . and lifting activity (e.g. work) out of place (e.g. the office) to distributed locations, including those on the move' (Line, Jain, and Lyons, 2011: 1490). Indeed, the dissolution of corporate contact systems has already proceeded sufficiently to mean that 'business travel can be a fundamental, repetitive (even mundane) everyday working process' (Beaverstock and Faulconbridge, 2010: 60). So much so, that it can be argued that 'in economic terms, business travel now appears to be the fundamental production process in constructing and reproducing the "Network Society" and the global knowledge-based economy that have come to be the hallmarks of contemporary capitalism' (Beaverstock et al., 2010: 2). At one extreme, then, are

Table 6.1 Percentage of respondents engaging in work-related email and mobile phone use, 2008

	Often	Sometimes	Rarely	Never
Check work-related email when on the go[a]	7	6	5	75
Make work-related calls when on the go	12	17	18	53

Source: reproduced from Rainie and Wellman (2012: 187).

[a] figures do not sum to 100 as 8% declared there was no email at work.

a privileged set of workers or 'globals'. At the other extreme are those who labour in the slow lane, at least partly it seems, in service of such globals. Thus the data presented in Table 6.1 highlight only the proportion of presumably globals making work-related email and mobile phone contacts while on the move but also the greater proportions of those who do not.

The Fast Subjects of Globalization

With regard to such globals, 'the decisive shift from internationalization to transnationalization is . . . registered in the proliferation of business workers—cosmopolitan "fast subjects"—who dwell in . . . [a] space of flows, to-ing and fro-ing between the hubs and spokes of the global economy' (Budd and Hubbard, 2010: 90–1). Here, then, is a picture of places as the primary containers of economic activity dissolving into Webber's (1964) 'community without propinquity' of professional and social networks.

This labour on the move is one component of the interplaces that I consider in this chapter. However, it is worth remembering that, in reality, 'companies use a range of types mobility, long and short-term, to acquire and transfer expertise between their own sites and those of their clients or collaborators. Business travel is one form of this mobility' (Salt, 2001: 107).[1] Nevertheless, Lassen (2010: 177) cites data from the World Tourism Organization from 2005 to note that 19 per cent of all international travel was business travel and that it more than doubled from 1990 and 2001. Indeed, some indication of the rising significance of international business travel is provided by the fact that Haynes (2010, cited in Lyons, 2013: 50) was able to note recently that it exceeds the total international air travel undertaken as recently as 1980. Using Office for National Statistics data Beaverstock and Faulconbridge (2010: 62) show that in the case of the United Kingdom alone 'since 1977 the numbers of overseas residents' visits to the UK and UK residents' visits abroad for the main purpose of business have both increased by over three-hundred fold'.

Time is money, so the saying goes, and that expression highlights an assumption that has become increasingly untenable in policy circles that the demand for travel is assumed to be derived—that is, a demand that is not for travel itself but as a means to do something or to get somewhere else is 'dead time' from the perspective of work and its value to the economy. And yet, all around us we see people working while on the move in cars, trains, and airplanes. The economic value of travel is routinely underestimated in

---

[1] Millar and Salt (2001) have itemized 8 types of mobility which companies employ as part of a portfolio of human resource strategies. These are: (1) permanent recruitment through external or internal labour markets; (2) long-term assignments of (1–4 years); (3) short-term assignments (3–12 months); (4) commuter assignments; (5) rotation; (6) extended business travel; (7) business travel; and (8) virtual mobility.

cost-benefit analyses of major infrastructure investments and their time-saving potential, since travel is essentially regarded as non-productive time spent getting to and from places of work or leisure. Even so, 'as currently judged within transport economics, business travel accounts for a major part of the economic value of time invested in travel overall' (Lyons, 2013: 50). Three per cent of all domestic trips in the UK in 2011 were for business, the figure being identical in the US.

The advent of ICTs in particular has rapidly and markedly increased the economic potential of travel, leaving multitasking as something of a '"forgotten dimension" of time use in travel behaviour research' (Kenyon and Lyons, 2007: 162). Multitasking may appear to register a strong measure of virtuality or synchrony in the contemporary economy in which actors are in two places at once (Marginson, 2010; Thrift and Olds, 1996). 'Global synchrony, which is the achievement of a common timespace and rhythm with people located across national borders who could be anywhere in the world, is the temporal partner of the spatial practice of global-de-severing, which is the process of imagining ourselves close to those in distant locations' (Marginson, 2010: 135). The greater penetration of ICTs into almost all working lives has rapidly increased this synchrony in many working lives, though most notably perhaps in those of what Urry terms the 'globals'. If not on collective terms, then at least on a personal level such synchrony is ambiguous in its implications, since 'the desire for global synchrony is as universal as the desire for global mobility. The forces of global mobility and global synchrony allow us to expand connectivity while sustaining the self. We can be open and bounded at the same time' (Marginson, 2010: 136).

Failure to consider multitasking leads to the under-reporting of activities and presumably economic activities. For example, 99 per cent of respondents to one survey reported some multitasking at some point in their week. Indeed multitasking is estimated in this survey to add 46 per cent to the time of each waking day (Kenyon and Lyons, 2007: 168). For 84 per cent of the time they travel a person will be doing at least one other task. This is higher than when at home suggesting that travel is no barrier to additional activity per se although it may be a barrier to work/economic activity specifically, though the most common activities with which travel is most commonly teamed with are not work related (Kenyon and Lyons, 2007: 171). Thus, once the value of working time per person as opposed to the value allocated to simply travel is taken into account 'in spite of their small share of overall (domestic) trips, in terms of assumed economic impacts of travel, business trips account for a substantial portion of total travel' (Lyons, 2013: 50).

A more accurate picture of work on the move is provided by fragments of various surveys that have attempted to capture a sense of how much time spent travelling is at least partly used for work purposes. Moreover, one recent

Table 6.2 Work-related tasks on business trips

	Never	Occasionally	Frequently
TRAIN JOURNEY IN CARRIAGE			
Interactive tasks	73%	16	11
Independent tasks	8%	12	80
PLANE JOURNEY: WITHIN DEPARTURE AREA			
Interdependent tasks	66%	23%	12%
Independent tasks	27%	31%	42%
PLANE JOURNEY: ON BOARD			
Interdependent tasks	89%	8%	3%
Independent tasks	45%	29%	26%
CAR JOURNEY: WITHIN SERVICE STATION			
Interdependent tasks	47%	34%	19%
Independent tasks	46%	33%	21%
CAR JOURNEY: WHEN PARKED AT SERVICE STATION			
Interdependent tasks	30%	20%	49%
Independent tasks	32%	32%	37%

Source: reproduced from Hislop and Axtell (2015).

survey conducted in the US asked where respondents had ever conducted work-related activities in a series of 'locations' in the past month. The results are revealing of the large proportion of work-related activities that now take place in an advanced economy like the US in locations associated with transport and mobility and on the move. Whilst the large majority of work-related activity outside of specifically designated corporate workplaces took place at home, work activities are distributed across a range of locations including those associated with mobility. So, fully 40 per cent of respondents indicated that they had undertaken work while in the car and at least 10 per cent takes place in airports, depots or at platforms, in planes, trains, or subways. The fact that at least 10 per cent of respondents indicated having undertaken work in the likes of parks and cafes further underlines the growing complexity and fundamentally distributed nature of work (Lister and Harnish 2011: 20). Table 6.1 is reproduced from Hislop and Axtell's (2015: 7) recent survey of behaviour to business travel work conducted at key modal ports (at airports, in motorway service area buildings, or car parks) or on the move (in train carriages and on board planes). It provides one of the most recent snapshots of the economy on the move in between and a backdrop to some of the discussion later in this chapter.

Thus 'The sleeping body of the business traveler . . . is therefore also a significant object of knowledge production' (Sharma, 2014: 40) associated with all technologies of mobility. Nowhere is this more so than in the case of air travel. However, this international business travel in particular also highlights growing inequalities in society which reverberate as we saw in Chapter 4 at the urban and inter-urban scale. That is, 'the societal stratification of transportation systems is not only enduring, in the case of commercial aviation at least, it seems to be deepening' (Bowen, 2010: 11). In particular, then, 'globalization has engendered wider levels of income inequality which simultaneously stretches the linkages of everyday life across continents and oceans. Together, these trends have fostered a proportionately larger global transnational capitalist class, the target market for long-haul business class services' (Bowen, 2010: 28).

Labour in the Slow Lane

It is hard to deny the idea that 'not only do we possess a certain hyperactive potential, defined in terms of the ownership of machines for moving information and the body through space and time, we have also been inclined to increase our use of these machines over time' (Buliung, 2011: 1371). Notwithstanding a generalized increase in physical and virtual mobility and a generalized speeding-up of work and social life for the vast majority in the global north, it is also true to see a continuing measure of complementary fixity and slowness in a set of other work activities. Indeed, a strong and continuing measure of slow, place-bound economic activity attends, and indeed is required by, the most mobile of economic activities and people.

The physical and virtual mobility that transportation and ICT technologies facilitate 'is the dynamic equivalent of location, then mobility is the dynamic equivalent of place' (Cresswell, 2006: 3). As already discussed in Chapter 4, something of this is found in Laurier's (2002) suggestion that mobile work involves the accomplishment of the region—it involves workers in large measure putting the region back together on behalf of public organizations and private corporations. That is, movement has in some senses as its logical counterpart—the production of a measure of fixity and place in various guises.

The self-provisioning and self-organizing of work has been one major component of how individuals help put the region back together in an era of dissolution of corporate contact systems in disorganized capitalism. Some of the inherent difficulties of increasing productivity in service industries has meant that self-servicing has for some time now been an important ingredient of the industrialization of service industries (Gershuny, 1978). New technologies appear to have extended this principle into the realms of the self-organization of work often away from the single office work environment to which one might have reported exclusively in the past and across a variety of locations, modes of physical and virtual mobility.

Partly as a result, 'there is now a reduced (and reducing) dominance of the clock-controlled industrialized time and a resurgence of the pre-industrial task-oriented concept of time' (Holley et al., 2008: 32) and instead the emergence of new 'time identities' in the organization of the working day. Most IT workers in one study fell somewhere between two extremes of 'clock timers' (adhering to rigid work times and sharp distinctions between work and leisure) and 'task timers' (with flexible timing of work activities and where there was no symbolic distinction between work and leisure) (Westenholz, 2006, cited in Holley et al., 2008: 33). 'The existence of more than one time perspective has implications for business travel time due to its potential to *decouple* travel time (and its use) from the traditionally assumed association with what takes place at the origin and destination' (Holley et al., 2008: 32, original emphasis). This unravelling of the single idea of clock time associated work has a lot to do with the emergence of relatively autonomous, self-organized, workers to some extent reproducing and remapping the contact systems once organized within major corporations, as discussed in Chapter 4. Despite all this, and despite the clear visible evidence of its likely quantitative and qualitative importance, we still can only guess at the significance of the work tasks undertaken in such a self-organized fashion (Holley et al., 2008: 34).

Moreover, 'the affective dimensions of laboring in the global economy cannot be levelled out in such a way as to argue for the precarious position of the privileged when we know that here is so much invested in rescuing these bodies' (Sharma, 2014: 69). These affective dimensions of labouring depend on an economy of care whose economic significance is barely recognized at all but which when an audit is taken and when properly valued amounts to perhaps half of all economic activity according to some estimates (Gibson-Graham, 2008: 617). The privilege of globals depends on a fixity of workers in particular places. This is certainly a picture of polarization that has become apparent over recent decades in many world cities (Sassen, 2000, though its causes and significance are debated and extend beyond the simple servicing of the mobility of one professionalized class by another less mobile class of workers, not least because of the migrant divisions of labour associated with the latter (Huws, 2014; May et al., 2007). 'Rather than restrict accounts of migrant workers to their role in servicing those functions usually attributed to a city's "global city" status then, we need to recognize the role such workers play in keeping the city as a whole "working"' (May et al., 2007: 161).

Yet even some globals are hardly hypermobile. Indeed some presumably are actually quite privileged in terms of their attachment to place in the form of the transformed nature of residence as in outlined in Chapter 4. With just 2.9 per cent of the US workforce engaged in teleworking—defined in terms of home being the primary location of work—teleworking is currently very much a minority form of employment in advanced economies. Yet its potential is considerable given that the same research suggests that as much as 45 per cent of the US workforce holds a job that it is compatible with at least part-time tele working (Lister and Harnish, 2011: 4).

Some portion of the economy of the interplaces of personal mobility centres not on the value added to productive processes while on the move in the form of business travel, but on the sheer amount of consumption of goods and services that has come to be associated with physical and virtual mobility. However, 'the impact of ICT on travel and physical mobility are extremely unclear for a number of reasons—the complexity of motivations for travel, the long versus short term impacts of ICT, the multiple effects of substitution and complementarity between the two and the two-way relationship between ICT and physical travel' (Aguilar et al., 2012: 666). 'The collection of places contained within any cybermediated container of spatial knowledge is expected to be enormous, including a vast range of geographical locations—some rarely, if ever, physically contacted—and virtual worlds hosted on remote computers. Local knowledge, developed from immersion with the built environment of the city, could melt away, as ICT-enabled spatial leapfrogging increasingly draws distant and virtual locations into individualized processes of production and consumption' (Buliung, 2011: 1375).

Consumption figures strongly as part of the virtual mobility of the internet since 'when human sociality is mediated by telecommunications systems . . . the internet is thus constituted as a vast virtual shopping mall' (Huws, 2014: 15). Yet this is sedentary shopping even by the standards of a drive to the out-of-town mall.

The Economy on the Move

The Airport as Flow

As inter-urban locations, airports are developments that have made their contribution to urban sprawl. However, according to Kasarda and Lindsay (2011: 10) 'if you look closely at the aerotropolis, what appears to be sprawl is slowly evolving into a system of reducing both [time and cost]' (Kasarda and Lindsay, 2011: 10). This places airports at the heart of an economy which—as a result of the systemic properties of automobility and aeromobility—is becoming increasingly finely, almost infinitely, sliced into segments of time-space. Thus 'the time and energy once wasted on conquering distance are reinvested in the exchange of goods and information' (Kasarda and Lindsay, 2011: 161). This is the airport and the flight itself as superdconductor promising yet less resistance to the friction of distance and even zero resistance (Kasarda and Lindsay, 2011: 167).

Airspace, like logistics space, is organized into corridors and 'the corridors not only materially support working life in knowledge organizations but also function as a logic of action. It is a selection mechanism, which picks and chooses so that the traveler is distributed in accordance with the logic of the corridor—a logic anchored in the "space of flows"' (Lassen, 2009: 178). The limited evidence that does exist suggests a modest economy taking place in these corridors—the flow of air travel; a modest economy paused or on the move in between. Figures from Hislop and Axtell's survey of business travel behaviour indicated that nearly 30 per cent of respondents surveyed in departure lounges at airports used technologies for work tasks quite a lot or a great deal. At between 10 and 15 per cent of respondents the figure was rather less for the conduct of work on board the plane in flight (Hislop and Axtell, 2015: 7).

Working in Carriage

The fact that air travel is by far the most important mode of international business travel centred on the UK, despite rail and sea also playing a role provides no easy clues as to the variable importance of work on the move supported by these different technologies of mobility. The role played by Eurostar in increasing the importance of rail for business travel (and therefore presumably work while on the move) has been countervailed by the emergence of low-cost airlines (Beaverstock and Faulconbridge, 2010). Nevertheless, what these findings also imply is that the impacts of successive technologies of mobility are unlikely to be stable over time or across different national and continental settings—it will be fascinating to see the implications of extensive development of high-speed rail in China for example, and the effects this may have upon business travel and the economy on the move in between.

For Axtell et al. (2008) train travel occupies something of an intermediate form of mobility given that work on trains is essentially stationary relative to the immediate physical context yet also mobile in relation to places being passed while in carriage. The relative fixity or place bound nature of work on trains actually presents significant constraints on both the amount and type of work that can be done effectively while on the move. In particular, Axtell et al.'s (2008) evidence from surveys of those working on trains suggests that it is the more routine tasks described by Thorngren (1970) (see also Chapter 4) that can be done independently and not the more strategic or 'orientation' tasks that require a good measure of social interdependency and interaction tasks that typically are performed on trains.

Holley et al. (2008) have reported on a 2004 UK National Rail Passengers survey to explore the potential for work to be conducted while on the move on trains. The figures reported by Holley et al. indicate that as many as 86 per cent of surveyed rail travellers suggested a potential for rail travel to be used for work purposes when indicating that some of their paid work could be carried out on the train. However, the extent to which this potential is reached in actual use of time on trains for work was limited. Only 51 per cent and 31 per cent of those surveyed used some and most of their time for working or studying respectively and a further 22 per cent and 2 per cent and 15 per cent and 1 per cent respectively had used some and most of their time responding to and making work-related texts and telephone calls (Holley et al., 2008: 37). Figures from Hislop and Axtell's (2015: 7) more recent survey of business travel behaviour suggest that the use of the time spent travelling on trains for work is stable or may be on the rise. The figure of over 40 per cent of respondents who made use of technologies to undertake work tasks in train carriages 'quite a lot' or 'a great deal' is somewhere between the upper and lower figures in Holley et al.'s (2008) earlier research reported above.

Working in the Car

While much economic activity takes place in buildings, office parks, and new nodal points such as motorway service areas located alongside or in close proximity to road infrastructure, it is also the case that much economic activity takes place on the move while driving along such roadways. Clearly much of the work associated with whole industries such as transportation and distribution is directly concerned with facilitating the circulation of goods and people. However, some portion of the work associated with plenty of other industries and occupations takes place on the move. As Laurier (2004: 262) explains, 'there are plenty of groups, such as commuters, lorry and bus drivers, sales representatives and so on, who spend years of their lives driving along the motorway's parallel lanes'.

Indeed the work done on the move in this way is part and parcel of the idea of the distributed workplace and its effects on corporate contact systems introduced in Chapter 4. Yet the remarkable thing about such profound changes in the organization and distribution of economic activity is how poorly planned they appear to have been. As Laurier explains 'there was a surprising lack of deliberate planning by companies who did not yet treat the growing daily mobility of their personnel with the same precision as the long-standing logistics of their products. Little recognition has been given to the fact that, when changes in technology and commercial company policy move staff out of their traditional office and on to the roads in their regions, then not all the work can be divided so that *one* person in *one* car can do it appropriately, safely and in coordination with their non-proxemic co-workers, given that they are also responsible for transporting themselves' (Laurier, 2004: 263–4, original emphasis).

Despite major improvements in the speed, efficiency, and reliability of vehicles and indeed massive improvements in mobile telecommunications a considerable measure of inefficiency inheres in this work on the move. 'Large journey times, which are common in large company regions, or delays in slow-moving traffic mean that days on the road tend to be driving mostly and very little "work", that is, if driving was really the only thing that business persons did on motorways' (Laurier, 2004: 263). The porosity of the working day is, for example, something that developments in mobile telecommunications promise to make greater use of. There is an accompanying assumption that a degree of organizational expectation drives the use of mobile devices in cars. However, the use of mobile devices for work is not especially high as yet. Moreover, the indications are that driving is not especially conducive to work that is qualitatively difficult or important since it was the simplicity of the call in one study that seemed to be the main determinant of whether a telephone call was taken in a car or not (Hislop, 2012). Thus, while ICTs may facilitate the coordination and management of work tasks in the new distributed work environment, 'the evidence suggests that in aggregate they have not yet given rise to a new approach to travel, and more broadly the organization of work within the firm' (Aguilar et al., 2012: 666) they accentuate practices that already exist.

In sum, commuting produces a sense of habitation produced inside the bus, train, or car which is folded together with a sense of those places passed on the journey (Cresswell and Merriman, 2011). Some of these places passed on the journey represent little more than an affective moving landscape seen while in carriage. Others—such as airports, motorway service, and railway stations—in their functional fixity are most definitely economically important places even if we do not always recognize them as such.

Conclusion

At first sight the fact that the infrastructures and technologies associated with progressively enhanced personal physical and virtual mobility should produce some of the best examples of fixed places that are in between seems a paradox. Taken as a whole, the apparatus associated with such mobility is an immensely important part of the global economy in both quantitative and qualitative terms. The paradox quickly recedes from view when we realize that mobility inhabits a middle ground (Cresswell, 2006) and that journeys generate interplaces (Casey, 1993). Here I have attempted to provide some sense of the economic importance of these interplaces as the largely 'new' places associated with fixed infrastructures for trains, planes, and automobiles, on the one hand, and the liminal spaces of transit, on the other hand.

My effort here was hampered by some of the real difficulties of accurately gauging how much and what type of work is carried out in such interplaces and the as yet limited empirical studies to draw upon. However, the evidence that does exist suggests that this particular manifestation of the economy in between is significant and growing even if there are real limits to what practically can be done while on the move.

7

Policy Mobility

Introduction

As Rodgers (1998: 5) reminds us, 'Atlantic-era social politics had its origins not in its national-state containers, not in an hypothesized "Europe" nor an equally imagined "America", but in the world between them.' That is, the process of policy mobility 'transcends both the national and the international and... takes place "in the spaces within and between"' (Stone, 2004: 561–4). On the one hand, consideration of policy mobilities undermines an exclusively territorial perspective in economic geography. Yet, on the other hand, as McCann (2011: 109) notes, 'The circulation of knowledge is paradoxically structured by embedded institutional legacies and imperatives... Thus the "demand side" of policy transfer and conditions under which adopters of "best practice"... operate must be acknowledged in combination with the study of the practices of "supply side" policy mediators, such as consultants.' This interplace economy is one that is materialized specifically in the technocratic landscapes of consulting and the technologies that support them (Prince, 2015).

The subject of policy mobility is one that signals a relational economic geography. It embodies the tension between the fixity and mobility of capital, between sedentarist and nomadic perspectives in geography. Yet it cannot be reduced to one or other in these sets of antimonies. Indeed, as MacFarlane (2011) elaborates, the processes that constitute the city are strongly rooted by the very nature of the learning process—as ones that involve not just translation but also dwelling in situated contexts. In general, then, consideration of urban policy mobility entails integration of idiographic and nomothetic outlooks—a careful treading of the line between local specificity and attention to global interconnection (Peck and Tickell, 2002). That is, 'Connections, even close ones, can exist, and differences can be discerned and acknowledged, without preventing the development of a universalist discourse whose terminology may not always be universally understood or accepted' (Saunier, 2002: 522). Arguably the market for all things urban has taken on increased significance and intensity in the present second global economy in which 'the urban does nothing in itself; its role is that of a dynamic socio-spatial sphere in which the *betweenness* of people is ever so much more intense' (Merrifield, 2013: 916, emphasis added). However, little of what is by now a vast literature has been concerned with what is surely a sizeable economy associated with these 'ideoscapes' of modernity (Appadurai, 1996).

It should come as no surprise that the in-between world of policy mobility rests on its own set of intermediaries. Less appreciated is that such intermediaries have long existed and that the state itself might now be classed as such. There has been and continues to be a variety of motives for, and mechanisms and agents involved in, urban policy mobility. On the one hand, urban policy mobility has not consisted entirely in the naked exertion of political, administrative or economic power as part of weak forms of competition. On the other hand, neither can urban policy mobility be held up simply as a progressive process of learning and exchange which results in gains to society. In between these two possibilities lie mechanisms of urban policy mobility such as the power of *seduction* which appear to represent an ambiguous middle ground of latent political and economic desires being unleashed.

The network metaphor is an important one for understanding 'weak' intercity competition and policy mobility in the present. However, it is also a metaphor that, alongside that of the agglomeration, speaks to some of the possibilities for mobilizing 'strong' competition and cooperative place-based alternatives. These two coexist with the enclave—a denuded and narrower counterpart of the agglomeration—and one promoted significantly as part of weak forms of inter-urban and international competition.

Cities for Nations, the World in Cities: The Rise of Urban Policy Intermediaries

The emergence of a first global economy by the late 1800s and its re-emergence as a second global economy from the 1970s onwards were inextricably intertwined with multiple mechanisms or modes of power through which national and urban policies have travelled from one context to another and in the process been translated, adapted, and modified, to the point where it is often difficult to judge their antecedents (Bunnell, 2015).

Braithwaite and Drahos's (2000) account highlights a number of distinct mechanisms by which 'global' regulatory principles have established themselves over the course of history.[1] From a different disciplinary context, Allen

---

[1] These include: military coercion, economic coercion, modelling, reciprocal exchange, non-reciprocal exchange, capacity building, and technical assistance.

(2002) alights on some of the same modes power but alerts us to the power of *seduction*. One can hardly consider modernity at large in a first and second global economy without considering this often underappreciated desire among consumers—politicians, policy-makers, citizens—to mobilize aspects of the urban. Doubtless, it is some of these desires that intermediaries of various sorts fed on in a first global economy. The commodification of place is something that has begun to be promulgated more fully in recent decades in a policy-making process that has itself become more 'roundabout' (Majone, 1989).

Urban Policy Mobility in the First Global Economy: Cities for Nations

Modern nation states were fashioned in Europe from smaller kingdoms and city states from the 1700s. Yet it is worth remembering that by the 1800s already 'ideas and political movements jumped across oceans and borders from country to country' (Bayly, 2000: 3). The modernity of a first global economy that culminated in the Atlantic era of policy exchange prior to World War I, was one that produced what we would recognise today as considerable hybridity in the sphere of urban policy.

Some sense of the economic importance of the places mobilized—to become, in a sense, interplaces—that had developed by the mid to late 1800s is provided by the considerable sums of money spent on advertising campaigns by railroad companies in the US. The Illinois Central Rail Road, for example, marketed the land it was granted and partially developing in the US to investors as far afield as Britain, Germany, and Scandinavia, while its marketing and disposal costs amounted to 10 per cent of the revenues gained from the sale its land holdings (Ward, 1998: 13). It was during this time too that the first real organized and concerted efforts were made by local elites to promote their respective cities with the opening of the 'New World' presenting a 'market' for many brand new settlements (Ward, 2003).

It is worth remembering that for all the genuine competitive spirit that pitted city against city within individual nations, municipal pride and planning at this time actually served to underline national identity. As King describes 'urban planning becomes on the one hand a step towards the social construction of "the nation" . . . and on the other a step towards the strengthening of the idea of the state' (King, 2003: 5). That is, 'in the multiple processes . . . by which a state acquires its identity as a state, as a *particular* state, and as a *modern* state, it represents itself in space, marking itself so to speak, inscribing itself urbanistically over its own territory' (King, 2003: 5, original emphasis).

Yet, it is equally no surprise that there was 'a professional class which served and indeed had a stake in the national system but which, as a distinct interest within the world system, readily transcended national boundaries' (Sutcliffe, 1986: 6). Among European nations, this professional class did so as part of imperial expansion. Pretty quickly these sorts of transnational exchanges led to hybrid national and urban modernities (Bayly, 2000) and played their own part in a first global economy (Jones, 2005). Groups of intermediaries were important in the building of colonial cities but these colonial cities more than most embodied 'plural societies, multiple identities and "intertwined histories"' (Nasr and Volait, 2003: xxi). In the construction of colonial cities we can observe 'go-betweens, advisors, mediators, who have their feet planted firmly in particular places and act as channels to the world at large', producing a 'complexity in urbanistic exchanges' in which it is often unclear what is local and foreign (Nasr and Volait, 2003: xv and xiii–xiv).

The urban policy mobility of the first global economy culminated in what has been regarded as an Atlantic era (Rodgers, 1998) in which the city came to the fore as the object of concern and territory of action (Saunier, 2001: 382). Urban policy mobility in this era produced a field in between—'an environment where ways of judging, apprehending and acting on the city were defined, where expertise and professional legitimacies were created, where knowledge and disciplines were constructed, and where the profiles of politicians responsible for urban issues were modified' (Saunier, 2001: 382). Arguably, one legacy of this era for the time between the two global economies was that 'the West remained a spatial and ideological construct that existed only under American guarantee' (Ward, 2003: 102). This is all the more curious for the fact that 'in a story that is littered with paradoxes, the most important of these is that the US has never developed an urban planning tradition commensurate in influence with its broader global significance' (Ward, 2003: 102).

Urban Policy in the Second Global Economy: World Cities and the Transnational Capitalist Class (TCC)

The intermediaries that were apparent historically in the planning and development of cities bound together as part of the empires of European nations might be taken as the forerunners of a global intelligence corps (GIC) (Olds, 2002) or transnational capitalist class (TCC) (Sklair, 2001). During the nineteenth and early twentieth centuries, then, planners, architects and civil engineers formed something of an internationale (Osterhammel, 2014; Saunier, 2001) in which 'model cities and architectural styles interacted with each other in different ways. The latter could be more easily copied than the former, but the cultural "spirit" of a city almost not at all' (Osterhammel, 2014: 312). Although there were very few multinational planning consulting companies formed at this time, nevertheless there was considerable work to be had based on the 'global imbalances between the perceived demands for and supply of the new planning expertise' (Ward, 2005: 136). Indeed, 'in some

cases, especially in the French and Japanese empires, colonies served as relatively unconstrained legal test beds for planning powers that were only later
adopted at the heart of empire' (Ward, 2005: 129). However, for Ward, the
British planning consultants involved in designing cities in the colonies of the
time did not amount to a GIC.

Nevertheless such a GIC or TCC does appear to be significant to understanding the interplaces of urban policy mobility in a second global economy. This
grouping is important to understanding the economic content of inter-urban
competition and spatial switching of capital in the present. A significant
measure of contemporary urban policy mobility should be understood in
terms of its relationship to the capitalist economic system in which places
are valorized by virtue of the need to complete the circuit of capital in
particular places.

The TCC is most relevant to understanding the dynamics of a group of
world cities.[2] It is the last part of Friedmann and Wolff's (1982) world city
definition—that the elite of world cities increasingly constitute a transnational social class—that has been taken up since by Sklair who sees the
emergence of a TCC as a class in itself and for itself. He identifies four fractions
of the TCC—globalizing politicians and bureaucrats, MNE executives, global
consumer elites. Each of these fractions has a vested interest in the health of
world city economies in something akin to a world city growth machine
(Molotch, 1976). Politicians may be partly dependent on the health of the
local economy. MNE executives seek to gain benefit for their corporations
especially those involved in real estate and infrastructure development. Consumer elites have the disposable income to speculate on rising residential
property prices partly in the process stimulating a distinct set of transnational
residential property and relocation service industries across the Pacific Rim
(Olds, 2002), and between world cities twinned by the migration of skilled
workers (White and Hurdley, 2003). Notably, for example, the TCC is quite
central to contemporary instances of policy mobility based on the likes of
iconic architecture. Here Sklair (2005) notes how it is the TCC and no longer
religious institutions or governments that have been responsible for the
skylines of cities. The growth of global architectural practices and the significant commissions for iconic buildings that they compete for is one indication
of the size of the interplace economy associated with policy mobility.

---

[2] Friedmann and Wolff (1982) originally identified five features of world cities. (1) World cities
articulate regional, national, and international economies into a global economy and serve as the
organizing nodes of the global economy. (2) Elsewhere major regions of the word are excluded
from these cores and live instead in an economic periphery or semi-periphery. (3) World cities
are large urbanized spaces of intense social and economic interaction. (4) The group of world
cities is itself a hierarchical system of major cities. They can be ranked. (5) The elite of world
cities increasingly constitute a transnational social class. A social class who are the product of global
capitalism and who act to ensure its survival.

Despite rapid urbanization across the global south, there is a strong measure of inertia with regards to the cores of this world cities network and even to the historic economic connections built-up as a result of empires. That is, 'contemporary globalization has a structure resulting from geographical (physical and politico-cultural) diffusion from the prime globalization arenas (northern America, western Europe and Pacific Asia) and...these regional imprints remain very evident' (Taylor et al., 2002: 2388). Carroll's (2010: 231) examination of the existence and evolution of a TCC through the prism of corporate interlocking directorships stakes out 'a middle ground between simple acceptance or rejection of the notion of a TCC' noting also that 'analyses in this field should resist abstract, polarized characterizations'. Just as Held and McGrew (2000) note that the globalization of economic activities calls forth counter-movements, so too Carroll argues that 'the TCC is not the product of a globalizing teleology but rather more a tendency dialectically linked to counter-tendencies' (Caroll, 2010: 235). Significantly, intermediaries play a key part in any such dialectic as Carroll suggests: 'The service of lawyers, consultants, academics, retired politicians and the like is integral to corporate business today. In the structure of economic power such advisors are subordinate...yet in the political and cultural fields they often lead the way in representing corporate interests or in mediating between these interests and others' (Carroll, 2010: 6).

The Weakness of Contemporary Inter-Urban Competition

While inter-urban competition registered in the likes of place marketing and branding has garnered much intellectual and practice-based attention recently, it was immediately apparent in an early review that 'what is lacking is any consensual understanding of how entrepreneurialism differs from previous forms of urban governance and local growth alliance or how it relates to broader dynamics of advanced capitalism' (Hubbard and Hall, 1998: 3).

The rise of a TCC may constitute one new dynamic in this regard. Leitner and Sheppard (1998) have emphasized the uncertainties that have accompanied the breakdown of the Fordist regime of accumulation in processes on inter-urban competition. Peck (2002) sees the replacement of Keynesian-welfare state with Schumpeterian Workfare or neoliberal state models in the west driving a measure of 'fast' policy mobility. Both appear likely to have made a contribution and to be mutually reinforcing. However, as I go on to argue, perhaps the signature of the contemporary betweenness of urban policy mobility is the manner in which inter-urban competition is mediated by the state.

Between Strong and Weak Competition

Notions of intercity and international competition often centre on what Cox and Mair (1991) term 'weak' forms of competition. On the one hand, 'paradoxically, much of local politics is not about localised social structures per se. Rather, insertion of localised social structures in wider spatial and scale divisions of labour means that local politics very often centres upon the way the locality is to be defined relative to the wider world and upon the ways in which subsequent action taken locally can suspend any contradictions between local actors and that wider world' (Cox and Mair, 1991: 202). These 'weak' forms of competition are not new. They have a lineage in a long-term decline in traditional forms of social relations which has 'left a potentially alienating void in self-understanding and in related concepts of community'—a gap left in which local business coalitions can offer 'pseudo-community', intervening with the aim of providing legitimations for their own version of community (Cox and Mair, 1988: 317).[3]

On the other hand, 'strong' forms of inter-urban competition, in which localities and their institutions might be said to display agency, involve the inverse process whereby 'powers are developed locally in order to improve the position of local actors in wider scale and spatial divisions of labour' (Cox and Mair, 1991: 205). Schumpeterian notions of creative destruction inhere within strong forms of competition and they have a paradoxical relation to the sorts of pseudo-place agendas mobilised by business and political interests as part of weak competition. Generally, weak forms of competition between cities elicit only muted local conflict within those cities. Yet, 'while local dependence is revealed to be one root of the antagonisms, at the same time it provides a basis for the suspension of conflict in favor of a solidarity within each locality: a solidarity that can then be turned against the locally dependent in other localities' (Cox and Mair, 1988: 307).

The contradictions inherent to the capitalist economic system ensure that it is an economy that is caught between the antinomies of the locational fixity required in order for labour to be reproduced, the forces of production to be fully unleashed and for fixed investments to be amortized, on the one hand, and the movement necessary in search of new sources of profit on the other. The fixity of capital and labour in place produces tendencies towards geographical concentration of economic activity and is representative of their use values above all else in the form of the dedicated land, property, skills etc. that compose significant agglomerations of economic activity. To the extent that

---

[3] Coincidentally the interests of business coalitions have tended to operate at the scale at which labour is reproduced and that scale has continued to increase to the point that Lefevre (1998: 22) notes how cities in Europe are now dependent on their (commuting) hinterlands to bolster them in inter-urban competition.

the logic of economic agglomeration stands for much of the 'authenticity' of place, then it is clear that strong forms of inter-city competition seek to fashion a measure of agglomeration. For Molotch, such authenticity is part and parcel of the way 'places produce stuff, but not just in the obvious sense that everything has to be made and distributed somewhere, the nature of a place affects what stuff can actually become because locale contains the ingredients...that go into making up goods' (Molotch, 2004: 161). In addition to the concept of external economies introduced in Chapters 2 and 3 (see Table 2.2), agglomeration is open to several other interpretations. Clark (1993) emphasizes the role of sunk costs and price competition in promoting periodic crises.[4] For Gough (1992) the spatial fixity of agglomeration is revealing of the structure that inheres in places.[5] Arriving from a different disciplinary starting point, Kolb (2008) makes a similar distinction between the structures of places and their relationship to systems.[6] For Harvey (1985), places can have 'structured coherence', representing propitious capital-labour combinations. For Cox and Mair (1988, 1991) scale dependency is what determines both the attachment of industry to place in economic terms but also the private sector's involvement in policy-making. It is the distinctive articulations between private sectors and institutions that imply local modes of social regulation (Peck and Tickell, 1992).

It is the exchange value of labour and capital that promotes tendencies towards the dissolution of economic agglomerations (and the very fabric and culture of places) with the dispersal of economic activity and geographical equalization of rates of profit. For orthodox economics, it is the positive urban externalities of agglomeration that have turned negative which drive their dissolution. Congestion, high labour and land prices prompt the relocation of industry to the suburbs and beyond. It is a familiar refrain in many policy circles but the evidence from enduringly successful urban agglomerations suggests instead that 'overheating' is a symptom of success. For political economy perspectives it is the capital concentration of economic activities and vertical integration into larger productive units that undermines the value of external economies (Harvey, 1985; Walker, 1981) and ensures that the forces that promote agglomeration are ephemeral.

---

[4] Type 1 markets are highly contestable. The prevalence of sunk costs make type 2 markets less contestable. For firms in the first type of market, places and their sites of production are expendable while exogenous economic events can produce local economic crises. In type 2 markets, exogenous events need not produce local crises in such immediate ways.

[5] Gough (1992) argues that competition in space cannot be understood in market (systems) terms but as dialectic between structure and system. Abstract structures are developed into spatially specific forms.

[6] 'Commodity places are structured for efficiencies that care little about human welfare or local peculiarities except to market them as images. This simplifies them for quick recognition and persuasion' (Kolb, 2008: 84).

The question that emerges is 'is the city a work or a product?' (Lefebvre, 1991: 73). The economic realities described in processes and patterns of urban policy mobility are ones that suggest that it is both. There are no places that are fully commodified and yet all places are commodified to an extent (Kolb, 2008: 83). There is 'a dialectical relationship in which works are inherent in products, while products do not press all creativity into the service of repetition' (Lefebvre, 1991: 79). Or, at least not yet? As Lefebvre also concedes, spaces can dissimulate—they can lie. And it is just possible that this is what a considerable element of contemporary place branding is about as I discuss further on pp. 250–4.

Most urban places, then, have only been partially commodified as a result of urban policy mobility and inter-urban competition. Instead, the fixity of capital is part and parcel of the uniqueness of urban places and is the basis of 'strong' competition between places, where strong competition is based on the fact that place provides opportunities for super-profits and is far from perfectly substitutable (Cox, 1995). That is, 'in addition to adjustment within a given set of conditions—technologies, labour, skills, products etc.—firms step outside circulation and seek a competitive advance by revolutionizing production' (Cox, 1995: 218).

The dialectic between these two antinomies in the logic of capitalism—of fixity and motion and associated strong and weak forms of competition between places—has also generated a variety of terms to capture the spatio-temporal dynamics produced. Harvey has referred to both 'spatial switching' and 'leapfrogging' as characteristic of the geography of capitalism. Smith observed a 'see-saw' effect as flows of investment moved back and forth between locations. One curiosity is that it is this relational sense of place in its most insecure aspect which invites the futile and destructive comparison and evaluation of weak forms of competition rather than a search for the novelty and distinction of strong forms of competition. A further curiosity is that much recent academic commentary could be said to have emphasized the prevalence of weak forms of competition, rather than reading for difference (Gibson-Graham, 2008) and strong competition alternatives. For its part, urban politics and policy discourse has been contradictory in its rhetorical emphasis on the distinctiveness of places while at the same time accepting the seeming inevitability of weak competition with all that this implies regarding the substitutability of places.[7]

---

[7] The same contradictions appear in present policy obsession with 'regional competitiveness'. On the one hand, 'Competitiveness is portrayed as the means by which regional economies are externally validated in an era of globalisation' (Bristow, 2005: 285) yet this same 'competitiveness discourse eschews consideration of the relations between regions focusing only on the imperative of building capacity within regions' (Bristow, 2005: 294). 'There is thus an inherent paradox here in that whilst the discourse emphasises the importance of factors endogenous to the region in

The business community and political coalitions produce pseudo-places in the manner intimated by Cox (1995) and these might be seen as a middling sense of place that can be produced from the inherent tensions in place marketing described further in Chapter 10. In this connection, 'the real world falls somewhere between...two hypothetical extremes, of immobile communities and immobile capital and labour. Capital, labour and communities are all mobile to some extent. Yet it tends to be presumed that if the invisible hand metaphor holds for the extreme cases it must also be true for more realistic intermediate situations' (Sheppard, 2003: 179). The economic geographic landscape is, of course, not a simple one of successful and abandoned places but one in which places are revealing of an elaborate division of labour in which elements of uniqueness and substitutability are apparent.[8]

For Lefebvre (1991: 62, emphasis added) 'when the forces of production make a leap forward, but the capitalist relations of production remain intact, the production of space itself replaces—or, rather, is *superimposed* upon—the production of things in space'. If the urban agglomerations associated with strong competition have been undermined, another of the geographical formations described in Chapter 3—the enclave—has emerged strongly in the second global economy as a superimposition of space as part of weak forms of competition. These enclaves are zones carved out of nations and urban territories and offer the prospect of unique advantages but which rarely develop into self-sustaining urban economic agglomerations. The enclaves that existed historically have been joined by the likes of Enterprise Zones (EZs), Business Improvement Districts (BIDs) but also the Export Processing Zones (EPZs), Free Ports and offshore financial centres, which I discuss in Chapters 8 and 9.

The State as Intermediary in Competition

It can be tempting to see hegemonic processes of neoliberalization promoting a 'significantly more limited role for the state' (Leitner et al., 2007a: 3). Yet, arguably the state plays a more pervasive role in policy mobility within regulatory capitalism. The economy centred on urban policy is mediated by central and local states since a large part of that economy is funded through the public purse. Governments absorb much of the risk associated with urban mega projects. Here, then, 'There is a paradox...At the same time as many

shaping firm performance, the key ingredients for success are uniformly prescribed making for a "one-size fits all" approach to regional economic development policy' (Bristow, 2005: 293).

[8] Describing the functionally polycentric character of the urban system in Europe, for example, Pain and Hall (2008: 1074) describe how 'For firms, it is relationships within First Cities and between them and with the other major business cities they relate to that predominate—a spatial scale of inter-city relations and functional complementarity that allows information and knowledge to be produced, exchanged, and circulated through different modes.'

more and much larger infrastructure projects are being proposed and built around the world, it is becoming clear that many such projects have strikingly poor performance records in terms of economy, environment and public support' (Flyvbjerg, Burzelius, and Rothengatter, 2003: 3). On the one hand, in those instances where the state is a major sponsor and underwriter of mega-projects and where politicians and bureaucrats are seduced by the idea of particular projects, the huge scale of the economy associated with policy mobility becomes apparent. The Valencian regional government's pursuit of several mega-projects including Santiago Calatrava's monumental City of Arts and Sciences (Vento, 2016) is a salutary reminder that every model city—a Bilbao or a Barcelona—is likely to have its anti-model counterpart. On the other hand, while 'weak competition' between places can prove a particularly destructive 'race to the bottom' it is also the case that some of the worst excesses of this competition are, at least to some extent, mitigated by states.

Policy itself emerges as a mediating force in a capitalist economic system. Competition between places may appear to imply an extension of the logic of perfect competition between capitalists. However, the state mediates any such perfect competition in numerous ways (Sheppard, 2003). For example, cities are embedded in national and subnational institutions and regulatory systems. Higher levels of the state are spatially selective such that each city has its own unique trajectory (Sheppard, 2003). The unique trajectories of urban economies rest in part on the acknowledgement that there is no necessary connection between the intensity of inter-urban competition bearing down on cities and the policy response; such a response is contingent on a number of factors. For Gordon (1999: 1013) 'even a much strengthened demand side for competitive action does not generate a "supply side" capacity to achieve this'. Moreover, how important specifically urban attributes are to the competitive position of firms—and hence how salient corresponding collective actions or policy interventions are—is unclear given the changing geographic scale at which external economies are open to businesses (Gordon, 1999).

The emergence of elements of global regulation is as good an indication as any of an economy centred on inter-urban competition but also is an indication of the way in which such inter-city competition is 'a site where cultural and economic speculation intersect' (Goodwin, 1993: 145). Inter-urban competition and the urban policy mobility associated with it serve to reduce the uniqueness of places to a single economic common denominator. That is, 'the act of selling places clearly conflates history and memory in the cause of meeting economic needs' (Kearns and Philo, 1993: 26). In this way, the cultures of particular places are 'not so much presented as foci of attachment and concern but as bundles of social and economic opportunity *competing* against one another in the open . . . *market* for a share of the capital investment cake' (Kearns and Philo, 1993: 18). The re-presentation of places or 'the promotion of new urban images, of new lifestyles and of new "city myths", is often a necessary prelude to the establishment of new urban economies' (Goodwin, 1993: 149). In all of this, the irony is that 'for places the idea is not so much that they try to be genuinely different from one another but that they harness their surface differences in order to make themselves in a very real sense nothing but "the same"' (Philo and Kearns, 1993: 20).

The Weakness of Contemporary Policy Mobility

On first inspection the judgement that 'geography has generally failed to incorporate a systematic analysis of markets within the study of places' (Ashworth and Voogd, 1990: 22) might seem a harsh one. Clearly, much of the early staples of economic geography were concerned with essentially market processes as these were seen to produce industrial locations or central places. Harvey (1989) laid out some of the same trends that motivated Ashworth and Voogd to speak of the increasing application of techniques from marketing to the making of place within what he termed a transition from urban managerialism to urban entrepreneurialism.[9]

The full scale and variety of an economy based on what Harvey (1989) termed the 'speculative construction of place' has perhaps only loomed into full view in the past two to three decades. From the present vantage point it seems banal to acknowledge that today 'the world is one market. The rapid advance of globalization means that every country, every city and every region must compete with every other for its share of the world's consumers, tourists, investors, students, entrepreneurs, international sporting and cultural events, and for the attention and respect of the international media, of other governments, and the people of other countries' (Anholt, 2007: 1).

Places are argued to be different from products both because they are composites and because of the way place is used by the consumer (Ashworth and Voogd, 1990: 18). This is true to the extent that place is synonymous with agglomeration but not if it manifests in the form of an enclave—at which point it becomes necessary to remember that the consumption of place is often associated with place in a packaged and tightly defined form. Inter-urban competition and policy mobility are bound up with the phenomenon and practice of place or city branding but also the creation of tourism enclaves, both of which form a part of the cognitive-cultural economy and its mobilizing of an economy of signs and symbols that I discuss in Chapter 10.

A potential blessing of the consumption of urban places is that they may be less subject to major secular trends of growth and decline associated with

---

[9] Specifically, he identified four strategies: tourism, defence, inward investment, corporate control and command functions.

many 'old' industries. At the same time, places are less likely to possess the structural coherence of genuine agglomerations but rather to have a fleeting moment in the limelight or to be permanently prone to substitution as implied with the notion of the tourism enclave (Britton, 1982). From the point of view of their being ever more centred on consumption, towns and cities may quickly become obsolete. That is, 'places can be literally consumed; what people take to be significant about a place...is over time depleted, devoured or exhausted by use' (Urry, 1995: 1–2). Places can 'seem worn out and exhausted, and consumers and related investment moves elsewhere' prompting the 'periodic reconstruction or theming of place' (Urry, 2014: 122).

The progressive character of an earlier Atlantic era of policy mobility has been overlain today by policy mobility of an altogether more regressive character centred on experiments such as EZs, BIDs, and workfare policies. The idea of EZs is one that has travelled from the UK to the US following Peter Hall's typically provocative last ditch, only partly serious, thought-experiment, solution for the ills of the UK economy in the late 1970s (Allmendinger, 2012). Shorn of some of its original ingredients, it was adopted as a significant 'area-based' urban policy experiment in the UK during the 1980s by Conservative governments in two phases through the 1980s and 1990s and resurrected in a further modified guise in by the Conservative–Liberal coalition and Conservative governments elected in 2010 and 2015. The area-based nature of the policy ensures that it has the features of an enclave in which exceptions to normal planning and other regulations are made and where special incentives to business operation are offered. By the same token, they are subject to the limitations of area-based policies such as the localized displacement of existing rather than the addition of new economic activities. While the scale and economic impact of these EZs has been modest to say the least, it was a policy idea that also found a ready audience in the US.

BIDs apparently have disseminated as a policy in the opposite direction across the Atlantic having originated in Canada in the 1960s (Tait and Jensen, 2007 with more than another 300 such zones established in Canada alone by the mid-2000s (Ward, 2006). Kahn (2002: 242, quoted in Tait and Jensen, 2007: 120), outlines how 'technically, a BID is a legislative and financial mechanism that operates as a selftaxing enclave; it can only be formed by a majority of local property owners', though the exact legal and financial arrangements adopted vary from city to city and nation to nation. Typically BIDs spend their tax revenues on security, cleaning, and marketing efforts. Framing their empirical study using actor network theory, Tait and Jensen (2007) note the significant mythology that can surround particular policies and their supposed origins. While mythologies can form an important ingredient in the seduction associated with policy mobility, as I discuss on pp. 168–71, they also tend to obscure the pragmatic appeal and the effects of some policies as apparent solutions to problems facing actors in particular places at particular times. They also obscure the fact that such policy solutions are often not new at all (Rodgers, 1998: 414). Here, then, it is not just the policies that circulate but the understandings of underlying urban problems in diverse economies either side of the Atlantic (Peyroux, Pütz, and Glasze, 2012). Similar developments which occurred later in the US, and specifically those in New York, proved a 'policy "hot spot" in the geographical imagination of UK policy makers' (Ward, 2006: 60) where these too appear to have become an apparently permanent feature of the urban management scene (Magalhaes, 2012).

Peck has concentrated on the mobility of neoliberal policies of 'workfare'. He describes how in this particular 'fast' policy regime 'new "agents of persuasion" seek explicitly to disembed and circulate suggestive and loaded policy signifiers and reform texts' (Peck, 2002: 349). Significantly,

> policy advocates, consultants, and emulators foster and circulate essentialized readings of effective local programs in which a small number of supposedly decisive (and *potentially replicable*) design features are privileged and promoted. In the process, the complex and locally embedded interventions are rendered as simplified, disembedded, and reproducible administrative routines... This disembedding process establishes the basis for a national and international market for transferable policy lessons and strategies (Peck, 2002: 349, original emphasis).

This is a picture in which cities—as urban economic agglomerations—have continued to serve as 'relay stations, and experimental sites in the roll-out of neoliberal modes of governance... and have been epicentres of contestation and transformative struggle' (Leitner, Peck, and Sheppard, 2007b: 315). In this instance, policy mobility and the intermediaries associated with it appear to have reinforced notable world cities as important concentrations of economic activity since 'the new transnational flows of policy signs and programming technologies are nowhere more intense than between hegemonic "centers of persuasion" like Washington D.C.; technocratic "epicentres of reform", like Wisconsin; and sub hegemonic "centers of translation", like London' (Peck, 2002: 349).

The Ordinariness of Strong Forms of Competition

Many of the 'strong' competition alternatives to the weak competition outlined above could be said to rest on promoting place-based agglomeration or on seeking to take places and their products out of wide circulation. Here, territorial and non-territorial conceptions of contemporary economic life are hardly separable since the reconstitution of place—agglomeration—often rests on the mobilization of alternative imaginaries within policy networks. Somewhat paradoxically some of the world's leading agglomerations—world cities—have generated a policy discourse that is closely associated with the promulgation of weak forms competition. In opposition, an 'ordinary cities' literature has argued that 'instead of seeing only some cities as the originators of urbanism, in a world of ordinary cities, ways of being urban and ways of making new kinds of urban futures are diverse and are the product of the inventiveness of people in cities everywhere' (Robinson, 2006: 1).

Non-capitalist Competition

Much of the extant literature on the learning represented by urban policy mobility has tended to be imbued with an overt sense of economic competition (MacFarlane, 2011). However, 'when it comes to "the economy", reframing has been an important strategy used by working people since the Industrial revolution' (Gibson-Graham, Cameron, and Healy, 2013: 9) indicating a history of urban and economic policy alternatives as long as capitalism and urban policy mobility in the modern era itself. There is also, then, literature that speaks to learning associated with informality, inclusion, and social and environmental justice even if the economic content of such policy mobility has not been the main subject of writing on such alternative imaginaries. Such alternative 'imaginaries promote collective over individual interest; collaboration rather than competition; recognition and respect for diversity rather than commodification of individual identity; and care for the environment over productivity/growth/exploitation' (Leitner, Peck, and Sheppard, 2007a: 12).

While acknowledging that some alternative economic forms may in some instances continue to be subordinate to fully capitalist economic relations, Gibson–Graham (2008) reconstitute the capitalist economy into alternatives composed of: transactions that can be 'alternative market' and 'non market'; alternative paid and unpaid labour; and non-capitalist forms of enterprise. They have gone on to add non-capitalist property and finance relations (Gibson-Graham, Cameron, and Healy, 2013). Taken together, these different manifestations of alternatives to mainstream capitalist relations indicate that '"marginal" economic practices and forms of enterprise are actually more prevalent, and account for more hours worked and/or more value produced, than the capitalist sector. Most of them are globally extensive, and potentially have more impact on social well-being than capitalism does' (Gibson Graham, 2008: 617). For example, practices of care across the world account for up to half of economic activity (Gibson-Graham, 2008: 617) while some estimates suggest that cooperative forms of enterprise employ more people worldwide than the multinational enterprises (MNEs) that are the subject of Chapter 8.

Much of the discussion centres ostensibly on the extrication of places from the worst excesses of weak forms of inter-locality competition since 'relocation redraws the boundaries of an economic community' (Gibson-Graham, Cameron, and Healy, 2013: 63). Alternative economic imaginaries focus on reconstituting some element of agglomeration or the place-bound nature of production and consumption. Gibson-Graham, Cameron, and Healy (2013) note the importance of alternative currencies in many national contexts which represent one way of underpinning the coherence of local economies not least by stimulating the induced linkages of local consumption. Experiments with local currencies have been quite widespread in the nations of the global north. There are over 600 local currencies in Japan (Gibson-Graham, Cameron, and Healy, 2013).

If alternative urban economic imaginaries are often centred on agglomeration as an economic geographical formation, the network metaphor is hardly absent since it is present in the empowerment and mobilization of diverse social movements as a result of the Internet and other mobile communications technologies. Indeed several geographically extensive transnational policy networks—such as the International Observatory on Participatory Democracy (IOPD) and United Cities and Local Governments (UCLG)—now exist to facilitate the movement of the likes of participatory budgeting (more on which below) and other municipal reforms and which could be said to embody horizontal rather than hierarchical linkages between cities and across continents.[10]

A different example of networks of progressive policy is provided by the ethical consumption movement which I also touch on later when describing global production networks (GPNs). These 'alternative trade networks enrol consumers and producers in a new international community in which an ethic of care for distant others is built into the pricing mechanism' (Gibson-Graham, Cameron, Healey, 2013: 103). As a result, 'revolt, too, can (and does) circulate like fictitious money capital: almost illusory, passing across frontiers and drifting through global space, often through cyberspace, exchanging itself, getting converted into other denominations of place-specific radicalism' (Merrifield, 2010: 16). Indeed some of the urban policy mobilities literature does identify how 'the travels of consultants, politicians, policy professionals and their policy models are in many ways paralleled, if not necessarily equalled, by the mobilities of NGOs and activists who find ways to disseminate alternative and innovative policy prescription' (McCann, 2011: 122). Here it is important to remember that 'place, mobility, networking across space,

---

[10] Figures quoted in Peck and Theodore (2015:198) suggest that the UCLG encompasses 1,000 local governments in 95 countries along with more than 100 Local Government Associations, while IOPD has 500 government and NGO members.

and scale each can play an important role in the mobilization, practices, and efficacy of contestations. Yet there is an unfortunate tendency... to prioritise one spatiality, thereby obscuring the significance of others' (Leitner, Peck, and Sheppard, 2007a: 19). Partly as a result, 'a paradox of resistance is its capacity to reify the very force that it contests' (Leitner, Peck, and Sheppard, 2007a: 5).

Innovation in Urban Policy: A Global Shift?

It is worth recalling that much of the history of urban policy mobility in a first global economy was borne of what might broadly be described as a progressive concern with improving the sanitary and housing conditions of the city of 'dreadful night' (Hall, 2002) before it shed some of these progressive credentials in favour of shaping the city as beautiful or efficient. Here standards developed across the Atlantic were and to some extent continue to be exported. Perhaps the most notable instance in this regard is the new town concept which in turn developed, in Britain, from Ebenezer Howard's garden city manifesto. Indeed, 'the concept of a new town is a planning idea which has truly travelled the world' (Ramsay, 1986). Yet, of course, 'the new town idea as we have come to understand it this century in fact arose out of the very specific economic and political conditions of European urbanization' (Healey, 1986: 132). It is the spatial arrangement, of garden cities (and by extension new towns)—their distinctly in between geography as the best of both urban and rural—that is most familiar to us. Yet the progressive credentials of Howard's original garden city idea and the British new towns are often overlooked. These include the importance of the ownership of land which provided the basis for leveraging on gains in land and property values (to fund infrastructure and amenities) and the balanced nature of the communities (in terms of work and residence and social classes). However there is little doubting that 'the variety of projects realized in the name of this concept, and the multiplicity of political and planning purposes to which they are designed to serve, is immense' (Ramsay, 1986: 87).[11]

In recent times the garden city/new town planning model has been eclipsed by others—such as compact, sustainable, or eco-cities and The New Urbanism—equally malleable in the hands of planners and politicians. Paradoxically, and echoing McCann's juxtaposing of dwelling and mobility, visual

---

[11] In particular, new town policies have appeared in a number of guises as: (1) a new community with different ways of organizing social and economic life; (2) part of regional spatial strategy; (3) as urban design at settlement/neighbourhood level, and; (4) a different approach to the financing and organizing of capital, land and building resources, and governance (Healey, 1986). The lineage of a number of contemporary planned eco-cities can be seen in the garden city/new town idea so that one could add to this a fifth guise of the new town as: (5) different technical arrangements for environmental sustainability.

techniques of inhabiting deployed by global planning consultancies are commonly used in order to mobilize sustainability principles (Rapaport, 2015). A generous interpretation of the prognosis for the settlements built or planned in the names of compact, sustainable, eco, and new urbanist principles might preserve something of the intentions associated with these planning concepts. However, these models have inherent contradictions that are exacerbated when rubbing up against the specifics of local contexts in which they are implemented. Notably, the sustainability credentials of individual developments become meaningless when separated from their wider hinterlands (Haughton, 1999) and urban systems (Neuman, 2005) given the potential for the displacement of environmental externalities. As such, geographical dimensions of equity become important but rarely are practised in the form of relational senses of place either at the inter-local or international scale (Haughton, 1999).

Latin America is notable for the analytical tradition of *dependencia* (Cardoso and Faletto, 1979) with its trenchant critique of the potential for extant social and economic relations to deliver inclusive national and urban economic development. The Latin American tradition is intriguing for several reasons but notably, for my concerns, this tradition draws attention to the enclave as an economic geographical formation with malign effects.

Latin America has been a fertile if fraught ground for analysis, politics, and policy-making critical of the iniquities of extant capitalist social relations. Among notable global models (with greater or lesser progressive credentials) to have emerged from this part of the world are Curitiba (bus rapid transit), Medallin, and Porto Alegre (participatory budgeting). The latter in particular, illustrates the importance of local context and historical conjunctures in the production of radical solutions. As Peck and Theodore (2015: 211) argue 'the direction of causality here is vital. Participatory budgeting was an organic product of this conjuncture' such that participatory budgeting 'was a profoundly endogenous creation, deeply embedded in a unique (and essentially nonreplicable) political context'. Yet, 'for a while, in the early 2000s, "learning from Porto Alegre" was the thing to do, particularly, it seemed, for left-leaning local and regional governments in Europe', with the city being deferred to as a place of 'policy origination' regarding participatory budgeting (Peck and Theodore, 2015: 182 and 170 respectively). Of course, 'the upside of left localism is that this can be an effective scale for mobilization and for the development of grassroots, organically embedded projects. There is a potential downside, however, especially if localist projects are disconnected from supportive structures at higher spatial scales and from redistributive financing channels, because in the context of isolated initiatives, local actors must often accept the role of rule takers rather than rule makers' (Peck and Theodore, 2015: 220). This indeed appears to be what has happened as the participatory budgeting processes pioneered in Porto Alegre have been mobilized far and wide often to the ends of weak forms of competition. For Peck and Theodore (2015: 221), then, 'there is a cruel irony in the way that some forms of PB have been folded into the very neoliberal hegemony that the original model was designed to contest. What began as a left success story seems consequently to have morphed into yet another dispiriting tale of conservative annexation.' Yet they also note 'the fact that PB experiments have been constrained in some places, and co-opted in others, and the fact that there is now a large hinterland of benign and managerialist "distortions" of the Porto Alegre model, should not be taken as a negation of the progressive potential of this enabling political technology' (Peck and Theodore, 2015: 156).

The provincial city of Solo (also known as Surakarta, see Figure 5.3) in Indonesia gained notoriety mainly within Indonesia as the proving ground for current President Joko Widodo (Bunnell, Miller, Phelps, and Taylor, 2013; Phelps, Bunnell, Miller, and Taylor, 2014). In Solo, Widodo helped to initiate and reinforce a series of reforms that centred on addressing issues of the relocation of informal settlers and street vendors in humane ways as well as experimenting with strategies of restricting the development of supermarket chain stores and shopping malls that otherwise might undermine vendors with precarious livelihoods. The progressive case of Solo has travelled within Indonesia but also internationally as depicted in crude terms in Figure 7.1. Solo became the subject of interest within Indonesia. Moreover, Jokowi himself took many of the policies developed in Solo with him through his rise to power as first governor of Jakarta (the capital city) and then President. The economic effects of these humane relocations of street vendors have been reported to have been mixed with early and better resourced relocations to purpose-built markets having been more successful than later moves and with some of the street vendors seeking to return to their former street side venues.

Curiously, the case of Solo provides a contemporary vantage point not only on the much longer standing travels of aspects of Javanese culture specifically but also the cultural or aesthetic logics to urban policy mobility more generally. 'The export of Javanese civilisation took place . . . partly through force of arms and partly through the sheer éclat and glamour it possessed for those outside it. Java's glamour and power was felt in Bali and Kalimantan, in the Lampungs, in Jambi and Palembang, in the states of the Malay peninsula, in mainland south-east Asia' (Kumar, 1997: 27). It is to the subject of the distinctly ambiguous power of seduction within urban policy mobility that I now turn.

The Power of Seduction

The preceding discussion highlighted 'regular' business or market transactions in processes of policy mobility and inter-urban competition. Historically, it is

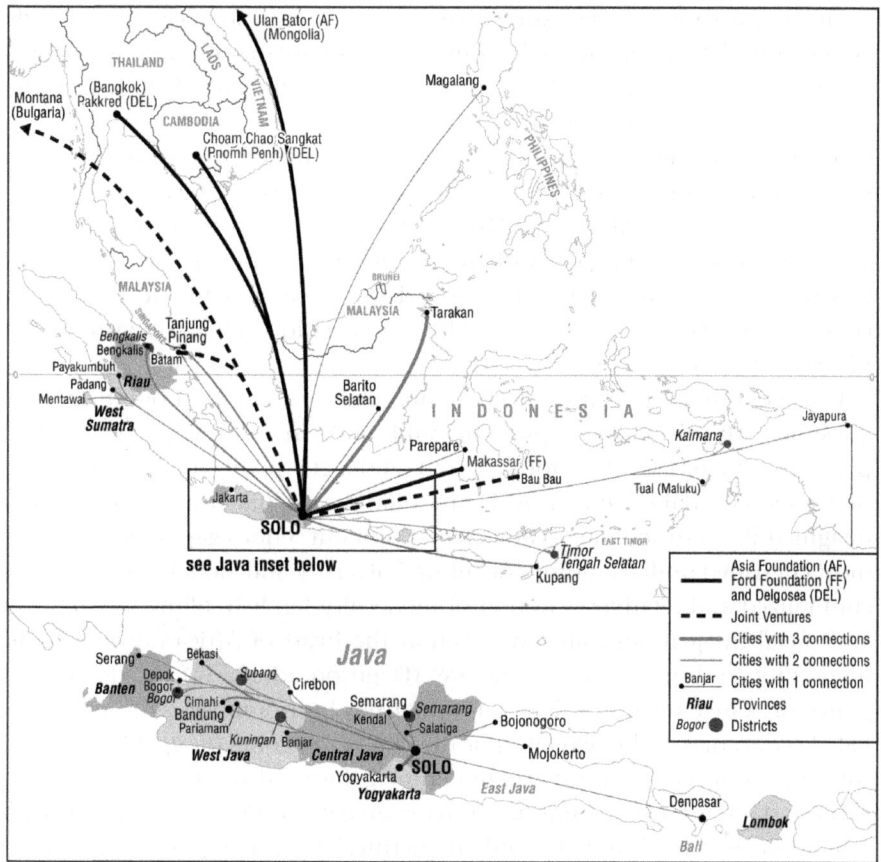

Figure 7.1 A snapshot of Solo's travels
Source: reproduced from Phelps et al. (2014).

hard to distinguish the influence of commerce from the military and economic coercion that were part of the imperial relations of a first global economy. However, for further insights into the *demand* for the mobilization of
urban policies we can turn to anthropology and sociology.

The power of seduction has been identified by Allen and underlined by
others. Miller in his discussion of the consumption of stuff notes how we have
moved 'from thinking of technologies of communication as merely things, or
capacities, and started to see them more as analogous with the arts of seduction' (Miller, 2010: 114). The power of seduction in the present era of urban
policy mobility is significant although it is hardly new. Processes of seduction
can be liberating and can contain the seeds of a radicalism whose 'critical
power doesn't come from coercion but from an ability to disrupt and reinvent,
to create desire and inspire hope' (Merrifield, 2010: 18).

There is a case for suggesting that we have underappreciated the early emergence of desire including its contribution to urban economic agglomerative processes. As Murphy (2010: 97) describes 'the British ruled their empire through hierarchy, through law and through aesthetic abstraction. As a general rule, hierarchies were loathed, laws were of mixed value, and aesthetic power was the most effective and least dispute causing means of exerting power at a distance' (Murphy, 2010: 97). Cities were one of the most important venues for exerting such aesthetic power. Moreover, such aesthetic power was not merely cultivated and projected from the west in the nineteenth century but involved elements of 'self-westernization' apparent within colonial cities (Osterhammel, 2014: 291).

The mobility of policies reflects desires that are 'tightly bound up with questions of inequality, aspiration, and rank in an imagined "world"' (Ferguson, 2006: 19). Thus, for Ferguson (2006: 20) 'taking a hard, and sometimes uncomfortable, look at African aspirations to "likeness" with real and imagined Western standards can help to point out serious gaps in some of our most cherished understandings of cultural diversity and global order', since 'a culturalized and relativized notion of modernity tends to allow the material and social inequalities that have been at the heart of African aspiration to modernity to drop out of the picture' (Ferguson, 2006: 34). Academic and policy discourse on the African continent has been imbued with a sense of failed economies and failed cities or the city yet to come (Roy, 2009). Yet, in this latter respect, Ferguson has underlined the need to take aspirations to western standards of consumption and material possessions seriously. 'African aspirations to "development" and "modernity" have always been shadowed by such questions surrounding the authenticity of the copy. The twin fears that the copy is either too different from the original or not different enough' (Ferguson 2006: 16).

The picture Ferguson paints is of an economy that it lies between subject and object as part of a dialectical process by which capitalism produces a stream of new 'stuff' whose meanings for us as consumers are ambiguous (Miller, 2010). Or, as Ashworth and Voogd (1990: 3) have it: 'For whatever reason urban societies have become more variegated, individualistic, internationally aware, and oriented to lifestyles based upon a fashion-conscious and rapidly shifting consumerism.' It is the stuff of place that fuels desire since 'it is possible for localities to consume one's identity so that such places become almost literally *all-consuming* places' (Urry, 1995: 2).

The thought that 'places are in a sense consumed, particularly visually' (Urry, 1995: 1) is important from the perspective of desires that have seen a place like Singapore emerge strongly as a model within and beyond Southeast Asia. Certainly the Singapore skyline has a visual allure for many across Southeast Asia. Yet the power of many cities to seduce is one that has tended to be underplayed in the present literature on policy mobility. The Malaysian government has traditionally looked to Singapore as something of a benchmark for its own experiments with modernization in the form of industrial and spatial planning projects, including the multimedia supercorridor (Bunnell, 2004) and technology parks (Phelps and Dawood, 2014). However, Kuala Lumpur and the nearby multimedia super corridor have themselves subsequently become models for authorities in India—a process that Bunnell and Das (2010) have referred to as serial seduction. Such patterns and processes of urban policy mobility centred on India appear to be a case of the search for cities that seemingly are 'free not just of infrastructure struggles but of the messiness of democratic politics' (Bhan, 2014: 3).

If the landscapes of modernity are manifestly urban, international, and shot through with power (Appadurai, 1996), then for Anholt (2007: 127) 'competitive identity is about making people want to pay attention to a country's achievements, and believe in its qualities. It is the quintessential exemplar of soft power' (Anholt, 2007: 127).[12] Arguably, the reach of such soft power exerted by places has increased since, as Urry notes, there has been a 'democratization' of the tourist gaze enabled by technologies and implied in the thought that 'everyone in the West is now entitled to engage in visual consumption, to appropriate landscapes and townscapes more or less anywhere in the world' (Urry, 1995: 176). We can speculate that there has been a *democratization of the policy gaze* of local and national government bureaucrats and politicians. This is a greedy gaze that has enveloped those in the global south as much as those in the global north and it is one that in many instances has rested on the emulation of neoliberal policy experiments or exceptions in a desire to 'look like a state' (Pritchett, Woolcock, and Andrews, 2013).

The Latent Strong Competition of Ordinary Cities?

Before we get carried away with the progressive credentials of the policy fomentation and mobility among cities of the global south, it is as well to remember that urban informality while representing a resource of great diversity is also one that is perceived in altogether narrower economic terms by national and transnational economic elites. That is, 'the differential value attached to what is "formal" and what is "informal" creates the patchwork of … space that is in turn the frontier of … accumulation' (Roy, 2009: 826). It is a frontier open to 'accumulation by dispossession' (Harvey, 2003, 2005)

---

[12] Nye (1990: 168) defines soft power as 'the ability of a country to structure a situation so that other countries develop preferences or define their interests in ways [that are] consistent with its own. This power tends to arise from such resources as cultural and ideological attraction as well as rules and institutions of international regimes.'

seen in the redevelopment of urban villages and resistance (in the form of 'nail houses') in China or the clearance of farmers at the fringes of Indian cities to make way for high-tech campuses (Das, 2015).

Moreover, this world of urban policy fomentation opening up to view also contains distinctive regional differences (Roy, 2009). While some of these regional traditions clearly contain important alternative, non-market, strong forms of competition, the progressive credentials of other traditions is less clear. Perhaps only East Asia really stands out as a region in which urban policy mobility has a primarily economic content as a product of the mobilization of transnational labour flows centred on enclaves, though such weak competition can be found elsewhere too. 'In the past two decades, Chinese and Indian urbanization have posed a significant challenge to urban theory by forcing us to think through what it means for large scale urbanization to take place through the production of enclaves, special economic zones and spaces of exception' (Bhan, 2014: 1). The economy in between of urban policy mobility registers itself in new enclaves that beg the question: 'What does it mean for the city to be born as an enclave, for it to eschew any notion of historical settlement and evolution?' (Bhan, 2014: 2). Here, then, the sorts of policies being mobilized may be altogether less subtle and more complete—offering the promise of being transportable as in the case of Dubai Logistics City: 'Accumulation through dispossession of land and substantive citizenship rights, managed through the production of securitized logistics space, is the ominous model that US port cities are borrowing from Dubai' (Cowen, 2014: 123). Indeed, Dubai Logistics City (DLC) has become the model incrementally replicated internationally. 'While DLC may be exceptional in its particular coupling of frenzied economic activity and anaemic political rights, it is precisely this exceptional form that is serving as the model for the protection of infrastructure and trade flows and reshaping of ports across the global north' (Cowen, 2014: 167). It represents a peculiarly denuded model in economic terms too given that 'portal cities have been the most palpable points of interaction *between* civilizations' and 'provide entrepotic services and ecumenical intelligence to drive inter-civilizational trade and traffic' (Murphy, 2010: 24 and 25 respectively).

Some further qualifications can be added on the latent strength of competition among ordinary cities. First, Gordon (1999) notes the irony of intercity competition being vigorous in Europe where states have a strong tradition of welfare and have been supported at the supranational scale in objectives of social cohesion compared to the US with its tradition of local boosterism. 'If networks simply elevate inter-urban competition from the urban to the network scale, with collaboration occurring primarily either between prosperous cities or between urban elites pursuing a common agenda, the interests of disadvantaged cities and social groups, are unlikely to be adequately addressed' (Leitner and Sheppard, 1998: 307). Indeed, supranational organizations such as the European Commission (EC) may unwittingly have sponsored weak forms of inter-urban competition in the name of social cohesion (Gordon, 1999). My own research on a network of self-styled European edge cities indicated that local government network members were often highly attuned to using such collaborative opportunities to bolster their competitive position (Phelps, McNeill, and Parsons, 2002).

Second, any countervailing force assumed for welfare states or NGOs in challenging weak forms of competition among cities cannot be assumed. 'Subalterns can only compensate for the dominant bloc's inherent advantage in the control of vast pools of dead labour by building associations of living activists, armed with a willingness to act. Given the power differential, globalization-from-below occurs in *response* to the social and ecological dislocations and crises that follow in neoliberalization's train' (Carroll, 2010: 222, emphasis added). Moreover, while many NGOs may be part of a countervailing force favouring strong forms of competition, they are, as a result of financial dependence on major donors, also as likely to contribute to the weak form of competition signalled in attempts of governments to 'look like a state'.

Third, much policy 'learning' amounts to little more than copying. This is the case not just in the weak forms of inter-urban competition found across much of the global north but also notably the appearance of what has been observed as a peculiarly Chinese idiom (Roy, 2009) further afield. Thus we have the apparent paradox of inter-urban competition potentially drawing sustenance from and heightening the particularity of place while at the same time contributing to greater uniformity in the search for best practice 'off the shelf' solutions. The economic content of urban inter-referencing is open to question since it is clear that much of it may not revolve around reproducing the sorts of Chamberlinian competition said to characterize the contemporary cognitive-cultural economy (Scott, 2008).

Conclusion

'Cities remain crucibles for new ideas, are where most people live and/or work, and are characterized as the scale at which state policies and practices are particularly sensitive to democratic pressure and local agendas. For all these reasons, successful implementation of neoliberal urban policy agendas has been key to neoliberalization' (Leitner, Peck, and Sheppard, 2007a: 2). Something of both the lineage of (neo)liberal competition and associated policy mobility among cities was traced to the first global economy. In this respect there are fundamental continuities in the role played by policy intermediaries in both eras. Yet, in the second global economy of the present, 'an image . . . begins to form of the city as a "node" of global networks, where local identity and the urban territory, as a stratified deposit of natural and cultural assets, no longer have a value for what they are but for what they become in the process of valorization' (Dematteis, 2000: 63).

On one level, there is little to disagree with in this repositioning of the plight of governments, businesses, and citizens. Moreover, the network metaphor contains within it the seeds of a global sense of place (Massey, 1994) vital to forestalling the worst excesses of weak competition among places. However, without reference to the enduring importance of urban agglomeration and enclaves as counterpart economic geographical formations, the network metaphor can provide an overly restricted perspective on the interplace economy. We have seen how 'weak' forms of inter-city competition mostly aim, only superficially, to fashion a sense of place as economically productive agglomeration. Arguably, strong competition and cooperation alternatives also seek a deepening of place as agglomeration—as much for reasons of social as economic solidarity. Yet, the exceptionalism represented by enclaves has also been a very important part of the weak forms of competition in which national and subnational governments have participated. In each of these cases the territoriality of economic life has been the object of networks of actors.

In all of this, 'The heroic modernity of cities is a fleeting moment that sometimes lasts just a few decades: an equipoise of order and chaos, a conjunction of immigration and functioning technical structures, an opening of unstructured public spaces, a flow of energy in experimental niches' (Osterhammel, 2014: 248). The fleeting balance achieved by some cities as international models is perhaps above all else a manifestation of the fragility of the interplace economy associated with urban policy mobility.

Part IV
The International Economy

8

The Multinational Enterprise

Introduction

Barnet and Muller (1974: 14) once claimed that 'the global corporation is the first institution in human history dedicated to centralized planning on a world scale' and that as a result 'industry has transcended geography' (Barnet and Muller, 1974: 26). With hindsight their claims appear overstated. It may be more accurate to argue instead that 'Global corporations present increasingly significant economic forces in the world. But the geography of multinational corporations is more difficult to locate than the geography of nations' (Klingmann, 2007: 256). In a fundamental sense multinational enterprises (MNEs) and their overseas subsidiaries as transnational formations in and of themselves do transcend the geography of places to orchestrate an economy in between; while statistics are very difficult to come by, one stylized fact pertaining to OECD country trade is that as much as one-third is *within* MNEs (Lanz and Miroudot, 2011: 5).

Yet the fact that 'it is difficult simultaneously to conceptualize economic activities...on the one hand, and territorially defined economies, on the other' (Dicken and Malmberg, 2001: 345) nevertheless means that we are forced to consider this interplace economy as one where the impulse of the MNE is also to leverage on the advantages and distinctiveness of places. Indeed, national and subnational borders present significant discontinuities in the location decision (Beugelsdijk and Mudambi, 2013). MNEs deploy in enclaves and organize through networks and hierarchies in a global economy that remains far from borderless (Yeung, 1998) even as their strategies seek to effect seamless transnational integration.

The earliest MNEs—the colonial trading companies of the British and Dutch East India Companies and their descendant trading MNEs could be regarded as corporate networks (Jones, 2005), yet their actual operations overseas often manifested as enclaves, not least as a consequence of territories being wrested from local populations. The modern MNE that replaced these trading companies from the late 1800s to the 1980s actually became organized significantly more so around the territoriality of nation states. That is, the presence of MNEs in agglomerations of economic activity went hand in hand with the development of national economies (Agnew, 2005; Kobrin, 2001). Finally, in the present day, MNEs have been seen, once again, to have adopted network organizational structures. Most notable in this respect are an ascendant group of MNEs operating at the point of final consumption— retailers and branders without factories (Gereffi, 1999).

The history of the MNE, then, is one that provides a warning against overly strident views regarding the theoretical primacy of either territorial or non-territorial perspectives on the organization of economic activities. Chapter 4 noted the potential dissolution of hierarchical corporate contact systems and the implications for the inter-urban economy. This process is best viewed as a reconstitution of such contact systems in which elements of hierarchical organization persist. It can be seen at the international scale too. As Kellerman 2012: 61) argues 'it does not seem real to assume that hierarchical business organization is about to disappear in the networking era. Though hierarchical business organization might have been weakened through internal networking, the very integration of "old" hierarchical and "new" network cultures and technologies of management has permitted the contemporary management of companies and transactions typified by unprecedented scales of size and volume respectively.'

In this chapter I examine the economic geography of the MNE as one that pushes in the direction of analysis necessarily somewhere between one of a fully territorialized organization and one that transcends the economies of cities and nations. This is a difficult analytical task, though it is not a task resolved by resorting to singular metaphors—whether network or agglomeration. The way that MNEs touch down at home and abroad reflects the need for a 'spatial fix' (Harvey, 1985) and, of necessity, an element of experimentation. Such spatial fixes and the experimentation they entail cannot be understood solely with reference to non-territorial metaphors. Moreover, enduring elements of territoriality in the organization and influence of the MNE are especially revealing of the power wielded by both MNEs and states.

History and the MNE

International organizations such as the United Nations (in its Conference on Trade and Development, UNCTAD) and scholars have preferred the term transnational corporation (TNC). There are several reasons why I use the term MNE. First, since I am interested in an economy that is distinctly *inter*national, the term MNE captures this better than the term TNC which tends to present an image of an already fully integrated international or global economy in which businesses are not constrained by borders (although see Dicken, 1994; Dicken and Malmberg, 2001; Dicken, Peck, and Tickell, 1997).

Second, while elements of a post-Westphalian order have been detected, we live in an international economy that will continue for some time to be distinctly Westphalian. As Whitley (2009: 161) notes, 'the coordination of economic activities in different countries does not...necessarily produce distinctive cross-national collective capabilities. Only in particular circumstances do forms of transnational capabilities emerge. For MNCs to become distinctive kinds of organizations as a result of operating across national borders, they have to "learn from abroad" in the sense of incorporating novel ideas, skills and technologies from innovating subsidiaries in other parts of the organization. So it is the combination of diversity of markets, employees, business partners, and institutions within systematic integration of organizational innovations within ownership-based boundaries that makes MNCs particularly significant different kinds of economic actors' (Whitley, 2009: 146). It is the *combination* of elements of hierarchy and network within MNEs which is distinctive, not *either* hierarchies *or* networks.[1] Moreover, in legal terms, MNEs are strings of national business entities that continue to engage in arbitrage based on this fact while at the same time avoiding many of the obligations that flow logically from a genuinely post-Westphalian international regulatory environment (Kobrin, 2009).

Third, UNCTAD (1993) reported an estimated 37,000 or more parent TNCs controlling over 170,000 overseas subsidiaries. While legitimate concerns arise over the intra-corporate trade and transfer pricing of the largest of these, the majority of MNEs in the world are actually small and transcend national boundaries only by virtue of operating in just one or a very limited number of markets internationally. Many of these MNEs are cautious in their internationalizing to countries that are physically or culturally proximate producing significant clustering of FDI (Petri, 1994). In sum, 'the idea that there is a distinctly transnational model of the MNC has been considerably overstated' (Whitley, 2009: 162).

From Network to Hierarchy and Back Again

Some popular and academic accounts extrapolate the trends of the immediate present. Yet an historical perspective often provides antecedents for what

[1] In this respect, the modern MNE as it emerged for much of the previous century hardly appears distinctively multinational but rather almost a national firm when seeking to exploit home-derived ownership advantages abroad.

appear to be new phenomena. So it is with MNEs and aspects of the way in which they have organized themselves. History suggests an international economy in between in which the territoriality of MNEs and their deployments—notably in their external engagement with nation states through the interplaces that are enclaves—can coexist and has coexisted with network forms of organization, notably within and between MNEs.

The trading companies that grew in tandem with the expansion of major empires during the eighteenth and nineteenth centuries effectively became the first modern MNEs. The British and Dutch East India Companies and their descendant trading MNEs could be regarded as corporate networks. Here, then, 'it is noteworthy that organizational forms characteristic of the first global economy remained vibrant during the second global economy' (Jones, 2005: 183). These companies mobilized through co-ethnic enclaves (Magee and Thompson, 2010) and in this respect, they made their own contribution to the significant migrations that held together the first global economy and the diasporas that have been re-energized in the present, second global economy.

Thus, 'in the nineteenth century too, the life of something did not always unfold on a joined together territory. The most important type of discontinuous social space is a diaspora' (Osterhammel, 2014: 108). An important element of these diaspora spaces operated through enclaves such as treaty ports and concessions. The trading company MNEs were similar to many service-sector MNEs of the present era in terms of their characteristic ownership advantages. Their advantages lay in soft skills embodied in people, knowledge, information, and human relationships (Jones, 2005). Their expertise in this regard was often quite regionally specialized. Moreover, this network form of organization was in no way antithetical to the hierarchy of the modern MNE. As Kumar (1997: 23) noted of the VOC (the Dutch East India Company): 'its capitalization at foundation . . . its phenomenally well-developed and comprehensive accounting system, its extensive political reportage, put it . . . in a class of its own for an institution of that period. Equally, its bureaucratic organization, reaching all regional branches and all levels of its organization, was probably one the earliest examples of the modern bureaucratic form.'

As Jones (2005: 296) warns, then, 'the history of multinationals and the creation of global capitalism have been distinctly non-linear. Periods of global integration have alternated with periods of global disintegration.' An important characteristic of the period after the birth of the modern nation state system was 'the developing symbiosis between emerging state systems and growing cosmopolitanism' (Hopkins, 2002: 24) though between then and now was a period when borders became less porous. It is this non-linear history that prompts Jones to speak of two global economies in the modern era—one in the nineteenth century based on the early mercantile MNEs and a present second global economy of today which began to emerge from the 1970s and 1980s onwards. Thus, 'if the formation of worldwide networks can be described as "globalisation" ... then the period from roughly 1860 to 1914 witnessed a remarkable surge of globalisation' (Osterhammel, 2014: 710–11). In terms of economic geography it is tempting, following the 'borderless world' (Ohmae, 1999) and 'the end of distance' (Cairncross, 2001) theses, also to imagine that present processes of international economic integration in the advent of a second global economy are more far reaching than those of the past, first global economy. Yet, as Jones (2005: 38) notes, unlike the first global economy, substantial parts of the world—notably the African continent—remain largely outside of the contemporary, second, global economy. Whole parts of the world previously separated off from capitalist economic relations have once again become incorporated into them though at very different speeds and depths including in terms of subnational patterns of economic development. Others such as in Latin America have struggled on and off to become reintegrated into globalization processes in ways that have produced sustained national and subnational economic development.

Moreover, historically speaking, the birth of the modern world produced the sorts of hybridity in almost all spheres of human organization such as religion, state, and private-sector forms (Bayly, 2000), which we are accustomed to overemphasizing from our present perspective. Prefiguring the sorts of connections that Cowen (2014) re-establishes between the military and economy in the contemporary pre-eminence of logistics, we can pause to note that 'the savage European ideological wars of the seventeenth century had created links between war, finance, and commercial innovation' (Bayly, 2000: 62).

As we saw in Chapter 3, with good reason there is a long tradition of understanding industry agglomerations in terms of territorially circumscribed processes. Yet, in this first—western-dominated—global economy, international movements of capital had already become quite complex (Bayly, 2000: 238), including in their conjoining network forms of MNE parent companies with the enclaves of, and agglomerations surrounding, their overseas deployments. In this way, 'these rapidly developing connections between different human societies during the nineteenth century created many hybrid polities, mixed ideologies and complex forms of global economic activity' (Bayly, 2000: 1).

Finally, then, it is important to acknowledge elements of an evolutionary perspective on the MNE well in advance of that today. Wilkins' (1974) pioneering work on the evolution of US investment abroad had already detected the emergence of a polycentric MNE organizational structure from earlier monocentric ones and was part of a wider academic interest at the time in the growing cosmopolitan nature of the international economy organized by MNEs (Perlmutter, 1972). Such evolutionary perspectives of the time proved premature and perhaps extrapolated on the basis of the narrow source of FDI that was the US at the time. Nevertheless, in some respects, these accounts have been vindicated in the reality of the contemporary orchestration of international trade and production by MNEs.

The modern MNE grew out of both the further processing of the produce of extractive and plantation industries and the production of new goods for growing markets of the west pioneered by the colonial trading companies (Dunning, 1983). It is important to recognize that the organization of these MNEs and their overseas activities generally began to reinforce the meaning and impermeability of nation state borders and hence the significance of the territories of nation states as the primary containers of economic activity of all sorts. The internal economy and organization of these new manufacturing MNEs grew significantly with US MNEs sequentially carving out monopolistic or oligopolistic market shares in separate overseas markets. By today's standards, the status of 'global scanners' accorded to these companies by Vernon (1979) may seem premature. For all their scale in their orchestration of economic activities across national borders, modern MNEs associated primarily with manufacturing industries of all sorts helped partition the international economy into distinct national markets and production systems. Paradoxically then, the expansion of these global leviathan manufacturing MNEs actually was associated in this period with national partitioning in an interregnum between two global economies (Jones, 2005). In particular, 'after 1930, multinationals were less drivers of global integration, than part of the process of disintegration ... Although extensive multinational operations remained in place, they functioned in more "national" ways' (Jones, 2005: 31).

It was not until the 1970s and 1980s that a second global economy slowly began to emerge as a product of reductions in tariffs under the various rounds of GATT (General Agreement on Tariffs and Trade, now subsumed within the World Trade Organization) negotiations and the creation and deepening of regional integration agreements such as the NAFTA (North American Free Trade Agreement) and the EU (European Union). As these have been overlain by numerous bilateral investment and trade agreements and as the capacity to organize across borders and time zones offered by information and communications technologies (ICT) have come more fully to bear from the 1990s onwards, the second global economy has involved significant offshoring and outsourcing.

The MNE as Container and Contained

MNEs had been experimenting with organizational structures to manage their home and overseas operations as much as a result of their increasing scale and internal divisions of labour as of the increasing variety of overseas national markets they were operating in. The most obvious organizational innovation adopted was the replacement of geographical divisions with product divisions. Many major US MNEs, for example, continued to operate an international division as an appendage to domestic product divisional organizational structures into the 1960s. They were joined in the 1960s and 1970s by experiments in what were described at the time as more world-wide, global, and even grid-like (later referred to as matrix) organizational structures (Wilkins, 1974: 382).

Initially, these organizational developments within the MNE were rendered in terms of the logic of internalization. In the late 1960s Hymer (1979) asked the apparently simple question of why go multinational? The answer lay in the ability to exploit monopoly advantages overseas by way of internalization. Hymer's insights were formalized significantly in subsequent treatments, which saw the MNE as a hierarchical organization with a single locus of authority and strategy making (Cowling and Sugden, 1998) and with a logic of internalization driven by the desire to economize on the transaction costs (Buckley and Casson, 1976); that is, the costs that might be borne by the MNE sought to secure overseas production through market transactions such as licensing technology or through subcontracting or franchising arrangements, especially when the quality and supply of these through such arm's-length arrangements could not be guaranteed and when there were factors such as language and culture that added significantly to the ability to eliminate such uncertainties.

By the 1970s, Wilkins noted how the enormous growth of FDI by US MNEs had 'contributed to the shrinking of the world's geography', but that 'this is still a world of individual nations' (Wilkins, 1974: 395). As Agnew (2005: 441) explains, 'territorialization of political authority was further enhanced by the development of mercantilist economies and, later, by an industrial capitalism that emphasized capturing powerful contiguous positive externalities from exponential distance-decay declines in transportation costs and from the clustering of external economies (resource mixes, social relations of production, labor pools, etc.) within national-state boundaries'. In this respect, the activities and organization of the 'traditional' MNE 'did not compromise sovereignty in any fundamental sense. It . . . may be said to have placed some limits on the *implementation* of internal sovereignty. However, the MNE reinforced the critical system defining construct of external sovereignty, mutually exclusive territoriality, borders, and geographically based political and economic governance' (Kobrin 2001, 185). This pattern of industrial capitalism in which MNEs played a central role had reached its zenith by the 1980s, but from the early 1900s to this time there was a remarkable coincidence in the organizational principles adhered to both by MNEs and by governments.

Many MNE parent companies had constructed vast organizations with a presence in each and every national market of 'miniature replica' subsidiaries (White and Poynter, 1984). These miniature replicas, although shorn of higher management functions, nevertheless replicated much of the rest of the original parent company business proposition from which they were cloned, notably in terms of reassembling systems of suppliers within each national territory.

The pathology of these miniature replicas was, to return to the concepts elaborated earlier in Chapter 3, that of overseas deployments or enclaves. They amounted to the insertion of islands of home country culture and business practice within overseas markets and this pattern of organization was typified by the overseas operations of MNEs from the US—the leading capital exporter of the time. The overseas operations of US MNEs were an important component of the extraterritorial power exercised in the 'American imperium'. As Katzenstein (2005: 215) describes 'American expansion is not the acquisition of foreign territory and the power to control but the penetration of foreign society and the ability to operate there freely'. On occasions the exercise of political power through the overseas deployments of MNEs was quite apparent.[2] For the main part, as interplaces in their own right, these overseas enclaves entailed the logic of deploying home derived product and process technological advantages abroad (Mansfield and Romeo, 1980; Teece, 1977) with a raft of attendant concerns emanating from host countries about the lack of diffusion of technology, the origins of key personnel, and the presence or absence of research and development activity.

The diffusion of technology had followed a relatively orderly pattern relating to the life cycle of the products (Vernon, 1966) which had accelerated as MNEs gained experience of operating abroad (Vernon, 1979). In fact, by the 1980s the evidence was that overseas MNE subsidiaries tended to use process technology every bit as advanced as in the home country even if products continued to be older and adapted to overseas market preferences. Nevertheless elements of this picture that had become reinforced significantly in the west were about to change quite rapidly.

The MNE as a Network within Networks

Since this time, then 'the boundaries of the firm have ... simultaneously shrunk organizationally and expanded geographically, while also becoming

---

[2] The role of US MNE ITT in the military coup overthrowing Salvador Allende in Chile is well reported as perhaps the highpoint of the political behaviour of private enterprises since the emergence of the modern MNE.

more porous' (Contractor et al., 2010: 1418). For Iammarino and McCann (2013: 12) 'we are, without doubt, in an age of outsourcing, offshoring, alliances, partnerships, networks, core capabilities and competencies, and clusters. Organizations which once strove to internalize functions—up and down the supply chain—now strive to source them.' The refrain was sounded earlier by other commentators. Thus, for Reich (1991: 81) 'The modern corporation at the close of the twentieth century bears only a superficial resemblance to its midcentury counterpart...It is increasingly a façade, behind which teems an array of decentralized groups and subgroups continuously contracting with similarly diffuse working units all over the world.' Indeed, 'so fragmented, or dislocated are some firms that it is hard for an outside observer and sometimes hard even for the company's own management, to tell who is "inside" or "outside" and who is local or foreign' (Contractor et al., 2010: 1428) such that Reich (1990) earlier posed the question: who is us?

Reich likens the organization of the modern American MNE to a spider's web, though the metaphor of choice across disciplines has been the network. Urry (2003: 57) argues that 'most of the transnational companies currently roaming the planet are organized through GINs [globally integrated networks]'. That is, 'major corporations work in a strategy of changing alliances and partnerships specific to a given product, process, time and space. Furthermore, these corporations are increasingly based on the sharing of information. These are information networks, which, in turn limit, link up suppliers and customers through one firm, with this form being essentially an intermediary of supply and demand' (Urry, 2003: 9). For Dicken and Malmberg (2001) the MNE as a major political actor as well as orchestrator and strategizer of international trade, production, and knowledge is rendered instead as a 'network within a network'. In each of these perspectives there is a danger that the firm—the parent company as a locus of strategic control—itself recedes from view. Attention has instead turned to a variety of actors (including different of states, NGOs, labour organizations, and civil society groups) which shape development outcomes within geographically extensive, global, production networks (GPNs).

These perspectives are the subject of Chapter 9. However, it will become clear that I believe that the network metaphor on its own offers at best only a very partial insight into the contemporary international organization of trade, production, and knowledge and that some sense of the MNE parent as a locus of hierarchical power and the enclave and the agglomeration as complementary concepts must be retained if we are to understand geographically uneven development. At least some of these same sentiments appear to resonate in the international business and comparative institutionalist literature. Morgan and Kristensen (2009: 168), for instance, emphasize how 'multinationals...are reconstituting hierarchical and lateral relationships between centres of power and influence in order to produce a new network of power that is distinctive in its nature'.[3]

Capitalism's Great Growling Engine Shifts Eastward

'In The Enemy in the Blanket, Anthony Burgess foresaw the 'dangerous Western engine' moving eastward, long before this global shift became apparent in academic commentary'. The growing competition that had been faced by US and EU MNEs during the 1960s, 1970s, and 1980s notably from Japanese MNEs in iconic industries such as automobile and electronics manufacture became patent as a 'global shift' (Dicken, 1988). It was the emergence of Japanese MNEs with their distinctive conglomerate parent company oganizations, 'just-in-time' production processes (Estall, 1985; Mair, 1993) and allied work practices that fuelled a fascination with the process of 'Japanization' of host economies via their 'transplant' FDI in the US and the UK (Dunning, 1986; Mair, Florida, and Kenney, 1988; Oliver and Wilkinson, 1992; Peck and Stone, 1993) and revisions of the theory of the MNE along network lines. As the origins of worldwide flows of FDI have continued to diversify to include other newly industrializing countries of East Asia (such as Taiwan, South Korea) but also the BRICS (Brazil, Russia, India, China, South Africa) so a greater appreciation of different varieties of capitalism (Hall and Soskice, 2001) and national business systems (Whitley, 1992) and their implications for the organization of MNEs has continued unabated.

For Dicken and Miyamachi (1998) the *sogo shosha* (general trading companies) are a uniquely Japanese institution as MNEs. As the earlier European trading company MNEs dwindled, the *sogo shosha* persisted and expanded globally to stand today at the head of extensive federations of connected businesses across a wide range of industries. Intriguingly, in a world that can appear distinctly disintegrated, their main (but not their exclusive) function is to act as financial intermediaries for group companies. As such the uniqueness of Japanese MNEs has been summarized in five key features: a high degree of inter-corporate shareholding; a good degree of intra-group assignment of executives; guidance by a presidential council; a participation in each major industry; and organization around a core bank and a general trading company (Dicken and Miyamachi, 1998). Moreover the large industrial concerns that are integrated into such large conglomerate groups in this way are themselves organizations that have close relationships with suppliers in a Japanese system of just-in-time (Sheard, 1983).

In all of this, the network metaphor of the heterarchical MNE organization has itself remained far from unchanged as a result of successive shifts in the world centre of gravity regarding the origins of FDI. Katzensten distinguishes

---

[3] Morgan and Kristensen (2009) also liken the MNE to a court society in which there are internal conflicts that directly result from elements of both hierarchy and networks.

the networks deployed by Japanese MNEs from those utilized by Chinese MNEs and entrepreneurs. If 'Japanese networks are closed, vertical, Japan-centred and long-term, Chinese networks are open, horizontal, flexible and ephemeral' (Katzenstein, 2005: 68). Thus, for Katzenstein, 'what is distinctive about Chinese business networks, compared to those in Europe or in the United States, is the vast distances they cover, the large amount of interpersonal trust they embody and the lack of formal institutionalization they exhibit' (Katzenstein, 2005: 66).

Indeed, Chinese capitalism has re-emerged as perhaps the dominant mode of economic organization in East and Southeast Asia, partly as a result of the quantitative significance of FDI across these regions and partly as a result of its distinctive qualities (Yeung, 2004: 1). For Yeung (2004), Chinese capitalism has four defining features. First, 'Chinese capitalism refers to an institutionalized mode of economic organization that, until recent decades, has operated largely outside mainland China' (Yeung, 2004: 5) and is, secondly then, not a territorially bounded mode of economic organization. Third, it has nevertheless achieved a degree of coherence including a defined spirit as, fourthly, 'an actor-centred rather than institution-specific' mode of economic organization (Yeung, 2004: 8). While the local embeddedness of Chinese capitalism in often hostile host environments represents a key ownership advantage it is an advantage that continually forces hybridity through adaptation such that 'changes and transformations are endemic to Chinese capitalism itself' as a result of these properties (Yeung, 2004: 32).

MNE Subsidiary Autonomy

Even as the uneven development associated with MNEs was being elaborated by Hymer (1979), Fröbel et al. (1981), and Henderson (1989), contemporary evidence had begun to indicate elements of a decentralization of production via FDI, and the increasingly rapid switch to overseas production missing out the stage of exports hypothesised in the product cycle (Vernon, 1979). As the full range of the ownership, location, and internalization advantages open to MNEs effectively itemized by Dunning (1979) have come into sight in the years following, the metaphor of the MNE as hierarchy has been overtaken by the metaphor of the MNE as a network or heterarchy. Here, heterarchy entails 'a geographical diffusion of core strategic activities and coordinating roles, a break with the notion of one uniform hierarchy of decisions as well as organization positions' (Hedlund and Rolander, 1990: 15).

The ability of a subsidiary to develop resources as much as be assigned them is recognized in this metaphorical shift in theoretical language. Perspectives have also sought to be evolutionary in that they recognize MNEs as organizations that 'draw upon regular and cumulative flows of knowledge

187

and capabilities from locationally differentiated sources' (Cantwell, 2009: 39). This is a picture of the MNE in which subsidiaries perform specialized roles within corporate strategies seeking to produce optimal configurations of host locations and production activities. Here, 'the desire to produce a greater variety of products or services... within a networked system appears to have led to major changes in the role played by subsidiaries' (McCann and Mudambi, 2005: 1863).

One outcome of these developments in the theory of the MNE has been an interest in elaborating different subsidiary roles, constituted by the bundling of resources, development of capabilities, competitive strategies and relationships with parent companies and local host territories and their institutions (Andersson et al., 2007). Early studies identified a series of different subsidiary roles as MNEs sought to reorganize in the face of trends in regional economic integration agreements. White and Poynter's (1984) approach emphasized the product range and market scope of subsidiaries. Their work and subsequent research deploying this framework (Young, Hood, and Dunlop, 1988) found an evolution away from the 'miniature replicas' associated with multi-domestic structures operated by MNEs in Europe in the 1950s towards 'rationalized manufacturers' and 'product specialists' by the 1980s. Coming as it did at a time before the full implications of regional and international economic integration had yet to take effect on company organizations, White and Poynter's research spoke to the 'head office assignment' of subsidiary capabilities and roles within hierarchically organized MNE parent companies. The problem was that this perspective had 'not been very helpful for understanding some of the higher value-adding activity that has emerged in subsidiaries, nor for understanding the process of subsidiary decline' (Birkinshaw and Hood, 1998: 777).

Subsequently, Bartlett and Ghoshal (1989) sought to elaborate the implications of processes of regional and international economic integration for the organization of MNEs and their subsidiaries. Their approach viewed the emerging heterarchical or matrix form of organization being adopted by MNEs as better balancing the increased need for responsiveness to local markets when set against the continued imperative of integration of operations across borders. Building largely upon the resource-based view of the firm, subsidiary role is consequently defined in terms of the internal resources controlled and the external resources incorporated by way of country-specific advantages (Hennart, 2009). Interestingly, while 'these idealized [heterarchical] organizations had many resemblances to the business groups which had developed in the nineteenth century, especially in respect of their use of networks rather than hierarchy... and use of shared cultural norms as binding agents' (Jones, 2005: 181), the introduction of the likes of matrix organizational structures often proved rather problematic.

Birkinshaw and Hood (1998) were able to interpret evolution in subsidiary roles and capabilities as an outcome of parent company assignment, subsidiary choice, and host territory environments. The process of evolution in subsidiary capabilities can lead in different directions: 'Subsidiary development consists of capability enhancement and charter establishment; subsidiary decline consists of capability atrophe and charter loss' (Birkinshaw and Hood, 1998: 783). Their approach is notable, then, for the emphasis placed upon the relationship between subsidiary evolution and the winning of mandates and charters (Birkinshaw, 1996). In this respect they highlight the contestable nature of evolution in subsidiary capabilities, since 'it is . . . the latent mobility of charters and the competition between subsidiary units for charters that is one of the fundamental drivers behind the subsidiary evolution process' (Birkinshaw and Hood, 1998: 782).[4]

Despite work having addressed these issues during the 1970s under the guise the branch factory (Hood and Young, 1976) or branch plant syndrome (Watts, 1981), comparatively few studies have attempted to focus on the relationship between subsidiary capabilities and territorial economic development. In contrast to some of the subsequent thrust of economic geography research, Phelps and Fuller (2000) saw the potential for autonomy in, and even subversive strategies of, subsidiary development within managed and open processes of intracorporate competition to be constrained within MNE parent structures. At best, there were opportunities for economic development of territories into 'semi-peripheries'—a pattern of territorial economic development somewhere *between* the vibrant economic agglomerations of the cores of the international economy in which economic processes are to a great degree locally concentrated, on the one hand, and the denuded branch plant or enclave economies of the peripheries of the international economy on the other hand (see Figure 8.1).

Rugman et al. (2010) sought to extend the 'integration and responsiveness' framework of Bartlett and Ghoshal (1989) when focusing on the continued division of labour within the MNE leading to the 'fine slicing' of corporate functions. That is, 'the value chain is no longer divided into large groupings such as R&D, production, or marketing. The functions and operations within each category can be sliced into dozens or hundreds of sub-activities' (Contractor et al., 2010: 1419), such that subsidiaries can occupy multiple, and sometimes divergent, specialized roles within their parent organizations.

---

[4] Interestingly, also, and in comparison to the decades of the New World Order in which developing nations sought with considerable difficulty to extract technology transfer and other economic development benefits from MNEs and their overseas subsidiaries, the designation of mandates and higher order functions to emerging markets is now something undertaken voluntarily as a means of accessing important markets, localized pools of labour and gaining legitimacy (Contractor et al., 2010).

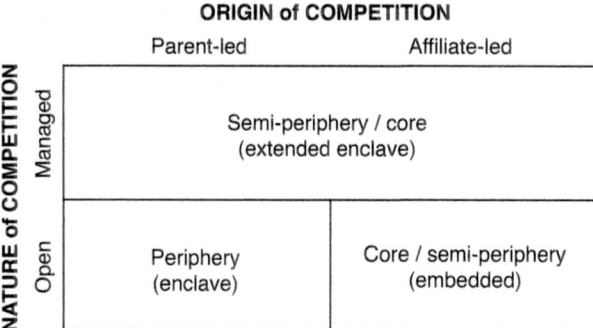

Figure 8.1 Scenarios of intra-corporate competition and local economic development
Source: reproduced from Phelps and Fuller (2000).

Such arrangements have arisen from the ability of MNEs to access locational resources from a broader range of host countries, and more advanced forms of internal coordination exercised by parent companies. Subsidiaries are therefore multiply attuned to, or detached from, aspects of their host territory environments and institutions. From a policy point of view, such developments represent a further evolution in the spatial divisions of labour highlighted by Massey (1984) and might be a cause for concern since there may be little or no connection between the slices of the value chain found at individual subsidiaries and territorial economic development prospects.

In light of these developments, the MNE has been interpreted as a 'differentiated network' in which subsidiaries have a degree of autonomy with parent companies often working in 'sheer ignorance' of the activities of their subsidiaries (Andersson et al., 2007). As the range of ownership advantages deriving from various home country locations has expanded from that which informed much of the theory of the MNE, so strategic variety among and within MNEs, and in their relations with home and host countries has risen (Pearce and Papanastassiou, 2009). As Iammarino and McCann, 2013: 304) summarize: 'Today's MNEs are . . . able to better match the production and knowledge characteristics of the individual subsidiary establishment to the knowledge and cost features of the specific location than at any time in the past'.

Moreover, 'fine sliced chains calls for a better understanding of the processes of bundling location advantages' (Rugman et al., 2010: 4). Such a *process* view of MNE subsidiary roles, resources and capabilities has emerged largely as a by-product of concern to classify different subsidiary roles. As a result, evolution is *implied* rather than specified in terms of distinct processes of change in the scale, degree of specialization, and range of capabilities found at subsidiaries over time. Thus, Thompson (2004) notes how the network metaphor has tended to de-emphasize the predictable, calculable, standardized, and routinized when posing the question: 'Where and when do the fluid performances by the actors stop and a relatively fixed representation emerge?' (Thompson, 2004: 420). Phelps and Fuller (2016) summarize the development of subsidiary capabilities in terms of six processes of change: expansion/contraction, reduction, involution, incorporation, accretion, and replacement (Figure 8.2). There are processes of change that imply only quantitative changes in the resources brought to bear (expansion/contraction), others that imply a qualitative transformation (for example, replacement) in resources and the presence of dynamic capabilities and those that represent specialization (for example, involution). Specifically, we sought to emphasize and provide a means of understanding processes of change that lie somewhere between the extremes of inertia (that seem a relic of the modern MNE as it emerged up to the 1970s) and the incessant change emphasized in current literature.

Some of the issues that emerge from this perspective are: (i) The central importance of peripheral sources of change and innovation within societal systems and, by extension large organizations such as, MNEs. Such peripheral sources of innovation in MNEs have been noted (Glückler, 2014) and can be seen in terms of 'springboarding' strategies (Pla-Barber, 2011) open to MNE parent companies via their subsidiaries. (ii) The connection between particular and generally positive types of changes in subsidiary capabilities and the extra-territorial strategies of nation states such as Singapore and Ireland. Increasingly, both these two 'network developmental states' (O'Riain, 2005) have gone furthest in positioning themselves not merely in terms of their host country locational advantages but as locations from which to configure a footprint of multiple business operations in a region—a theme I take up in Chapter 11.

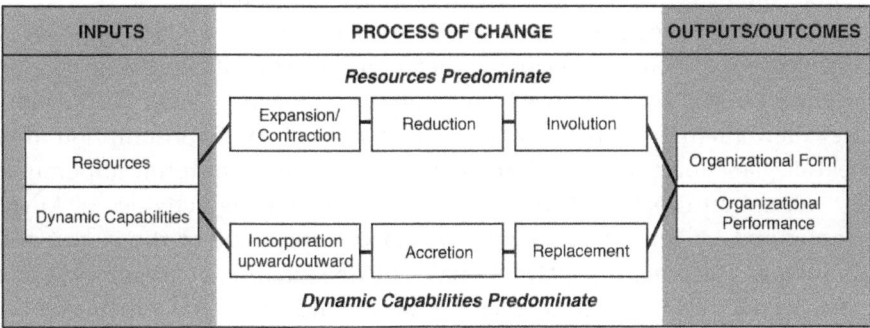

Figure 8.2 Processes of organizational change and the development of MNE subsidiary capabilities

Source: reproduced from Phelps and Fuller (2016).

Retail and Service Sector MNEs

I touch on the concept of GPNs in Chapter 9, but much analysis with reference to this concept has focused on those activities orchestrated not by the sort of manufacturing oriented-MNE as it was depicted in much extant theory of the MNE but upon those driven by buyers—the rapidly growing number retail or brand-oriented MNEs. Some MNEs have operated their own factories as overseas deployments in a nomadic fashion. Despite some of the sunk costs involved in establishing overseas factories, these hardly represent a spatial fix at all. Instead, doubtless aided and abetted by generous grant and other aid, such investments have been amortized rapidly, to allow footloose behaviour in search of low-cost locations on an international scale (Donaghu and Barff, 1990). Other MNEs were effectively 'born global' without factories (Cavusgil and Knight, 2015): 'one of the most notable features of buyer-driven chains is the creation since the mid-1970s of prominent marketers whose brands are extremely well known, but that carry out no production whatsoever. These "manufacturers without factories"... literally were "born global" since their sourcing has always been done overseas. As pioneers in global sourcing, branded marketers were instrumental in providing overseas suppliers with knowledge that later allowed them to upgrade their production in the apparel chain' (Gereffi, 1999: 46).

In this latter case, intermediaries of various sorts are important actors in the GPNs organized by such MNEs. In the case of relatively 'simple' products such as textiles and apparel, company or independent buyers with considerable regional knowledge of supply sources act—rather as in the days of the trading companies—on behalf of parent company organizations. In the case of more complex mechanical, electrical and electronics products, a whole class of major companies—major MNEs in their own right—have become coordinators of production on behalf of others. Perhaps the most notable of these is the Taiwanese company Foxconn which coordinates production of Apple's various products in China and which I discuss further below.

While widely regarded as having been overstated, Barnet and Muller's *Global Reach* nevertheless was prescient in other terms since they drew attention to the importance of consumption which I pursue further in Chapter 10. Notably, they drew attention to the emergence of 'communities of consumption' that held allegiance only to particular company brands and to the future importance of 'cultural anthropology' to the competitive marketing activities of MNEs (Barnet and Muller, 1974: 33 and 30 respectively). Some of the largest and most rapidly growing and internationalizing MNEs in the contemporary period have been MNEs whose business propositions and ownership advantages are intimately involved with understanding consumption patterns.

Notable among the growth of service sector MNEs has been the rise of very large retail MNEs. The largest 14 retail TNCs with over $10 billion international revenues by 2003 typically operated in 10–30 countries and are now as multi-national as many manufacturing MNEs (Wrigley, Coe, and Currah, 2005). Multinationalization of these companies has gone hand in hand with processes of consolidation in home markets but has also involved an element of diffusion to second mover indigenous companies in host markets (Coe and Wrigley, 2007). Some elements of the research agenda for understanding these retail MNEs are little different to those pertaining to manufacturing MNEs—notably on issues to do with the supply chain. However, the agenda differs precisely on the observation made some time ago by Barnet and Muller (1974) regarding the extent to which such MNEs are socially and culturally embedded in a way that many manufacturing companies have ceased to be. While manufacturing MNEs have been subject to both the fine slicing of value chains and heterarch-ical parent organizational structures, retail MNEs also have experienced the challenges of knowledge mobilization across 'differentiated networks' (Currah, 2004). However, perhaps in contrast to the role played by virtuality in manu-facturing companies which have gradually been able to partially disembed or insulate themselves from home and host territory market volatility by way of global sourcing and rationalization of individual markets, the likes of e-commerce developments appear to have underlined the distinctive territorial embeddedness of retail MNEs.

Retail MNEs (and other service sector MNEs intimately involved with final consumption) have been significant investors in real estate markets. These MNEs have been characterized as 'replicators' (Winter and Szulanski, 2001). It is tempting to dismiss such strategies as involving overseas deployments of little commitment; however, replication 'requires the capability to recreate complex, imperfectly understood, and partly tacit productive processes in carefully selected sites, with different human resources every time' (Winter and Szulanski, 2001: 731). Such strategies therefore entail significant investments. That is, 'the key feature of the retail TNC [transnational corporation] is...the need for an unusually high level of *investment in embeddedness* in host markets. Retailers need to sink capital into physical assets in markets simply to access them' (Wrigley, Coe, and Currah, 2005: 441, original emphasis). In this way the process of market expansion drives a measure of organizational deepening whereby eventually 'each retail store is potentially an autonomous centre of innovation' (Wrigley, Coe, and Currah, 2005: 440).

Enclaves: The Logic of Deployment in the MNE

It might be tempting in all of this to view the modern MNE as simply a network—hardly territorial in any serious way. Yet the manner in which the MNE touches down can hardly be described as a series of 'point instants' to prefigure Chapter 9. Instead, these point-instants are best considered as deployments or enclaves. Consideration of the logic of the enclave is important to understanding not only the organization of the contemporary MNE itself but also its economic development contributions at home and abroad and its interaction with governments—the potential for 'strategic coupling' (Coe and Hess, 2011; Yeung, 2016). Conceivably, it is the pathology of the hierarchical MNE that best fits with idea of the overseas operations of MNEs as enclaves, and yet Latham's (2000) inspiration for term deployment derives from a consideration of the network form of organization assumed by colonial trading companies.

Enclaves represent territories within territories—places carved out of existing national and urban 'containers' of economic activities and they are revealing of shifting relationships between MNEs and states. Historically, the concessions granted to overseas powers (and which MNEs governed on their behalf), were territories physically in, but not of, the host nations concerned, having different legal and administrative arrangements from the remainder of the national territory. Shanghai's bund would be a good example (Taylor, 2002). Areas in the Middle East set aside for European expatriate residents who benefitted from 'special legal codes and taxation regimes' (Bayly, 2004: 178) might be another example. These enclaves were an important ingredient in the emergence of a first global economy. Territorial deployments, whether of the operations of an individual company or those of a group of companies, have always been evident as an important manifestation of MNEs though the role of states in their facilitation appears to have waxed either side of the effective partitioning of the international economy into strongly regulated and less permeable national economic spaces from the inter-war years to the 1970s or so. Yet in the contemporary second global economy, then, many smaller and island states have been highly creative in mobilizing their geographical peculiarities for economic development purposes when partially uncoupling state from territory (Baldacchino, 2010).

The MNE Overseas Subsidiary as Enclave

Latham depicts the MNE and its overseas subsidiaries as a transnational formation in its own right akin to a series of military camps. The image of the MNE in its overseas deployments and the enclave territoriality of collectivities of business (such as the Taiwanese, South Korean, and Japanese MNEs that have clustered in particular industrial estates and towns in China and Indonesia) this conjures is one around which there appears to be no process of osmosis with the host economy. Yet, for all the attempts of MNEs to internalize ownership advantages, there are always environmental, political, and economic spillovers surrounding such deployments. Thus: 'even the lightest of deployments can affect considerably life within the locale it enters...there is something uniquely powerful about the narrowness of deployments that works to their advantage in local contexts' (Latham, 2001: 81). This is the power to abdicate responsibility—for human rights and the environment—and the possibility of not being constrained by the broader political and social environment of the host territory. A more subtle gloss is put on this in Katzenstein's (2005: 215) notion of an American imperium whereby the presence of US MNEs contributed to 'the penetration of foreign society and the ability to operate there freely' (Katzenstein, 2005: 215). Deployments have waned as a means of exerting power. Evidence of the American imperium is now found in the arenas and networks I speak of in Chapter 11. However, the historical significance of overseas deployments in the Latin American setting seems clear. Here, 'foreign trade and enclave economies first, and domestic markets and nationalist, militarist, or populist regimes later, have given the United States the instruments to wield its influence south of the border' (Katzenstein, 2005: 228). Little wonder that *dependencia* theory (Cardoso and Faletto, 1979) was so trenchant on the enclave.

For some, this may represent a narrow casting of MNE subsidiaries since the MNE 'provides a culture in which identities are constituted and interests constructed from the perspective of membership of at least two states and one firm' (Tétreault, 1999: 71) and there is good reason to believe that 'since transnational deployments are narrow in scope and often temporary in status they are unlikely to be very good conduits as constitutions of order, even if they sought to be so' (Latham, 2001: 85). Yet, it is also clear that the private sector has been the main force promoting the emergence of elements of global business regulation (Braithwaite and Drahos, 2000). Spillovers have been apparent in terms of MNEs being conduits for business and regulatory practices from one context to another in the search for conducive business environments (Phelps, and Wu, 2009).

Even when viewed as overseas deployments, a measure of the home business system spills over from MNE subsidiaries to host economies. This is the sense of the MNE which inheres in established theories of the projection of home-derived ownership advantages overseas and summarized in the interaction of home locational advantages and ownership advantages (Dunning, 1979). MNEs have at times acted in ways that go beyond those of their own purely private interests to blur with those of wider corporate and national interests of home countries (Boddewyn, 1988). Before we consign this form of geoeconomic or geopolitical influence in the international economy to history we might note that the rapid emergence of sovereign wealth funds and their strategic investments in overseas headquartered MNE parent companies has reignited concerns over the exercise of particular national interests through FDI (Haberly, 2011).

From Imperial Enclaves to Branch Plants and Customized Spaces

The deployment character of the trading companies of the nineteenth century at least partly reflected the nature of imperial expansion by military force. While some element of this enclave nature of FDI disappeared in the era of the modern MNE where much FDI flowed between, was secured within, and reinforced, the territorial integrity of developed nations, it never disappeared entirely. Indeed, some element of the enclave nature of FDI was registered in the branch factory or branch plant syndrome widely reported in the UK and the US in the 1960s, 1970s, and 1980s. The fact that sizeable FDI sites projected home-derived ownership advantages—hence their description as cloning spatial structures (Massey, 1984) or miniature replicas (Whyte and Poynter, 1984)—not only confirms this but also hints at their sealed or enclave character. One irony is that in an international environment that has become newly neoliberalized, enclave forms of FDI have re-emerged in some notable instances regardless of the security and state of development of host economies.

The term deployment used by Latham (2001) encapsulates many of the long-standing concerns of communities and local and national policy-makers with the enclaved character of MNE subsidiaries. The enclave concept emerged most strongly in Latin America as part of the *dependencia* theoretical and ideological perspective (Cardoso and Faletto, 1979; Weisskoff and Wolff, 1977). Elsewhere it emerged in muted, less overtly ideological, terms in the guise of the branch plant (Watts, 1981), or branch factory (Hood and Young, 1976) syndrome and the problems of external control (Firn, 1975). Here the large self-contained vertically integrated operations of MNEs were considered to have a number of inter-related deficiencies including a lack of certain segments of the occupational hierarchy, local backward linkages, lower levels of product and process technology. The evidence has never been conclusive—not least because of the difficulties of establishing the counterfactual situation or indeed an underlying implicit sense of comparison with idealised conceptions of indigenous companies (Phelps, 1993). Yet, while some of these concerns were partially revised in literature of the 1990s and 2000s which pointed to a re-synthesis of the division of labour and the embedding of MNEs, concern remained. Indeed, the more critical strands of this revisionist literature pointed to the potential for the branch factory syndrome to extend to entire production complexes—clusters of businesses—assembled around the subsidiaries of MNEs (Amin and Robins, 1990; Phelps, Mackinnon, Stone, and Braidford, 2003), giving the false impression of agglomerations that might endure.

The 1990s witnessed a period of intense inter-locality competition for very large 'flagship' FDI projects across the Europe and US. The provision of 'customized spaces' for the projects became part of the bloated incentives packages offered to secure investments. Here then part of the sunk costs of MNE deployments (including access roads and power generation and sometimes elements of the initial training of employees) have been borne by local government and development agencies. Such 'customized spaces' included sites with problematic status in planning terms—previously not zoned for development, zoned for other land uses or protected by environmental designations. In the UK this phenomenon began with Nissan's investment in Sunderland (Peck, 1996) but extended to several ill-fated projects by Korean investors LG, Samsung and Hyundai (Phelps and Tewdwr-Jones, 1998, 2001). Moreover, the centrality of spatial planning to the provision of customised spaces in this way raised issues regarding the accountability and potential capture of democratic institutions (Phelps, 2000; Phelps and Tewdwr-Jones, 1998, 2001). A prime case would be an investment by the South Korean conglomerate LG in a large, multifaceted production site in South Wales (figure 8.3). The project attracted what was at the time the biggest-ever incentives package offered to an inward investor to the UK. It also entailed a

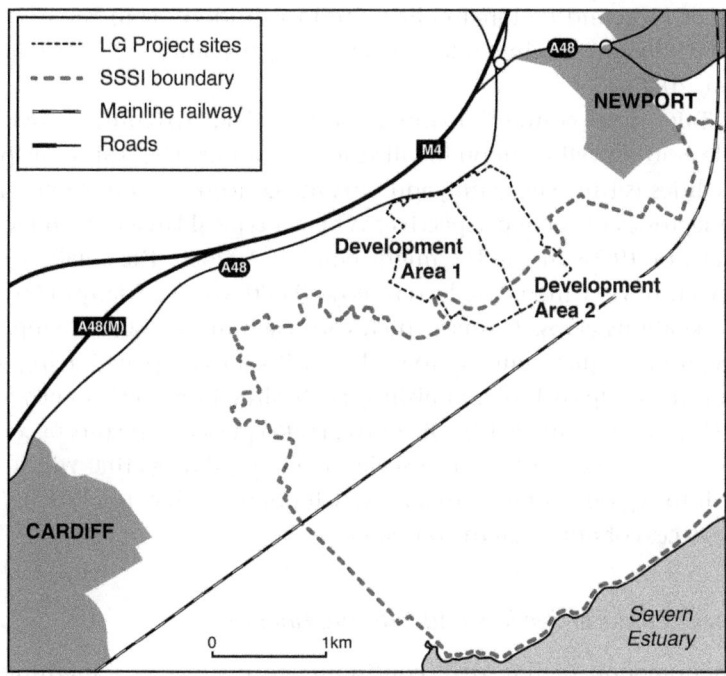

Figure 8.3 The LG site in South Wales
Source: reproduced from Phelps and Tewdwr-Jones (1998).

customized space previously earmarked for a mix of smaller-scale businesses and retained as a green wedge to prevent coalescence between Cardiff and Newport and subject to several planning constraints and environmental designations. The investment—particularly the higher skilled jobs desired by the Welsh Development Agency—never fully materialized and LG ceased operations a little over a decade later. Many of the same issues revealed themselves in the US (Yanarella and Green, 1990) where the issue could become politically charged given the longer-term mortgaging of local governments to particular investors through the issue of bonds to finance incentives packages.

While the controversies surrounding the provision of customized spaces have receded since this time, the fashioning of enclave spaces for major investors has hardly disappeared. Indeed, there is ample evidence that the branch plant syndrome may be alive and well elsewhere across the globe. The branch factory syndrome has to a great extent been offshored from the US itself to neighbouring Mexico, most notably in the cities that have grown along the border under the maquiladora programme (Sklair, 2011). In Europe, some facets of the branch factory syndrome have been offshored from the likes of the UK, France, and Germany to the Central and Eastern European peripheries of the EU. Here an extreme dependence on FDI with as yet limited local linkages appears to have been associated with significant corporate capture of local and national policies and institutions as in the case of the automobile manufacturing industry in Slovakia (Pavlínek, 2016; Pavlínek and Žížalová, 2016).

The Taiwanese contract manufacturing MNE, Foxconn, provides an example worth dwelling upon for all kinds of reasons. The scale of its production facilities is truly staggering and puts the concerns of a previous era over branch factories in some perspective. Where a typical large branch factory of the 1960s or 1970s in the UK might employ 2–5,000, the smallest of Foxconn's factories in China is said to employ 20,000 workers. Many of Foxconn's larger operations across China (which can reach up to 400,000 employees), exist as purpose-built company townships with the company having secured much of the set-up costs of establishing such 'sites' from the host city governments (Ngai and Chan, 2012). Of course, it also presents the prospect of such enclaves—by virtue of their sheer scale—having spillovers that will see them mutate into agglomerations—that is, were it not for their extreme dependence on the success of one western company.

Securitized Producer Services and Offshore Finance

The phenomenon of the MNE continuing to operate as something of an enclave overseas extends beyond extractive or manufacturing industries. Indeed, many of the same branch plant and enclave features remain apparent in the case of the deployments of service sector MNEs. Indeed, highly securitized enclaved environments are a feature of MNE coordinated GPNs in the present era (Kleibert, 2014, 2016).

After the initial decades of decentralization from major cities to provincial towns and cities within the global north, the back-office and data-processing requirements of many industries have now in large part been routinely offshored (Dossani and Kenney, 2007) to enclaves of some description in many developing countries across the world. In Europe, for example, half of all establishments in one survey were already carrying out at least one function remotely using telecoms (Huws, 2014: 53). The variety of activities offshored is revealing of a more complicated picture than would be suggested by much of the established theory of the modern hierarchical MNE as it existed until the 1980s, with some advanced functions found in emerging markets (Jensen and Pedersen, 2011). The human capital endowment supplied by educational and research institutions in Bangalore, Hyderabad, and Delhi are argued to have prompted significant flows of business services FDI into India (Patiblanda and Petersen, 2002). In addition it appears that domestic companies have further developed aspects of the outsourcing model (Athreye, 2004). As a result, 'some Indian companies have already moved to intermediary positions in the value chain and are outsourcing to other destinations including Russia, Bulgaria, Hungary, and the Philippines' (Huws, 2014: 55). Moreover, the division of labour may well be elaborated *within* some of these newer producer service employment locations. Evidence suggests that these business service enclaves have had different generative effects on the economies of different cities in the Philippines, for example (Kleibert, 2014).

'In these special "digiports"—high capacity, product specific, satellite infrastructures—are being combined with export processing zone, tax haven status, and ultra-reliable water and power networks to support enclaves of maximum global connectivity and minimum local connectivity for transnational foreign investors and information service forms' (Graham, 2004: 232–3). The International Technology Park (ITP) in Bangalore was described in Chapter 5 and provides one example of the fine-slicing and geographical extension of the division of labour in the activities of established MNEs and the rise of service sector MNE GPNs. It began life as a joint venture development between the governments of Singapore and India in 1992, generating a renewed interest in development to the east of the city as a secondary IT node. The district of Whitefield near to the airport at the edge of the city of Bangalore has grown as a major international hub of back-office producer service and software industry and it has grown typically in the form of a series of enclaves—either as individual corporate campuses of major companies such as Microsoft or as securitized high-technology parks such as the original seed provided by ITP. FDI exists in such enclaves as both physical and digital infrastructure has otherwise remained poorly developed in this booming city-region. Echoing the ideas discussed in Chapter 5, the style of this development has followed an idealized image held by Indian authorities. Heitzman (2004: 204) quotes the Indian National Task Force on IT industries: 'International experience has shown that hi-tech industries flourish essentially in the rural hinterland adjacent to cities with modern telecoms and communication infrastructure and top class hi-tech educational/research institutions. India will promote such "hi-tech habitats" in the rural hinterland adjacent to suitable cities.'

The pattern is also one that is seen elsewhere in India not least because of espoused aims to create as many as 100 such smart cities. Many of these appear set to be based on particular international experiences (Das, 2015; Datta, 2015). Although in India the smart-city narrative has been synonymous with green-field sites (Datta, 2015), as Das (2015) and Datta's (2015) accounts of Dholera show, these are hardly blank canvasses since these enclaves nevertheless have entailed the use of state-created special vehicles for the expropriation, the expediting of infrastructure development and planning, and the development of land. Nevertheless the scale of these enclaves is worth remarking upon for the economic opportunities for FDI across a range of sectors that they signal. Dholera Smart City is planned to cover 903 km^2—twice that of Mumbai at present—and cost US$9–10 billion, with public sector investment expected to leverage private sector investment on a ratio of 1:9 (Datta, 2015).

Conclusion

Notwithstanding the analytical dangers of over-privileging the agency of MNEs in an analysis of the international economy (Walker, 1989), it is important to retain a sense of the hierarchy of and the power exercised by MNEs as perhaps *the* key actor both within its own organization and in GPNs. The lineage of GPN analysis lies in defending the centrality of MNEs to an understanding of contemporary global trade and production (Dicken and Thrift, 1992; Dicken, 1994). Yet, this original emphasis now sits uncomfortably with the theoretical preferences of GPN analysts to de-emphasize the MNE as an actor. For Dicken, Kelly, Olds, and Yeung (2001) the emphasis has been on the distributed power exercised *through* GPNs rather than power exercised *within* such networks (Sheppard, 2002). There is a danger here that the MNE disappears from view within GPN inspired analysis. Yet 'the metaphor of the MNC as a system of exploitation highlights the awareness of these corporations as independent powerful stakeholders' (Mir and Sharpe, 2009: 248). It could be argued that to ignore MNEs as independent powerful stakeholders may seriously undermine an appreciation of the significant exploitation that occurs in the international economy. As Barnet and Muller (1974:

336) argued some time ago, 'the raison d'être of the global corporation is planning for growth on a global scale. It is the institution ... most directly responsibile for producing malignant growth in modern society, and accordingly ... it is the one institution on which hopes for benign growth must rest' (Barnet and Muller, 1974: 336).

In this respect, and seen in historical context, the economic geography of the MNE emerges as one that has for much of the time involved quite complex coexistence of hierarchy and networks in parent organizations and the production of enclaves and agglomerations centred on deployments at home and abroad. It has, to use a term popular in the present, involved considerable hybridity. The MNE as a corporate personality is a creature that continues to organize trade, production, and knowledge in a way that reflects the inherent tensions between a desire to transcend national and subnational places in a bid to centralize and universalize business processes and the necessity to evolve as an entity somewhere between being of and in these same places.

Just as significant from an academic point of view, is the potential for research focusing on GPNs to underplay the 'dark side' (Coe and Hess, 2011) of geographically uneven development. That is, there is an important part of the GPN research agenda to be developed in a way that acknowledges and incorporates notions of the enclave and the branch plant economy (Kleibert, 2016; MacKinnon, 2012; Phelps, Atienza, and Arias, 2015). One lesson inherited from this earlier stable of research is that questions over the economic development impacts of MNEs and their FDI at home and abroad are not ones that can be resolved with recourse to strong universalistic ideological or theoretical positions. Instead they are questions for largely empirical, albeit theoretically informed, research and associated progressive but pragmatic development of policies based on disaggregation even to the level of individual investments (Bergsten et al., 1978).

9

Global Production Networks

Introduction

'Somehow everything must... "lash-up" such that the otherwise loose elements adhere; only then can there be a new thing in the world' (Molotch, 2004: 2). These geographically extensive lash-ups have come to be analysed almost exclusively within one of several competing theoretical frameworks—global commodity chains (GCCs, Gereffi, 1999), global value chains (GVCs, Kaplinsky, 2000) and global production networks (GPNs, Henderson et al., 2002). They are evidence of the fact that 'fewer products have distinct nationalities' and are 'international composites' (Reich, 1991: 112 and 113 respectively). Writing from their preferred GVC perspective Neilson and Pritchard (2011: 8) argue that 'the broad field of product/commodity analysis is now encumbered by a diversity of alternative models each seeking to "bring in" geography in its own unique way'. Regardless of the competing claims of these related approaches, none of them totally undermines the idea of the territoriality of economic life.[1]

The literature adhering to these closely related approaches has tended to focus to a great extent on either extreme of activities composing the production and consumption of particular commodities. Even so, there remain notable omissions despite the volume of scholarship involved. There is relatively little written on agricultural or extractive industries from within this perspective (Bridge, 2008)—industries, which are inherently territorial.

---

[1] The contestation between these approaches can hardly be said to amount to hair-splitting; however, the expansionist claims of each have also at times appeared to consume energy that might have been spent on deepening some of their respective core concepts. There is also a sense in which the academic debate and positioning involving these different perspectives are revealing of the power relations within and between the sociology, development studies, and geography disciplines themselves. I am ambivalent about the use of any one of these approaches in particular but in what follows I refer to global production networks (GPNs).

Nevertheless, recent contributions within, without, and tangential to the concerns of these three approaches have begun to address the role of circulation through the likes of logistics industries and intermediaries (Coe, 2014; Cowen, 2014; Hesse, 2010). This chapter on GPNs is an appropriate place to dwell at length on intermediary actors, communities, and industries since 'standing between maker and end user are a series of intermediaries that include wholesalers, retailers, and people who buy for others use...Because attention to goods so often focuses on their means of production...and their consumption...the "middle" can be missed' (Molotch, 2004: 131).

The invisibility of some of the economic, ecological, and social costs of GPNs serves a purpose in terms of value extraction but also poses a major problem regarding public policy. As Cowen notes, 'the use of the virtual space of the Internet as a metaphor for the actual material space of supply chains is fascinating and ironic....If the Internet connects people and movements even as it subjugates them, so too does the "physical Internet", paradoxically in ways that are often *more* material and *less* visible' (Cowen, 2014: 229). It might be easy to celebrate the hybridization that occurs in the creation and circulation of stuff however such 'meldings take place under all sorts of conditions, benign, authoritarian, and in-between' (Molotch, 2004: 114). It is worth dwelling on this 'dark side' of GPNs (Coe and Hess, 2011).

'For the end of the Western pattern was the conquest of time and space. But out of time and space came point-instants, and out of point instants came a universe', wrote Anthony Burgess in *Time for a Tiger*. This universe of 'point-instants' is perhaps the corollary of mistaking the abstract for the concrete in the metaphor of the network. This is a universe reminiscent of that fashioned in renaissance thinking in which place was reduced 'to a pinpoint spot in a massive matrix of relations' (Casey, 1997: 138). However, even in a world made smaller by the extension of GPNs, territoriality, in the form of agglomerations and enclaves, remains much more than point instants. GPNs touch down in the enclaves operated by individual MNEs and those that have been specially created for *collectivities* of companies by states. These are the export processing zones (EPZs), special economic zones (SEZs), offshore finance centres (OFCs) which have proliferated in recent years, despite having their lineage in the concessions and treaty ports of a first global economy. The international economy is one whose developmental outcomes are ambiguous and likely to centre as much on these enclave formations as on agglomerations. What the vast volume of empirical work based on GPNs may yet tell us is that much economic activity takes place in forms that represent neither the highs of industry agglomerations or lows of enclaves but outcomes somewhere in between (Phelps, Atienza, and Arias, 2015).

Global Production Networks

In Chapter 8 I discussed how the MNE is a transnational formation in itself. It seems clear that vertical disintegration and outsourcing among MNEs coupled with the many more MNEs born global have seen the emergence of GPNs. As Princen et al. (2002: 15) notes, the value of these approaches is that they remind us 'that consumption decisions are heavily influenced, shaped and constrained by an entire string of choices being made, and power being exercised as commodities are created, distributed, used, and disposed of'. When GPNs touch down they do so in terms that are territorial—in new agglomerations associated with industry upgrading or in enclaves with their dubious records in delivering sustained local economic development or, worse, outright exploitation.

Despite claims that a major contribution of GPN analysis has been to globalize research on regional development (Coe, Lai, and Wojcik, 2014), there is a considerable measure of *déjà vu* about this and related approaches. Indeed, Casson (2013: 12) argues that 'from an economic point of view, a "global supply chain" or "global value chain" is not a new phenomenon that needs a new theory to explain it, but an old phenomenon in a new guise. Modern supply chains have clear precedents in the trading systems of the Roman Empire, the British Empire, and the Venetian state among others.... Its economic logic is timeless but whether this logic dictates its emergence depends on conditions prevailing at the time.' In important respects the GPN and related GCC and GVC approaches have a lineage in earlier theoretical statements such as the Law of Uneven Development (Hymer, 1979) and the New International Division of Labour (Fröbel et al., 1981)—albeit shorn of some of their pessimism and sense of geographic and organizational hierarchy (Dicken, 1994). Moreover, much of the agenda of GPN analysis and closely related approaches was prefigured by the policy-facing research of the United Nations (UNCTAD, 1993).

An interest in global commodity chains (GCCs) was developed by sociologist Gereffi in the 1980s and evolved out of Wallerstein's world systems views (Gereffi and Korzeniewicz, 1993). It is now used interchangeably with the term 'global value chains' (GVCs) as a perspective that has been taken up primarily within sociology and development studies with influence on policy (UNCTAD, 2013). The main advantage of this approach—yet one also considered a disadvantage—is its parsimony when focusing on a limited number of explanatory variables: input–output structure, governance structure, territorial coverage, and institutional framework (Gereffi, 1995). In practice, GCC/GVC analysis has tended to concentrate on the governance variable. In this respect an initial focus on buyer- and supplier-driven chains has, for example, given way to extended typologies of GCCs/GVCs as ones displaying hierarchy, captive, relational, modular, and market forms of organization (Gereffi, Humphrey, and Sturgeon, 2005) or arm's length, network, hierarchical, and quasi-hierarchical forms of governance (Humphrey and Schmitz, 2002).

Elements of the GPN approach in economic geography originated around the same time (Dicken, 1994; Dicken and Thrift, 1992), though the distinctive conceptual features of its approach were crystallized later.

> GPNs do not only connect firms functionally and territorially but also they connect aspects of the social and spatial arrangements in which those firms are embedded and which influence their strategies and the value, practices and expectations of managers, workers and communities alike. The ways in which the different agents establish and perform their connections to others and the specifics embedding and disembedding processes are to a certain extent based upon the 'heritage' and origin of these agents (Henderson et al., 2002: 451).

GPNs are described as a heuristic device for dealing with economic activities, actors, and processes apparent at multiple geographical scales and over time (Coe, Dicken, and Hess, 2008b). The GPN approach 'combines insights from GCC/GVC analysis with ideas from the actor network theory (ANT) and varieties of capitalism/business systems literatures' (Coe, Dicken, and Hess, 2008a: 267).

It is not without good reasons that the GPN approach has proved enormously attractive as an organizing framework for much empirical work within economic geography. One of these perhaps is our neediness as academics to appear global and inclusive in our world view. However, the fruits of this approach are 'vast quantities of empirical work on particular chains and the experiences of particular firms and regions in them, and relatively little theoretical work attempting to account for these findings in a systematic and integrated way' (Peters, quoted in Yeung and Coe, 2015: 31). Setting itself firmly against parsimony, the scope of the GPN approach continues to be expanded to the point where it does indeed appear to be largely a synonym for global capitalism.

In one stock-tacking exercise (Coe, Dicken, and Hess, 2008b) it is acknowledged that the GPN approach could do more to consider circulation processes, theorize the firm and the natural environment. Over time, more and more conceptual content has been poured into the GPN approach. Some of these concepts—such as the notion of strategic coupling (Coe and Hess, 2011; Yeung, 2016)—clearly have a greater emphasis on the territoriality of economic relations and have also been taken up enthusiastically, possibly because they are more empirically tractable than the original conceptual basis of the approach. As Yeung and Coe (2015) concede, the original concepts and the causal links between them have not been developed and specified.

Most recently, then, three competitive dynamics—optimizing cost-capability ratios, sustaining market development and working with financial discipline—are developed in a 2.0 version of the approach in order to address some of these issues.

The GPN approach is founded on the significance of the network metaphor, though the criticisms of the GPN approach noted lead to the thought that this metaphor has been overdone. To the extent that part of the purpose in the GPN approach is to 'elevate the tension between territorial relationships and transterritorial developments' (Hess, 2004: 178), then its aims are in keeping with the sentiments of the original relational approach that I wish to preserve here. However, as a fourth generation of relational economic geography (Yeung, 2005), the GPN approach can at times appear a long way removed from the original social relations of production incarnation of relational economic geography and its sentiments and methods when deploying metaphors such as the rhizome (Hess, 2004) or focusing on 'power geometries' (Yeung, 2003), which appear to emphasize the non-territorial character of GPNs.[2]

At the time of writing the contribution of GPN 2.0 remains to be seen. Notably, the integration of the three dynamics promises a potentially more parsimonious framework, one more attuned to some of the core concerns of international business scholars and, partly as a result, one more centred again on the MNE as the key actor within GPNs.

Intermediation in GPNs

Curiously, despite the aspirations of the GPN approach to offer a means of depicting a broad range of network actors beyond MNEs as lead firms, the latter have nevertheless been the most tractable entry point from which to study particular GPNs. In contrast, 'past research has not paid much attention to these power brokers, who enable the effective functioning of global production networks' (Coe and Yeung, 2015: 51). These power brokers or intermediaries come in different forms and have a variety of positive market creating effects for the private sector but also negative welfare-reducing impacts on communities. In their recent work, Coe and Yeung (2015: 51) focus on 'new' intermediaries in financial, standards and logistics sectors, arguing that 'the

---

[2] There are non-trivial difficulties of conducting and resourcing the multi-sited ethnography implied with such an extensive approach (Phelps and Waley, 2004; Coe, Dicken, and Hess, 2008b). These difficulties are magnified when one realizes some of the influence of actor network theory (ANT) on the GPN approach. Within ANT 'all that is required is to describe the network as fully as possible' (Murdoch, 1997: 747). The word describe is alarming since 'in the face of this methodological requirement to simply describe . . . it is not always possible to capture all the network elements; sometimes the sheer complexity of the relations might be almost impossible to follow through all their twists and turns' (Murdoch, 1997: 747).

undertheorization of these new intermediaries in global production networks, nevertheless represents a missing link in our knowledge base'.

The stretching of GPNs offers interstices into which an intermediary economy of signs and symbols has inserted itself as I discuss in Chapter 10: 'as the institutional and spatial journeys of commodities grow more complex, and the alienation of producers, traders, and consumers from one another increases, culturally formed mythologies about commodity flow are likely to emerge' and 'as distances increase, so the negotiation of the tension between knowledge and ignorance becomes itself a critical determinant of the flow of commodities' (Appadurai, 1986: 48). There is a 'politics of the product' which Miller and O'Leary (1993: 189) define as 'a field of intersecting and often competing arguments, proposals and counterproposals deployed by a variety of interested parties, such as professional associations, government agencies, organized labour, and employers' federations'. While Princen et al. (2002) have argued persuasively regarding the invisibilities of some forms of consumption and its costs hidden throughout GPNs, it could also be argued that the activities of MNEs in constructing GPNs have called forth a countervailing response from civil society, international organizations, and NGOs. The outcome of this politics of the product remains to be seen.

A politics of the product is registered in the value added by business service industry intermediaries in the innovation process. Less straightforwardly it is registered in the enormous collateral impact of financial intermediaries upon any number of seemingly unrelated economic activities. It is also apparent in what Neilsen and Pritchard (2011) term the value chain struggles of labour to appropriate value; in the partly connected rise of ethical consumption and corporate social responsibility (CSR) initiatives and campaigns and their reverberations along GPNs, and; in debates over the value to be attached to nature and second nature. This by no means exhausts the variety of intermediary activities important to understanding GPNs but in what follows I examine each of these in turn.

Ethical Consumption

Ethical consumption campaigns are multi-stakeholder initiatives which might be seen as countervailing civil society responses to the concentration of power lurking behind global networks of trade and investment. Indeed, the emergence of GPNs has driven the desire to make the shrouded inequities of consumption visible in campaigns for ethical consumption (Hughes, Buttle, and Wrigley, 2007: 492). Globalization contains within it:

> contradictions such as competition among economic players for markets and for profits, discrepancy between the banalization of products and the search for

quality, and finally, the lack of congruency between the increasingly homogeneous consumption of major international brands, on the one hand, and regional and cultural diversity, on the other. These contradictions create opportunities for alternative forms of production and distribution to become more viable, and they open the way for strategies aimed at developing certain products on the basis of specific qualities. These strategies are facilitated by the emergence of new patterns of consumption on the basis of new values that are socially created and shared in a context of growing social differentiation   (Renard, 1999: 484).

The differentiation of products and the possibilities for niche markets within GPNs open possibilities for strategies based on mobilizing the symbolic values of products. In the case of foods, authenticity, social solidarity, ecology, hygiene, and safety and health each offer possibilities for the symbolic value of products to be enhanced (Renard, 1999).

However, 'Theorizing about global political responsibility requires more than just telling stories about spatially extensive networks of connection and entanglement' (Barnett et al., 2011: 9) it requires an appreciation of how the power to influence patterns of consumption is widely distributed as a result of its being bound up in a variety of shared political projects. For Amin (2004), such initiatives might be examples of the emergence of 'micro-worlds of regulation' which do not correspond with territory, state, and nested hierarchy (Amin, 2004: 226, quoted in Hughes, Buttle, and Wrigley, 2007).

If the constitution of GPNs provides opportunities for a politics of the product based on alternative forms of production, circulation and consumption, MNEs have not remained passive, given that 'corporate knowledge generating and disseminating practices are central to the circulation of ethical knowledge with ramifications for the governance of GPNs' (Hughes, Wrigley, and Buttle, 2008: 346). MNE retailers now provide glimpses of the GPNs that deliver stuff to us. An example would be the workings of bakeries to shoppers inside supermarket stores. 'This kind of "visual marketing" which consists of setting up a "transparent" staging of a product's distribution path is an obvious attempt at clearing away the foolish fears of consumers—a hole pierced in the shop's walls so they can see beyond' (Cochoy, 2007: 124). These instances of corporate knowledge are found, mobilized, and enhanced, by a host of intermediaries whose role in adding value to corporations, on the one hand, and to place or social communities, on the other, remains highly ambiguous. Such ethical consumption is shot through with its own conflicts and no little mythology. An economy of signs and symbols interlocutes regarding knowledge of production and knowledge of appropriate consumption—the aesthetic, technical, and moral knowledge surrounding the life story of particular commodities—though it is as well to remember the scope for powerful mythologies to offset or obscure ethical claims. It is in this connection that the depth of some strategies of corporate social responsibility (CSR) might be questioned.

Innovation

Reich (1991: 33) argues that 'global insight partnerships specializing in particular problem-solving,—identifying, and brokering are becoming important points of intersection in rapidly expanding global webs'. For some, knowledge intensive business services (KIBS) are developing into a second (private) knowledge infrastructure alongside that in the public sector (den Hertog, 2000). Knowledge intensive business services act as interfaces where 'these interfaces are the focus of a good deal of the service innovations, though innovation studies with their focus on mass manufacturing, have tended to overlook changes occurring in these industries'. These service industries are facilitators, carriers, and sources of innovation since 'KIBS operate as catalysts which promote a fusion of generic and quasi-generic knowledge and the more tacit knowledge located within the daily practices of the firms and sectors they service' (den Hertog, 2000: 505).

This interface is one that is particularly relevant to understanding the small firm sector. Rantisi (2014: 957) highlights how 'in a global and information-rich economy...It is increasingly acknowledged that few firms have the resources to continuously identify and exploit new ideas on their own'. The reason for this is that 'many clusters lack the presence of large firms, and the small and medium sized firms (SMEs) that constitute these clusters have limited resources or know-how to assume a lead role in pipeline construction. In such cases, intermediaries (or "brokers") may take over a coordinating role' (Rantisi, 2014: 959). Elsewhere, 'The interface between the more bureaucratically structured form of the R&D technologist in the flagship firm and that of the university scientist is often to be mediated by the artisanal *bricoleur* within the context of the small service company' (Loveridge, 2009: 221).

This has led Howells (2006) to identify ten roles played by innovation intermediaries and to provide a comprehensive view of the market creating as well as the market protecting roles that intermediaries may play in given instances.[3] Some of these—such as gatekeeping, brokering, accreditation, validation, and regulation—each juxtapose a positive and negative aspect of the role in terms of the value potentially added. However, 'Assessing the impact of innovation intermediaries is...difficult, given their indirect (and indeterminate) effect on a business value chain, but the growth in the number and range of these actors within the system belies the benefits they create to their clients and to the innovation system overall' (Howells, 2006: 726).

---

[3] These are: (1) Foresight and diagnostics, (2) scanning and information processing, (3) the combination and recombination of knowledge, (4) gatekeeping and brokering, (5) testing and validation, (6) accreditation, (7) validation and regulation, (8) protecting investments, (9) commercialization, (10) evaluation of outcomes.

Logistics

The logistics system centred on the twenty-foot equivalent (TUE) container forms part of a rather forgotten set of spaces that is nevertheless central to the functioning of GPNs (Birtchnell and Urry, 2015: 26). As an industry involved with the circulation of goods, logistics can be seen as an activity playing an intermediary role within GPNs—'magically' linking production and consumption. Thus, Birtchnell and Urry (2015: 26) have recently spoken of the need to examine 'the history and future of cargo as the culmination of three currently separate domains: the forgotten space (distribution), the magic system (marketing) and the consumer "cults" at the core and the periphery (consumption)'. Software code now mediates these separate domains in the form of enterprise resource planning (ERP) and supplies much of the magic to the logistics system. It is hard to overstate the importance of logistics and software code to the contemporary economy (Cowen, 2014). As Kitchin and Dodge (2011: 201–2) note 'while the product names of ERP systems are generally unknown to the general public, they have a major effect on the running of contemporary society. The market leader R/3 is so successful that it has made its developer, SAP, into the third largest software company in the world, after Microsoft and Oracle, with revenues of $14 billion in 2007.'

A world drawn near through GPNs is one of 'logistics space' (Cowen, 2014) which embodies a 'geopolitics of in-betweenness' (Birtchnell and Urry, 2015: 26) and has been closely linked to the processes of offshoring so characteristic of recent geographical extensions of GPNs. However, the territoriality of economic organization and the state are not absent in this set of interplaces. 'From its history as a military art in service of the national, territorial, geopolitical state, logistics became a technology of supranational firms operating in relational geoeconomic space. In contrast to the absolute territory of geopolitical calculation associated with colonial rule, geoeconomics relies on the unimpeded flow of goods, capital, and information across territorial boundaries' (Cowen, 2014: 50–1). This imperative for the unimpeded flow of goods has seen new geographic formations produced in the guise of logistics corridors. However, 'while logistics space collides with and corrodes national territoriality, it by no means marks the decline of territory' (Cowen, 2014: 10). Instead, key to the sorts of geoeconomic transformation precipitated by logistics spaces is the rise of new 'transversally bordered spaces that not only cut across national borders but also generate new types of formal and informal jurisdictions . . . deep inside the tissue of national sovereign territory' (Sassen, 2013: 23, quoted in Cowen, 2014: 10). That is, enclaves are also part of the way the logistics industry mediates between production and consumption in the contemporary workings of GPNs.

If the field of logistics is central to the construction of GPNs, it has also given rise to specific logistics intermediaries. Here 'the commodity trader or "merchant"... is neither purely a "global buyer" nor a "global supplier" but both. Indeed it is exactly the information uncertainty between buyers and suppliers across global markets on which the trader typically capitalizes' (Jacobs, 2014: 485). These intermediaries are not necessarily associated with intermediate locations, since it is the usual roster of world cities in which they are primarily located. Nevertheless, as a specific group of actors within the logistics industry itself, they have been significant enough to have promoted the further development of one or two exceptional port cities where logistics and advanced producer services are concentrated.

Finance

Financialization, in the form of 'capital markets and intermediaries have become more important in shaping the successful relations of corporate, household, and individual agency, rendering finance ever more central to understanding economic geographies' (Pike and Pollard, 2010: 33). For Pike and Pollard (2010: 33) financialization means that 'existing and new institutions are increasingly becoming drawn into disintermediated financial markets through their investments in equity, debt, pensions, mortgages, infrastructure, investment funds, and insurance'. In this way 'risk, uncertainty, and volatility are now more thoroughly embedded within urban and economic geographies of the financial system' (Pike and Pollard, 2010: 33). These urban and economic geographies are in, some instances, in between in character. It is also clear that, following the emphasis of this book, the rise of financial intermediation involves 'broadening and deepening the array of agents, relations and sites that require consideration in economic geography and is generating tensions between territorial and relational spatialities of geographic differentiation' (Pike and Pollard, 2010: 29).

In some instances, traditional financial intermediaries have declined but in general the trend has been towards the creation of new intermediaries and intermediary markets in finance. Thus, 'Although transaction costs and asymmetric information have declined, intermediation has increased. New markets for financial futures and options are mainly markets for intermediaries rather than individuals or firms' (Allen and Santomero, 1998: 1461). Other financial industry intermediaries have had a role in creating new markets. In life assurance new conventions have had to be created where none existed in the process of product development, which in turn has shaped the regulatory environment (French, 2000: 110). However, 'just as knowledge is unstable, contested, fuzzy and relational so are these intermediaries, intermediaries that are defined and redefined in interaction with each other and various other networks' (French, 2000: 110).

For Miller (2010: 75) 'key processes in contemporary finance start not with doing something, but with an act of reconceptualization'—acts of reconceptualization in which financial intermediaries play a prime role. Financial analysts have been argued to occupy a role analogous to critics. 'Like film reviewers, food experts or wine connoisseurs, analysts bring a social dimension back into decision-making' (Beunza and Garud, 2007: 14). That is, they are frame-makers since 'market actors respond to information but interpret this information within a social context of controversy. This controversy plays out as rivalry in frames, nested frames and self-imposed milestones' (Beunza and Garud, 2007: 35) and the abandonment of particular frames at particular moments.

Credit rating agencies can be considered to be intermediaries involved with the creation and sale of new knowledge. They appear to have acquired the authority of regulatory agencies since 'it is no exaggeration to say that the fate of nations hangs on the way these firms decide to "brand" them. To make matters worse, their conclusions are arrived at by methods which are not even published: they are considered trade secrets' (Anholt, 2007: 41). Moreover, the global geography of this set of intermediaries is particularly skewed as Anholt (2007: 41) goes on to note: 'America may have lost something of its skill at managing its own brand, but when it comes to branding other countries, it is still a world leader' (Anholt, 2007: 41). Credit rating agencies are not just market forming but also 'ratings themselves, as expressions of "neutral" judgement about a corporation can often take on a life of their own and "crowd out" analysis by the investor' (Sinclair. 1994: 149).

Interestingly, it is with regard to finance that the GPN approach has perhaps come closest to addressing the sorts of concerns I have in mind here in this book. Thus, in seeking to integrate finance into the GPN approach Coe, Lai, and Wojcik (2014: 764) emphasize not only the role of advanced business services in the intermediation of the economic activities composing GPNs but also, thereby, the manner in which the network metaphor central to the approach can be integrated, to an extent, with considerations of the territoriality of agglomerations (in the form of world cities and enclaves (in the form of offshore jurisdictions).

Labour

An important corollary to the rise of particular intermediary industries and occupations is evidence of the way in which value added in GPNs is dispersed. The statistics quoted by Reich (1991: 104) are that more than 85 per cent of the cost of producing a car went to pay routine labour and investors in 1920 but by today, in comparison, only 6 per cent of the costs of a semiconductor device are accounted for by routine labour whereas over 85 per cent is accounted for by specialist design and engineering services and on patents and copyrights.

It might be tempting to concentrate on the world city agglomeration high points of the intermediary economy associated with GPNs. However, there are likely to be just as many low-productivity, poor working condition, low wage, low points that make up a dark side of GPNs (Coe and Hess, 2011). In a passage that echoes, in a rather darker way, Anthony Burgess' *Time for a Tiger*, Lefebvre (1991: 318–19) argues that 'to the extent that capitalist enterprises create enclaves of complete dependence and subjugation of workers, these remain isolated within the space where the "freedom" of the individual, and that of ... capital itself, hold sway. However, to the extent that these enclaves tend to link up, they constitute a fabric well suited to the emergence of a totalitarian capitalism (founded on the fusion of the economic and the political)'. Thus, 'it is not only parcels and policies that are circulating in contemporary supply chains; people are also on the move' (Cowen, 2014: 124). Well in fact, of course, some are nearly constantly on the move and arguably have only a shallow attachment to places—the global knowledge workers seen in Chapter 6. Indeed, the labour market for many of these corporate elites is mediated by labour recruitment specialist intermediaries. Thus, 'Whilst the disintermediation of many services has been reported—in particular due to the rise of the internet—the executive search industry has actively entrenched its position as an essential intermediary through internationalization' (Faulconbridge et al., 2008: 217) not least as a result of their market-making.

Other segments of the workforce are rather more settled and attached to places, home or abroad, precisely in service of movements of all sorts of people, goods, and services. Here 'one of the ironies of the present situation is that many of the most fixed jobs are often carried out by the most footloose people, when some of the most footloose jobs may be carried out by people with deep ancestral roots in the location in which they work' (Huws, 2014: 49). That is, 'one implication of such power relations is the growing number of people who have to be immobile at any given time in order to serve the seemingly growing virtual and physical mobilities of others' (Kellerman, 2012: 31). Moreover, 'the traditional diurnal rhythms of life are disrupted by requirements to respond to global demands ... with ... the expectation that it is normal for everything to always be open. This normalization process is accelerated by the existence in each city of growing numbers of new residents whose comparative frame of reference is spatial not temporal' (Huws, 2014: 58).

The upshot of the speed with which stuff of all sorts flows to us from across the globe, is that it remains critically dependent on labour that is, comparatively speaking, fixed. That is, a sense of 'temporal divisions of labour' (Sharma, 2014) can be added to the more familiar spatial divisions of labour (Massey, 1984) implicated in production. Huws prefers the term 'fracturing' to capture precisely the in-between character of the working experiences of the majority of what she refers to as the 'cybertariat'. As she explains, 'in a fractured existence, the characteristics of fixedness and footlooseness are in constant, tense interaction with each other. Rooted real time activities... are constantly interrupted by "virtual" ones... while "virtual" activities... are disturbed by the physical realities of the situation in which one is placed' (Huws, 2014: 57).

A different set of labour market intermediaries, temporary staffing agencies, are 'remaking the "rules" of disadvantaged urban labor markets' (Peck and Theodore, 2001: 474). 'Staffing firms are not simply supplying services; in their role as private labour market intermediaries they are a major new *institutional* presence in liberalizing economies. They facilitate new kinds of inter-mediated employment practices and forms of labour contingency that otherwise would be logistically and socially infeasible' (Peck, Theodore, and Ward, 2005: 4). Here, any value added to corporations is matched by an altogether more pernicious impact upon communities as a result of discriminatory hiring practices (Peck and Theodore, 2001: 493). 'In the Chicago case, in particular, the presence of a large... infrastructure of temp agencies has come to exert an important influence on the path of labor–market restructuring, facilitating as it has the simultaneous suburbanization and flexibilization of jobs by opening up low-cost recruitment channels within the contingent labor pools of the inner city' (Peck and Theodore, 2001: 494).

For organized labour, fixed in places but exposed to employment organized within GPNs, there nevertheless are opportunities. As Cowen (2014: 96) explains, 'the problem of disruption in a world built on fast flows takes on epic proportions; the reliance on speed combines with the interconnectivity of supply chains to propel disruption in one seemingly discrete locale to system-wide crisis'. The just-in-time production philosophies associated with the orchestration of many GPNs are vulnerable to industrial disputes that can quickly reverberate at an international scale (Herod, 2000). Indeed, such vulnerabilities are the point of departure Cowen takes for understanding the violence and securitization surrounding the logistics spaces of GPNs. That is, 'globally the new military urbanism is being mobilized for the securing of the strung-out commodity chains, logistics networks, and corporate enclaves that constitute the neoliberal geoeconomic architectures of our planet' (Graham, 2010: 77, quoted in Cowen, 2014: 186). If the most globalized segments of intermediary occupations are important constituents of the relatively open agglomerations of economic activity concentrated in world cities, others, including those less globalized, also shape the fixity of labour in 'regimes of control' apparent in the more tightly delimited production enclaves such as those found across East Asia (Kelly, 2001, 2002).

Nature

The distancing between activities that occurs within GPNs is something that severs the ecological feedback on consumption (Princen et al., 2002). The tendency to follow the life of commodities to the final product within GPN analysis 'obscures sight of a vast range of intermediary things that are actively consumed in production and circulation' (Herod et al., 2014: 424) and many of the environmental costs that are externalized by major beneficiaries such as extractive MNEs. Watts (2004: 254), speaking of the 'oil complex' in Nigeria, notes the striking 'invisibility of both transnational oil companies (which typically work in joint ventures with the state) and the specific forms of rule associated with petro-capitalism'. This results from the sheer complexity of calculating the various economic let alone social and environmental costs of extractive industries when these are distributed across local, national and international scales (Eggert, 2001).

Speaking of the environmental consequences of the activities of MNEs, Barnet and Muller (1974: 344) argued that 'the interest of the corporation is to ignore and, where necessary, to obscure such consequences'. Much has changed with the vertical disintegration of many MNEs (including those involved with extractive industries), with respect to civic, corporate, and regulatory attitudes toward the environment since they wrote. However, unless we think that Barnet and Muller's evaluation continues to overstate the case, it is as well to remember that 'the internationalization of production of goods and services through FDI increases the likelihood of the extension of any related environmental damage to a greater number of countries and, therefore, to a larger part of the world's environment' (UNCTAD, cited in Miles, 2013: 130). For Miles, the law on international investment continues to be steeped in the aims and interests of the early MNEs that were implicated in imperial expansion. 'In engaging with the environment of non-European nations Colonial administrators, trading companies, and foreign investors had a targeted focus—the efficient exploitation of natural resources for European purposes, the subjugation of nature to enable commercial enterprise, and the management of supply lines of raw materials to Europe' (Miles, 2013: 43–4). This emphasis in international law remains due to effective reposts from those same interests to efforts of post-colonial states, advocates of alternative legal doctrines, and environmental groups.

Miles concedes that environmental concerns have made inroads into this dominant framing of international investment law primarily through the pressured or 'voluntary' adoption of corporate codes of conduct with respect

to the environment. That is, 'the deepening reach of transnational capital...
has its counterpoint in a proliferation of social movements' (Watts and Peet,
2004: 4). Regardless of whether one interprets these as simply corporate image
making or a 'social license to operate', it seems clear that it is the distributional
claims of environmental and civic groups on companies that have produced a
decentring of 'the corporation' away from objectives focused purely on capital
accumulation and politics away from that focused solely on the capital–labour
relation (Gibson-Graham and O'Neill, 2001). Gibson-Graham and O'Neill
(2001: 57) provide an account of the AUS\$650 villagers were able to extract
from BHP Billiton in compensation for the effects of downstream pollution
from one of its mines in 1996 noting how 'What was inimical to BHP—
apparently contrary to its nature and well-being—has become integral as
part of its official identity and program.'

Across much of Africa, the picture that can be painted is less positive. Here
insecurity provides the justification for what are narrow deployments in
Latham's (2001) terms in which any number of responsibilities are abdicated.
For Leonard and Strauss (2003) it is precisely the enclave nature of production
that ensures that it is an economic formation that can survive in spite of the
failure of nation states. The failure of states is intimately associated with the
exploitation of nature in enclave formations precisely because of the opportunities for predation. In Nigeria 'the discovery of oil and annual oil revenues
of \$40billion currently has ushered in a miserable, undisciplined, decrepit,
and corrupt form of "petrocapitalism"' (Watts, 2004: 251) in which living
standards of the majority of the population have hardly increased from those
at Independence in 1960 despite oil providing three-quarters of government
revenue and virtually all export earnings. In this particular intersection of
state, corporations and communities 'oil politics produces particular sorts of
enclave economies...characterized by violence and instability' (Watts, 2004:
254). This much is made clear in Ferguson's depictions of resource extraction
in Africa where 'Vast areas of the continent have been effectively abandoned
by their national states, subject instead to the...authority of warlords and
private armies and to the economic predations of resource-extracting multinational firms operating in secured enclaves' (Ferguson, 2006: 13).

While there are a number of aspects upon which GPN analysis sheds light
on extractive industries, nevertheless 'the persistence of core–periphery structures and the centrality of the state in extractive GPNs is somewhat at odds
with the emphasis in the GPN literature on the rejection of hierarchy' (Bridge,
2008: 413). At the height of the perceived economic and political power of the
MNE, Barnet and Muller (1974: 94) were able to observe how 'despite its
extraordinary command of financial and technological resources, the global
firm has less military potential than its eighteenth-and nineteenth century
predecessors'. Yet in many respects this ignores the present role of states in

offering up the conditions under which violence is implicated in resource extraction. Watts (2004) is able to depict the horrific state, corporate but also community-come-vigilantism-fuelled violence and predation surrounding oil in Nigeria while Cowen (2014) underlines how corporate and military logics have been entangled from the start in the field of logistics and now drive the extension of GPNs.

Ferguson (2006: 201) provides a glimpse of the manner in which networks and enclaves combine within GPNs when suggesting that forms of mineral extraction have become more 'oil-like'. The picture painted is one in which 'MNEs are organized *de facto* as networks of nodes, and that capital does not flow across the globe but hops from discrete point to discrete point' (Ferguson, 2006: 38), though as I have argued it is not possible to reduce economic geography to one of point instants. Neither can the environmental, distributional, and representational politics associated with extractive industries be reduced to a single—network—geographical metaphor since 'the politics of the environment seems to embrace a wide range of terrain' (Watts and Peet, 2004: 5), which includes transnational networks of social movements but also action centred on arenas such as the World Bank (the example cited being the Global Environmental Facility).

What we are presented with, here, is 'the increasingly bizarre and bitter disjuncture between a fluid core of producer-consumer practices . . . and an impoverished periphery in which something close to anarchy often reigns in what is often an extended battlefield . . . that the modern state is meant to banish. . . . The disjuncture is only underlined by the fact that some of the same companies are involved in both worlds, participating in both a new kind of capitalism and in primitive accumulation' (Thrift, 2006: 300). It is a disjuncture that encompasses the different logics of networks, agglomerations, enclaves, and arenas.

For Smith (2007: 38), then, there has been a 'vertical integration of nature into capital'. Not only is this a product of the invisibility of the environmental effects associated with the consumption, production, and disposal of products circulating within global production chains and networks but also a 'lack of . . . reflexivity has not only facilitated a massive industrial transformation of nature but also fostered a broad-based societal blindness about the destructive results of this process' (Smith, 2007: 27–8). Indeed, perhaps more than anything, what the growing complexity and geographic extension of GPNs signifies is 'a major strategy for ecological commodification, marketization and financialization which radically intensifies and deepens the penetration of nature by capital' (Smith, 2007: 20).[4]

---

[4] The specific example that Smith cites in this regard is the creation of wetland credits. Here, then, 'Nature has . . . become a new frontier, and not unlike earlier "frontiers", that frontier became almost instantaneously financialized' (Smith, 2007: 24).

There are distinct logics, governance structures, and pathways concerned with second-hand products and recycling of products (Herod et al., 2014) to the point that Herod et al. (2014) argue in favour of analysing these as distinct 'global destruction networks'. Here again we should be alert to the ambiguous role that intermediaries might be said to play in GPNs. If 'capital relies not only on the symbolic conquest of nature . . . it also requires semiotic conquest of local knowledges, to the extent that "surviving nature" demands the valuation of local knowledges of sustaining nature' (Escobar, 1996: 334), then intermediaries such as environmental groups and experts have been enveloped into helping extractive MNEs in the resignification of nature in the guise of 'sustainable development'; that is, in the creation of knowledge that can re-inscribe nature into the law of value. Paradoxically, then, 'nature is shrinking, but the signs of nature and the natural are multiplying, replacing and supplanting "real nature". These signs are mass produced and sold' (Lefebvre, 2003: 27).

GPNs and Agglomeration

It is important to retain an appreciation of the territoriality of business participation in national and urban economies since place in some way or other mediates the international relations that constitute GPNs. As Molotch (2004: 163) notes, 'at the heart of the production apparatus—even a in a world of e-commerce, globalism, and virtual simulations—it's still location, location, location and all accoutrements of milieu that influence what stuff can be. Local geography—the nature of cities and regions – subtly permeates virtually all aspects of stuff' (Molotch, 2003: 160). Much of the attention in economic geography continues to be focused on the spikes of the international economy (Iammarino and McCann, 2013) in the guise of cities and industry agglomerations. Indeed, an emphasis upon documenting instances of industrial upgrading and agglomeration might even be considered a point of commonality among GCC, GVC, and GPN approaches.

One celebrated case of an ostensibly new agglomeration borne of the extension of apparel GPNs is that of the Torreon jeans industry in Mexico (Bair and Gereffi, 2001). Bair and Gereffi (2001) highlight not only the significant growth in jobs that had occurred in Torreon in the space of just ten years but also a qualitative development of the activities taking place there from simple assembly to all elements of the chain of production except design, the growth of local full-package suppliers to retailers in the US, with consequent impacts in terms of rising wages and local content.

Other prominent examples of sizeable agglomerations of production might be the footwear industry of the Sinos Valley in Brazil and the Sialkot medical instruments industry in Pakistan. Schmitz (1995a) originally drew attention to the role of export agents in helping to stimulate this concentration of 400 companies in Brazil's Sinos Valley and its sizeable direct employment and the impressive range of the value chain found in this one place. This 'supercluster' had grown from one oriented to the domestic to the international market. He later reported how the prospects of this concentration appeared mixed since, despite further upgrading in production activities, exports and profitability had fallen (Schmitz, 1999a).[5] The longer-term prospects of a large agglomeration such as the Sialkot medical instruments industry in Pakistan are also open to question despite it embodying a sizeable core of 300 producers surrounded by 2,500 specialist suppliers of one sort or another (Nadvi, 1999).

Some of the dangers of too readily reading for new sustained agglomerations on the basis of the activities generated by the extension of GPNs are revealed in the case of a cluster of suppliers predicted at the outset around Nokia in Beijing (Yeung, Weidong, and Dicken, 2006). Apart from questions regarding the nature of that agglomeration as production complex style agglomeration (Gordon and McCann, 2000), Nokia's rapid fall from pre-eminence in the mobile phone industry highlights many of the fragilities of the branch plant economy. Helpfully, in this regard, Felker (2003) uses the term 'contingent clusters' to signal the manner in which the extension of GPNs and the newly found presence of MNEs in Southeast Asia produces industrialization without urbanization (at least not in the fullest economic sense implied in the word agglomeration). These clusters did not involve a great deepening of the division of labour locally and were instead '"local" in only a very abstract sense' (Felker, 2003: 267).

It could be suggested that the development studies literature deploying the terms GCC and GVC has more readily become attuned to the 'dark side' of GPNs—those instances where the extension of GPNs has largely failed to make lasting and deeper contributions to local economic development in many developing countries-than the GPN approach. The optimism surrounding the possibilities for mobilizing collective efficiencies through joint action (Schmitz, 1995b, 1999b), soon evaporated in the face of the evidence regarding the failure of industry agglomerations in developing countries—despite superficial similarities to those in the third Italy (Weijland, 1999)—to develop more elaborate local divisions of labour and deepen production capabilities. Notable agglomerations of businesses in single or closely related industries can be seen in developing countries but little or no vertical division of labour has developed. Instead major centres of production such as the wooden furniture

---

[5] Interestingly he also drew attention to the fact that the dynamics of this agglomeration were not easily captured in a simple likening to the districts of the Third Italy nor simple periodization of a transition from Fordism and flexible specialization.

industries in Indonesia in Jepara and in Sukoharjo are for the most part composed of many small firms which are horizontally specialized around simple product differentiation using traditional methods that have changed little (Phelps and Wijaya, 2016). The predominance of hierarchical govern-ance structures of GPNs was highlighted as one factor precluding sustained and sustainable agglomeration in many developing countries (Humphrey and Schmitz, 2002) and an important strand of work in the GVC tradition has continued to highlight the potential for 'trading down' (Gibbon and Ponte, 2005) among localities and nations woven into various GPNs as a result.

There is a long history and specific structures to disconnects between local agglomerations in developing countries and major markets elsewhere (Perlin, 1983) that in many instances can render the global meta-theoretical orienta-tion of GCC/GVC/GPN approaches rather clumsy in analysing this 'dark side'. For instance, while GCC/GVC/GPN approaches are well disposed to analysing the articulation of major formal-sector export-oriented industry agglomer-ations into production networks, they typically have less purchase on the prospects of the numerous craft based local agglomerations which struggle to export to any significant degree (see, for example, Dicken and Hassler's 2000 account of the Indonesian textile and clothing industries). Some of the specificity of these disconnects relates to the quite complex ways in which they are mediated or doubly mediated not just by buyers but by local agents acting as intermediaries between buyers and local producers who in turn source from home workers in many instances (Hassler, 2005). It is at this point that we become aware of some of the ostensibly 'local' limits to any claims of GPN analysis to have globalized regional studies.

GPNs and Enclaves

A sense of the continued territoriality of GPNs as they touch down in the form of enclaves is vital if a dark side of GPNs is not to be overlooked. The enclave endures because 'for a business firm, the ideal economy is a frontier economy' (Princen et al., 2002: 104). Yet, 'although there are few, if any, true frontier economies today...policy makers and business people...continu-ally try to construct them' (Princen et al., 2002: 104). The numerous and diverse enclaves of the present extend well beyond the extractive sectors to provide interplaces where manufacturing, business service, consumer and financial service activities organized into GPNs can touch down. There typically has been far less recent interest in the 'dark side' of GPNs repre-sented by enclaves—despite the rich theoretical *dependencia* tradition and the empirical tradition of the branch plant syndrome (Watts, 1981). Rarely have these enduring concerns been married to the GPN approach (although see Kleibert, 2016). Between the highs of industry agglomerations and lows of the worst of enclaves is an economic landscape in between (Phelps, Atienza, and Arias, 2015).

The enclave concept has from the outset been more attuned to both multi-scalar and, in particular, international linkages or relations than conceptualizations of networks or agglomerations (Phelps, Atienza, and Arias, 2015). Between the two ideas of industry agglomeration and enclaves themselves lies a middle ground of outcomes of industrialization. Figure 9.1 provides examples of the variety of outcomes in the case of extractive industries,

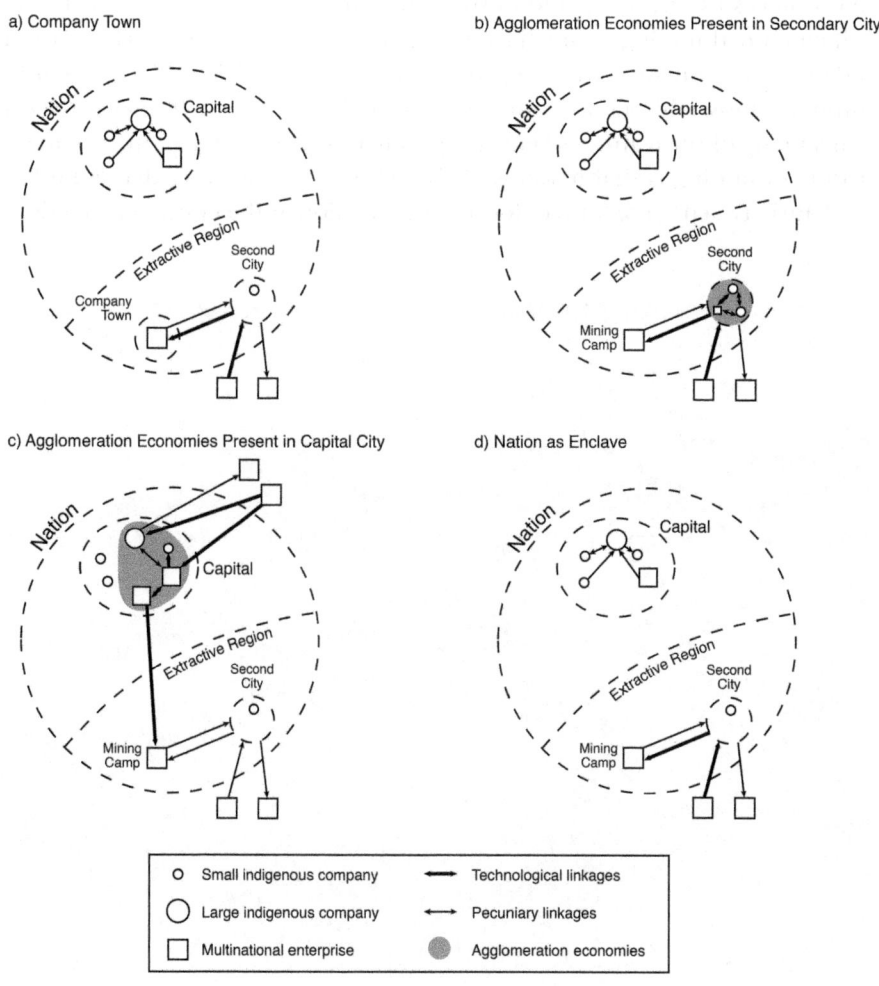

Figure 9.1 The evolution of the mining town
Source: Phelps, Atienza, and Arias (2015).

though doubtless there are other examples that might fit other industries such as manufacturing, tourism, and producer and financial services.

The paradigmatic example of the historic enclave nature of the activities of MNEs is provided by extractive industries. Chile's Atacama desert region of Antofagasta contains many abandoned mining town enclaves such as Pedro de Valdivia (Figure 9.2). These were self-contained towns developed for exploiting nitrates, silver, and ores for producing copper and other metals. They were often small but self-contained towns with churches, markets, hotels, and theatres and even their own currency (designed to limit labour turnover) developed around a vertically integrated enterprise. They did not promote broader urbanization and industrialization based upon processes of vertical and horizontal disintegration (Scott, 1983, 1986). Self-contained mining towns have largely disappeared in Chile. The pattern today—as elsewhere—has changed to one in which labour is flown into mining camps. Although no longer associated with the enclave at the local scale, many of the features of enclave production remain apparent. The main feature of mining is that it seems likely to promote outcomes that are intermediate between some form of local agglomeration at the point of extraction,

Figure 9.2 The former mining town of Pedro de Valdivia
Source: author's photograph.

on the one hand, and none at all at any point within the Chilean urban system; the likelihood is that the enclave features of mining in Chile may be associated with a measure of further industrialization and urbanization in the capital city Santiago. Questions remain, then, over the future of extractive region secondary cities such as Calama and Antofastasta. Antofagasta has grown to the fourth largest city in Chile—a regional core city with a population of around 350,000 at some distance from remaining mining activity (Fernandez and Atienza, 2011). It has boomed as a result of the consumption associated with migrant workers who have fuelled the retail and residential real estate sectors in the city. However, it continues to have almost no breadth or depth to its economy (Arias, Atienza, and Cademartori, 2014) since it neither plays a role in the further processing of raw materials nor is it a base for suppliers to the mining industries.[6] Indeed, although estimates vary, at best the Antofagasta region has less than half the number of suppliers one might expect according to its contribution to national GDP (Phelps, Atienza, and Arias, 2015).

Enclaves as Intermediate Locations

The enclave represents an interplace by virtue of being tightly and often formally and physically delimited but also penetrated by international economic relations. As Graham (2004: 232) argues, 'newly constructed spaces for foreign direct investment in both the "north" and the "south", show similar combinations of intense "glocal" infrastructure connections and attempts at the careful "filtering" of local connections. Such spaces are increasingly equipped with their own self-sufficient assemblies of customized "glocal" infrastructure networks, which allow the immediate locale to be transcended.'

Enclaves retain a salience today and have been argued to be a key political principle through which place and space are organized (Sidaway, 2007). They illustrate the power exercised not merely by MNEs but also by nation states, since states have been significantly implicated in their creation. I touched upon examples of the deployments associated with individual MNEs in the previous chapter. Such deployments are also visible in enclaves that cater to collectivities of businesses and they come in many varieties. One of particular note can be described as the logistics city 'model' already discussed in

[6] The figures reported in a recent OECD (2013) study comparing the industry shares of regional and national GDP are revealing. In Chile as a whole manufacturing accounted for 11.6% of GDP in 2012 but in Antofagasta it was just 4.4% despite the obvious potential for the manufacture of various inputs to mining and possibly an element of further processing. Transport accounted for 7.2% of GDP nationally but only 4.7% in Antofagasta despite the importance of transportation and port activities to mining. Finally, financial and business services produce only 2.2% of Antofagasta GDP compared to 19.7% of national GDP underlining the lack of value adding service industries around mining.

Chapter 6. The logistics city provides an ideal starting point for the discussion as it has been described in terms very close to the vocabulary used by Latham (2001) introduced in Chapter 3. For Cowen (2014: 181–2), then, 'the logistics city is more than a free trade zone, combining the discipline of the military base with the exceptionality of the camp. If the export processing zone is an exceptional zone of hyper exploitation and spatial discipline focusing on production, the logistics city is all this and more, dedicated to servicing the system of stuff in motion' (Cowen, 2014: 181–2).

Enclaves figured as interplaces at the inter-urban scale in Chapter 5. They are also associated with the emergence of some intermediate places at an international scale. Recognition of an economic geographical landscape of intermediate places has come historically from the situational perspective in which locations are defined and explained in relational terms. Situation has been revived recently by Sheppard underlining the inertia that exists in settlement patterns internationally despite advances in transportation technologies. 'Any general increase in space-transcending techniques is unequally applied geographically . . . enhancing the positionality of some places related to others the steamship, airplane, and telegraph generally enhanced transoceanic mobility, but historically were applied first to the routes along which large shares of commodities and information *already* flowed' (Sheppard, 2002: 319, emphasis added).

Recognition of intermediate places comes also from the field of transport geography. Hesse (2010: 76) has argued that 'GCC discourses need to consider the issue of material flows more precisely, particularly because the role that physical distribution and logistics management play in determining the extent, origin, destination, volatility and governance of the chains' (Hesse, 2010: 76). In part, the value of a logistics and transport perspective within GPNs is that it draws attention to the fact that one outcome of the extension of such networks is that this process produces intermediate geographies—intermediate places. As Fleming and Hayuth (1994: 4) note, 'locations between important origins and destinations—locations that are chosen as way stops, route junctions, break-in-bulk points, gateways etc. These concepts have abstract relational meaning as well as a clear, geographical connotation.' More particularly, such intermediate places highlight relational geography since 'the two locational attributes, centrality and intermediacy, combine at various geographical scales to define particularly strategic locations within transportation systems' (Fleming and Hayuth, 1994: 18). By definition, 'intermediate places or hubs are neither central place nor gateway, but are located in between other paces. They specialize in relation to them, mostly based on connectivity, and emerged as intermediate places primarily thanks to a strategic location along a transport axis or with regard to market areas' (Hesse, 2010: 82).

'Strategic location in relation to other places—both in terms of space and time—is the most important property of intermediate areas' (Hesse, 2010: 83) but at the same time there is a sense that some of the intermediate places engendered by the logistical requirements of GPNs are temporary. On the one hand, the prospect of 'manufactured accessibility' also ingrains places with a sense of vulnerability to the flux of changing technologies. This implies a rather insubstantial physical, urban economic geography in-between. These places might be considered to take on some of the here today, gone tomorrow characteristics of temporary clusters (Bathelt, Malmberg, and Maskell, 2004). On the other hand, there is the prospect of new and enduring economic centres born of intermediate locations. If there is some sense in much recent economic geography literature that a space of flows will supersede space of places, then:

> site would no longer determine situation, but a seamless organization of flows would be decisive for the site. Site and situation would thus tend to converge, mobility would become a constitutive framework condition for urban develop-ment, not only a by-product of change. This is not the case, except for some very rare cases   (Hesse, 2010: 87).

We can only speculate on the isolated instances where enclaves as legal or regulatory creations or new intermediate places borne of accessibility have stimulated agglomeration.

EPZs

Enclaves represent interplaces in another respect; they often embody a fun-damental meeting of minds between states and MNEs over the value of limited territorial deployments. If private capital's search for order rests on the preference for a relative lack of order, or for very particular types of order, then states have often done their best to provide such space for capital in the form of export processing zones (EPZs), free trade zones (FTZs), and offshore financial centres. The ideal-type of a deployment or an enclave as a trans-national formation is 'only approached by TNCs in free trade zones around the world' (Latham, 2001: 83).

EPZs have a recent history but have proliferated in recent decades. The first was created in 1959 at Shannon Airport in Ireland. As late as the mid-1960s there were only two, but in 1986 there were 116 and by the time Palan was writing there were over 700 worldwide (Palan, 1998: 68 and 70). By 2007 there were approximately 3500 in 130 countries (Boyenge, 2007, cited in Farole and Akince, 2011: 5). This world of FTZs, EPZs, and offshore financial centre enclaves is actually extremely diverse:

Ask three people to describe a special economic zone (SEZ) and three very different images may emerge. The first person may describe a fenced-in industrial estate in a developing country, populated by footloose multinational corporations (MNCs) enjoying tax breaks, with laborers in garment factories working in substandard conditions. In contrast, the second person may recount the 'miracle of Shenzhen,' a fishing village transformed into a cosmopolitan city of 14 million, with per capita gross domestic product (GDP) growing 100-fold, in the 30 years since it was designated as an SEZ. A third person may think about places like Dubai or Singapore, whose ports serve as the basis for wide range of trade- and logistics-oriented activities   (Farole and Akince, 2011: 1).

The definition that the World Bank offers of special economic zones (SEZs) underlines the territorial nature of these formations. They are considered to be 'demarcated geographic areas contained within a country's national boundaries where the rules of business are different from those that prevail in the national territory. These differential rules principally deal with investment conditions, international trade and customs, taxation, and the regulatory environment; whereby the zone is given a business environment that is intended to be more liberal from a policy perspective and more effective from an administrative perspective than that of the national territory' (Farole 2011: 23). Modern enclaves are a mixture of different types of zones created around one company or a collectivity of companies which in some instances are companies linked by nationality of origin, ownership or long-term contractual relations or all three.

The diversity of modern enclaves summarized in Table 9.1 presents a 'challenge of saying anything specific about such a heterogeneous policy tool' (Farole and Akince, 2011: 1). Regardless, they are fundamentally compatible with the network metaphor for understanding the geography of the global economy: 'the global trade and investment environment is changing in a way that may no longer support the traditional EPZ model.... [Their] growth was enabled by the vertical and spatial fragmentation of manufacturing into highly integrated "global production networks"... this era may have come to an end.' (Farole and Akince, 2011: 5–6). Not surprisingly EPZs have a mixed record. They typically offer positive but static benefits in the short run but fail to generate dynamic (spillover) benefits since broader urbanization and industrialization is rarely sustained in the longer term. Interestingly, then, individual country experiments and even individual EPZs have been subject to quite markedly different interpretation.

The Dominican Republic's experiment with FTZs and EPZs began in 1969 and 'is probably the Western hemisphere's most widely recognized success story in the literature on free zones' (Burgand and Farole, 2011: 159). However the experiment was argued to have contributed to the commodification of manufactures and an 'immiseration' of the work force due to a race to the

Table 9.1 Summary characteristics of different SEZ enclaves

Type of zone	Development objective	Typical size	Typical location	Activities	Markets	Examples
Free trade zone (commercial free zone)	Support trade	<50 hectares	Port of entry	Entrepot and trade-related activity	Domestic, re-export	Colon Free Zone (Panama)
Traditional EPZ	Export manufacturing	<100 hectares	None	Manufacturing and other processing	Mostly export	Bangladesh, Vietnam,
Free enterprizes (single unit EPZs)	Export manufacturing	No miniumum	Countrywide	Manufacturing and other processing	Mostly export	Mauritius, Mexico
Hybrid EPZ	Export manufacturing	<100 hectares (only part of area is EPZ)	None	Manufacturing and other processing	Export and domestic	La Krabang, Thailand
Freeport/SEZ	Integrated development	>1000 hectares	None	Multi-use	Internal, domestic and export	Aqaba, Shenzhen

Source: Farole and Akince (2011).

bottom of low-cost exports—chiefly textiles and garments mainly to the US (Kaplinsky, 1993). Subsequent accounts consider the country's experiment with EPZs to have had immediate positive effects but to highlight 'the limitations of FZ [Free Zone] programs that rely on sources of competitiveness that are unlikely to remain sustainable—specifically, low wages, trade preferences, and financial incentives' and which fail to 'address the structural changes that are required' (Burgand and Farole, 2011: 161 and 172).

Experiments in African nations present a less positive experience. Here 'with the possible exception of Ghana, African zones show low levels of investment and exports and their job creation impacts have been limited' (Farole, 2011: 3). None of the special economic zone programmes in Africa studied in this report had 'played any significant role in facilitating upgrading or catalyzing wider reforms; and integration between the zones and their wider domestic economies is limited'. Kenya's Athi River EPZ outside of Nairobi (Figure 9.3) has been the location for much of the expansion of the garments industry in the recent past under the African Growth and Opportunity Act preferential trade access to the United States market. While direct job creation has been significant, the wider benefits to the local or national economy in terms of

Figure 9.3 Athi River EPZ
Source: Photograph courtesy of Roseline Wanjiru.

backward linkages have been extremely limited (Phelps, Stillwell, and Wanjiru, 2009). However, some distance from the main port of Mombassa and disconnected from the Nairobi economy, it has also provided a prime example of the sorts of poor infrastructure and accessibility of EPZs in many other African nations. The impacts of new incubator programmes designed to stimulate the formation and development of indigenous companies on the zone (Farole, 2011: 229) remain unclear.

Conclusion

In *The Enemy in the Blanket,* another of his *Malayan Trilogy,* Anthony Burgess glimpsed the coming global shift of the 'dangerous Western engine' eastward, long before academic commentary. It is *some* of the realities of this global shift that have figured strongly in the emergence of the GPN approach. In particular, it is the geographical extension of trade and production implicated in this shift that can usefully be depicted in terms of the network metaphor.

However, it is important in any relational perspective that understanding of GPNs is not reduced to a flat ontology of a universe of point instants—to invoke again the excerpt from *Time for a Tiger.* The territoriality of both the state and the MNE are central to understanding the uneven geography and impacts of GPNs (Selwyn, 2015). A fuller understanding of the hows and whys of strategic coupling, decoupling, and recoupling entails the sort of return to literature on the enclave and branch plant economy brought to bear by Kleibert (2016) and MacKinnon (2012).

Moreover, to be meaningful as a depiction of the uneven development of contemporary capitalism in a second global economy, this metaphor needs to be allied to others. As we will see in Chapter 11 it is another geographical organizing principle, the arena, that sets much of the context for understanding the 'strategic coupling' of actors within GPNs.

10

The Cognitive-cultural Economy

Introduction

Vladimir Nabokov's puzzling and unresolvable story *Signs and Symbols* in which 'everything is a cipher and of everything he is the theme' treads a path in human affairs between, on the one hand, the causal associations of signs apparent in the natural world and the ambiguity of the symbols that are language. Treading this middle path is difficult but important since 'things are objectifications in a more complex sense than the doctrine of the arbitrary sign would have it, their malleability is overdetermined as they genuinely mediate—indexically—social processes' (Myers, 2001: 22 and 23 respectively). Instead, then, 'in their materiality objects are subject to forces of natural meaning or causality. But as tokens in a social world they are always subject to transformation as bearers of non-natural meaning' (Keane, 2001: 70). For Gottdiener and Lagopoulos (1986: 17) urban space is produced by semiotic processes *and* non-semiotic processes such that 'signs of place are mediations. They are vehicles for the organization of group action rather than the reified elicitators of action' (Gottdiener, 1986a: 211).

Can a geography of the cognitive-cultural economy (Scott, 2008) tread a middle path between signs and symbols without succumbing to the sort of 'referential mania' that was likely the intended effect of Nabokov's story (Leving, 2012)? That is an open question, and it is perhaps the most troubling for the economic geography of interplaces presented in this book. Some element of the in-between economy of interplaces revolves ever more so around factors which are not easily subjected to empirical verification of any sort, let alone quantification. Yet a retreat into the realm of affect is not something that I am totally comfortable with as an economic geographer. Instead I approach the subject of the economy of cultural affect indirectly through the social life of commodities, processes of intermediation and market making, and the way in which affect is leveraged to create brand value and stimulate consumption.

Consumption of all sorts has attended human existence though its organization and the meanings associated with, and reproduced through it have evolved over time. Indeed, consumption 'is always beyond commerce' as the way in which we make sense of the world (Douglas and Isherwood, cited in Lury, 2011: 14). Evidence suggests that the consumption of luxuries was important historically to the rise of capitalism in Europe (Appadurai, 1986: 37) where it became freed from political constraints, setting in train the development of the division of labour surrounding the production not only of 'necessaries' but also the 'elegancies' as Adam Smith referred to them (Phelps and Ozawa, 2003). Consumption was the necessary prelude to the extension of the commercial apparatus of European manufacturers as they wove Asian producers into their realm (Perlin, 1983).

Nevertheless it is in contemporary second modernity that the cognitive-cultural dimensions of the economy have emerged forcefully within a recognizably independent sphere as 'consumer culture' with an optimism generally surrounding contemporary analysis when compared to the earlier pessimism of the Frankfurt School (Kloosterman, 2015). It is to the seemingly paradoxical qualities of this less or non-material world that I now turn.[1] 'In contemporary consumer culture what it is to be a person is linked to the accumulation of discrete, separable or alienable things, owned by individuals as private property' (Lury, 2011: 35). The signature of the contemporary cognitive-cultural economy is that, 'even though objects still have a physical existence, the way in which we relate to them is increasingly organized in terms of knowledge and imagination' (Lury, 2011: 29). In these ways consumption is a process of value creation rather than mere passive acquiessence (Miller, 2001: 109). Ideas of the 'social life of commodities' (Appadurai, 1986), an economy of signs (Lash and Urry, 1994), the 'economy of qualities' (Callon et al., 2002 and the 'politics of the product' (Miller and O'Leary, 1993) can each shed light on aspects of the cognitive-cultural economy but take us well beyond either the material or quantifiable.

All four of the economic geographical formations highlighted in this book have a salience in the cognitive-cultural economy. Some elements of consumption continue to take place within specialized enclaves, as we saw in Chapter 5. However, the processes of intermediation and economization that are central to an economy of signs and symbols also take place in specialized arenas. To the extent that the distributed networks of cognitive-cultural

[1] Among these are the transformation of natural objects in circulation that take on symbolic meaning (Keane, 2001) and the thoughts that 'inalienability comes mainly through the consumption of commodities and the power of consumption to extract items from the market and make them social or personal' and that the gift 'has emerged as one of the few arenas in which a relatively precise assessment of a social relationship . . . is made and translated into a price' (Miller, 2010: 95 and 99 respectively).

intermediation concentrate in world cities, the economy of signs and symbols that emerges is one in which agglomeration and networks can also be seen as complementary organizing principles.

Intermediaries, Arenas, and the Social Life of Commodities

For Lash and Urry (1991: 10) the 'cosmopolitan presupposes patterns of mobility...and an ability to reflect upon and judge aesthetically between different natures, places and societies, both now and in the past'. Given the continuities that have existed across two global economies of modernity and second modernity, some care may be needed when adopting Thrift and Glennie's (1993: 43) related thought that what is different about contemporary consumption is that 'in the past, this reflexivity was predominantly cognitive and normative but increasingly it is also aesthetic'.

One way of interpreting these intermediary industries is in terms of the role they play in providing 'expertise regarding the technical, social or aesthetic appropriateness of commodities' (Appadurai, 1986: 54). Intermediaries provide knowledge vital to geographies of circulation as Cook et al. (2000: 252) have suggested regarding the use of management strategizing within GPNs. In the modern cognitive-cultural economy moreover these intermediaries are, one might argue, vitally important to the specifically *transnational* character of the networks through which commodities are produced, circulated, and consumed, as we saw in Chapter 7 on policy mobility and in Chapter 9 on GPNs. Intermediaries of all sorts emerge in the cognitive-cultural economy as important to aesthetic reflexivity in the construction of the social lives of commodities. A role for cultural intermediaries has been outlined specifically by Bourdieu (1984). However, more broadly, a role for intermediaries is implied in the 'prosumption' that characterizes the contemporary economy, the emergence of specialized arenas in which 'tournaments of value' take place and the speeding up of capital circulation apparent in this cognitive-cultural economy.

'Prosumption' in the Cognitive-cultural Economy

Cultural intermediaries may be an important part of the cognitive-cultural economy and associated GPNs since 'taste is what brings together things and people that go together' (Bourdieu, 1984: 241). If 'consumption is...a stage in a process of communication...which presupposes proactive or explicit mastering of a cipher or code' (Bourdieu, 1984: 2), it is a class of cultural intermediaries that does much of the work of encoding and decoding in a world of images 'situated at the edges of what exists, between the shadows and the light, between the conceived (abstraction) and the perceived (the readable/ visible)...Always in the interstices' (Lefebvre, 1991: 389).

For Reich (1991) this class of cultural intermediaries has become more fully corporatized in character in today's economy. That is, 'corporations no longer focus on products as such; their business strategies increasingly center upon specialized knowledge' (Reich, 1991: 84) and in this and their web- or net-work-like properties described in Chapter 8 they rely on a set of intermediaries that Reich terms 'symbolic analysts'. These symbolic analysts are engaged in activities such as (i) problem solving, (ii) problem identifying (that is, helping customers understand their needs), and (iii) strategic brokering which consists of bringing these two together. 'Symbolic analysts solve, identify, and broker problems by manipulating symbols, they simplify reality into abstract images that can be rearranged, juggled, experimented with, communicated to other specialists, and then, eventually transferred back into reality' (Reich, 1991: 178). They 'rarely come into direct contact with the ultimate beneficiaries of their work' (Reich, 1991: 178).[2]

Sometime earlier Barnet and Muller (1974: 352) had already argued that 'the most profitable sort of innovation for a large corporation is what is known as product differentiation'. The principle in which the affective qualities of products (as manipulated by way of the symbols attached to them) is one that has seen the advertising industry rise to prominence. It is this scale of adver-tising, marketing, market research, and the like that provide at least one indication of the scale of the symbolic economy associated with interplaces and the desire of large corporations to transfer community and national loyalties to themselves (Barnet and Muller, 1974: 356). As Barnet and Muller (1974: 353) went on to argue 'The consumer must, of course, pay the price of his [or her] seduction'. To an extent this rather understates the price paid since consumers are by now doubly implicated in the seduction process—being sold products or services they often have co-produced.

For Appadurai (1986: 31) since 'consumption is eminently social, relational, and active rather than private, atomic, or passive', it follows that commodities have a far greater social potential than credited in much of economics and political economy. This social life of commodities reveals itself along the trajectory of a commodity from production, exchange, distribution to consumption.[3] Similarly, for Callon et al. (2002: 196), the product is best

---

[2] As with the site selection professionals as intermediaries (discussed in Chapter 11), it is unclear whether these activities although adding value to individual consumers also improve societal welfare (Reich, 1991: 185).

[3] He identifies three aspects of commodity-hood: the commodity phase in the life of a thing; the commodity candidacy of a thing, and; the commodity context of a thing. 'In modern capitalist societies it can safely be said that more things are likely to experience a commodity phase in their own career, more contexts to become legitimate commodity contexts, and the standards of

examined as a process in which 'economic agents devote a large share of their resources to positioning the products they design, produce, distribute or consume, in relation to others' (Callon et al., 2002: 196). The nonmaterial, cognitive-cultural, value of products—is registered in their Chamberlinian properties notably in terms of what these signal in terms of the reputation of the seller.[4] Significantly these qualities of products are reworked in the interaction of producers and consumers. 'The qualities of a product depend on the joint work of a host of actors and there is no reason to believe that consumers do not participate, like other actors concerned, in the objectification of those qualities' (Callon et al., 2002: 202–3). It is this that has led some to speak of the rise of the 'prosumer' whereby 'consumers have become involved in the production of commodities and particular commodities which themselves generate value, by fostering allegiance, by offering instant feedback and by providing active interventions in the commodity itself' (Thrift, 2006: 290). Here, then, 'markets become less simple means of selling products composed at the terminus of a value chain . . . products and services are *not* the basis of value. Rather value is embedded in the experiences co-created by the individual in an experience environment that the company co-develops with consumers' (Thrift, 2006: 290). For Thrift (2006: 283) this prosumption is a 'new kind of efficacy'— 'one in which the process of satisfactory encounter with the commodity is central'. The co-production, prosumption or tournaments of value that shape so many of the GPNs that are the subject of Chapter 9 play themselves out in new specialized arenas in which economic efficacy 'lies between business and art' (Thrift, 2006: 297).

The Arenas of the Cognitive-cultural Economy

The social life of commodities can also be understood with reference to there being an economy of qualities (Callon et al., 2002) and a politics of the product (Miller and O'Leary, 1993). Each suggest that 'tournaments of value' shape the symbolic content of material objects (Appadurai, 1986). Some element of the re-working of the qualities of products can happen as a result of the tournaments of value that take place within places familiar within economic geography. The concept of the politics of the product (Miller and O'Leary, 1993) pays particular attention to the nature of the workplace and how this plays into the non-material value of products. However, it is also apparent that 'the

commodity candidacy to embrace a larger part of the world of things than in noncapitalist societies' (Appadurai, 1986: 15).

[4] Chamberlinian competition is based on a measure of monopoly enjoyed by a product such that it is not perfectly substitutable for another.

complete conversion of commodities into signs' (Appadurai, 1986: 51) in modern economies has taken place in new *arenas* especially created for such tournaments of value. The example that Appadurai alights on is that of financial futures markets where 'the tournament occurs in a special *arena*, insulated from practical economic life and subject to special rules' in which 'there are specific ways in which the reproduction of the larger economy is articulated with the structure of the tournament economy' (Appadurai, 1986: 50, emphasis added).

The examples of arenas I discuss in the next chapter pertain to the non-territorial realm (Ruggie, 1993) of the international economy. Others have noted the importance of award ceremonies or 'tournament rituals' that have become associated with products, services, and fields of knowledge, which are considered to have a symbolic structure distinct and recognizable from regular activity involving a selective judgement of worth (Anand and Watson, 2004: 60). Elsewhere Lampel and Meyer, 2008: 1026) identify 'field configuring events' as arenas formed of 'temporary social organizations such as trade-shows, professional gatherings, technology contests, and business ceremonies that encapsulate and shape the development of professions, technologies, markets, and industries'.

Here the 'prosumer' emerges less as a heroic individual agent than one whose actions are mediated and organized by emergent institutions of shared responsibility as Barnett et al. (2011) detail regarding the growth of ethical consumption. The power to influence the production, circulation and consumption of commodities is widely distributed as a result of new organizations and institutions that orchestrate a sense of shared responsibility (Barnett et al., 2011). 'Ethical consumption as an organized field of strategic interventions, seeks to use everyday consumption as a surface of mobilization . . . for wider, explicitly political aims and agendas' (Barnett et al., 2011: 13). Consumption emerges here as a subject of interest which acts to blur the boundaries between economy and politics, between economy and culture etc. It is this that has led Amin and Thrift (2002) to argue forcefully for geographers to adopt the unitary term cultural-economy. It is also the logic that lies behind Scott's (2008) treatment of the cognitive-cultural economy. The deployment of such terms cannot easily be dismissed since as Barnett et al. describe in connection with ethical consumption:

> The potentials of ethical consumption might be *less* significant in purely economic terms than is often claimed, in so far as it does not represent a spontaneous expression of consumer demand. It also means that ethical consumption might be *more* significant in political terms than is often acknowledged, in so far as it is an aspect of new forms of organization, campaigning mobilization . . . that stretch the understanding of what is political and how being political can be performed
>
> (Barnett et al., 2011: 202).

235

Finally, the social life of commodities implies the creation of myths surrounding them—those created by producers, those by consumers, and those fashioned by a growing legion of cultural, business service and financial 'intermediaries'. While commodities have 'had the least time to accumulate an idiosyncratic biography or enjoy a peculiar career at their point of production', it nevertheless 'may not be accurate to regard knowledge at the production locus of a commodity as exclusively technical or empirical and knowledge at the consumption end as exclusively evaluative or ideological. Knowledge at both ends has technical, mythological, and evaluative components' (Appadurai, 1986: 41–2). The fashioning of specialized arenas in which these tournaments of value take place appears to open a particular and important role for *intermediaries* in the creation of myths attached to products in their *circulation*. Such specialized arenas might be one important locale for the social innovation that Gershuny (2000) sees as driving changes in the use of time.[5]

Signs, Symbols, and the Velocity of Commodities

Time is an important consideration in an understanding the contemporary economy. Indeed, from a social accounting perspective, one can conceptualize individual choice, structural economic change and in particular apparent paradoxes surrounding consumption in terms of changes in the use of time (Gershuny, 2000). For Lash and Urry (1994: 242), 'there are two transformations which have taken place: the realization of an immensely long, imperceptibly changing, evolutionary, or glacial time; and of a time so brief, so instantaneous that it cannot be experienced or observed. Clock-time lies in the middle and it is clock time that has been the organizing principle of modernity.' The implication here is that the clock-time of modernity is being overtaken by a more instantaneous sense of time which, by virtue of modern technology and the loading of commodities with symbolic value, has become both more perceptible and more invested with experience and meaning. This implies that the sort of economy in between perspective I had in mind for this book is, to some extent, presently being undermined.

[5] For Gershuny (2000: 77) three levels of theoretical perspectives on the use of time including for consumption—namely micro sequential theory, micro aggregate theory and macro aggregate theory—are reconciled by recognizing the processes of individual adjustment of daily sequences and institutional level adjustments as ones of intermediation. That is, constraints operate on the use of time at each level but are mediated by processes of adjustment. Over time the process of social innovation implied in individual and institutional-level adjustments produces historic societal shifts in the use of time (Gershuny, 2000: 103).

An historical view helps to clarify that it is not the degree of commodification that sets the contemporary cognitive-cultural capitalism apart from non-capitalist societies 'but rather that the consumption demands of persons in our own society are regulated by high turnover criteria of "appropriateness" ... in contrast to the less frequent shifts in more directly regulated sumptuary or customary systems' (Appadurai, 1986: 32).

> It is in the interests of those in power to completely freeze the flow of commodities by creating a closed universe of commodities and a rigid set of regulations about how they are to move yet the very nature and contests between those in power (or those who aspire to greater power) tends to invite a loosening of these rules and an expansion of the pool of commodities   (Appadurai, 1986: 57).

Here, such elite politics can take different forms: 'the politics of diversion and of display; the politics of authenticity and of authentification; the politics of knowledge and of ignorance; the politics of expertise and of sumptuary control; the politics of connoissorship and deliberately mobilized demand' (Appadurai, 1986: 57). This is what Appadurai refers to as an aesthetics of the decontextualization of commodities—a process whereby the symbolic, non-material, value of a commodity is preserved and enhanced. He goes on to argue that processes involving the decontextualization of commodities have promoted an acceleration of the materialization of symbolic value in exchange, which has been apparent at junctures historically and presently (Appadurai, 1986: 28). Indeed, such diversions 'of commodities from specific paths is always a sign of creativity or crisis, whether aesthetic or economic' (Appadurai, 1986: 26).

Lash (1999: 342) notes how 'symbolic objects which circulate in markets and through markets come to constitute an horizon. ... there is a vast expansion of things that think, of objects with information, and memory, of objects that talk, judge, police and seduce'. Not only is there a vast expansion of things but the velocity with which such things circulate has accelerated. Increasingly, the manipulation of the properties of commodities in order for them to take on cultural associations is important, to the point where there is 'aesthetic obsolescence' and the rapid churning of the particular cultural associations signified and symbolized (Lee, 1993, cited in Lury, 2011: 63). 'As more and more needs, wants and desires are brought into the realm of signification, individuals lose autonomous control and surrender to the code' (Lury, 2011: 68).

The increased velocity of the production, circulation, and consumption of commodities apparent in the contemporary cognitive-cultural economy is a product of the way in which tournaments of value produce a churning of the symbols attached, detached, and reattached to commodities. As a result of such acceleration, something of a paradox is produced in that consumption becomes both more rational and more emotional.

In the economy of qualities it is preferable for the service provider to cooperate with the consumer and therefore to deal with a calculating consumer at least on a regular basis without long intervals in-between. This is possible only by limiting the periods of routine attachment and by constantly calling into question the singularization of products proposed in order to launch new negotiations and adjustments of their (re) qualification   (Callon et al., 2002: 211–12).

The very language and images which are part and parcel of this acceleration of commodities have also permeated the organization of business more broadly—new visual and linguistic metaphors have emerged as aids to refigure business organization and their relationship to the world (Thrift, 1996: 40).

Cognition and Aesthetics

Objects have been progressively emptied of material content to be increasingly loaded with informational content. Lash and Urry (1994) note that there are twin logics—cognitive and aesthetic—to this loading of objects with signs and symbols, and they place considerable emphasis on the aesthetic value in objects. This has led Lash (1999) to equate the first modernity with 'hard' cognition and the second modernity of the present with expression and cultural experience. Moreover, for Lash and Urry (1994) and Scott (2008) the cognitive-cultural economy of signs and symbols is one that concentrates or agglomerates in major cities.

Urban Agglomeration and the Cognitive-cultural Economy

Lash and Urry (1994) identify the likely distributed nature of this new economy. Yet, they also present a rather staid economic geographical interpretation of the new economy of signs and symbols. The core of the economy of signs and symbols is centred on the head-office business producer service complex found in the largest metropolitan areas. This is a way, of course, of reinterpreting continuities in the agglomeration of economic activities in the highest cost central areas of cities.

This depiction of the agglomeration of the cognitive-cultural economy in the world's largest cities is one that is elaborated more fully by Scott (2008). For Scott, while large metropolitan areas house many low-wage manufacturing and service jobs, these are increasingly intertwined with, and dependent upon, the cognitive-cultural talents that abound there:

the core sectors of the new economy include technology-intensive manufacturing, services of all kinds (business, financial, and personal), cultural-products industries (such as media, film, music and tourism), and neo-artisanal design-

and fashion-oriented forms of production such as clothing, furniture, or jewellery. These allied industries have now supplanted much of the mass-production approaches as the main foci of growth and innovation in the leading centres of world capitalism where they constitute the main sectoral foundations of . . . a new economy (Scott, 2008: 12).

While he highlights these sectors as important today he does acknowledge that some aspect of the cognitive and cultural has been present in earlier versions of capitalism (Scott, 2008: 64–5). However, in the contemporary cognitive-cultural economy 'rational and emotional faculties of the labour force are being dramatically revalorized in the workplace' (Scott, 2008: 65). He alights on four most salient features of the cognitive-cultural economy: (i) the radical flexibilization and destabilization of work; (ii) the prevalence of Chamberlinian forms of competition among businesses; (iii) the centrality of digital technologies within the sectors concerned, and; (iv) the role of the leading sectors alluded to in the quotation above.

Of the leading sectors of the cognitive-cultural economy, he notes how the particular segment constituted by the cultural/creative industries proves rather problematic for economic geographic inquiry due to their aesthetic and semiotic content (Scott, 2008: 84). He acknowledges that they can constitute an incoherent set of industries but notably they share three main properties: (i) they are subject to Chamberlinian dynamics of competition; (ii) they are generally subject to Engels Law;[6] and (iii) they are involved with the creation of sign or symbolic value. Scott (2008) has little interest in differentiating the city-regional economy nor in considering the inter-urban economy. The emphasis is rather on highlighting how we have 'entered into a historical and geographical moment such that the axes of the world system are in major measure defined by large city-regions that function more and more as the concentrated points of economic and social order and as the central reference points of symbolic value' (Scott, 2008: 156). To the extent that the cognitive-cultural economy is one centred significantly on processes of intermediation, it is also one that reinforces processes of agglomeration in the world's largest cities. It is a refrain familiar from the world cities literature (Friedmann and Wolff, 1982). It might be subject to the critique of simply recasting this literature (with its emphasis on business and financial services) into one in which the leading sectors are cognitive-cultural—though this does conceivably leave it less exposed to criticism of its ignoring the worldliness of cities of the global south (Robinson, 2006).

---

[6] Engels Law refers to the fact that as personal income rises proportionately less of that income is spent on basic necessities and proportionately more on luxury items.

The Aesthetic in the Cognitive-cultural Economy

Echoing earlier debates on the nature of the service economy (Walker, 1985), Allen rightly points out some of the inadequacies of thinking about the contemporary cognitive-cultural economy in terms of wholesale transitions from one particular sector of an economy to another, arguing instead that the dynamics of the cognitive-cultural economy pervade all sectors to a greater or lesser extent (Allen, 2002). However, for Allen, in their discussion of the aesthetic value of objects, Lash and Urry (1994) have reduced an understanding economic knowledge to the cognitive and codifiable—in effect codifying the uncodifiable. Allen identifies similar tendencies in Reich's (1991) *The Work of Nations*, Coyle's (1999) *The Weightless World*, and Leadbeatter's (2000) *Living on Thin Air*. Instead, then, he is suspicious of attempts to divide up economic activity along cognitive or aesthetic lines in preference to acknowledging 'the entangled nature of economic knowledges which shape much of what we take to be creative know-how' (Allen, 2002: 54).

Drawing on Cassirer's writings on symbolic knowledges—which are those that do not simply reflect the observable world but provide a means of apprehending and comprehending it—Allen argues that 'the relationship between symbolic knowledges and the material world is a mediated one, therefore, in which meaning is dependent not upon particular numbers, musical sounds, specific images or the marks we place on a piece of paper, but upon their symbolic function: what they express, represent or signify' (Allen, 2002: 49). Cassirer distinguished three types of symbolic functions: expressive symbolism; representation (a middle ground which is ambiguous); and signification (where there is a one to one correspondence). Allen highlights the full implications of the expressive symbolism inherent in the cultural-cognitive economy to emphasize that 'there is a creative context to such affects that cannot readily be measured by any cognitive yardstick' (Allen, 2002: 50).

> The practice of negotiating unformed feelings as part of a fuzzy work life is not something that captures the attention, but it is nonetheless a key dimension of economic know-how today. To think otherwise is to cede the economic landscape of the symbolic and the affective to the encoders, whether in the fields of finance, services, manufacturing or indeed agro-chemicals   (Allen, 2002: 55).

For many economic geographers this terrain is an unfamiliar and rather unknowable one since 'as the site of playful representation, the semiotic work of advertising, branding and the like, involves the skillful deployment of symbols regardless of whether or not the signs themselves represent anything in particular' (Allen, 2002: 51).

Here, we arrive at a thoroughly ambiguous middle ground we know well in our life experiences though it sits uncomfortably with our roles as academics—encoders of sorts. From an analytical point of view it can easily produce the sort of referential mania that was the subject of Nabokov's *Signs and Symbols* since 'there is no way out of the game of culture' (Bourdieu, 1984: 12). Little wonder, then, that Lash and Urry and others have retreated into summarizing the cognitive-cultural economy in terms of particular industries or the cognitive rather than the aesthetic. For McFall (2014: 50) 'the problem with cultural intermediary accounts...has been a tendency to get carried away with all that symbolism, signification and taste-making at the expense of the more mundane work involved in market making'. Culture and economy are inextricably intertwined in a way in which 'the world of signs passes itself off as a true world...This is a fraudulent world...When there is talk of art and culture, the real subject is money, the market, exchange, power. Talk of communication actually refers only to solitudes. Talk of beauty refers to brand images' (Lefebvre, 1991: 389).

Brands and the Symbolic Economy of Consumption

A fundamental paradox regarding the cognitive-cultural economy centres on the thought that, 'Function cannot be everything to do with form as there is simply too much variety in form persisting in stuff for functional explanations' and that 'a theory of representation...tells us little about the actual relationship between persons and things' (Miller, 2010: 48). Instead, 'the power of material things is their immateriality...the less visible things are the more power they are able to exert on behavior' such that it is our 'exterior environment that habituates and prompts us' (Miller, 2010: 51). Here, the work of intermediaries such as designers, prompts a bigger question regarding the economy of interplaces since as Molotch (2004: 53) notes 'the great form versus function debate within design reflects analogous controversy in society.... If not one or the other, then where should the "compromise", the "balance", the "line", be located?'

In this connection, Miller rejects a purely non-representational theoretical approach that appears to be the logical outcome of Allen's writings discussed above. Instead he returns to the idealist strand of Hegel's dialectical reason rather than Marx's materialist reversal of it, opting to 'replace a theory of stuff as representation with stuff as one part of a process of objectification or self-alienation' (Miller, 2010: 60). This is not a comfortable middle ground of middling theory or of theory that privileges either representation or affect. Instead it is the uncomfortable ground in-between in which ultimately there is no separation between objects and subject—though it might be better served by a return not to Hegelian dialectic but to other versions of dialectic reason that entertain absence as discussed in Chapter 2. It is this shifting middle ground between representation and affect on which economic geographers must try to stand when considering the consumption of brands.

For Scott (2008: 1474) 'commodity production itself becomes ever more deeply infused with aesthetic and semiotic meaning'. As a result, a whole global marketing and advertising industry apparatus might be taken as the signature of the cultural-cognitive economy. The basic reason for this is that 'commodities must be seen to be useful to their purchasers—to have value and this in turn implies that they are seen as meaningful in the context of their life worlds. Such meanings may relate to strongly utilitarian aspects of commodities . . . or, increasingly . . . their affective dimensions and culturally coded symbolic meanings' (Hudson, 2008: 429). Despite the intangible nature of the affective dimensions and symbolic meanings carried in brands, their monetary value is calculated such that they have become 'a financial asset class' listed on balance sheets. Such valuation of brands can determine access to capital, share prices, and significantly shape corporate strategy. Suitably protected in intellectual property rights, brands can generate significant rents as a result of franchising, licensing, and merchandising (Pike, 2013: 322).

As Anholt (2010: 21) argues 'globalization has created a vast, planet-sized network of individuals working, communicating and trading together . . . on a rational basis of earned trust. Human society therefore ultimately depends on a vast and complex system of brand value in order to operate at this scale'. As a consequence brands are intimately related to the geographic extension of GPNs discussed in Chapter 9. That is, 'brands are a necessary consequence of the growing distance between buyer and seller; and this distance is a necessary function of the desire to expand the business to benefit from a wider market place' (Anholt, 2010: 22). In this way, brands have spatial connections and connotations as a result of their travels and as a result of their attachment to services and products (Pike, 2013). Some of these brands are sufficiently globally recognized to be ubiquitous, others are defined by country of origin or territorial denominations.

In sum, 'brands and branding depend on and are constitutive of the spatial differentiation of economy and society because the actors involved are compelled by the dynamics of accumulation and differentiation to search for, create, exploit, and (re)produce economic and social inequalities over space and time' (Pike, 2013: 322). This uneven geography associated with brands and branding can be seen at the international scale with regard to the promotion of nations to investors.

Investment Promotion

In one of the few systematic treatments of the activity, investment promotion is defined as 'advertising, direct mailing, investment and seminars, investment missions, participation in trade shows and exhibitions, distribution of itineraries for visits of prospective investors, matching prospective investors with local partners, acquiring permits and approvals from various government departments, preparing project proposals, conducting feasibility studies, and providing services to the investor after projects have become operational' (Wells and Wint, 2000: 8). Much of this investment promotion is undertaken by a growing number of investment promotion agencies (IPAs). One estimate suggested there were around 250 national and 160 subnational IPAs of which only a handful existed twenty years prior to this (Morisset and Andrews-Johnson, 2004: 1). This number must surely have increased significantly. In 2013 the World Association of Investment promotion Agencies had 170 fee-paying members from 130 countries.[7] The resources, position within, and access to national and local government machinery of these IPAs vary considerably (UNCTAD, 2001). Some, such as Singapore's Economic Development Board (EDB) and Ireland's Industrial Development Authority (IDA), have been credited with the transformation of their respective national economies—partly by thinking extra-territorially, as I explain in Chapter 11. Many are not merely national or local organizations but international in their reach—operating networks of overseas offices.

In as much as IPAs can help reduce the information costs associated with FDI location decisions, they have been interpreted as intermediaries in the market for capital—that is, FDI flows. 'Because no investor has access to all the information needed to make a decision, they fill in the gaps by making assumptions, extrapolating based on known information and relying on the advice and opinions of others (including the media, consultants, and competitors)', such that one key task of an IPA is to 'facilitate the flow of information to the investor' (MIGA, 2000: 3). The argument has been made more explicitly by UNCTAD: 'A case can be made for investment promotion and the creation of an investment promotion agency (IPA) purely on the basis of market failure. Conditions in a particular host country (including resource endowment, policies and practices, and feasible projects and their likely outcomes) are not known to all foreign investors; and any one foreign investor (particularly its international track record and capabilities) is not known to all host countries. Similarly, all potential foreign investor partners are not known to all prospective local joint venture partners, and vice versa. It is not surprising, therefore, that virtually every developed and developing country has a type of IPA(s), most of which have some degree of government involvement' (UNCTAD, 1997: 19).

---

[7] www.waipa.org (accessed 26 October 2015).

Many IPAs attempt to bridge a gap that exists between what they as promotional bodies see as the economic realities of their home territories and the perceptions of foreign investors. Perhaps the key examples in this respect are the many nations of sub-Saharan Africa that remain largely at the margins of the second global economy, despite national governments and international organizations having been very active in terms of investment promotion. Here, there are significant problems regarding the image of the continent as a whole and subsequently that of individual nations when it comes to the attraction of FDI (United Nations, 1995). As a recent review underlines: 'African nations need to work on long-term strategies to develop positive images of their countries, based on concrete developments, and tangible improvements that counter the negative image or at the very least initiate strategies to accentuate the positive aspects of their country's image while changing the negative realities that create negative perceptions. This would see the development of a sustainable Investment Brands for individual countries which would then positively contribute to the continent's overall image as an investment destination' (Matiza and Oni, 2014: 267–8).

The question of whether the activity of IPAs is cause or effect of FDI flows—whether the economic geography of the investment promotion industry facilitating FDI doesn't simply reflect extant distributions of wealth and flows of FDI—is one that is difficult to resolve. Evidence suggests that investment promotion efforts do stimulate FDI flows (Harding and Javorcik, 2011; Morisset, 2003; World Bank, 2012). Harding and Javorcik (2011) estimate that a dollar spent on investment promotion leverages US$189 of FDI inflows. The evidence of the effectiveness of IPAs in different environments is less clear. In one early study of 58 IPAs, performance was highly dependent on the extant economic and political environment (Morisset, 2003). A more recent study of 124 countries suggested that investment promotion worked in developing countries but not in industrialized countries (Harding and Javorcik, 2011). Examples of best practices can emerge as pockets of excellence in varied circumstances (World Bank, 2012). However, those IPAs from the poorest nations are the least able to be effective at attracting investment (Morisset, 2003). The World Bank's monitoring of global investment promotion best practice since 2006 suggests that sub-Saharan Africa has been the weakest region in terms of overall investment facilitation, with around three-quarters of its 46 IPAs offering a very poor service to investors (World Bank 2012: 14).

Moreover, the line between correcting market failures that derive from missing or incomplete information on the one hand and image-making or brand enhancement on the other hand is a distinctly blurred one. While nation branding for investment promotion purposes can indeed be based on the enduring assets and qualities of places it can and often does extend well beyond these. Anholt's (2007, 2010) likening of place promotion to the skills of state craft and diplomacy highlights the way in which some states have been very successful in such a diplomatic role in support of economic activities. IPAs are important organizations through which states seek to exert such soft power since the scope of IPA advocacy includes 'representing interests of transnational entrepreneurs and firms to foreign governments and multilateral agencies' (Riddle, Brinkerhoff, and Nielsen, 2008: 57). Moreover, one of the few studies of the efficacy of IPAs suggests that those that devote more resources to policy advocacy are more effective in attracting FDI (Morisset, 2003).

The brands of nations have been ranked and valued including the brand as it relates to the climate for investment (Table 10.1). Presumably—given the sums of money tied up in the realised and potential flows of investment—brand image represents a sizeable economy. The gloss put on such place branding and promotion directed at inward investors emphasizes how 'a strong nation brand helps to cut through the information glut that is inherent in the modern business news both locally and internationally. It also supports investor confidence in the value of a country' (Brand Finance, 2014: 11). However, such promotion is treated with some scepticism by corporate investors themselves, while it is often considered part of a 'cognitive problem' of misinformation by the specialist site selection consultants that I discuss in the next chapter. Indeed, Klak and Myers (1997: 137–8) are scathing of the 'depiction, fiction and omission' that make up the 'discursive tactics' used to present an image of African nations to foreign capital: 'context is generally highlighted only to the extent that it adds charm or additional opportunities for profit to the generic features that are pro-foreign industrialist'.

Intermediaries in the market for FDI have undoubtedly been an important force promoting the widespread liberalization of FDI policy, regulation, and

Table 10.1 Top ten investment brands 2014

Top performers		Top movers	
Country	BFI score	Country	BFI score increase
Singapore	79	Norway	4
Switzerland	78	Switzerland	3
Sweden	76	Finland	2
Germany	75	Singapore	2
Norway	74	New Zealand	2
United States	73	South Africa	2
United Kingdom	73	Denmark	2
Denmark	73	Luxembourg	2
Finland	72	Iceland	2
Netherlands	72	Netherlands	2

Source: Brand Finance (2014).

law in the past three or four decades. 'There has been a remarkably rapid unification of policy around a neoliberal development model across the third world' to the point where 'the guidebooks differ in terms of the extent to which they offer investors glimpses of the less-than-fully-neoliberal and less "civilized" societies behind the mediascapes' (Klak and Myers, 1997: 146 and 147 respectively). The intense interest shown by international organizations concerned specifically with investment promotion activities in African nations is indeed strongly imbued with a particular set of practices (Phelps, Power, and Wanjiru, 2007).

Certainly, corporate mobility, the use of specialist intermediary site selection consultants and promotional or industrial recruitment activities, has long been part and parcel of American arm's-length capitalism (Cobb, 1993; Thomas, 2000). It is also apparent that elements of the American 'model' have been strongly promoted abroad within what Katzenstein (2005) terms the American Imperium. Nevertheless, elsewhere with colleagues I have emphasized that, whilst in broad terms this remains a reasonable depiction of events, it is a singular story in need of some finessing, since there are frequently a number of geographical or regional sub-plots, not all of which sit comfortably with the story of a US imperium and its close associations with processes of neoliberalization. In the case of Aceh, the attempt to assert a strong measure of independence from the rest of Indonesia has meant the search for economic development imaginaries, several of which are not easily classed as neoliberal, despite a context in which both armed conflict and the natural disaster of the 2004 Tsunami presented the pretext for the insertion of a broad-based neoliberalization of urban and economic policies of all sorts, including the attraction of investment (Phelps, Bunnell, and Miller, 2011). Prior to the widespread liberalization of FDI laws and regulations from the late 1970s onwards, many nation states continued to have sectoral restrictions on FDI or to set performance requirements on FDI. Partly as a legacy of this, there are many nations where investment promotion is a less prominent part of economic development policy and where international organizations and intermediaries involved with the reform and development of investment promotion have had a less prominent role. Thus, what Thomas, (2000, 2011) has referred to as 'the market for capital' in a second global economy is hardly a single market but rather is partitioned into ones that offer distinctly different 'markets for social order' (Bornschier and Trezzini, 2001; Phelps and Wu, 2009).

Consuming The City, Consuming The Enclave

If brands come to reflect the uneven geography of the services and products to which they are attached, detached, and reattached, then this uneven landscape includes not only the peaks of world city agglomerations but also the troughs of the international economy found in enclaves. However, 'moving beyond the polarized views in recent geographic debates, theorization of the geographical association of brands and branding can more usefully address their expressions in spatial circuits as relational and territorial, bounded and unbounded, fluid and fixed, territorializing and deterritorializing' (Pike, 2013: 324). Here Pike underlies the potential for geographical formations—the network and agglomeration (and the enclave and arena I might add)—to coexist as *complements* in the contemporary cognitive economy. Returning to the language mobilized in Chapter 3, if 'the local must always be understood to be a juncture point between arenas, networks and deployments', then, for Latham (2001: 84), 'the problem is that the politics of these junctures rarely unfold on equal terms, as capacities to shape images in international arenas, or the terms and currency of network exchanges have been historically uneven'. We can view the uneven geography of brands with regard to urban agglomerations we call cities and their counterpart enclaves.

The Enclave as a Place of Consumption

Many aspects of city branding represent little more than the commodification and hence the homogenization of place into non-places. On the one hand, the commodification implied in the branding of cities implies a measure of cosmopolitanism within inter-city competition by dint of the relational construction of such brands. Yet, on the other hand, 'such cosmopolitanism is based not so much on any notion of universal or world citizenship, but rather on a conception of the free-floating investor or consumer who has no primary affiliation other than to the optimization of investment return or lifestyle satisfaction, irrespective of where that may be achieved' (Malpas, 2009: 192). While we can associate the consumption of places in a cognitive-cultural economy with the Chamberlinian sense of competition among more or less unique cities discussed in Chapter 7 and by Scott (2011), it is also the case that much consumption of places—including that in a cognitive and aesthetic register—takes place in enclaves. I introduced the retail mall as a suburban economic enclave in Chapter 5. Here I dwell briefly on this economic geographical formation again. In addition I consider enclave tourism as a 'highly ambiguous' development strategy based on tourism (Britton, 1982: 332). Both these examples of enclaves of consumption highlight the fundamentally ambiguous properties of this particular geographical formation as discussed in Chapters 2 and 3.

Consumption has come to play a role that is central to the transformation and survival of capitalism (Clarke, 1997: 222) in which there is 'the substitution of seduction for repression, public relations for policy, advertising for authority, needs-creation for norm imposition' (Bauman, 1987: 167–8, quoted in Clarke, 1997: 219). Little wonder, then, that the enclave nature of the retail mall is open to interpretation as the sort of managed playground open to all to engage in the sorts of post-modern reflexivity previously reserved for the flaneur. However, and to prefigure the example of tourism enclaves below, the seduction brought to light in retail enclaves amounts to a 'package deal' (Clarke, 1997: 232) in which 'today's underdogs are nonconsumers' (Bauman, 1995: 204, quoted in Clarke, 1997: 232). The rise of consumer society is inextricably bound up with an extreme reliance on the market as an allocator of resources (Clarke, 1997: 233) in which 'objects are no longer commodities: they are no longer even signs whose meaning and message one could decipher and appropriate for oneself, they are *tests'* (Baudrillard, 1994: 75, quoted in Clarke, 1997: 233). These are tests that all of us will be subjected to perpetually by way of the sorts of processes of economization (involving market-making devices and techniques, co-production and prosumption) and tournaments of value that make up the social life of commodities described earlier; 'the entire sphere of consumption possesses the character of an indefinite referendum' (Clarke, 1997: 233).

The mall as an enclave is a pseudo space. While we should be careful with such pejorative language, the term highlights the fundamental ambiguity of the shopping mall as an enclave. The symbolism associated with the mall provides an insight into the ambiguity of this enclave. As Goss (1993: 19) describes it: 'in recognition of the culturally perceived emptiness of the activity for which they provide the main social space, designers manufacture the illusion that something else other than mere shopping in going on, while also mediating the materialist relations of mass consumption and disguising the identity and root-edness of the shopping center in the contemporary capitalist social order'. The symbolic economy of the mall is one that seeks to assuage the guilt and alienation that might otherwise be associated with acts of consumption: landscaping in malls stands in some contrast to the degraded second nature of the suburban environments in which they are often located, naturalizing the act of shopping; the innocence of shopping is affirmed in symbolic appeals to history; pieces of art lend a non-commercialized aesthetic to an otherwise thoroughly commercialized setting (Goss, 1993). The power of the mall as an enclave is 'its ability to contrast positively with the experience of the everyday environment in the surrounding space' (Gottdiener, 1986b: 295). Moreover, the ambiguity or pseudo place credentials of malls are given in their attempts to 'recreate the urban space of agglomeration and reproduce in a temporary setting the urban scale of population density' (Gottdiener, 1986b: 295).

Lest we think that there is an easy way out of the referential mania produced by the ambiguity of the mall as enclave it is as well to remember some of the limits to tactics of resistance: 'There are...inherent limits to...[the]

subversion of commodity symbolism, in that while temporarily challenging the established order of the image, it still employs the object code and is thus relatively easily coopted - radical soon becomes radical chic' (Goss, 1993: 41). Some indication of the lure and scale of the symbolic economy of retail malls is provided by the statistics quoted by Goss (1993: 18 and 42 respectively) that only time spent at home and at school or work exceeds time spent in malls and that 25 per cent of visitors to malls in the US did not purchase anything.

If 'tourism is typically divorced from the historical and political processes that determine development' (Britton, 1982: 332) then, while dependency-theory literature has been subject to important critique, it nevertheless retains a salience to understanding the enclave formation. Indeed, some aspects of the contemporary appear highly conducive to the appearance and multiplication of the enclave. For Urry (1995: 1) 'places are increasingly being restructured as centres for consumption, as providing the context within which goods and services are compared, evaluated, purchased and used'. That is, 'a country's tourist product may be easily substituted by foreign companies and tourists of that of an alternative destination' (Britton, 1982: 340). Just as the tourist gaze produces its own contradictions, so too we can consider some of the contradictions of the *policy gaze* and its democratization via the Internet and in an era of unprecedented movements of images, experts, and finance. These contradictions are the contradictions of time-space compression identified by Harvey (1991): (i) accentuation of volatility and ephemerality associated with places as commodities; (ii) instaneity and disposability of character of place-based experiences; (iii) short-termism; (iv) signs and images are the most exemplary of time-space compression, and; (vi) images often involve simulacra. In this way places as commodities have continually to be produced and reproduced by the attachment of the meanings and associations of signs and symbols. The latter aspect in particular also makes it clear that performative and affective elements are important to the in-between economy of tourism since different consumer-producer relations are apparent in enclaved and heterogenous tourism spaces (Edensor, 2000).

Studies of tourism enclaves make it clear that the local economic benefits are rarely of the scale or quality hoped for. Despite tourism having grown to be the second most important industry in Botswana by the year 2000, the prevalence of foreign ownership of tourism facilities, the repatriation of revenue, the dominance of expatriates in management positions, and the under taxation of enterprises are part of the picture in which this growth industry has failed to alleviate poverty in the Okovango delta (Mbaiwa, 2005).[8]

---

[8] The figures reported by Mbaiwa (2005) suggest that: over half of tourism enterprises in Okovango delta area were foreign owned; over 70% of tourism revenue has typically been repatriated; and that as few as 11% of tourism enterprises had been paying taxes.

Elsewhere, tourism enclaves are very much the deliberate creation of major business interests closely linked to states. One example would be the Bintan Beach International Resort on the island of Bintan opposite Singapore. This is a major enclave of 23,000 hectares covering 100 km of coastline in which several separate exclusive resorts have been developed (Bunnell, Muzaini, and Sidaway, 2006; Hampton, 2010). This tourism enclave is essentially an extension of the Singaporean economy, with 70 per cent of visitors to the island being Singaporeans and presumably many non-Singaporeans transiting through Singapore. The first resort was opened in 1994 and up to 2008 this economic zone had attracted US$800 million investment. With some backward linkages and some unanticipated spillovers to the rest of the local economy, it nevertheless exhibits most of the characteristics typical of the tourism enclave and more besides. The creation of this particular enclave entailed the forced eviction of, lack of or variable compensation paid to, and loss of livelihoods of members of, the local population (Bunnell, Muzaini, and Sidaway, 2006).

As places that are consumed every bit as much as the heterogeneity of cities, tourism enclaves are 'designed for gazing' and to stimulate consumption and desires (Edensor, 2000); they are economic spaces in which particular and often lucrative types of performance and particular types of affects are mobilized but in which these are also carefully balanced between novelty and security (both literal and of the familiar) (Britton, 1982).

City Marketing

Our lived experience is played out between apparently simultaneous processes of individualization and universalization (Miller, 2010) and these inhere in the form of the built environment itself—or what Scott (2011: 309) refers to as 'aesthetized land use intensification'—though it also runs much deeper. As Zukin (1998: 835) explains, 'most women and men live in the spaces between the images manipulated so prominently in the past 30 years by identity politics and "lifestyle magazines" and the desire to live as good a life as possible in their own neighbourhoods. Yet the diversity of their lives is often submerged by the increasing standardization of consumption spaces, even at their most spectacular.' The search for cultural capital drives the production of urban lifestyles and cultural consumption (Zukin, 1998) and strategies of redevelopment centred on a 'symbolic economy based on such abstract products as financial instruments, information and "culture"—i.e. art, food, fashion, music and tourism' (Zukin, 1998: 826). In this way 'urban cultural diversity holds a curious and yet wonderful mirror to the paradox of polarization: while cities become more like other places, they continue to attract the extremes of poor, migrant and footloose urban populations and the very rich'

(Zukin, 1998: 837), prompting Zukin (1998: 826) to ask the question; 'are populations now divided along lifestyle lines [rather] than race, ethnicity and social class?'

The proliferation of slogans in a 'slogosphere' of city branding 'are among the most "economical" forms of communication in the economy of signs' (Anttiroiko, 2014: 78). Indeed, in this connection, 'rankings provide a short cut to the symbolic battlefield of cities or . . . to the symbolic economy. We may even hypothesise that the normal aspect of competition between cities in the contemporary world relates to league tables and rankings' (Anttiroiko, 2014: 15). Before we accord too much significance to an economy of symbols in the contemporary cognitive-cultural economy, it is as well to remember that 'the image of the city does not float above the oppositional nature of society . . . it belongs at the level of group interaction and as a banner in the fight between contending social interests' (Gottdiener, 1986a: 216). In this way, 'spatial systems of signification in Late Capitalist urban environments . . . are directed by a dialectic between closed instrumental functions and open social levels of connotation' (Gottdiener, 1986a: 213). That is, 'competition exists between places over the attraction of resources but symbolic appeals alone rarely play a determining role in this process. More likely they are conjunctural mediators, working together with other, non-symbolic factors' (Gottdiener, 1986a: 209).

The interplace character of cities promoted through branding is registered in a number of respects which can be seen to engender the sort of referential mania I alluded to in the introduction to this chapter. First, the in-between nature of city marketing can be seen in its simultaneous basis in the uniqueness of place and its homogenization. City marketing 'has a tensional inner logic because . . . we should locate ourselves where the needs and desires of our target audiences take us into the symbolic space, but at the same time . . . positioning should place the city outside of the gravitational field of competitors' (Anttiroiko, 2014: 74). The fact that 'the process must be globalized in reach and understanding of the international world elites, cosmopolitan in its appeal to sophisticated observers of difference, and parochial . . . in its accurate reflection of a local sense of being and belonging' (Donald, Kofman, Kevin, 2009: 8) appears to present branding as an inherently contradictory and potentially maddening process.

Second, the spatial logic of this economy bound up with city branding revolves around processes of *re*territorialization as much as those of the *de*territorialization implied in the circulation of signs and symbols. 'The sort of "economies of signs and space" that become pervasive in the wake of organized capitalism do not just lead to increasing meaninglessness, homogenization, abstraction, anomie and the destruction of the subject. Another set of radically divergent processes is simultaneously taking place. These processes may open up possibilities for the recasting of meaning in work and leisure, for the reconstitution of community' (Lash and Urry, 1994: 3). Indeed, for Thrift, locality is key to ameliorating the excesses of the symbolic nature of consumer culture. For him, 'soft capitalism, though global in character, will still be strongly oriented to the local as organizations attempt to replace this information loss and diminish ambiguity' (Thrift, 1996: 59). In more practical terms, 'the production and reproduction of the "cosmopolitan city" involves a symbolic and material territorialization of difference, involving a "normalized" fixing in place of "acceptable" and "unacceptable" difference' (Young et al., 2006: 1689, quoted: Hatziprokopiou, 2009: 15). Ready acceptance of the pre-eminence of an economy of signs and symbols can tend to give the impression of an economy detached from its basis in material reality and nature. This is an economy of symbols which replaces an economy of signs and in which places increasingly therefore lose meaning to become placeless. However, we should not be too hasty to dismiss the sorts of new places thrown up by cultures of consumption as inauthentic.

Third, 'every inhabited place has a reputation, just as products and companies have brand images' and while 'the reputations of places tend to come about in a more complex and more random way' (Anholt, 2007: 7 and 8 respectively), city branding is contradictory in its inevitably being a partial representation of elements of a city and its culture and history by politicians and marketing professionals, on the one hand, and yet taken as a shorthand summation of that city by consumers (including counterpart policy-makers and politicians) of that place. That is, 'paradoxically it is not always clear which side of the process, sender or receiver, has the upper hand in determining the life of a brand in the long run' (Anttiroiko, 2014: 54). There is a contradiction regarding the completeness of a brand in relation to the city to which it is attached. This does not prevent policy-makers and politicians from trying to brand or sell cities as wholes, nor consumers from seeking to taste their essence. One reason for this is that 'we all navigate through the complexity of the modern world armed with a few simple clichés and they form the background of our opinions' (Anholt, 2007: 1). If 'the cultural aspect of national image is irreplaceable and uncopiable' (Anholt, 2007: 99) then nations at least have yet to travel in the imagination of consumers in quite the same way that cities appear to have done. If anything, cities appear more prone to 'travel' as wholes a result of image production within city marketing efforts ostensibly being about modifying existing images. The contemporary consumption of cities by tourists but also by policy-makers and politicians seems only to highlight how shallow such contemporary policy mobility can be to the point where 'places themselves are seen as travelling' (Urry, quoted in Kellerman, 2012: 15). Indeed, much of this superficial use of culture and history is made by economic elites in their promotion of cities and not by citizens and tourists as consumers of places in which they live or travel to (Kearns and Philo, 1993).

One reason for this is that the uniqueness of places is inevitably implicated in the lash-ups that produce stuff within GPNs (Molotch, 2004). Indeed, 'the local has more consequence because it can so vastly move out through the goods to so many other settings' (Molotch, 2004: 192) which brings us to questions of the mechanisms or modes of power by which policies travel including 'regular' business transactions or market mechanisms. It is these more than anything else perhaps that ensure that 'for something to happen, including a product, a place must forge linkages...across diverse spheres' (Molotch, 2004: 163).

However, the processes of city branding coupled with contemporary inter-urban competition have also made their own distinct contributions such that 'the functions of the city or region, or *the city or region as a whole*, must be commodified, that is, treated as a product or set of products which must be positioned' (Ashworth and Voogd, 1990: 80 and 29–30 respectively, emphasis added). Little wonder, then, that, 'design is whole-city big. Boosters now sell their cities as sculpture: places advertise themselves not in terms of their entertainments or their people's folkways, but the look and texture of their built environments' (Molotch, 2004: 212). Indeed, the symbolism of toponymy—of place names—has itself become commodified as city author-ities, institutions, and businesses seek to convert cultural or symbolic capital into money capital by selling naming rights (Light and Young, 2015). Argu-ably 'the economic dimension of naming urban places is becoming more significant owing to contemporary shifts in the political economy of cities and the development of new forms of public-private-sector collaboration' (Light and Young, 2015: 441) which have seen the exchange value of the names of streets and whole districts realized sometimes at the expense of some of the use value to residents. The revenues generated from naming rights can be significant lines of business in their own right with the leading professional football clubs in England generating in excess of £10 million per annum (Light and Young, 2015).

Moreover, the public sector is now as likely to lead as it is to follow the private sector in this process by which cultural or symbolic capital is converted into economic capital. For Pasotti (2010: 13), 'politics and markets are conver-ging in their operational logics as well as their respective relationships to voters and consumers. The basis for this convergence is that entrepreneurs in both spaces increasingly pursue their goals of consensus and profit maxi-mization by manipulating preferences and striving to shape new values and identities.' Here then, 'brand politics initiates reform by relying on the direct communication with the electorate of new values, identities, and symbols' (Pasotti, 2010: 9). Thus, for Pasotti 'subject for decades to entrenched legacies of poor government, patronage, corruption, lack of development, social conflict, and political apathy, cities have made a transition to brand politics' (Pasotti, 2010: 2). The examples of Naples, Bogota, and Chicago that Pasotti draws on 'show that mayors in cities with direct elections, weak parties, and tight fiscal constraints tend to mobilize support through the construction of brands: innovative visions of what it means to be a citizen that undermine pre-existing cleavages' (Pasotti, 2010: 227). Politics as branding ensures that cities travel as models: 'the Neapolitan example was nicknamed the Vesuvian model and was adopted throughout the South . . . Bogota's inventive approach was emulated by several Colombian cities and in particular Medallin . . . and some ideas spread as far as London' (Pasotti, 2010: 233). Brands contribute not just to the celebrity but also the velocity of places as they are mobilized (Kolb, 2008: 118).

As Cox (1995) notes, the opposition between community and capital is a false one in that some element of community is composed of capital. In similar vein, Anttiroiko's approach to the value and meaning of city branding is one instead that 'is located somewhere in the middle of the realm of business and civil society. As local government as a public hierarchy must find its own way in branding, there is an inherent interplay between ProLogo and NoLogo aspects in its endeavour' (Anttiroiko, 2014: 157). As he elaborates:

> branding at least to some extent is a reflection of institutional exchanges, calculation and competition but in today's world such a dimension simply reflects the de facto relationality associated with attraction-oriented global intercity competition. This does not imply that city branding needs to be one dimensional; it can also be a community-wide process of learning, inclusion, resource generation and self-sustainability   (Anttiroiko, 2014: 167).

The problem is that for any progressive potential, city branding can also become one focused narrowly on the opinions of elite intermediaries. Thus 'branding has a potential to help in intermediating dominant selective processes directed at small groups of target organizations and key individuals . . . This is the area in which visibility in global media, including rankings, is an important part of global city branding' (Anttiroiko, 2014: 141).

Conclusion

The proliferation of stuff challenges many of our preconceptions as economic geographers. 'once the "economy" becomes a seemingly ineluctable reality . . . capital and the struggles around it must broach the question of the domestication of all remaining social and symbolic relations . . . It is no longer capital and labor that are at stake per se, but the reproduction of the code' (Escobar, 1996: 334). Consideration of the cognitive-cultural economy—an economy between sign and symbol—takes us close to a sense of an underlying code to capitalism. However, it also takes us close as consumers and as analysts to the sort of referential mania that Nabokov sought to induce in his *Signs and Symbols*.

The economy between sign and symbol is a particularly hard middle ground to penetrate in analytical terms but also in normative terms. It is this economy of signs and symbols that best illustrates the strengths of post-modern analysis but which least lends itself to clear and unambiguous policy interventions since politics and policy pronouncements are open to infinite critique for their cultural intolerance or insensitivity.

The economic geography of the signs and symbols of the cognitive-cultural economy is one that demonstrates the complementarities that can exist between different economic geographical formations. In particular, the apparent ethereal and elusive properties of the signs and symbols mobilized by networks of intermediaries actually are often rather concretely urban—concentrated in world city agglomerations. Away from these agglomerations, possibilities for consumption in the cognitive-cultural economy produced in GPNs also touch down as specialized retail or tourism enclaves. Less familiar are the arenas which provide important locales of sorts—the institutional infrastructure—in which tournaments of value are played out. As we will see in Chapter 11, these have become a newly important part of the international economy.

11

The Non-territorial Realm of the International Economy

Introduction

In Chapter 3 I introduced the idea that the economic geographical formations that make up contemporary economies could be described in terms of agglomerations, deployments (enclaves), arenas, and networks. In the preceding chapters I dealt with some of the enduringly territorial manifestations of economic activity orchestrated at the international scale within the MNE itself, partly by the MNE and other actors within GPNs and even in the way networks of intermediaries—so important to the cognitive-cultural economy—agglomerate in world cities. In this chapter I emphasize how the fashioning of the international economy in modern times has itself entailed experimentation with distinctly new economic geographical formations—arenas—for the regulation of many aspects of business. These arenas exist as important new places of sorts in the international economy and coexist with networks of intermediaries, enclaves, and agglomerations as part of the variegated landscape of global capitalism.

The number of international organizations (IOs) and international non-governmental organizations (INGOs) has risen exponentially since the early 1900s and this alone provides a measure of the growth of global governance (Boli and Thomas, 1999) or a 'global civil society-state complex' (Carroll, 2010: 205). The growth of global governance is also, as these figures attest to, a comparatively recent phenomenon stemming initially from the end of a first global economy but coming to a much broader reach and fuller effect since the Second World War as part of a second modernity. In comparison to the networks, agglomerations, and enclaves which have been *reproduced* over time as some of the most important economic geographical formations within capitalism, arguably such *arenas now exist as ostensibly newly produced spaces of regulatory capitalism*. The logic of convocation is found in the *arenas* of various worldwide conventions that populate 'a sort of spaceless "international realm"' (Latham, 2001: 72).

Arenas constitute a new and important ingredient in what Ruggie (1993) has referred to as a non-territorial realm of the international economy. This is a realm of legal, regulatory, and policy activity that involves both the private and public sector—and indeed NGOs and civil society—with the distinctions between these different sectors at times becoming blurred. As Held and McGrew (2002: 20–1) describe, 'Many new sites of rule-making and law-making have emerged, creating a multitude of "decentred law-making processes" in various sectors of the global order...Many of these have come into existence through processes of self—validation in relation to technical standardization, professional role protection and transnational regulation of multi-national corporations, and through contracting, arbitration and other elements of *lex mercatoria* (the global framework of commercial law)' (Held and McGrew, 2002: 20–1).

In this chapter I argue that, on its own, the network metaphor again is inadequate to the task of capturing this apparently non-territorial realm of the global economy. For sure, various networks 'are of a purely bureaucratic nature but they have also become primary mechanisms through which civil society and corporate interests are effectively embedded in the global policy process' (Held and McGrew, 2002: 71). However, new arenas might also be seen as part cause and part consequence of the emergence and rationalization of the institutions of global governance that has ushered in an era of regulatory capitalism (Levi-Faur, 2005: 13) in which 'democratic governance is no longer about the delegation of authority to elected representative but a form of second-level indirect representative democracy—citizens elect representatives who control and supervise "experts" who formulate and administer policies in an autonomous fashion from their regulatory bastions'. Regulatory expansion has acquired a life and dynamic if its own—the policy-making process has itself become more roundabout in nature as we saw in the case of urban policy mobility in Chapter 7. Here, then, communities of experts help to mediate economic relations in the international economy and they do so as much in arenas as they do in networks.

The concept of the arena and its associated logic of convocation is an important addition to our vocabulary alongside the metaphors of the network and the enclave and agglomeration. This is not least because 'the rise of the modern corporation has been paralleled by an extraordinary rise in the activities and pretensions of the modern nation-state' (Barnet and Muller, 1974: 74). Some of these pretensions have seen the creation of an array of specialist arenas as part of the very supranational organizations that appear to undermine the nation state. These supranational organizations and the decision-making and regulatory arenas associated with them might appear distinctly cosmopolitan in complexion. However, it would be a mistake to see them as harbingers of a post-Westphalian system of transnational economic regulation let alone cosmopolitan democracy (Held, 1995). As with a nascent transnational capitalist class (Sklair, 2001), they remain only partially detached from distinctly national economic interests.

Laws are defined and interpreted, policy discussions held and decisions adopted in important arenas. These are periodic meetings held under the auspices of organizations and institutions in particular places; sometimes the same place on a regular basis, sometimes peripatetically in different places but under largely the same rules and procedures. These events and the arenas in which the likes of the law regarding international investment takes shape are perhaps more similar to the 'temporary clusters' that Maskell, Bathelt, and Malmberg (2006) see as comprised of the conferences, exhibitions and trade fairs that form part of the relational economic geography of 'buzz in global pipelines'. Not only is the international economy stitched together—like a patchwork quilt—by treaties and legal agreements that are of various extents in territorial coverage, it is designed, promoted, regulated, and adjudicated through a complex mixture of professional networks operating in and through notable arenas. That is, the non- territorial realm of the international economy is hardly that at all. It remains in important respects partially territorialized including around the nation state but also in the interplaces that are the arenas in which so much of international economy is decided upon.

The Non-terrritorial Realm

Interestingly, the implications of what Ruggie from an international relations and international political economy perspective refers to as the non-territorial realm of the international economy have barely been touched upon by international business scholars. Extant frameworks within international business have set discussion of evolution in MNE subsidiary roles and capabilities with reference to only parent company, subsidiary, and host territory forces shaping such evolution stressed in a seminal contribution of Birkinshaw and Hood (1998). Yet regulatory activity and processes of international economic integration and their ramifications in terms of the character FDI and MNE subsidiary capabilities can hardly be understood without reference to Ruggie's non-territorial realm of the international economy—a realm that exists beyond and encompasses the environment represented by individual nations. Important extant theoretical frameworks (Birkinshaw and Hood, 1998) leave the two-tier parent–subsidiary relationship without a logical counterpart in terms of a parallel (if extremely messy) two-tiered environment external to the MNE. Here it is also important to understand the emergence of this non-territorial realm from the perspective of nation states, which continue to project and share power within what has been characterized as a multi-polar system (Djelic and Sahlin-Andersson, 2006; Morgan, 2009).

The Projection and Sharing of Authority in Enclaves

State extra-territoriality has a long and generally only dimly appreciated history in shaping the character of MNEs and their FDI. It is as well to remember at least two ingredients of this history. First, this history is one in which the roles of early MNEs and states in shaping global business regulation were barely distinguishable (Bayly, 2000; Jones, 2005). The earliest overseas trade organization even preceded the trading companies that were to form the first multinationals. The Company of the Merchants of Staple, for example, was created in the fourteenth century to help replenish the royal treasury and gradually shared some element of economic and political power with the Crown (Barnet and Muller, 1974: 72). Moreover, much of the present reshaping of the international investment regime—including significant modifications to the approach of capital exporting nations such as the US—is closely associated with the state-linked or sovereign character of FDI emanating from the new FDI origin countries (Sauvant and Alvarez, 2011).

Second, the coupling of nation and state as the primary jurisdictional 'container' and regulator of economic activity from the Treaty of Westphalia *preceded* the rise of capitalism. As such, 'competition in the world market is not directly between individual capitals, but is mediated by state boundaries . . . this enables the state to organise the external projection of national class interests through foreign policy, diplomacy and military force' (Lacher, 2005: 39). State strategies of extra-territoriality in this respect point to the present tendency towards 'the willingness of states to share authority in the face of environmental, economic, and social problems that go well beyond their individual capacity to manage on their own' (Agnew, 2009: 111–12).

One can argue that the real purchase of this projection and sharing of sovereignty on economic processes—including flows of trade and investment—might be thought of as deriving specifically from its *territoriality*. Indeed, there is a paradox of globalization in that rampant economic liberalization and space-time compression have eroded borders, on the one hand, and yet at the same time jurisdiction as a resource has been used to create space by engineering 'inner space' within national territories (Baldacchino, 2010: 138), on the other hand. Thus, 'the contemporary world has a staggering number of "jurisdictional enclaves" which occupy the fuzzy middle ground between full sovereignty and conventional municipality' (Baldacchino, 2010: 19).

These exceptional territorial manifestations of regulation in the non-territorial realm of the international economy have been around since the process by which nation states were formed. Their history dates to the numerous 'accidental' enclaves and exclaves left as national borders began to be defined. They are also seen in deliberately created enclaves dating to the likes of the bunds of treaty ports (Taylor, 2002) but most recently in the likes of Free Ports (Wang and Olivier, 2006), Export Processing Zones, Tax Havens (Hudson, 2000) or Zones of Economic Integration (such as the Indonesia-Malaysia-Singapore-Growth Triangle IMS-GT), which are delimited territories within or across national territories. They are both territory as anachronism and territory as a powerful new 'abstract expression of the collective effects of the state, corporate, and business elites of the world to avoid the very laws and regulations that they have collectively designed' (Palan, Murphy, and Chavagneux, 2010: 6).

For Palan, Murphy, and Chavagneux (2010: 19) globalization actually works in and through a modest number of financial service enclaves or Tax Havens which are 'merely another type of economic speciality promoted by states'. Tax havens might be seen as differential space produced for and suited to the needs of particular branches of capital. They estimate there are between 46 and 60 active such tax havens worldwide and that these Tax Havens are home to around two million international business companies, with nearly one-third of the world stock of FDI and one half of all bank lending registered in them (Palan, Murphy, and Chavagneux, 2010: 5). As such 'tax havens are among the most significant, if persistently overlooked, structural factors that are determining the distribution of the benefits and costs of globalization among the world's peoples' (Palan, Murphy, and Chavagneux, 2010: 7). As enclaves which articulate global flows of finance they are nevertheless the products of the nation state system; they are the in-between by-products of the territoriality of nation states and an inter-national system in which territory, sovereignty, and the legality of business are not synonymous. The proliferation of sovereign states has brought with it unintended cracks and loopholes relating to the regulation and taxation of business entities. More particularly it is the proliferation of new sovereign territories with the breakup of the British, Dutch, and French empires that is closely associated with the growth of tax Havens (Palan, Murphy, and Chavagneux, 2010: 141).

In this respect island states and protectorates are especially well suited to exploiting their physical or temporal 'inbetweenity' or 'in betweenness'. For Baldacchino (2010: 141) 'in a world of multi-level governance, islands continue to serve as epitomes of offshoring; they embody how economies can strategically reconfigure intimate relationships *between* identity, function, and location' (Baldacchino, 2010: 141, emphasis added). Here, then, 'island entrepôts have acted as magnets for significant incoming and circulating population movements and diversity; they are also well placed to exploit their "in betweenity" in another manner: to accumulate fiscal, human, and material capital for development' (Baldacchino, 2010: 170).

Enclaves have developed around some curious niche markets besides high finance. One such is Geneva Freeport which exists as 'a massive high-spec warehouse of treasure' (Bonnett, 2014: 162) such as fine art, rare wine, cigars, and the like. Originally established in 1888 it has gradually acquired this niche role to house a value of art alone that is estimated at $100 billion. It exists then as 'the world's central repository for a new kind of global investment system based on the buying and selling of objects of high value' (Bonnett, 2014: 162–3) even though it now has spawned similar such Freeports in Singapore and Beijing. Moreover, 'the trajectory towards ever more storage-housing challenges the idea that ours is an age of the virtual; an era in which real objects are increasingly irrelevant' (Bonnett, 2014: 164–5). It also actually puts a rather different gloss on the geography of the cognitive-cultural economy discussed in Chapter 10. Although urban, these art objects remain sequestered barely seeing the urban light of day—locked instead in 'offshore' tax-free limbo somewhere between buyer and seller.

At larger geographic scales, the spatially delimited nature of formal government-to-government agreements can also be seen in the form of bilateral investment treaties (BITs) and free trade agreements. BITs have proliferated significantly in recent decades (Elkins, Guzman, and Simmons, 2006). They effectively *envelop* or join the territories of two or more nation states. These are not enclaves or exclaves carved out of national territories but rather hint at a formation of spaces that are beyond the analytical framework and scope of this book. One way of interpreting the emergence of these greater-than-national territorial envelopes is to recall that the division of labour and external economy effects that drive urban agglomeration now are often generated by markets that are larger than those represented by the largest world cities and in recent decades by markets that are larger than all but the most populous nations. Moreover, international organizations, western states, and networks of legal professionals have played an important role in the bounded rationality apparent in the rapid and widespread adoption of these BITs by enhancing the availability of 'short, predefined, and simple treaty texts' despite the potential liabilities for and their provisions contradicting important constitutional and other aims of developing countries (Poulsen, 2014: 5).

Regional integration agreements have also proliferated in the post-war era. Their formation and deepening clearly has, to varying degrees, shaped the geography of economic transactions of all sorts and the organization of production. Indeed, for a while literature spoke to the apparent regionalization of the world economy and associated international relations and public policy formation. However, the strong sense of a world partitioned into self-contained regional blocs has receded somewhat in favour of the view of porous regions and moreover regions still noticeably within the orbit of an American Imperium (Katzenstein, 2005).

The Networks and Arenas of the International Economy

Notwithstanding the observations made above regarding the enduring territoriality of the apparently non-territorial regulatory realm of the global economy, networks, and arenas have become an increasingly important channel through which states can exert their interests and authority extra-territorially, though necessarily in less individualistic and uni-vocal terms than associated with the enclaves of MNE deployments. One important development has been the rise of regulatory and policy activity affecting economic activities within a non-territorial (Ruggie, 1993) or transnational (Djelic and Sahlin-Andersson, 2006; Morgan, 2009) sphere of the international economy.

For Ramamurti (2001), legal and regulatory activity in this non-territorial sphere is sufficiently important and hierarchical in nature for it to have resulted in an upper tier (tier-1) of bargaining processes distinct from an extant lower tier (tier-2) of one-to-one bargaining processes between individual MNEs and their subsidiaries and individual host territory governments. As Ramamurti (2001: 24) explains it, 'the industrialized countries have used tier-1 bargaining to weaken the hand of host governments in tier-2 bargaining while strengthening that of their MNCs . . . and have been more successful at doing this in some countries and sectors than others'.

However, for others, this transnational regulatory sphere of the international economy is one that is noticeably multipolar (Djelic and Sahlin-Andersson, 2006) and one in which 'as states form coalitions and constellations beyond their territories; as they increasingly rely on neutralized discursive references to expertise and science, they may gain in the process significant leverage both over local constituencies and in transnational arenas' (Djelic and Sahlin-Andersson, 2006: 379). Both MNEs and nation states have actively fashioned this transnational sphere of the international economy, which is one that 'implies a more open-ended set of cross-border connections . . . in which the forms of interaction become more than simply the source of interactions between different "national" units: it constitutes a social space *sui generis* that cannot be reduced to the interplay of pre-existing national groups or interests' (Morgan, 2001: 115). This is a picture of states as autonomous yet embedded, as regulated as much their being regulators and as coherent and yet also fragmented institutions. However, while the landscape of globalization may involve a multiplicity of actors, the steady growth in the degree of its organization and scientization (Boli and Thomas, 1999; Drori and Meyer, 2006; Meyer et al., 1997) also suggests that behind this diversity lies a strong measure of convergence. In this respect, transnational arenas of governance are 'highly constrained and constraining... with an intense surface activity that tends to generate and reproduce order behind an appearance of complexity and competition' (Djelic and Sahlin-Andersson, 2006: 391).

This multipolar non-territorial realm actually exists, then, in the form of two rather different logics of transnational interaction—those associated with networks and arenas (Latham, 2001).[1] The logic of transnationalism within networks of experts involved with various aspects of policy and regulation impinging on FDI is one of *interaction* through which there is the transmission of norms and principles. The examples of the international investment, regulation, arbitration, and promotion communities considered later in the chapter are relevant here as they highlight the role of networks of experts in mediating global economic relations. In particular, 'states are increasingly subjected to numerous forms of regulative, inquisitive and mediative activities... As a consequence, states can be seen less as autonomous rule-making organizations than as organizations deeply embedded in their environments and scripted by wider systems of rules and ideas' (Jacobsson, 2006: 205).

Jacobsson describes inquisitive activities as those involved with the auditing and ranking of states and territories which can themselves lead inadvertently to the making of new rules and standards. Many of these inquisitive activities are carried out by networks of experts but also are closely associated with particular regulatory arenas in which the activities of states are discussed and compared and where ideas are generated and shared. Here, 'the idea that indicators and other quantitative ways of representing social phenomena can serve as technologies of governance has distinctive implications for the topology of global governance' (Davis, Kingsbury, and Merry, 2012a: 9). To the extent that the promulgation of such indexes represents a deepening of the activities composing a non-territorial or transnational realm of the global economy, then, it serves to underline the relatively recent rise of such a realm. That is, 'the rapid growth in prominent indicators in global governance is a time compressed phenomenon' (Davis, Kingsbury, and Merry, 2012a: 15). One recent account found a total of 95 major international rankings, ratings, and indexes across a number of issue areas, 17 of which covered business and economics (Cooley, 2015). The investment regulatory, arbitration, and promotion communities provide good examples of these mediative and inquisitive activities, which impinge on questions of sovereignty with regard to outward and inward FDI. In the case of investment promotion and the benchmarking and ranking of investment environments, for example, there is

---

[1] As Latham (2001) notes, the distinction between networks and arenas is not always clear—partly, as we might note with regard to our examples above, because key individuals are present in both types of transnational formations.

evidence that states and territorial bodies are intensely aware of, and indeed deliberately try to shape, these inquisitive activities (Schueth, 2011).

Arenas would be represented by the numerous but periodic and partly nomadic rounds of trade, intellectual property, and FDI regulatory meetings and negotiations and their logic is one of *convocation*. Linnros and Hallin (2001) are among the very few who have distinguished arenas as organizing principles in this way. They are concerned with the manner in which environmental politics has been played out in a number of formal and informal discursive arenas. Their discussion makes it clear that such arenas are hardly placeless since, in the form of courts of law or public spaces such as squares, such arenas are *of* places but not *in* place. In Linnros and Hallin's terms I am concerned with formal arenas. On the one hand, the word 'global' hardly denotes many true instances in which arenas are inclusive and planetary-wide in the discourses and regulation they channel. On the other hand, this non-territorial realm of arenas is not quite as non-territorial or *placeless* as it might seem. It might be said that the meetings that take place in such regulatory arenas occur in particular places but not of any place in particular. That is they take place for a limited duration at various venues of policy boards, IOs, and INGOs under the procedures of these institutions and organizations, sometimes in the same places, sometimes rotating nomadically among a series of venues.

The arenas that compose part of the transnational sphere of the global economy represent important new places in which the interests of a transnational capitalist class (TCC) are present, 'given the persistence of national corporate networks, we might say that the articulation of a transnational capitalist interest requires sites beyond the boardrooms—places where business leaders can come together' (Carroll, 2010: 37). Trade fairs and business conventions are another and longer-standing way for business leaders to come together. These might be assumed to be trivial arenas were it not for the fact that these 'temporary clusters' are interplaces with potentially important knowledge exchange functions (Bathelt and Glückler, 2011).

Beyond these arenas 'routinely' constituted from commerce are the sorts of international business policy-boards that Carroll focuses on as well as the sorts of law-making and regulatory arenas that significantly shape and structure international trade, investment and knowledge flows. These include the likes of the World Economic Forum (WEF), the World Business Council for Sustainable Development and they provide another very much private sector-initiated and organized set of arenas in the scheme presented in Chapter 3. More often than not, the scope and character of the work of these policy-boards has evolved over time, to incorporate representation from the likes of civil society groups and NGOs and has also produced counter-movements such as the World Social Forum counterpart to the World Economic Forum (WEF).

The organization and specialist activity of some of the largest IOs—the likes of the World Trade Organization (WTO), the United Nations (UN), the International Monetary Fund (IMF), the World Bank (EB), the Organization for Economic Cooperation and Development (OECD)—provide the prime examples of arenas that have rapidly become an increasingly important force regulating all aspects of global economic relations. So much so, that these same organizations are open to criticism for the particular interests that appear to belie their supposed autonomy and neutrality in economic affairs within an international interstate system. Thus as Peet (2003: 198) observes, 'even more than an institution, the WTO is a place, or a restricted discursive space, where intergovernmental meetings occur, experts congregate, expertise is employed, and decisions are made within a common understanding expressed in a specific, political-economic language'. One aspect of the work of the WTO is the arbitration of investment disputes under the International Court of Settlement of Investment Disputes (ICSID) to which I return later in this chapter as one very important international arena.

Investment Promotion Communities of Interest at Work

As we saw in Chapter 10, investment promotion has emerged as an important part of the branding of places as part of a cognitive cultural economy and is registered in the growing number of IPAs that seek to mobilize FDI flows. Site selection/investment promotion intermediaries stand at the heart of a process of location, relocation, and expansions and contractions and rationalizations that is charged with enormous symbolic content; the symbolic meaning of the investments themselves and the value of a presence in a particular territory to corporate and place images as well as the bottom line of corporate profits or gains in the welfare of communities. By turns, cities, regions, and nations have sought in the 1960s and 1970s to attract 'blue chip' MNEs, large flagship FDI projects in the 1990s and perhaps more recently 'green tech' or other sectors for what they confer on their image.

Mediating the Market for Location: Site Selection Consultants as Intermediaries

I place these intermediaries at the centre of Figure 11.1, not because they are the most quantitatively important among the economic actors and industries included but because they are the most centrally concerned with the location decision itself. Looking beyond the narrow core of site selection consultants at the centre of Figure 11.1, it is also clear that the boundaries with very closely related business activities are not especially clear. The boundaries of this

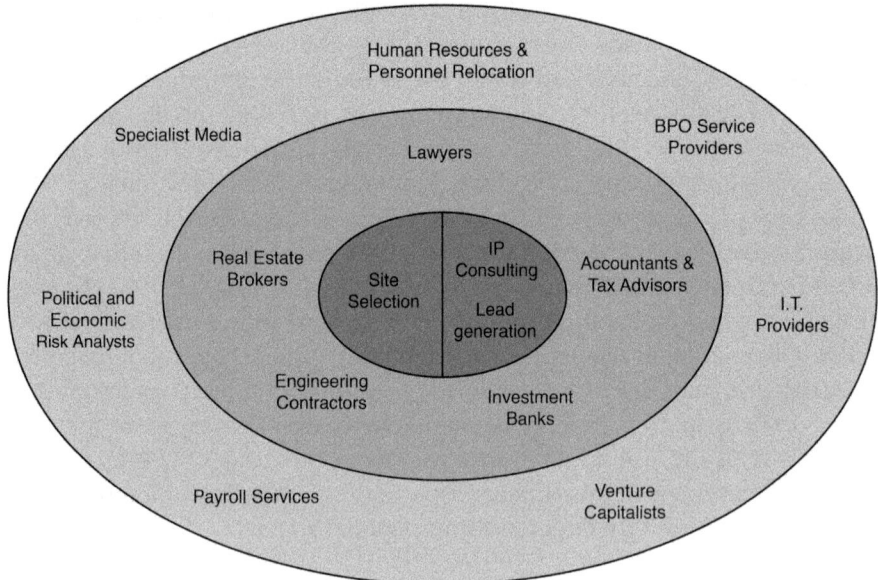

Figure 11.1 The site selection 'industry'

'industry' are, then, quite porous as companies diversify into and out of investment promotion activities from core businesses in human resources and personnel relocation consulting, plant and construction engineering contractors, real estate brokerage, and the like. Presently, for example, and despite outsourcing and offshoring being logically separate, widespread preferences among client multinationals for the outsourcing of certain functions and business activities have seen companies in ICT service and the business process outsourcing (BPO) industries begin to offer location search services as part of their services to clients. In Figure 11.1 therefore I depict the relationship of the core of investment promotion consulting activities as being surrounded by layers of more or less closely related activities.

The private-sector companies involved are also very diverse, ranging from specialized, one- person investment promotion consultants to giant accounting and management consulting multinational enterprises (MNEs) who offer a full service to investors and of course organizations that sit somewhere in between. As a result of the diversity within the private-sector investment promotion industry and its surrounding supportive industry contexts, the money to be made out of the industry surrounding FDI is derived in rather different ways (such as arbitrage, by time involved or flat-rate fees for standard discrete services).

There are several reasons as to why the industry of site selection and investment promotion experts are probably best considered as a loose network of intermediaries. First there are no real professional credentials that mark out coherent occupation and industry boundaries. Only recently in 2010, for instance, has a Site Selectors Guild been created in the United States precisely in order to establish a set of credentials of true site selection consultants.[2] Second, site selection and investment promotion consultants can hardly be considered an established industry.[3] Third, as I noted above, there is considerable mobility of individuals across established industry divides and public and private sectors. Fourth, at the international scale a sense of professional/ occupational identity is secured, not through professional associations, but through recurrent events such as conferences (such as those organized by the World Association of Investment Promotion Agencies (WAIPA) and Red Hot Locations) and technical assistance workshops (funded and organized by UNCTAD and UNIDO); Internet tools (such as FDI Exchange), and; to some extent continental or sub-continental networks of IPAs.

Earlier in Chapter 3, following the information economics perspective of Casson, I introduced a number of roles that market intermediaries perform. The role of site selection consultants is usually one in which the primary role is viewed—rather narrowly as it happens—as one of reducing the search costs of finding a location. Elsewhere (Phelps and Wood, forthcoming) with Andy Wood I have detailed how the role of site selection consultants is more than one of merely helping clients economize on search costs. Our findings are summarized in Table 11.1. Their role extends into the negotiation, specification, and enforcement of contracts in such a way as to positively add value—including through the entrepreneurial process itself—and create markets for MNEs through the location decision.

Site selection experts play an indirect role in enforcement of the business climate. The use of indexes to measure and compare different aspects of the business environment at the scale of nations and subnational territories has burgeoned in such a way that they are now seen to be a technology of global governance and exert a distinct influence on the forms, the exercise and distributions of power within particular issue areas within networks of global governance (Davis, Kingsbury, and Merry, 2012a,b). Indeed, *the* pioneering site selecting consultant firm—Fantus Factory Locating Service—also pioneered the use of indexes; offering from the 1950s its business climate index

---

[2] See www.siteselectorsguild.com.

[3] Site selection is included as one activity under the six-digit heading 541611 'Administrative Management and General Management Consulting Services' in the North American Industrial Classification System (NAICS, 2012) classification as part of 'Professional Scientific and Technical Services' (sector 54) (see http://www.census.gov/eos/www/naics/). However, it does not receive specific mention in the Nomenclature statistique des activités économiques dans la Communauté Européenne (NACE, 2008) classification (see http://ec.europa.eu/eurostat/ramon/nomenclatures/index.cfm?TargetUrl=LST_NOM_DTL&StrNom=NACE_REV2&StrLanguageCode=EN&IntPcKey=&StrLayoutCode=HIERARCHIC).

Table 11.1 The role of site selection consultants as bearers of information costs

Search	Specification	Negotiation	Completion	Enforcement
Tangible: collation and analysis of quantitative information	Integration: overcoming of disciplinary fragmentation in business case	Negotiation of incentives	No significant role	Indirect: communication of investment promotion 'best practice'
Tangible: site certification	Recognizing and realizing location as a focusing prism of business strategy			Indirect: production of proprietary rankings or indexes
Intangible: experience used in the interpretation of qualitative information				

as an aid to the location decision. More recently, indexes such as the *Doing Business* Index of the World Bank have come to be viewed as sufficiently important in terms of their influence on the perceptions of investors that they have been targeted specifically by the institutions of prospective host territories (Schueth, 2011).

It seems clear that this industry leverages location or place to add value to corporations. However, the industry's contribution to the net welfare of these same communities and places is less clear—since their involvement in the likes of negotiations for incentives and in indirectly enforcing a measure of behaviour among territorial organizations with regard to investors is open to significant criticism for unnecessarily raising the incentives on offer to investors or disciplining communities and conditioning investors to the sort of weak forms of competition discussed in Chapter 7.

Selling Location: The Geoeconomics of Investment Promotion

A 'continuing bias towards reordering imposed by the big states—new or old—should not hide the impact that small states have in rethinking and reconfiguring practices of diplomacy. What small states lack in structural clout they can make up through creative agency' (Cooper and Shaw, 2009: 2). Indeed, 'the so-called "small state" is the typical state size (as it has also been for most of recorded history)' (Baldacchino, 2009: 23). Moreover, as Baldacchino goes on to note, small states are most likely to be successful in creative diplomatic adventures in the issue area of financial or economic matters. Thus, 'resilience as motif has replaced vulnerability in a few small states, especially "developmental island states" such as Mauritius and Trinidad and Tobago. These states take their cues from other small developmental states such as Singapore . . . as well as Iceland and Ireland' (Cooper and Shaw, 2009: 6–7).

The mention of economic issues and of Ireland and Singapore is significant in this respect as these two states have had what are regarded as the two most effective investment promotion agencies (IPAs). Indeed, although the growth, status, and organization of IPAs is a subject in itself that I do not digress upon here, the significant growth of promotional activity in the public sector—the supply side of what has been termed the market for capital (Thomas, 2000) or the market for social order (Bornschier and Trezzini, 2001)—no doubt continues to fuel the growth of the private sector investment promotion industry itself as a result of the revolving door alluded to above.[4] Such 'investment promotion agencies have become a fully institutionalized element of the world polity' (O'Riain, 2005: 75). Moreover, IPAs are examples of territorial agencies that nevertheless are often highly internationalized (Paul, 2002) by virtue of their networks of overseas offices. The largest of these networks of overseas offices are maintained by national IPAs in OECD countries with an average of seven overseas representations (UNCTAD, 2001: 8) while only a third of sub-Saharan African IPAs had an overseas office.

The network nature of the organization of investment promotion professionals has begun to extend to the way in which territorial organizations such as IPAs are just beginning to promote their territories beyond national jurisdictions. Such thinking is, however, in its infancy. In reality, then, few nation states have recognized this role and those that have been most successful in this regard have been small nation states. One reason for the unique success of Singapore's EDB and Ireland's IDA in this respect might be found in the thought that 'a place that is not territorial, can survive only by turning extra-territoriality into an asset. Such places rely heavily on intelligence instead of conventional factors of production' (Murphy, 2010a: 27). In this way 'extra-territorial places become an asset by virtue of the fact that they provide attractive gateways for trading, exchanges, and contacts' (Murphy, 2010a: 27).

The IDA has been active in mobilizing the Irish diaspora of MNE executives and investment promotion professionals in both promoting new FDI to

---

[4] Although the number of national and subnational IPAs has expanded greatly in the past two decades, there are few reliable estimates of just how many now exist. Moreover, their status and organization vary enormously. Some are arms of government; some are separate though nonetheless public entities; others are quasi-public and some fully private entities charged with promotion of the national territory to investors. The internal organization and effectiveness of such IPAs also vary enormously. Sometimes promotional activities are separated from regulatory activities (such as the issue of licences) and sometimes not. Some are able to perform a very strong advocacy and policy formation role within their respective governmental machineries while others are irrelevant or ineffectual in such terms.

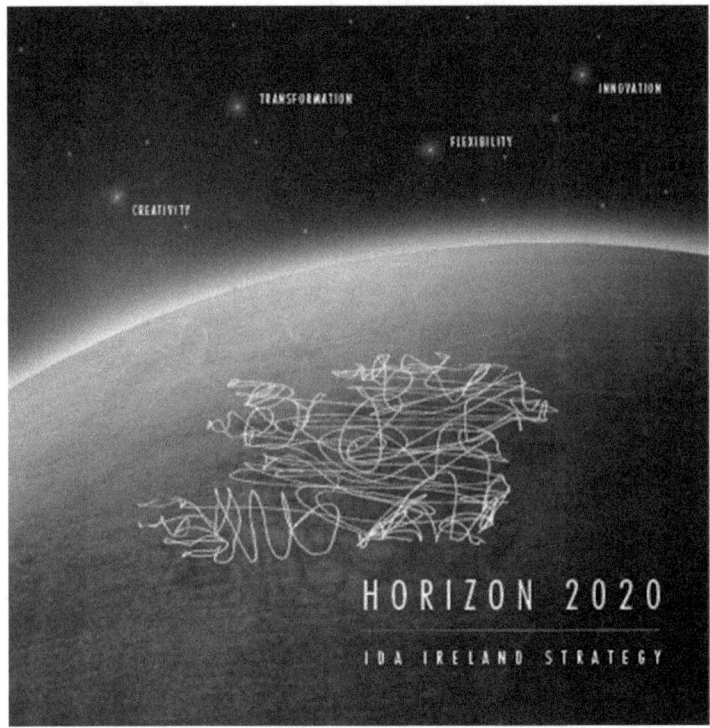

Figure 11.2 The imagery of the IDA's Horizon 2020
Source: reproduced with permission from IDA.

Ireland but also in securing in-situ upgrading of MNE subsidiary operations (O'Riain, 2005). The imagery of the IDAs former Horizon 2020 strategy document (Figure 11.2) appears to draw on the network metaphor while recent thinking takes this principle further—exhorting all fractions of the Irish diaspora to help promote FDI into the Irish economy. Here, then, the 'combination of its embeddedness in the most powerful fraction of capital in the Irish economy and its position of "autonomy with influence" within the Irish state made the IDA a potent force within the Irish industrialization policy regime and an effective competitor in the market for mobile investment' (O'Riain, 2005: 155–6).

For Singapore the deployment of 'soft power was a choice, not an inheritance' and forged out of an 'intermestic' condition of the domestic government having been forced into reacting to and anticipating international trends (Chong, 2009: 67). Singapore has used several channels to think extraterritorially (Phelps, 2007). It has sought to mobilize the diaspora connections that have resulted in its peculiar colonially produced domestic ethnic mix. Just as significantly, a series of overseas industry and technology parks have been developed through government-to-government agreements in Indonesia, Vietnam, China, and India as a means of providing a little piece of Singapore abroad and a place to which the orderly offshore movement of manufacturing activities can be organized retaining important effects on knowledge-intensive production possibilities at home. These industry parks offer both infrastructure hardware and administrative software of Singapore in an overseas environment via unique government to government agreements. Some of these parks—as in the case of Batamindo on the Indonesian island of Batam just 45 minutes' boat ride from Singapore—have achieved notable success and promoted the development of other industry parks and the wider industrialization and urbanization of a largely uninhabited island (Phelps, 2004b). Others in China, where the expectation was to leverage on Chinese diaspora connections and cultural similarities between Singapore and Chinese business systems, have been less successful (Phelps, 2007; Yeung, 2000).[5] In the case of Suzhou (see Figure 11.3), the jointly owned and administered park has remained exceptional in the China context despite the many visitations from park authorities elsewhere in China.

If Singapore and Ireland offer 'model' agencies in some respects, the IPAs of developing countries with more challenging propositions for FDI have also sought to mobilize diaspora communities. Here the expatriate communities that compose diasporas often have strong identification with their homeland that can be mobilized, though there is little in the way of an accepted understanding of how this can be done or indeed the results. The thinking here is that 'perceptions of ethnic advantage and altruistic feelings of homeland duty and obligation may motivate diaspora members' homeland investment interest even in the face of political and economic risk' (Riddle, Brinkerhoff, and Nielsen, 2008: 55) with the cases reported being Afghanistan, Ghana, and the Dominican Republic. As the same authors note, diasporas can play a catalytic role in creating home-grown MNEs since 'diasporas can play important intermediary roles between potential investors and homeland markets, either as interlocutors between cultures and/or as honest brokers who can facilitate trust' (Riddle, Brinkerhoff, and Nielsen, 2008: 55).

Singapore in particular also appears to have provided something of a model for China in the organized use of overseas industry parks and zones. Here, then, 'Beijing's use of economic statecraft reflects the internationalization of the developmental state, a process already well advanced among other East Asian nations' (Brautigam and Tang, 2012: 816). Thus 'it is important to note

---

[5] The overt mobilization of diaspora communities by Singaporean and Irish authorities only serves to underline what could be regarded—following Appadurai (1996) as the 'ethnoscapes' of modernity; the international flows and reverse flows of 'new Argonaut' high skilled labour that have to an extent underpinned the growth of different national and subnational economies (Saxenian, 2007).

Figure 11.3 Suzhou Industrial Park administration building
Source: author's photograph.

that, although it was once reasonable to talk of work being predominantly offshored "eastwards" from the "west"...There are now many patterns of offshoring, the most striking being movement of investment and employment from China to various other countries' (Urry, 2014: 39). A spread of 19 overseas industrial zones formally recognized by the Chinese government as of 2016 have been framed as part of a high visibility 'soft power' package of pledges, though these zones are generally company rather than government led developments (Brautigam and Tan, 2012: 810). These overseas enclaves or zones help raise production possibilities and promote structural transformation of the domestic economy while also projecting a measure of soft power—most notably in Africa (7 of the 19 zones are in African countries).

The View From Nowhere? The Arenas of the International Economy

Some arenas have struggled to gain the importance once envisaged for them by groups of national governments. The International Labour Organization (ILO) would be a case in point (Braithwaite and Drahos, 2000: 233). Similarly, the United Nations' Conference on Trade and Development (UNCTAD) had to struggle for recognition as an institution for negotiating trading rules and principles because GATT already existed. Eventually UNCTAD and UNIDO (United Nations Industrial Development Organization) carved out a role for themselves surrounding developing country interests in the likes of technology transfer and helped to change the balance of power between states during the 1970s (UNCTAD, 1985) though their outlook actually has converged with other major IOs such the IMF and WB since this time.

The organizational networks created by the planning movement during this first global economy and up to its demise as discussed in Chapter 7 were remarkably resilient 'in their capacity to transcend national boundaries, these networks, the literature they produced and the specific discursive events they organised were important media for the creation of a global epistemology of planning' (Ward, 2005: 136). The events of which Ward speaks have, if anything, become more systematized in the post war era under the auspices of the likes of the UN Habitat, which has itself also done much to publicize various city and planning models. Eugene McCann (2011: 119) notes how the World Urban Forum organized by UN Habitat in Vancouver in 2006 had 9,600 delegates from 100 countries and was perceived by the organizers as a node or 'globalized microspace'. Such periodic meetings are a complementary economic geographical formation to the professional networks that organize them. They are key 'relational sites' as McCann (2011) terms them and decisions on how and where to hold such meetings have implications for attendees, organizers, and host economies.

Indeed, the UN Habitat itself speaks specifically of policy arenas in relation to urban planning. Policy arenas are defined as:

> the institutional sites where members of policy communities come together to develop ideas and actions for urban futures. They act as nodal points for stakeholders and are places where critical decisions are made. Sometimes, they are fixed in time and space and are formally defined by planning rules, or they may be fluid and *ad hoc*. Such arenas may be a local council chamber, the office of a planning authority, a law court, a semi-judicial enquiry process, an informal community development group, or a business association. Such arenas occur at various locations and over time—for example, at different levels of formal government and/or in less formal *ad hoc* arrangements between key stakeholders
> (UN Habitat, 2009: 89).

However, as the same report goes on to note, even though orchestrated ostensibly by public bodies and officials and in the name of public policy and the public interest, such arenas are often characterized by inequalities of access. 'First, the more "open-access" arenas become segmented off from the main nodes for urban policy development.... Second, the agenda is set by the public sector and the participants are "the usual suspects" (i.e. the same group of people appearing in different arenas in slightly different combinations and compositions)'. Participation of any 'outside' stakeholders is marginal and policy is made, often behind closed doors, by a small, yet powerful, group of government officials and a few large businesses. Such marginalization of informal forums and their late inclusion in the process leads to a sense of democratic deficit and distance between governments and citizens in urban policy processes (UN Habitat, 2009: 90).

Other arenas have emerged from ostensibly private sector roots and from serving very particular private interests and issue areas to become extremely important shapers of global economic relations. Of note are organizations such as the World Economic Forum (WEF), which, as a new and influential arena, is essentially a delimited affair of heavily guarded invite-only delegates in meetings held each year in the Swiss ski resort of Davos. The exclusivity of the WEF as a new arena has nevertheless prompted the formation of the World Social Forum (WSF) in response.[6] I am less concerned in this book and in this chapter with the arena as a more open forum for discussion (see Chapter 3), though it is clear that the inclusive agendas of the likes of the WSF can entail arenas that, being city-wide, take on some of the properties of agglomerations; the city of Porto Alegre in Brazil (see Chapter 7) has become the spiritual home of the WSF. 'Porto Alegre has come to be seen . . . as a kind of anti-Davos, a paradoxical capital of the global justice movement, which as a "network of networks" of course eschews the very notion of coordinated control or hierarchical power' (Peck and Theodore, 2015: 147). As Peck and Theodore (2015: 147 and 182) go on to explain 'Porto Alegre was instead an open space of exchange and debate for the sprawling ecology of progressive networks'—the city as a whole is recovered as an arena with all of its carnival and chaos.

Most troubling of all may be those arenas related to the arbitration of international investment disputes and the regulation of trade related invest-ment measures (TRIMs) and trade related intellectual property (TRIPs) in which private-sector interests are overwhelmingly dominant. The develop-ment of the TRIPs provision of the WTO in 1994 was promoted by an ad hoc US business-centred grouping of the Intellectual Property Committee begun at the initiative of Pfizer and IBM. In this instance, 'In effect, twelve corporations made public law for the world' (Sell, 2003: 96, quoted in Kobrin, 2009: 355) having identified a trade issue and formulated and promoted a solution.

---

[6] At its formation in 2000 the World Social Forum declared that it is a 'plural, diversified, non-confessional, nongovernmental and non-party context that, in a decentralized fashion, interrelates organizations and movements engaged in concrete action at levels from the local to the international in order to build another world' (quoted in Peck and Theodore, 2015).

In sum, these specialized and delimited arenas are significant new elements in the non-territorial realm of the international economy. These interplaces are deserving of greater scrutiny within economic geography.

International Investment Arbitration

The networks and arenas of international investment arbitration have emerged as ones through and in which conflicting principles regarding the treatment of FDI and the balance of interests between states and MNEs are played out. On the one hand, 'international commercial arbitration is partly an epistemic community or issue network, but it is also an extremely competitive market involving big business' (Dezalay and Garth, 1996: 16). As such, lawyers involved in international investment arbitration appear as intermediaries. 'Located at the intersection of the world of business and that of law, these business lawyers serve as "lawyer compradors"—double agents serving their own interests as lawyers and those of their merchants who retain their services' (Dezalay and Garth, 1996: 119).

On the other hand, the field of investment arbitration presents 'a panorama of places of power and of potential intermediaries' (Dezalay and Garth, 1996: 211). Indeed, 'the competition in providing business justice leads to a compartmentalization of the market that the state judicial system is powerless to control... Justice is in effect shattered into pieces, divided between the different places or networks of power that claim to have a role in the regulation of economic relations. The diversity of forums, techniques, and operators, indeed, reflects and reinforces the competition that reigns in the field' (Dezalay and Garth, 1996: 210). These 'different places and modes of commercial conflict resolution exist only in relation to one another' (Dezalay and Garth, 1996: 120). Yet the growth of this particular market has led both to the dominance of some arenas and the creation of alternative arenas that perform differentiated roles (Dezalay and Garth, 1996: 123).

As a set of intermediaries in the market for FDI, the investment arbitration community represents a transnational formation which displays elements of both a network form of organization, when viewed as a community of elite individuals, and manifests in a limited set of arenas, when viewed as periodic discrete tribunal events. First, the in-between character of the economy centred on arbitration of investment disputes is registered in its being a further example of market intermediation—in this instance in the market for capital or the market for social order as was introduced above. The interpretation of international investment law can itself be an important moderating influence on the quantity and quality of demand of investment flowing to and from different home and host countries and from particular companies. Certainly, then, 'an aspect of the history of international investment law... is its emergence as a new professional specialization, outgrowing its origins in the fusion of elements of public international law and international commercial arbitration', that is, 'a new discipline requiring specialist (and expensive) knowledge and expertise, provided and supported by an "epistemic community", with its own networks, conferences, journals, newsletters, mailing lists etc.' (Mills, 2011: 473 and 486). As a relatively small community, investment arbitration lawyers might be regarded as a network of individuals repeatedly appointed to cases. Some reports have painted this group as a relatively 'closed homogeneous group comprised of "grand old men" and nationals of developed countries' (Kapelink, 2010: 77 and 79 respectively) though it should be noted that these repeat appointees came from a spread of 16 countries with the leading nations of origin being not the United States but France and Canada. Moreover some of the aura enjoyed by a generation of these 'grand old men' has been replaced by the professionalism of a new generation of technocrats (Dezalay and Garth, 1996). Like the investment promotion community, the intermediary role played in the market for FDI finds these individuals occupying different sides of the fence: 'because many elite arbitrators have established prestigious professional careers as practicing attorneys, it is not uncommon for them to serve as an arbitrator in one case while representing a disputing party as counsel in another case' (Kapelink, 2010: 65).

Second, however, there is a more fundamental sense in which international economic law is caught between antinomies. That is, the in-between, or ' "mixed" character of international investment law and arbitration' is a product of the fact that it 'inherently brings together apparently contradictory perspectives, and that it is the amalgam of these oppositions, of these "public-private" antinomies' (Mills, 2011: 477). 'International investment arbitration remains situated in the disputed territory at the boundary of the two "communities" of public international law and private international commercial arbitration, pervasively torn between these two identities' (Mills, 2011: 486). Drawing as they do upon Bourdieu's (1984) notion of cultural fields, Dezalay and Garth (1996: 127) note the intermediary position of lawyers involved in international investment arbitration in market creation and expansion: 'the inevitably ambiguous relations between law and business are essential to the construction and prosperity of a custom of justice built up half way between these two universes but this position of equilibrium between two fields of power is by definition precarious...New forms are born and develop as a complex function of new opportunities in the international scene' (Dezalay and Garth, 1996: 127).

Third, since international economic law can be seen as 'constitutive of social relations and relational identities' as Delaney, Ford, and Blomley (2001: xv) have it, it is fundamentally in-between in the sort of geographical perspectives it mobilizes. That is, there is a contradiction of geographic perspective at the heart of international law (Riles, 2001). Potentially, the law applied to international investment and closely related fields such as intellectual property and trade-related investment measures holds out the prospect of a view from nowhere in particular—the prospect of universality. However, given the vigorous competition that has existed between principles of treatment in the international sphere (Sornarajah, 2010), international investment law does mobilize often very particular perspectives drawn from particular parts of the world.

The negotiation of investment treaties takes place at locations in the respective countries, but arbitration takes place in a relatively limited number of arenas under particular procedures. To an extent these arenas might be regarded as of nowhere in particular. They are detached from the nation states they happen to be located in and also detached from those involved in the dispute. As Dezalay and Garth, 1996: 5–6) explain 'arbitration hearings typically take place on a "neutral site" away from the countries of the disputants but they may be set virtually any place where hotels and conference rooms can be found'. The two most frequently used arenas are the International Center for the Settlement of Investment Disputes (ICSID) created in 1966 and the World Trade Organization (WTO) but there are several others. Thus, while the network of individuals who make up the arbitration community are from particular parts of the world, their role as arbitrators in such 'neutral' locations can be seen to offer something of the view from nowhere. As Mills (2011: 87) recounts 'the "delocalised" forum provided by the ICSID was . . . regarded by capital exporting states as one of the most important features of the system'.

The orthodox view of law is that it is autonomous, rational, consistent and just and stands above and is closed off from the realities of society as a 'pervasive, yet contingent social vision' (Blomley, 1994: 12). In fact, and contributing to the view from nowhere in the realm of international law and disputes, 'One important way in which space appears in law, ironically, is an absence' (Blomley, 1994: 53). This is a view often held by lawyers themselves and to an extent resonates with the history of legal development which from an early point sought to adopt a globalizing and cosmopolitan stance (Riles, 2001, although see also Mills, 2011). That is, 'from the vantage point of the international lawyers' globalizing gaze, distant events "on the ground" were "spotted" as international issues, and the adjudication of international disputes was understood to take place on an "international plane" different in scale from these events themselves' (Riles, 2001: 277). However, this espoused view from nowhere has been argued by Miles (2013) to be part of an orientation within international investment law which has persisted from the days of European empires. She argues that 'international investment principles had been constructed, using the language of universality and neutrality, to create an ostensibly objective and apolitical regime, but, in fact, one that largely consisted of protection for investors and obligations for capital importing states to facilitate trade and investment' (Miles, 2013: 2–3). While arbitrators may hold onto the idea of a vantage point from no particular point of view they are, when acting as counsel, often using tricks of perspective to change the debate and establish the significance of a particular instance, where that perspective implies both scale and a particularity of the vantage point (Riles, 2001).

It would be easy to assume that this small community or network of individuals share a common view and have played their part in promoting the liberalization of investment law that has been witnessed over the past 30–40 years. Certainly it seems that there is some evidence that they have done much to uphold the rights of investors over states, though this in turn has promoted some significant revision of investment treaties as former capital exporting nations like the US have found themselves at the receiving end of FDI, the character of which may conflict with national interests and national economic development (Sauvant and Alvarez, 2011). This recent period of unfettered liberalization of FDI policy and law may already be at an end in a longer history of significant and enduring conflict regarding the nature and purpose of international investment law (Brown and Miles, 2011; Sornarajah, 2015). Investment arbitration and its effects have become a lot more visible (Sornarajah, 2015) and are now the focal points for concern among states and NGOs over environmental protection, and legitimate scope for state action. Moreover, 'with the advent of investor–state arbitration in the latter part of the twentieth century, new levels of complexity, uncertainty and substantive expansion have been emerging' (Brown and Miles, 2011: 3). This includes concerns over the biases or inconsistencies that might be associated with rulings made by a quite limited group of elite arbitrators appointed to preside on disputes and the way in which counsel, arbitrators, and expert witnesses switch roles over successive disputes (Brown and Miles, 2011: 5). Indeed, the lucrative nature of this industry has attracted attention. Corporate Europe Observatory reports that by 2011 151 investment arbitration cases involved costs of at least US$100 million and that the threshold for distinguishing oneself as an arbitration lawyer of note had reached a minimum of a US$350 million award at tribunal.[7] Peel and Croft (2010) cite figures from *Global Arbitration Review* that the four top legal companies handled 212 investment dispute cases of a value of US$71 billion in the two-year period 2007–09.

---

[7] See http://www.corporateeurope.org/2012/chapter-2-investment-ttreaty-disputes-big-business-arbitration-industry (accessed 10 April 2016).

Temporary Clusters: Trade Shows

The notion of temporary clusters or agglomerations might also be taken as an instance of what, following Latham (2001) in Chapter 3, I termed trans-national arenas whose logic is one of periodic convocation in particular places but not of any particular place. They have some of the same properties of physical propinquity of agglomerations but are held periodically and are of limited duration. As temporary clusters, trade fairs (Bathelt, Golfetto, and Rinallo, 2014; Power and Jansson, 2008; Ramírez-Pasillas, 2008) and the sorts of tournaments of value or tournament rituals (Anand and Watson, 2004), noted in Chapter 10, could be considered as important arenas within the international economy—they share a value to businesses as a means of garnering the symbolic capital associated tournaments (Power and Jansson, 2008). In light of what we have seen in the preceding chapters regarding the significance of intermediary organizations, industries, and occupations to the interplace economy, trade shows can offer a particularly effective way of garnering commercially valuable knowledge precisely because of the measure of disintermediation they allow in the direct contact between buyers and sellers. Indeed, as arenas, trade fairs are often organized in an almost continual cycle (Power and Jansson, 2008) such that the interplace qualities of these arenas are more continuous, or rather cyclical, than the term temporary cluster implies.

'Why have international trade fairs become central nodes in the global political economy? One of the most important reasons relates to the fact that such events compress an industry's entire world into a single place—albeit for a limited time period' (Bathelt and Glückler, 2011: 191). Trade fairs, conventions, exhibitions 'can be usefully characterized as temporary clusters that develop a unique information and communication ecology, referred to as global buzz' (Bathelt and Glückler, 2011: 190–1). Their importance to the organization of economic activity is highlighted by Bathelt and Glückler (2011: 175) who argue that these 'leading international trade fairs are critical events that bring together agents of a particular industry, technology field, or value chain from virtually all parts of the world. In addition to supporting knowledge flows about markets and innovations, these events create opportunities for agents to find new transaction partners and establish networks on a global scale' (Bathelt and Glückler, 2011: 175).

From their ancient origin in commodity fairs, trade shows have evolved into expositions and sample fairs with the industrial revolution to become specialized trade shows by the present day. Their importance as part of the emergence of a first global economy grew as colonial powers organized exhibitions during the latter half of the nineteenth century. These arenas thus provided a focus for what Magee and Thompson regard as the networks of people, goods, and capital that typified the mode of economic organization of the age and allowed the opening up of new channels of trade (Magee and Thompson, 2010: 151).[8] By today, they have become 'inter-organizational rituals' or 'specialized systems staged at regular intervals' (Bathelt, Golfetto, and Rinallo, 2014: 4 and 99). Reflecting this longer history, and with a 48 per cent share of world exhibition capacity in 2011, Western Europe has the most developed trade show industry in the world with shows that are on average larger and have a greater international reach than elsewhere. Here, 'insofar as trade show organizers and firms assume specific functions to trade shows through which they maintain territorial specificities'. Elsewhere, in North America however, trade shows do not reinforce territorial patterns of economic specialization. In China the trade show industry is developing rapidly emulating the structures found at shows in Europe and North America (Bathelt, Golfetto, and Rinallo, 2014).

Bathelt, Golfetto, and Rinallo (2014) use data from a trade show observatory, finding that in 2012 there were 7,900 events across the EU attracting 145 million visitors. Larger numbers of shows take place in North America depending on the size of event included. Some indication of the economic significance of trade shows is provided by the fact that 23–33 per cent of European manufacturing firms' communications budgets are spent on them. The largest exhibition centres organize between 40 and 70 events per annum and can themselves be substantial employers within their respective local economies. One estimate suggested economic development impacts of US $140 billion stemming from trade shows in North America in 2003 (Bathelt, Golfetto, and Rinallo, 2014: 125).

Bathelt, Golfetto, and Rinallo (2014) go on to identify several ingredients of the global buzz of these temporary clusters. Trade shows provide: dedicated co-presence of global supply and demand; intense temporary face-to-face interaction; temporary possibilities for dense observation; the generation of interpretative communities and shared understandings, and; multiplex meetings and relationships. Moreover, these ingredients are actively cultivated by the event organizers who seek to: set boundaries by including and excluding particular firms; improve the release and acquisition of knowledge; prevent undesirable knowledge spillovers; invest in new technological or market developments; and build the culture of the industry. Others have noted the value of trade fairs as arenas in the dissemination (Power and Jansson, 2008) and cross-fertilization of knowledge (Ramírez-Pasillas, 2008).

---

[8] The famous exhibition at Crystal Palace spawned a series of similar events internationally. Melbourne in Australia, for example, was host to six exhibitions from the mid to the late 1800s as well as a centennial exhibition in 1888–9 (Magee and Thompson, 2010: 150).

Conclusion

The observation that 'boundaries between major actors in the international system are less like lines in the sand than like frontiers encompassing broad areas of geographic and metaphoric overlap (Tétreault, 1999: 55) serves as a reminder of the metaphorical overlaps that have been emphasized from the outset and throughout this book and not just those apparent in the networks and arenas of the non-territorial realm of the global economy. The geographical metaphors of agglomerations, enclaves, networks, and arenas each remain relevant to a depiction of the production and reproduction of space in the in-between capitalism of a second modernity and a second global economy. Indeed they combine and coexist in complex and intriguing ways that can help depict the uneven development of the inter-urban and international economies.

Drawing on Latham's (2001) framework for analysing transnational formations, in this chapter I have emphasized the relative novelty of one particular geographical formation—the arena. It is a formation that has grown rapidly and significantly out of states' desires to undergird and project their national economic interests but also more recently from the networks of private and third sector actors as a key facet of global governance. These arenas and networks associated with the interplace economy reflect, to a significant extent, the emergence of a more fully regulatory capitalism and are deserving of greater scrutiny within and beyond the field economic geography.

Part V
Conclusion

12

Conclusion

What was Lost in Between

A fundamental dialectical tension has long been evident in our understanding of how human activity is organized as places and across space (Casey, 1997; Entrikin, 1991). I have highlighted agglomerations, enclaves, networks and arenas as formations (re)produced as part of the dialectical process of development of capitalism. That is, these four terms provide an expanded conceptual vocabulary and one way of further appreciating the contradictions of capitalism and their expanding depth and latitude. Of course, bearing in mind the sort of dialectic approach outlined in Chapter 2, there are—there must be—absences in the approach adopted here. Doubtless, it is some or all of these that can drive future consideration of an economic geography of interplaces.

There are, then, some important absences or near-silences in this book that need to be noted. First, I am less concerned here with elaborating at length subjective experiences that make up an economy of interplaces. These subjective experiences of interplaces have begun to be elaborated at some length though notably from the vantage points offered by sociology and cultural studies. It will be clear that I have erred on the side of the cognitive part of the cognitive-cultural economy implied in some of the formations implicated in the in-between economy of interplaces. In Chapter 10 I went as far as I wanted to as an economic geographer though it is clear that this is precisely where a social or cultural geographer might wish to depart.

Second, there is also comparatively little to be found in this book on the economic geographies of business services and finance capital when set against the volume of articles and books now focused on these industries. I have touched on the significance of the contribution of business service industries as intermediaries. Since financial services are currently receiving quite extensive treatment in economic geography and moreover by those far better placed than myself I leave an extended discussion of aspects of the in-between character of these industries to others.

Third, some may be disappointed that I have not spent longer discussing what is by now a vast literature on global production networks (GPNs). This is an approach in itself and I have instead here tried to focus my efforts on setting out a different, though not unrelated agenda. It simply has not been possible to do justice to the developments in this approach let alone the many empirical studies in this tradition.

Fourth, multiple 'temporal itineries' (Sharma, 2014) make up a good deal of the economy of interplaces. Here I have focused on the economic geography in-between but I have also been concerned with some of the temporalities of this economic geography. Admittedly these are primarily ones that speak to the longer-term historical continuities and discontinuities in geographical formations such as agglomerations, networks, enclaves, and arenas, rather than more immediate short-term shifts. It is clear, philosophically speaking (Casey, 1993, 1997), that time and place/space cannot be spoken of independently let alone in any economic geography of interplaces. Nevertheless, for all my discussion in the preceding pages, doubtless a 'sense of the multitude of time-based experiences specific to different populations that live, labor, and sleep under the auspices of global capital' (Sharma, 2014: 9) can be lost. If 'transit space is often posited as public space's denigrated other' (Sharma, 2014: 147), then potentially my emphasis here on the economic geographical formations that together can help understand a landscape of interplaces may also have the inadvertent effect of missing important points of political and policy leverage.

Fifth, the examples of the interplace economy presented here pay too little attention to the disadvantaged in society. In some respects entirely another book could and should be written from this perspective. Following May et al.'s (2007) work on global city economies, I might suggest that a raft of service workers are essential to the growth and continued development of the interplace. Here the book bears the burden of it being a way of drawing together my existing strands of research. Again, others are better placed than me to provide this alternative view on the interplace economy. I am sure that I have not always read for difference in quite the way hoped for by Gibson-Graham (2008: 618). In particular, the gendered character of the interplace economy is also something I feel poorly equipped to do justice to. A casual inspection of some of the substantive concerns of this book—for example, the transformation of suburbs and the work of various international arenas—makes it quite apparent that gender is an incredibly important dimension along which the geography of these economies is organized. Equally, I hope that it is clear that I have written not merely with 'scepticism and negativity' and instead sought to emphasize some of the present variety that exists in the geographical organization of economic relations.

Sixth and finally, while this book does attempt to bring together territorial metaphors such as the enclave and the agglomeration with non-territorial metaphors such as networks and the partially deterritorialized notion of the arena in a way not often encountered in the discipline presently, it does not—except in a very minor way when discussing the generalities of ICT and 'market devices'—delve into the non-human properties and human–non-human interactions of actor networks that have proved such an inspiration to much contemporary work in human geography.

In all of this and much else that was lost in the process of thinking and writing, this economic geography doubtless lies somewhere between a success and a failure.

Intervening In-Between

In this book I have emphasized the continued importance of 'old' territorial metaphors alongside the new analytical value offered in the likes of the network metaphor. The analytical limits of territorial metaphors and the value of new metaphors within a refigured economic geography (Thrift and Olds, 1996) seem clear. However, one concern I have had with the network as one example of a new metaphor in economic geography is the associated 'political danger in not recognizing the need to organize deliberately for a closure, to limit the possibilities associated with complete openness and a celebration of the unpredictability of the future' (Thompson, 2004: 421).

The power to see and use space as a container—to empty it, fill it, re-fill it, and reorganize it—means that socially constructed territory, events, and space are conceptually separable (Sack, 1992). That is not to say that the social construction of space is not without its unintended consequences. As capital produces space in its own image so the social construction of space is revealing of important contradictions such as the inertia that can characterize the built environment in the face of economic change (Harvey, 1989, 1985). The process of the social production of space goes well beyond its production as territory or container to be filled, emptied, and refilled—as the rise of new metaphors in economic geography indicates. Yet, we also saw in Chapter 2 that, following Lefebvre (2003), *the production of space involves the repetition of already produced space*. Putting the two observations together provides for a rather bleak outlook in any concluding chapter which serves as both a research agenda and policy prescription. It provides a bleak outlook of both capital and of politics and policy-making being condemned to repeat their own mistakes. To be sure, by now, many of us in most national contexts must already have a strong sense of *déjà vu* surrounding public policy and political debates. We have been here before as if the already long history of capitalism is like some circular and dreamlike Borges short story. For some, the bleakness is compounded by a recognition that 'the most oppressive use of theory tends to come dressed in the guise of critical or radical political endeavor, a claimed concern with the actually oppressed conditions of our humanity' (Miller, 2010: 80). Here I offer just a few thoughts based around a critique and reconstruction centred on the key concepts mobilized in this book.

Intermediaries Indicted

The role of intermediaries even in purely economic terms is highly ambiguous. It seems certain that they add value within a capitalist system—to the production of goods and services—to businesses in particular and hence to a particular class in society. However, in serving the lowest common denominator of money in a capitalist system, it is less clear whether they contribute to increases in the welfare of labour, communities, or the environment of places.

The dark and ironic side to the cosmopolitan world we live in and which is shaped seemingly by many intermediary or symbolic analytic occupations becomes darker still when we look beyond economic considerations. Those most skilled at dealing with economic abstractions (such as financial derivatives) may have difficulty with the particular abstractions of ethics, morals, and social welfare. As Reich (1991: 309) explains:

> For without strong attachments and loyalties existing beyond family and friends, symbolic analysts may never develop the habits and attitudes of social responsibility ... Without a real political community in which to learn, refine, and produce the ideals of justice and fairness, they may find these ideals to be meaningless abstractions.

The difficulties that intermediaries may have with the abstract ideals of justice and fairness of course are learned not solely from within a network, nor as part of an individual place (such as an enclave or an agglomeration) or part-place (such as an arena) but in the productive tension of being in place but connected to other peoples and places. This is what Massey (1994) identified as a relational sense of place and an accompanying relationally grounded ethics of care.

And if the cognitive-cultural economy of second modernity has become ever more about aesthetics rather than information, knowledge, or cognition, then there is the very real danger of the aesthetization of politics itself. This would be tantamount to a politics of taste escaping questions of the moral content of decisions and policies (Sayer, 1999). The cognitive-cultural economy discussed in Chapter 10 cannot be understood or analysed without reference to morals. This, as Sayer argues, is not just a reflection of a shift from normative to positive theory in social science, since that distinction has been a product of the changes in economy and society at issue. When it comes to moral positions the experience is almost always ambiguously in-between. That is, 'while it is possible to abstract out the moral from the instrumental and the conscious from the habitual, in practice behavior is often shaped by mixed motives and influence' (Sayer, 1999: 58).

As we saw in Chapters 5, 9, and 10 intermediaries have been intimately involved with the increased velocity with which products, services, and symbols circulate in GPNs. That is, they are implicated in the way 'temporal inequalities intensify when the dominant way of apprehending time is guided by the discourses of speedup' (Sharma, 2014: 138). Speedup and the discourses surrounding it are not likely to slow down any time soon. Yet 'the yielding of space to time not only dissolves the granularity of politics but also gives rise to a way of being in time that is adverse to a political public sphere' (Sharma, 2014: 6). Despite the fact that 'time is lived at the intersection of a range of social differences that includes, class, gender, race, immigration status, and labor' (Sharma, 2014: 138), 'shared space is quite often treated as an intrinsic social good, the condition of possibility for democracy.... But ... there is no common experience of time, no universal free time in which the spatialized ideals of democracy and social change can be realized' (Sharma, 2014: 146).

The Network Neutered?

Much criticism has been levelled during the course of this book at the metaphor of the network—or rather its overuse and overextension in recent economic geography. Doubtless, it will be countered that some of this criticism is misplaced or by now dated in the light of a more deft usage of this particular metaphor. It is certainly curious that within work on geometries of power, on GPNs, on actor network theory, that considerations of power often remain underdeveloped, or even, in some instances, lost entirely. In the partial recasting of MNEs as networks within the international business studies and economic geography literature, the MNE as a locus of power has at times receded from view in research on GPNs along with questions of its power over labour, communities, and states (MacKinnon, 2012). Moreover, it is vital to avoid simple oppositions between the hierarchical organization of MNEs and states on the one hand and the network form of grassroots political and NGO mobilization since, for example, 'globally, the role of NGOs has changed considerably in recent years. Not only are many in partnership with multinational corporations in varying degrees of closeness ... but many NGOs are entirely funded by multinationals' (Huws, 2014: 147).

Some of the mixed motives and influences that Sayer describes as underlying human behaviour are certainly played out in our relation to the actual production and circulation of the commodities we eventually end up consuming and our attitudes towards regulating the GPNs that were the subject of Chapter 9. As Princen et al. (2002: 127) describes, 'when cultural, bargaining and agency distances increase, the trade-offs between, say, restrained consumption and low prices, shift from the non-material (e.g. stewardship) to the material (immediate consumption). Responsibility for everyday production and consumption diminishes as distance increases'.

A relational geographical perspective makes these things clear analytically and is a prelude to conversations about what is to be done. For example, 'supply chains connect people across vast distances and provide the networked "grounds" for a commons. This is the potential of logistics space done differently' (Cowen, 2014: 229). Thus, transnational networks of unions have been able to fend off attacks on, or gain concessions regarding, pay and working conditions (Herod, 2000). Much of such networked political activity has been reactive rather than proactive such that 'the prospects for moving beyond global corporate power hinge significantly on discovering political methodologies that activate democratic social learning as to how we might live differently... This involves a logic of pre-figuration' (Carroll, 2010: 222–3).

The Enclave Excoriated

I have emphasized the enclave as a particular economic geographical formation that has been overlooked by economic geographers in recent years. As an interplace in its own right, the enclave is a geographical formation that appears especially problematic wherever and however it manifests. This is all the more troubling since the inequities for which it is economic geography's poster child have long been apparent.

I reintroduced consideration of the enclave in Chapter 3 by way of Latham's (2001) discussion of the deployments of MNEs. Collinson and Morgan (2009) suggest that the very idea of the MNE (and presumably its deployments) has been associated with two very different positive and negative images from the outset. To return to the discussion in Chapter 2 and the broader philosophical context of this book, theory which is overly dogmatic about this misses the point that the impacts of MNEs are an empirical question and one that is best dealt with in pragmatic policy stances (Bergsten et al., 1978). There is enough evidence by now to suggest that a measure of healthy scepticism within pragmatic policy stances based on incremental learning from interacting with MNEs has by now produced better economic development results than uncritically liberal policy attitudes.

Curiously, while the historical drift has been for individual deployments (or enclaves) of MNEs to have come under greater scrutiny, the enclaves fashioned by states for such MNEs and wealthy individuals remain some of the least transparent. As Urry (2014: 178) argues, 'the absolute requirement for good governance is transparency, and that is what secrecy jurisdictions preclude. There is here an offshoring of democracy, since money and resources are rendered invisible and unaccountable.'

Elsewhere in the economic landscape of interplaces, 'postwar suburbanization took the form of enclaves—sovereign, specialized land uses with limited automobile connections to other suburban sectors' (Mozingo, 2011: 219). At first glance, 'the persistence of this separatist geography is an essential problem for the future reform of the suburban landscape' (Mozingo, 2011: 220). Yet, on further reflection, the separatist nature of this corporate landscape in some respects surely actually aids its future redevelopment since rarely can large parcels of land in single ownership be found once the land development process has transformed undeveloped land for the first time. Of course, whether such redevelopment is put to socially useful and environmentally sustainable ends—to mark, for example, any 'sequel to suburbia' (Phelps, 2016)—is another matter.

There are questions of whether in the inter-urban sphere, to some extent, enclaves represent a commons; a limited commons or club good, as has been explained in relation to gated residential communities (Webster, 2002). In the case of gated residential communities then the balance sheet of economic and other effects of these enclaves is often less clear cut than much of the urban geography literature has cared to admit. Yet it does seem clear also that the sort of geographical fragmentation enclaves precipitate is antithetical to the inclusive politics and policy associated with a global sense of place. As Kolb (2008: 181) questions, 'can there be ways of acknowledging far horizons by gestures toward them . . . The aim would be to remind people that they live in networks and processes of change, and not just in the local enclave.' The same concerns are expressed by Gibson-Graham, Cameron, and Healy (2013: 148), who argue that 'in a community economy we begin to take responsibility not just for individual commons but for how our commons is interconnected with another and how our specific "we" is interdependent with differently constituted we's'.

Agin the Arena

In some respects the new arenas of the international economy are ones in which the aura of experts—such as international investment arbitrators—is on display. The arenas that have grown to represent relatively new productions of space in the second modernity of a second global capitalist economy appear particularly problematic. They clearly are dominated by and imbued with the interests of leading state interests that have their roots in empires. Far from representing the proto-sites of cosmopolitan democracy (Held, 1995), they may in fact be nearer to the sorts of nautonomic (or autarchic) sites that are its nemesis. At present then arenas like the WTO are partial. As a result of the much publicized 'banana wars' ruling 'the WTO agreement focuses on a narrow set of concerns—the market-place relationships between sellers and buyers. The agreement discounts a wide set of concerns about the human impacts of different forms of production. It also erases the environmental costs that go with ... large scale plantations' (Gibson-Graham, Cameron, and Healy, 2013: 101). While a measure of opening of WTO Ministerial meetings to a variety of NGOs and alternative economic interests has been apparent, it may also be the case that this contributes to 'the broad hierarchy of space and power within the WTO' (Wainwright, 2007: 197). In light of these and other concerns Peet (2003: 199) has argued how 'trade is a discursive space that has to be opened to a broader, democratic process, where social movements represented by highly informed NGOs are active agents, and alternative conceptions such as fair trade, under which workers get a living wage and environments are actively protected, contend with equal force'. The problem is, as Dezalay and Garth (1996) describe in the case of investment arbitration community and the sorts of arenas that it inhabits, that the growth of this market has tended to produce entirely new 'alternative' arenas rather than result in the modification of existing arenas.

The very recent emergence of the arena as a distinct economic geographical formation might be taken as the signature of regulatory capitalism. Certainly these apparently non-transparent arenas concentrate much economic, political, and even social power today. However, Levi-Faur (2005) argues that such centres of power are also open to collective action. That is, 'regulatory capitalism is much more open to collective action than is usually portrayed by both advocates and opponents of freer markets. While the regulatory instruments and institutions that were developed in the past two decades certainly marginalized the domestic and global poor, the growing reliance on regulation as a mode of governance reopens the field for a more balanced approach to the distribution of power and resources. This is indeed the great challenge of regulatory capitalism' (Levi Faur, 2005: 28).

In short, the problem with both the enclave and the arena as part-places is often the very narrow or specific purposes for which they are (re)produced. They are not places designed around, let alone to increase, variety and complexity; they are unlikely to amount to good places (Sack, 2003).[1]

---

[1] Good places can be thought of as those which 'expand our awareness of reality' and 'increase the variety and complexity of reality' (Sack, 2003: 6).

Agglomeration's Allure

The agglomeration of people and commerce is the sine qua non of the city and the city, in turn, has been taken as the crucible of democratic forms of politics and policy. For all that the city has long been associated with inequity and the extraction of economic surpluses (Walker, 2016), it should be of little surprise, then, that the concentration that is the logic of agglomeration continues to provide perhaps the most powerful means of transforming political and policy discussion…This appears to be thrust of what Thrift and Glennie (1993: 46) suggest when arguing that 'perhaps the only way left to provide a joint appeal to this whole unstable ambivalent mess of social groupings is by providing them with a "sense of place": as "sense of place" that invests the practices of buying and trafficking in commodities with localized meanings'.

Given the emphasis of this book from the start, perhaps it is fitting that we should end with agglomeration as a specific economic geographical formation. Although recast here as concentration—rather than bounded place as it has tended to be portrayed in some past work in economic geography—it is taken as perhaps the highest expression of the territoriality of human organization.

'Territoriality provides us with the places in which we can imagine ourselves to be and this allows us to think of ourselves as from somewhere else' but it also allows us to think of space 'as a container for the spatial properties of events' for 'without territoriality, although we would still possess a personal sense of place, this personal sense of place would not be inserted into any other kind of place' (Sack, 1992: 42). That is, the territoriality of agglomeration is an indispensable ingredient in a relational or global sense of place. Given that those people, processes, and meanings that are not anchored to a place are not essentially and necessarily of that place (Sack, 1992) there are some dangers implicit in too readily accepting that our cities are irremediably dissolute (Amin and Thrift, 2002), since this can produce a view from nowhere or propel us towards it. While methods and spatial imaginaries used in planning practice have sought to embrace a relational perspective (Healey, 2006), it is unclear what much of this amounts to or what real purchase it has had or can have on planning practice. In the UK context, such imaginaries might be considered largely empty of value, a technocratic or post-political planning of soft-spaces (Allmendinger and Haughton, 2012) while politics continues to inhere around distinct local government territories and their boundaries (Phelps and Valler, 2017).

For good reasons, it is hard to escape the practical point of departure for politics and policies based on a relational sense of place offered by agglomeration when compared to the likes of enclaves, networks, and arenas. For example, even something as apparently ethereal as branding initiatives find it difficult to deal with networks and flows and instead are better focused on territorial ingredients of cities—such as clusters (Anttiroiko, 2014: 156). Thus, 'in all this talk of global flows and nodes supplanting place and territories, it is important to remember that decisions about land use are still made by people working within a spatial imaginary of bounded territories who seek to incorporate flows of goods within a global network in a way that benefits each territory, in turn shaping the geography of the network itself' (Cidell, 2011: 834).

Developments in physical and virtual mobility appear to undermine agglomeration but it persists even in the present as a key geographical formation and organizing principle of economic relations. Thus, for the urban agglomerations of the cognitive-cultural economy, 'the policy and planning problems posed by the internal crises of modern cities have both recurrent and conjunctural rhythms just as they have both local and national dimensions, and these different time-space registers leave distinctive marks on policy-making and policy-implementation arrangements' (Scott, 2008: 34). Moreover, 'the currently emerging sophisticated technologies for virtual personal mobility do not necessarily involve spatial material change as they present a mode of adaptation to existing spatial structures. This indifference of mobile communications to urban spatial structure stands in sharp contrast to the automobile, which has simultaneously facilitated and demanded much of the urban spread typifying contemporary cities' (Kellerman, 2012: 145–6). In this respect, cities such as New York provide some grounds for optimism since it is the prime example of where 'A city may . . . lead in the production of virtual mobility and possibly also in its consumption, while preferring public and non-technological media for physical mobility' (Kellerman, 2012: 158). It may equally be that such technologies contribute to a measure of agglomeration in the mid-urban realms emerging in many countries. Although we may still have to live with an expanding urban universe for some time to come, there is also some prospect of continued concentration or even the re-concentration of population and economic activity in the form of urban agglomerations of some sort.

In other respects it would of course to be wrong to end up at agglomeration since the whole purpose of the book is not to argue the analytical primacy or virtues of one geographical formation over another. 'The places to which we are attracted are literally fields of care, settings in which we have had a multiplicity of experiences and which call forth an entire complex of affections and responses' (Relph, 1976: 38). However, intervention can never be solely about the places we call home and put above anywhere else. The view from interplaces is partly a product of a dual aspect of place itself. As Sack (1992: 22) reminds us 'the inside/outside character of place makes us aware of being somewhere, which allows us to see that we are free and morally responsible agents, while it also forces us to view the process from several perspectives, which has the moral virtue of placing us, quite literally, in the position of others'.

In Between Times

This book is a very personal one, as I alluded to in the Preface. In some senses then I am loath to attempt to set out a research agenda, since in a way it would be a very personal one and I must admit to some unease with the regularity with which major academic conferences have sessions and journals have special issues clearly designed to corral academic endeavour into what appear to be comparatively few dominant and sometimes aggressively promoted, and jealously policed, agendas. Nevertheless, this book like all publications is an act in persuasion and so I want here to briefly allude to where I might see an economic geography of interplaces leading in the future.

First, considerable emphasis has been placed on the concepts of mediation and intermediaries. It is these actors and processes—diverse as they are—that provide much of the dynamic to the production of space in contemporary society. Yet these concepts are hardly without their definitional difficulties. Assumptions of the value, status, and permanency of intermediaries are all too easily made. More might be done to consider the actual contributions and value of such intermediaries not just to economic activities and businesses but also to the welfare of communities and to provide fuller theoretical elaboration of those contributions. The brief discussions notably in Chapters 3, 4, 9, and 11 were just that and nothing more, as little appears to have been done to unify any cross-disciplinary field of intermediaries let alone a subdisciplinary field of economic geography of intermediaries specifically.

Second, I believe there are important research agendas that can centre on elaborating those geographical formations rather ignored in much of the present economic geography literature. In comparison to the long-standing and diverse body of research on the subject of agglomeration and the recent fascination with the network as a metaphor, it will be clear that I believe there are equally important research agendas to be pursued in connection with the enclave (Phelps, Atienza, and Arias, 2015) and the arena. Reconsideration of the enclave is important if we are to be able to consider, for example, the 'dark side' of GPNs and to integrate the many case studies of (potential) agglomerations with an overall sense of persistent global uneven development (Selwyn, 2015). The value of the concept of the arena has barely begun to be explored and yet these curiously temporary clusters or part-places have become incredibly important to the organization and regulation of economic activities of all sorts in recent times.

Third, I touched in passing on geographic formations that could also be the subject of greater attention. The focus of Chapter 5 was on megalopolitan regions in which the formations of the agglomeration, enclave, and network were visible. However, I left rather underexplored the fact that megapolitan regions—as the hinges between national and international urban economic systems (Gottmann, 1976)—are themselves in between economic-geographical formations. Chapter 11 discussed how much of the non-territorial realm of the international economy is hardly that at all since it might be considered to be organized in terms of a patchwork of overlapping supranational but distinctly territorially demarcated envelopes. Again, this thought has been left undeveloped, though it is possible that the nature and consequences of the organization of economic activities in such envelopes could form a distinct line of inquiry. The economy centred on the home was only briefly discussed in Chapter 4, but it is clear that it is an important place in which the material and symbolic in our lives are related (Blunt and Dowling, 2006). It too could usefully be a focus of continued research effort.

Fourth, it will be clear from the emphasis throughout much of this book that much of what is most intriguing in economic geography—including that of the economy in between—are the questions and agendas posed by the various rhythms, continuities, and discontinuities apparent in the workings of economic processes and the production of geographic formations over time. Some of the economic geographical formations—such as the agglomeration—that I have worked with as part of the conceptual basis of this book have endured over long periods of time and precede capitalism. The enclave, even if a formation that continues to be produced in general, is also, in individual instances, often deeply imbued—notably in the case of mining towns—with a sense of a finite existence rarely exceeded when, for example, producing or becoming part of a broader urban agglomeration. Others, such as the arena, are in their infancy and are a reflection of the present state of development of capitalism. We actually know very little about these peculiarly temporary economic geographical formations—their partial placeness—or the impacts of the economic activities they help to organize. Yet others such as the network can be associated with a flux in economic relations that is at times—as in the finance industry—virtually instantaneous. There is, then, a future research agenda that could focus on the different temporal geographies of economy.

References

Adey, P. (2010) *Aerial Life: Spaces, Mobilities, Affects*. Chichester: Wiley-Blackwell.

Agnew, J. (2005) 'Sovereignty regimes: territoriality and state authority in contemporary world politics', *Annals of the Association of American Geographers* 95: 437–61.

Agnew, J. (2009) *Globalization and Sovereignty*. New York: Rowman and Littlefield.

Aguilar, A., Guillot, C., and Rallet, A. (2012) 'Mobile ICTs and physical mobility: review and research agenda', *Transportation Research Part A* 46: 664–72.

Allen, F. and Santomero, A. M. (1998) 'The theory of financial intermediation', *Journal of Banking and Finance* 21: 1461–85.

Allen, J. (1988) 'Service industries: uneven development and uneven knowledge', *Area* 20: 15–22.

Allen, J. (2002) 'Symbolic economies: the "culturalization" of economic knowledge', in P. Du Gay and M. Pryke (eds), *Cultural Economy: Cultural Analysis and Commercial Life*. London: Sage, pp. 39–58.

Allen, J. (2011) 'Topological twists: power's shifting geographies', *Dialogues in Human Geography* 1: 283–98.

Allmendinger, P. (2012) 'Non-plan', in M. Tewdwr-Jones, N. A. Phelps, and R. Freestone (eds), *The Planning Imagination: Peter Hall and the Study of Urban and Regional Planning*. London: Routledge, pp. 162–76.

Allmendinger, P. and Haughton, G. (2012) 'Post-political spatial planning in England: a crisis of consensus?', *Transactions of the Institute of British Geographers* 37: 89–103.

Alonso, W. (1973) 'Urban zero population growth', *Daedalus* 102: 191–206.

Amin, A. (2004) 'Regulating economic globalization', *Transactions of the Institute of British Geographers* 29: 217–33.

Amin, A. and Robins, K. (1990) 'The re-emergence of regional economies? The mythical geography of flexible accumulation', *Environment and Planning D: Society and Space* 8: 7–34.

Amin, A. and Thrift, N. J. (2002) *Cities: Reimagining the Urban*. Cambridge: Polity.

Anand, N. and Watson, M. R. (2004) 'Tournament rituals in the evolution of fields: the case of the GRAMMY awards', *Academy of Management Journal* 47: 59–80.

Andersson, U., Forsgren, M., and Holm, U. (2007) 'Balancing subsidiary influence in the federative MNC: a business network view', *Journal of International Business Studies* 38: 802–18.

Angel, S. and Blei, A. (2016) 'The spatial structure of American cities: the great majority of workplaces are no longer in CBDs, employment subcentres, or live-work communities', *Cities* 51: 21–35.

Angotti, T. (2013) *The New Century of the Metropolis: Urban Enclaves and Orientalism.* New York, NY: Routledge.

Anholt, S. (2007) *Competitive Identity: The New Brand Management for Nations, Cities and Regions.* Basingstoke: Palgrave-Macmillan.

Anholt, S. (2010) *Places, Identity and Reputation.* Basingstoke: Palgrave-Macmillan.

Anttiroiko, A.-V. (2014) *The Political Economy of City Branding.* London: Routledge.

Appadurai, A. (1986) 'Introduction: commodities and the politics of value', in A. Appadurai (ed.), *The Social Life of Things: Commodities in Cultural Perspective.* Cambridge: Cambridge University Press, pp. 3–63.

Appadurai, A. (1996) *Modernity at Large.* Minneapolis: University of Minnesota Press.

Appold, S. J. (2016) 'Airport cities and metropolitan labor markets: a response to Cidell', *Journal of Economic Geography* 15: 1145–68.

Arias, M., Atienza, M., and Cademartori, J. (2014) 'Large mining enterprises an regional development in Chile: between the enclave and the cluster', *Journal of Economic Geography* 14: 73–95.

Ashworth, G. J. and Voogd, H. (1990) *Selling the City: Marketing Approaches in Public Sector Urban Planning.* London: Belhaven Press.

Athreye, S. S. (2004) 'The role of transnational corporations in the evolution of a high-tech industry: the case of India's software industry—a comment', *World Development* 32: 555–60.

Atkinson R. (2008) 'The flow in enclave and the misanthropy of networked affluence', in J. Blokland and M. Savage (eds), *Networked Urbanism: Social Capital in the City.* Aldershot: Ashgate, pp. 41–58.

Augé, M. (1995) *Non-Places: Introduction to an Athropology of Supermodernity.* London: Verso.

Axtell, C., Hislop, D., and Whittacker, S. (2008) 'Mobile technologies in mobile spaces: findings from the context of train travel', *International Journal of Human-Computer Studies* 66: 902–15.

Badcock, B. and Beer, A. (2000) *Home Truths: Property Ownership and Housing Wealth in Australia.* Melbourne: Melbourne University Press.

Baigent, E. (2004) 'Patrick Geddes, Lewis Mumford and Jean Gottmann: divisions over megalopolis', *Progress in Human Geography,* 28: 687–700.

Bair, J. and Gereffi, G. (2001) 'Local clusters in global chains: the causes and consequences of export dynamism in Torreon's blue jeans industry', *World Development* 29: 1885–1903.

Baldacchino, G. (2009) 'Thucydides or Kissinger? A critical review of smaller state diplomacy', in A. F. Cooper and T. M. Shaw (eds), *The Diplomacy of Small States: Between Vulnerability and Resilience.* Basingstoke: Palgrave-Macmillan, pp. 21–40.

Baldacchino, G. (2010) *Island Enclaves: Offshoring Strategies, Creative Governance and Subnational Island Jurisdictions.* Montreal: McGill-Queen's University Press.

Banham, R. (1971) *Los Angeles: The Architecture of Four Ecologies.* London: Allen Lane.

Barnes, T. J. (1996) *Logics of Dislocation: Models, Metaphors and Meaning in Economic Geography.* New York: Guilford.

Barnes, T. J., Peck, J., Sheppard, E., and Tickell, A. (2007) 'Methods matter: transformations in economic geography', in A. Tickell, E. Sheppard, J. Peck, Barnesand T. J. (eds), *Politics and Practice in Economic Geography.* London: Sage, pp. 1–24.

Barnet, R. J. and Muller, R. E. (1974) *Global Reach: Power of the Multinational Corporation*. London: Jonathan Cape.

Barnett, C., Cloke, P., Clarke, N., and Malpass, A. (2011) *Globalizing Responsibility: The Political Rationalities of Ethical Consumption*. Chichester: Wiley-Blackwell.

Bartlett, C. A. and Ghoshal, S. (1989) *Managing across Borders: The Transnational Solution*. Cambridge, MA: Harvard Business School Press.

Basten, L. (2017) 'In-betweens in time and space: the governance of suburbanism in the Ruhr', in N. A. Phelps (ed.), *Old Europe, New Suburbanization: Land, Infrastructure and Governance in Europe's Suburbs*. Toronto: University of Toronto Press, pp. 158–82.

Bathelt, H. and Glückler, J. (2011) *The Relational Economy: Geographies of Knowing and Learning*. Oxford: Oxford University Press.

Bathelt, H., Golfetto, F., and Rinallo, D. (2014) *Trade Shows in the Globalizing Knowledge Economy*. Oxford: Oxford University Press.

Bathelt, H., Malmberg, A., and Maskell, P. (2004) 'Clusters and knowledge: local buzz, global pipelines and the process of knowledge creation', *Progress in Human Geography* 28: 31–56.

Baudrillard, J. (1994) *Simulacra and Simulation*. Ann Arbor: University of Michigan Press.

Bauman, Z. (1987) *Legislators and Interpreters: On Modernity, Post-modernity and Intellectuals*. Cambridge: Polity.

Bauman, Z. (1995) *Life in Fragments: Essays in Post-modern Morality*. Oxford: Blackwell.

Bayly, C. A. (2000) *The Birth of the Modern World*. Cambridge: Cambridge University Press.

Beauregard, R. (2006) *When America Became Suburban*. Minneapolis: University of Minnesota Press.

Beaverstock, J. V. and Faulconbridge, J. (2010) '"Official" and "unofficial" measurements of international business travel to and from the United Kingdom: trends, patterns and limitations', in J. V. Beaverstock, B. Derudder, J. Faulconbridge, and F. Witlox (eds), *International Business Travel in the Global Economy*. Farnham: Ashgate, pp. 57–84.

Beaverstock, J., Derudder, B., Faulconbridge, J., and Witlox, F. (2010) 'International business travel and the global economy: setting the context', in J. V. Beaverstock, B. Derudder, Faulconbridge J., Witlox and F. (eds), *International Business Travel in the Global Economy*. Farnham: Ashgate, pp. 1–7.

Beck, U. (1992) *Risk Society: Towards a New Modernity*. London: Sage.

Beck, U., Bonss, W., and Lau, C. (2003) 'The theory of reflexive modernization: problematic, hypotheses and research programme', *Theory, Culture & Society*, 20: 1–33.

Bennett, R. J., Graham, D. J., and Bratton, W. (1999) 'The location and concentration of businesses in Britain: business clusters, business services, market coverage and local economic development', *Transactions of the Institute of British Geographers* 24: 393–420.

Bergsten, C. F., Horst, T., and Moran, T. H. (1978) *American Multinationals and American Interests*. Washington DC: Brookings Institution.

Beugelsdijk, S and Mudambi, R. (2013) 'MNEs as border-crossing multi-location enterprises: the role of discontinuities in geographic space', *Journal of International Business Studies* 44: 413–26.

Beunza, D. and Garud, R. (2007) 'Calculators, lemmings or frame-makers? The intermediary role of securities analysts', in M. Callon, Y. Millo, and F. Muniesa (eds), *Market Devices*. Oxford: Blackwell, pp. 13–39.

Bhan, G. (2014) 'The real lives of urban fantasies', *Environment & Urbanization* 26: 1–4.

Bhaskar, R. (1993) *Dialectic: Pulse of Freedom*. London: Verso.

Biblioteca Nacional (2012) Reportes estadísticos y comunales. Available at: http://reportescomunales.bcn.cl/2012/index.php/Colina#Indicadores_demogr.C3.A1ficos (accessed 15 September 2015).

Birkinshaw, J. (1996) 'How multinational subsidiary mandates are gained and lost', *Journal of International Business Studies* 27: 467–95.

Birkinshaw, J. and Hood, N. (1998) 'Multinational subsidiary evolution: capability and charter change in foreign-owned subsidiary companies', *Academy of Management Review* 23: 773–95.

Birtchnell, T. and Urry, J. (2015) 'The mobilities and post-mobilities of cargo', *Consumption Markets and Culture* 18: 25–38.

Blomley, N. (1994) *Law, Space, and the Geographies of Power*. London: Guilford Press.

Blunt, A. and Dowling, R. (2006) *Home*. London: Routledge.

Bock, R. (2015) 'Airports on the move? The policy mobility of Singapore's Changi Airport at home and abroad', *Urban Studies* 52: 2724–40.

Boddewyn, J. J. (1988) 'Political aspects of MNE theory', *Journal of International Business Studies* 19: 341–63.

Bogard, W. (2000) 'Simmel in cyberspace: strangeness and distance in postmodern communications', *Space and Culture* 4/5: 23–46.

Bogart, W. T. (2006) *Don't Call It Sprawl: Metropolitan Structure in the 21st Century*. Cambridge: Cambridge University Press.

Boli, J. and Thomas, G. M. (1999) *Constructing World Culture: International Nongovernmental Organizations since 1875*. Stanford CA: Stanford University Press.

Bond, D. W. (2014) 'Hegel's geographical thought', *Environment & Planning D* 32: 179–98.

Bonnett, A. (2014) *Off the Map: Lost Spaces, Invisible Cities, Forgotten Islands, Feral Places, and What They Tell Us about the World*. London: Aurum Press.

Bontje, M. and Burdack, J. (2005) 'Edge cities, European-style: examples from Paris and the Randstad', *Cities* 22: 317–30.

Bornschier, V. and Trezzini, B. (2001) 'World market for social order: embedded state autonomy and third world development', *Competition and Change* 5: 201–44.

Bourdieu, P. (1984) *Distinction. A Social Critique of the Judgement of Taste*. London: Routledge (translated by R. Nice).

Bowen, J. T. Jnr (2010) 'A people set apart: the spatial development of airline business class services', in J. V. Beaverstock, B. Derudder, J. Faulconbridge, and F. Witlox (eds), *International Business Travel in the Global Economy*. London: Ashgate, pp. 11–30.

Boyang, G., Weidong, L., and Dunford, M. (2014) 'State land policy, land markets and geographies of manufacturing: The case of Beijing, China'. *Land Use Policy* 36: 1–12.

Boyenge, J. P. S. (2007) *ILO Database on Export Processing Zones (Revised)*. Sectoral Activities Programme, Working Paper 251. Geneva: International Labour Organization.

Braithwaite, J. (2008) *Regulatory Capitalism: How It Works, Ideas for Making It Work Better.* Cheltenham: Edward Elgar.

Braithwaite, J. and Drahos, P. (2000) *Global Business Regulation.* Cambridge: Cambridge University Press.

Brand Finance (2014) *Nation Brands, 2014.* Brand Finance, London. Accessed at: http://brandfinance.com/images/upload/brand_finance_nation_brands_report_2014_final_edition.pdf (last accessed, 2 February 2017).

Brautigam, D. and Tang, X. (2012) 'Economic statecraft in China's new overseas special economic zones: soft power, business or resource scarcity', *International Affairs* 88: 799–816.

Breheny, M. (2001) 'Housing is not a disease: reflections on PPG3 and Regional Planning Guidance', *Journal of Planning and Environmental Law* 29: 79–89.

Brennan-Horley, C. (2010) 'Multiple work sites and city-wide networks: a topological approach to understanding creative work', *Australian Geographer* 41: 39–56.

Brenner, N. (1998) 'Between fixity and motion: accumulation, territorial organization and the historical geography of spatial scales', *Environment and Planning D* 16: 459–82.

Bridge, G. (2008) 'Global production networks and the extractive sector: governing resource-based development', *Journal of Economic Geography* 8: 389–419.

Bristow, G. (2005) 'Everyone's a "winner": problematizing the discourse of regional competitiveness', *Journal of Economic Geography* 5: 285–304.

Britton, S. G. (1982) 'The political economy of tourism in the third world', *Annals of Tourism Research* 9: 331–58.

Brown, C. and Miles, K. (2011) 'Introduction: evolution in investment treaty law and arbitration', in C. Brown and K. Miles (eds), *Evolution in Investment Treaty Law and Arbitration.* Cambridge: Cambridge University Press, pp. 3–16.

Buckley, P. J. and Casson, M. (1976) *The Future of the Multinational Enterprise.* London: Macmillan.

Budd, L. and Hubbard, P. (2010) 'The "bizjet set": business aviation and the social geographies of private flight', in J. V. Beaverstock, B. Derudder, J. Faulconbridge, and F. Witlox (eds), *International Business Travel in the Global Economy.* Farnham: Ashgate, pp. 85–104.

Buliung, R. N. (2011) 'Wired people in wired places: stories about machines and the geography of activity', *Annals of the Association of American Geographers* 101: 1365–81.

Bunnell, T. (2004) *Malaysia, Modernity and the Multimedia Super Corridor: A Critical Geography of Intelligent Landscapes.* London: Routledge.

Bunnell, T. (2015) 'Antecedent cities and inter-referencing effects: learning from and extending beyond critiques of neoliberalisation', *Urban Studies* 52: 1983–2000.

Bunnell, T. and Coe, N. M. (2001) 'Spaces and scales of innovation', *Progress in Human Geography* 25: 569–89.

Bunnell, T. and Das, D. (2010) 'Urban pulse—a geography of serial seduction: urban policy transfer from Kuala Lumpur to Hyderabad', *Urban Geography* 31: 277–84.

Bunnell, T., Muzaini, H., and Sidaway, J. D. (2006) 'Global city frontiers: Singapore's hinterland and the contested socio-political geographies of Bintan, Indonesia', *International Journal of Urban and Regional Research* 30: 3–22.

Bunnell, T., Miller, M., Phelps, N. A., and Taylor, J. (2013) 'Urban and regional development in decentralised Indonesia: Two progressive cases and their travels', *Pacific Affairs* 86 (4): 857–76.

Burgand, J.-M. and Farole, T. (2011) 'When trade preferences and tax breaks are no longer enough: the challenges of adjustment in the Dominican Republic's Free Zones', in T. Farole and G. Akince (eds), *Special Economic Zones: Progress, Emerging Challenges, and Future Directions*. Washington DC: World Bank, pp. 159–81.

Burger, M. J., Meijers, E. J., Hoogerbrugge, M. M., and Tresserra, J. M. (2015) 'Borrowed size, agglomeration shadows and cultural amenities in north-west Europe', *European Planning Studies* 23: 1090–109.

Buzzelli, M. and Harris, R. (2006) 'Cities as the industrial districts of housebuilding', *International Journal of Urban and Regional Research* 30: 894–917.

Cairncross, F. (2001) *The Death of Distance: How the Communications Revolution Is Changing Our Lives*. Cambridge, MA: Harvard Business Press.

Caliskan, K. and Callon, M. (2009) 'Economization, part I: shifting attention from the economy toward processes of economization', *Economy and Society* 38: 369–98.

Callon, M., Meadel, C., and Rabeharisaa, V. (2002) 'The economy of qualities', *Economy & Society* 31: 194–217.

Cantwell, J. (2009) 'Location and the multinational enterprise', *Journal of International Business Studies* 40: 35–41.

Cardoso, F. H. and Faletto, E. (1979) *Dependency and Development in Latin America*. Berkeley CA: University of California Press.

Carr, C. M. H. and Whitehand, J. W. R. (2003) *Twentieth-century Suburbs: A Morphological Approach*. London: Spon.

Carrión, F. (2005) 'El centro histórico como proyecto y objeto de deseo'. *Revista EURE*, 31: 89–100.

Carrión, F. (2007) 'El desafío político de gobernar la ciudad'. *Nueva Sociedad* 212: 36–52.

Carroll, W. K. (2010) *The Making of a Transnational Capitalist Class: Corporate Power in the 21st Century*. London: Zed Books.

Casey, E. (1993) *Getting Back into Place: Toward a Renewed Understanding of the Place-world*. Bloomington: Indiana University Press.

Casey, E. (1997) *The Fate of Place: A Philosophical History*. Berkeley CA: University of California Press.

Casson, M. (1997a) *Information and Organization: A New Perspective on the Theory of the Firm*. Oxford: Oxford University Press.

Casson, M. (1997b) 'Institutional economics and business history: a way forward', *Business History* 39: 151–71.

Casson, M. (2013) 'Economic analysis of industrial supply chains: an internalization perspective', *Journal of Supply Chain Management* 49: 8–13.

Castells, M. and Hall, P. (1994) *Technopoles of the World*. London: Routledge.

Castree, N. (2006) 'From neoliberalism to neoliberalization: consolations, confusions and necessary illusions', *Environment & Planning A* 38: 1–6.

Cavusgil, S. T. and Knight, G. (2015) 'The born global firm: an entrepreneurial and capabilities perspective on early and rapid internationalization', *Journal of International Business Studies* 46: 3–16.

Ceruzzi, P. E. (2008) *Internet Alley: High Technology in Tysons Corner, 1945–2005*. Cambridge, MA: MIT Press.

Charles, D. C. (2015) 'From technopoles to science cities: characteristics of a new phase of science cities', in J. T. Miao, P. Benneworth, and N. A. Phelps (eds), *Making 21st Century Knowledge Complexes*. London: Routledge, pp. 82–102.

Chong, A. (2009) 'Singapore and the soft power experience', in A. F. Cooper and T. M. Shaw (eds), *The Diplomacy of Small States: Between Vulnerability and Resilience*. Basingstoke: Palgrave-Macmillan, pp. 65–80.

Cidell, J. (2011) 'Distribution centers among the rooftops: the global logistics network meets the suburban spatial imaginary', *International Journal of Urban and Regional Research* 35: 832–51.

Cidell, J. (2015) 'The role of major infrastructure in subregional economic development: an empirical study of airports and cities', *Journal of Economic Geography* 15: 1125–44.

Clapson, M. (2003) *Suburban Century: Social Change and Urban Growth in England and the USA*. Oxford: Berg.

Clark, G. L. (1993) 'Costs and prices, corporate competitive strategies and regions', *Environment & Planning A* 25: 5–26.

Clarke, D. B. (1997) 'Consumption and the city, modern and postmodern', *International Journal of Urban and Regional Research* 21: 218–37.

Cobb, J. C. (1993) *The Selling of the South: The Southern Crusade for Industrial Development 1936–1990*. Champaign IL: University of Illinois Press.

Cochoy, F. (2007) 'A sociology of market-things: on tending the garden of choices in mass retailing', in M. Callon, Y. Millo,and F. Muniesa (eds), *Market Devices*. Oxford: Blackwell, pp. 109–29.

Coe, N. M. (2014) 'Missing links: logistics, governance and upgrading in a shifting global economy', *Review of International Political Economy* 21: 224–56.

Coe, N. M. and Hess, M. (2011) 'Local and regional development: a global production network approach', in A. Pike, A. Rodriguez-Pose, and J. Tomaney (eds), *Handbook of Local and Regional Development*, London: Routledge, pp. 128–38.

Coe, N. M. and Townsend, A. R. (1998) 'Debunking the myth of localized agglomerations: the development of a regionalized service economy in the South East of England', *Transactions of the Institute of British Geographers* 23: 385–404.

Coe, N. M. and Wrigley, N. (2007) 'Host economy impacts of transnational retail: the research agenda', *Journal of Economic Geography* 7: 341–71.

Coe, N. M. and Yeung, H. Y-C. (2015) *Global Production Networks: Theorizing Economic Development in an Interconnected World*. Oxford: Oxford University Press.

Coe, N. M., Dicken, P., and Hess, M. (2008a) 'Introduction: global production networks—debates and challenges', *Journal of Economic Geography* 8: 267–9.

Coe, N. M., Dicken, P., and Hess, M. (2008b) 'Global production networks: realizing the potential', *Journal of Economic Geography* 8: 271–95.

Coe, N. M., Lai, K., and Wojcik, D. (2014) 'Integrating finance into global production networks', *Regional Studies* 48: 761–77.

Contractor, F., Kumar, V., Kundu, S. K., and Pedersen, T. (2010) 'Reconceptualizing the firm in a world of outsourcing and offshoring: the organizational and geographical relocation of high-value company functions', *Journal of Management Studies* 47: 1417–33.

Cooley, C. H. (1894) *The Theory of Transportation.* Baltimore: American Economic Association.

Cooley, A. (2015) 'The emerging politics of international rankings and ratings: a framework for analysis', in A. Cooley and J. Snyder (eds), *Ranking the World: Grading States as a Tool of Global Governance.* Cambridge: Cambridge University Press, pp. 1–38.

Cooper, A. F. and Shaw, T. M. (2009) 'The diplomacies of small states at the start of the twenty-first century: how vulnerable? How resilient?', in A. F. Cooper and T. M. Shaw (eds), *The Diplomacy of Small States: Between Vulnerability and Resilience.* Basingstoke: Palgrave-Macmillan, pp. 1–18.

Cooper, F. (2001) 'Networks, moral discourse and history', in R. Latham, R. Kassimir, and T. M. Callaghy (eds), *Interventions and Transnationalism in Africa: Global-Local Networks of Power.* Cambridge: Cambridge University Press, pp. 23–46.

Corey, K. E. (2004) 'Moving people, goods, and information in Singapore: intelligent corridors', in R. E. Hanley (ed.), *Moving People, Goods, and Information in the 21st Century: The Cutting Edge Infrastructures of Networked Cities.* London: Routledge, pp. 292–324.

Cowen, D. (2014) *The Deadly Life of Logistics: Mapping Violence in Global Trade.* Minneapolis: University of Minnesota Press.

Cowling, K. and Sugden, R. (1998) 'The essence of the modern corporation: markets, strategic decision-making and the theory of the firm', *The Manchester School* 66: 59–86.

Cox, K. R. (1995) Globalisation, competition and the politics of local economic development', *Urban Studies* 32: 213–24.

Cox, K. R. and Mair, A. (1988) 'Locality and community in the politics of local economic development', *Annals of the Association of American Geographers* 78: 307–25.

Cox, K. R. and Mair, A. (1991) 'From localised social structures to localities as agents', *Environment & Planning A* 23: 197–213.

Coyle, D. (1999) *The Weightless World: Strategies for Managing the Digital Economy.* Cambridge, MA: MIT Press.

Cresswell, T. (2004) *Place: A Short Introduction.* Oxford: Blackwell.

Cresswell, T. (2006) *On the Move: Mobility in the Modern Western World.* London: Routledge.

Cresswell, T. and Merriman, P. (2011) *Geographies of Mobilities: Practices, Spaces, Subjects.* Aldershot: Ashgate.

Cresswell, T., Dorow, S., and Roseman, S. (2016) 'Putting mobility theory to work: conceptualizing employment-related geographical mobility', *Environment & Planning A* 48: 1787–1803.

Crowther, L. (2010) 'Et in suburbia ego: a cultural geography of craft in the London suburbs', *Journal of Modern Craft* 3: 143–60.

Currah, A. (2004) 'Networks of organizational learning and adaptation in retail TNCs', *Global Networks* 4: 1–23.

Cwerner, S. (2009) 'Introducing aeromobilities', in S. Cwerner, S. Kesselring, J., and Urry (eds), *Aeromobities.* London: Routledge, pp. 1–21.

Das, D. (2015) 'Hyderabad: visioning, restructuring and making of a high-tech city', *Cities* 43: 48–58.

Datta, A. (2015) 'New urban utopias of postcolonial India: "Entrepreneurial urbanization" in Dholera smart city, Gujarat', *Dialogues in Human Geography* 5: 3–22.

Davis, K. E., Kingsbury, B., and Merry, S. E. (2012a) 'Introduction: global governance by indicators', in K. E. Davis, B. Kingsbury, and S. E. Merry (eds), *Governance by Indicators: Global Power through Quantification and Rankings*. Oxford: Oxford University Press, pp. 1–28.

Davis, K. E., Kingsbury, B., and Merry, S. E. (2012b) 'Indicators as a technology of global governance', *Law and Society Review* 46: 71–104.

Dear, M. and Dahmann, N. (2008) 'Urban politics and the Los Angeles school of urbanism', *Urban Affairs Review*: 44: 266–79.

De Grazia, V. Ed. (1996) *The Sex of Things: Gender and Consumption in Historical Perspective*. Berkeley CA: University of California Press.

DeJong, J. K. (2014) *New Suburbanisms*. London: Routledge.

Delaney, D., Ford, R. T., and Blomley, N. (2001) 'Preface: where is law?', in N. Blomley, D. Delaney, and R. T. Ford (eds), *The Legal Geographies Reader*. Oxford: Blackwell, pp. xiii–xxii.

Dematteis, G. (2000) 'Spatial images of European urbanisation', in A. Bagnasco and P. Le Gales (eds), *Cities in Contemporary Europe*. Cambridge: Cambridge University Press.

Den Hertog, P. (2000) 'Knowledge intensive business services as co-producers of innovation', *International Journal of Innovation Management* 4: 491–528.

Dennis, R. (2008) *Cities in Modernity: Representations and Productions of Metropolitan Space, 1840–1930*. Cambridge: Cambridge University Press.

Dezalay, Y. and Garth, B. G. (1996) *Dealing in Virtue: International Commercial Arbitration and the Construction of an International Legal Order*. Chicago: University of Chicago Press.

Dick, E. and Reuschke, D. (2012) 'Multilocational households in the global south and north: relevance, features and spatial implications' *Die Erde* 143: 177–94.

Dicken, P. (1988) *Global Shift*. London: PCP.

Dicken, P. (1994) 'The Roepke lecture in economic geography global–local tensions: firms and states in the global space-economy', *Economic Geography* 70: 101–28.

Dicken, P. and Hassler, M. (2000) 'Organizing the Indonesian clothing industry in the global economy: the role of business networks', *Environment & Planning A* 32: 263–80.

Dicken, P. and Malmberg, A. (2001) 'Firms in territories: A relational perspective', *Economic Geography* 77: 345–63.

Dicken, P. and Miyamachi, Y. (1998) '"From noodles to satellites": the changing geography of the Japanese *sogo shosha*', *Transactions of the Institute of British Geographers* 23: 55–98.

Dicken, P. and Thrift, N. (1992) 'The organization of production and the production of organization: why business enterprises matter in the study of geographical industrialization', *Transactions of the Institute of British geographers* NS 17: 279–91.

Dicken, P., Peck, P., and Tickell, A. (1997) 'Unpacking the global', in Lee, R. and Wills, J. (eds), *Geographies of Economies*. London: Arnold, pp. 158–66.

Dicken, P, Kelly, P., Olds, K., and Yeung, H. W.-C. (2001) 'Chains and networks, territories and scales: towards a relational framework for analysing the global economy', *Global Networks* 1: 89–112.

Dietz, J. L. (1985) 'Export-enclave economies: international corporations and development', *Journal of Economic Issues* 19: 13–22.

Dixon, D., Woodward, K., and Jones, J. P. (2008) 'On the other hand... dialectics', *Environment & Planning A* 40: 2549–61.

Djelic, M. L. and Sahlin-Andersson, K. (2006) 'Institutional dynamics in a re-ordering world', in M. L. Djelic and K. Sahlin-Andersson (eds), *Transnational Governance: Institutional Dynamics of Regulation*. Cambridge: Cambridge University Press, pp. 375–97.

Dodgshon, R. (1987) *The European Past: Social Evolution and Spatial Order*. Basingstoke: Macmillan.

Dodgshon, R. (1998) *Society in Time and Space: A Geographical Perspective*. Cambridge: Cambridge University Press.

Donaghu, M. T. and Barff, R. (1990) 'Nike just did it: international subcontracting and flexibility in athletic footwear production', *Regional Studies* 24: 537–52.

Donald, S. H., Kofman, E., and Kevin, C. (2009) 'Introduction: processes of cosmopolitanism and parochialism', in S. H. Donald, E. Kofman, and C. Kevin (eds), *Branding Cities: Cosmopolitanism, Parochialism and Social Change*. London: Routledge, pp. 1–13.

Dossani, R. and Kenney, M. (2007) 'The next wave of globalization? Relocation of service provision to India', *World Development* 35: 772–91.

Dowding, K., Dunleavy, P., King, D., Margetts, H., and Rydin, Y. (1999) Regime politics in London local government. *Urban Affairs Review* 34: 515–45.

Drori, G. S. and Meyer, J. W. (2006) 'Scientization: Making a world safe for organizing', in M. L. Djelic and K. Sahlin-Andersson(eds), *Transnational Governance: Institutional Dynamics of Regulation*. Cambridge: Cambridge University Press, pp. 31–52.

Ducci, M. E. (2000) 'Santiago: territorios, anhelos y temores. Efectos sociales y espaciales de la expansión urbana'. *EURE (Santiago)* 26(79): 5–24. http://www.scielo.cl/scielo.php?script=sci_arttext&pid=S0250-71612000007900001(last accessed 13 January 2017).

Duncan, S. (1989) 'What is locality?', in R. Peet and N. Thrift (eds), *New Models in Geography*, Volume 2. London: Routledge, pp. 221–51.

Dunham-Jones, E. and Williamson, J. (2009) *Retrofitting Suburbia: Urban Design Solutions for Redesigning Suburbs*. Chichester: Wiley.

Dunning, J. (1986) *Japanese Participation in British Industry*. Beckenham: Croom Helm.

Dunning, J. H. (1979) 'Explaining changing patterns of international production: in defence of the eclectic theory', *Oxford Bulletin of Economics and Statistics* 41: 269–95.

Dunning, J. H. (1983) 'Changes in the level and structure of international production: the last one hundred years', in M. Casson (ed.), *The Growth of International Business*. London: Allen &Unwin, pp. 84–139.

Duranton, G. (1999) 'Distance, land, and proximity: economic analysis and the evolution of cities', *Environment and Planning A* 31: 2169–88.

Dutton, J. A. (2000) *New American Urbanism: Re-framing the Suburban Metropolis*. Milan: Skira.

Easterling, K. (1999) *Organization Space: Landscapes, Highways and Houses in America.* Cambridge, MA: MIT Press.

The Economist (2015) 'Home-field advantage: E-commerce in South-East Asia', *The Economist* 6 March, 414: 69.

Edensor, T. (2000) 'Staging tourism: tourists as performers', *Annals of Tourism Research* 27: 322–44.

Eggert, R. G. (2001) *Mining and Economic Sustainability: National Economies and Local Communities.* Mining, Minerals and Sustainable Development Paper 19. Available online: http://pubs.iied.org/pdfs/G00952.pdf (last accessed 13 January 2017).

Elden, S. (2010) 'Land, terrain, territory', *Progress in Human Geography* 34: 799–817.

Elden, S. (2011) 'What's shifting?', *Dialogues in Human Geography* 1: 304–7.

Elkins, Z., Guzman, A.T., and Simmons, B. (2006) 'Competing for capital: the diffusion of bilateral investment treaties, 1960–2000', *International Organization* 60: 811–46.

Elliott, A. and Urry, J. (2010) *Mobile Lives.* London: Routledge.

Entrikin, J. N. (1991) *The Betweenness of Place: Towards a Geography of Modernity.* Baltimore: Johns Hopkins University Press.

Erickson, R. A. (1983) 'The evolution of the suburban space economy', *Urban Geography* 4: 95–121.

Erickson, R. A. (1985) 'Suburban nucleations', *Geographical Review* 75: 19–31.

Escobar, A. (1996) 'Construction nature: elements for a post-structuralist political ecology', *Futures* 28: 325–43.

Estall, R. C. (1985) 'Stock control in manufacturing: the just-in-time system and its locational implications', *Area* 17: 129–32.

Farole, T. (2011) *Special Economic Zones in Africa: Comparing Performance and Learning from Global Experience.* Washington DC: World Bank.

Farole, T. and Akince, G. (2011) 'Introduction', in T. Farole and G. Akince (eds), *Special Economic Zones: Progress, Emerging Challenges, and Future Directions.* Washington DC: World Bank, pp. 1–21.

Faulconbridge J., Hall, S. J. E., and Beaverstock, J. V. (2008) 'New insights into the internationalization of producer services: organizational strategies and spatial economies for global headhunting firms', *Environment & Planning A* 40: 210–34.

Feagin, J. R. (1987) 'Thee secondary circuit of capital: office construction in Houston, Texas', *International Journal of Urban and Regional Research* 11: 172–92.

Felker, G. B. (2003) 'Southeast Asian industrialisation and the changing global production system', *Third World Quarterly* 24: 255–82.

Ferguson, J. (2006) *Global Shadows: Africa in the Neoliberal World Order.* Durham: Duke University Press.

Fernandez, I. and Atienza, M. (2011) 'Increasing returns, comparative advantage, and history: the formation of the mining city of Antofagasta', *Urban Geography* 32: 641–61.

Firn, J. (1975) 'External control and regional development', *Environment & Planning A* 7: 393–414.

Fishman, R. (1987) *Bourgeois Utopias: The Rise and Fall of Suburbia.* New York: Basic Books.

Fleming, D. K. and Hayuth, Y. (1994) 'Spatial characteristics of transportation hubs: centrality and intermediacy', *Journal of Transport Geography* 2: 3–18.

Florida, R. (2005) *Cities and the Creative Class*. London: Routledge.

Florida, R., Mellander, C., and Holgersson, T. (2015) 'Up in the air: the role of airports for regional economic development', *American Regional Science* 54: 197–214.

Flyvbjerg, B., Bruzelius, N., and Rothengatter, W. (2003) *Megaprojects and Risk: An Anatomy of Ambition*. Cambridge: Cambridge University Press.

Folmer, E. (2013) 'Entrepreneurship in the neighborhood: shifting patterns of economic activities in residential neighborhoods in five Dutch cities', *Journal of Urban Affairs* 36: 742–59.

Folmer, E. and Risselada, A. (2013) 'Planning the neighbourhood economy: land-use plans and the economic potential of urban residential neighbourhoods in the Netherlands', *European Planning Studies* 21: 1873–94.

Forsyth, A. (2002) 'Who built Irvine? Private planning and the Federal government', *Urban Studies* 13: 2507–30.

Forsyth, A. (2014) 'Alternative forms of the high-technology district: corridors, clumps, cores, campuses, subdivisions, and sites', *Environment & Planning C* 32: 809–23.

Forsyth, A. and Crewe, K. (2010) 'Suburban technopoles as places: The international campus-garden-suburb style', *Urban Design International* 15: 165–82.

Freestone, R. (2011) 'Managing neoliberal urban spaces: commercial property development and Australian airports', *Geographical Research* 49: 115–31.

Freestone, R., Williams, P., and Borden, A. (2006) 'Flybuy cities: some planning aspects of airport privatization in Australia', *Urban Policy and Research* 24: 491–508.

French, S. (2000) 'Re-scaling the economic geography of knowledge and information: constructing life assurance markets', *Geoforum* 31: 101–19.

Friedmann, J. and Wolff, G. (1982) 'World city formation: an agenda for research and action', *International Journal of Urban and Regional Research* 6: 309–44.

Fröbel, F., Heinrichs, J., and Kreye, O. (1981) *The New International Division of Labour*. Cambridge: Cambridge University Press.

Fuentes, L. and Sierralta, C. (2004) 'Santiago de Chile, ¿ejemplo de una reestructuración capitalista global?' *EURE (Santiago)* 30: 7–28. Available at: http://www.scielo.cl/scielo.php?script=sci_arttext&pid=S0250-71612004009100002 (last accessed 13 January 2017).

Fuller, G. (2009) '>store>forward>: architectures of a future tense', in S. Cwerner, S. Kesselring, and J. Urry (eds), *Aeromobilities*. London: Routledge, pp. 64–75.

Garreau, J. (1991) *Edge City: Life on the New Frontier*. New York: Doubleday.

Gereffi, G. (1995) 'Global production systems and third world development', in B. Stallings (ed.), *Global Change, Regional Response: The New International Context of Development*. New York: Cambridge University Press, pp. 100–42.

Gereffi, G. (1996) 'The elusive last lap in the quest for developed country status', in J. H. Mittelman (ed.), *Globalization: Critical Reflections*. Boulder CO: Lynn Reinner. pp. 53–81.

Gereffi, G. (1999) 'International trade and industrial upgrading in the apparel commodity chain', *Journal of International Economics* 48: 37–70.

Gereffi, G. and Korzeniewicz, M. (1993) *Commodity Chains and Global Capitalism*. London: Praeger.

Gereffi, G., Humphrey, J., and Sturgeon, T. (2005) 'The governance of global value chains', *Review of International Political Economy* 12: 78–104.

Gershuny, J. (1978) *After Industrial Society?* Basingstoke: Macmillan.

Gershuny, J. (2000) *Changing Times: Work and Leisure in Postindustrial Society.* Oxford: Oxford University Press.

Gibbon, P. and Ponte, S. (2005) *Trading Down: Africa, Value Chains, and the Global Economy.* Philadelphia: Temple University Press.

Gibson-Graham, J. K. (1996) *The End of Capitalism (As We Know It).* Oxford: Blackwell.

Gibson-Graham, J. K. (2008) 'Diverse economies: performative practices for "other worlds"', *Progress in Human Geography* 32: 613–32.

Gibson-Graham, J. K., Cameron, J., and Healy, S. (2013) *Take Back the Economy: An Ethical Guide for Transforming Our Communities.* Minneapolis: University of Minnesota Press.

Gibson-Graham, J. K. and O'Neill, P. (2001) 'Exploring a new class politics of the enterprise', in J. K. Gibson-Graham, S. Resnick, and R. Wolff (eds), *Re/Presenting Class: Essays in Postmodern Marxism.* Durham: Duke University Press, pp. 56–80.

Giddens, A. (1984) *The Constitution of Society: Outline of the Theory of Structuration.* Berkeley, CA: University of California Press.

Ginsburg, N. (1991) 'Extended metropolitan regions in Asia: a new spatial paradigm', in N. Ginsburg, B. Koppel,and T. McGee (eds), *The Extended Metropolis: Settlement Transition in Asia.* Honolulu: University of Hawaii Press, pp. 27–46.

Glaeser, E. (2011) *The Triumph of the City: How Our Greatest Invention Makes Us Richer, Smarter, Greener, Healthier and Happier.* Basingstoke: Macmillan.

Glasmeier, A. (1988) 'Factors governing the development of high tech industry agglomerations: a tale of three cities', *Regional Studies* 22: 287–301.

Glückler, J. (2014) 'How controversial innovation succeeds in the periphery? A network perspective of BASF Argentina', *Journal of Economic Geography* 14: 903–27.

Goddard, J. B. (1975) *Office Location in Urban and Regional Development.* Oxford: Oxford University Press.

Golubchikov, O. and Phelps, N. A. (2011) 'The political economy of place at the post-socialist urban periphery: governing growth on the edge of Moscow', *Transactions of the Institute of British Geographers* 36: 425–40.

Goodwin, M. (1993) 'The city as commodity: the contested spaces of urban development', in G. Kearns and C. Philo (eds), *Selling Places: the City as Cultural Capital, Past and Present.* Oxford: Pergamon, pp. 145–62.

Gordon, I. R. (1999) 'Internationalisation and intercity competition', *Urban Studies* 36: 1001–16.

Gordon, I. R. and McCann, P. (2000) 'Industrial clusters: complexes, agglomeration and/or social networks?', *Urban Studies* 37: 513–32.

Gordon, P. and Richardson, H. W. (1996) 'Beyond polycentricity: the dispersed metropolis, Los Angeles, 1970–1990', *Journal of the American Planning Association* 62: 289–95.

Gospodini, A. (2006) 'Portraying, classifying and understanding the emerging landscapes in the post-industrial city', *Cities* 23: 311–30.

Goss, J. (1993) 'The "Magic of the Mall": an analysis of form, function and meaning in the contemporary retail built environment', *Annals of the Association of American Geographers* 83: 18–47.

Gottdiener, M. (1977) *Planned Sprawl: Private Public Interest Suburb*. London: Sage.

Gottdiener, M. (1986a) 'Culture, ideology and the sign of the city', in M. Gottdiener and A. Lagopoulos (eds), *The City and the Sign: An Introduction to Urban Semiotics*. New York: Columbia University Press, pp. 202–18.

Gottdiener, M. (1986b) 'Recapturing the center: A semiotic analysis of shopping malls', in M. Gottdiener and A. Lagopoulos (eds), *The City and the Sign: An Introduction to Urban Semiotics*. New York: Columbia University Press, pp. 288–302.

Gottdiener, M. (2001) *Life in the Air: Surviving the New Culture of Air Travel*. Lanham MD: Rowman & Littlefield.

Gottdiener, M. and Lagopoulos, A. (1986) 'Introduction', in M. Gottdiener and A. Lagopoulos (eds), *The City and the Sign: An Introduction to Urban Semiotics*. New York: Columbia University Press, pp. 1–22.

Gottmann, J. (1964) *Megalopolis: The Urbanised Northeastern Seaboard of the United States*. Cambridge, MA: MIT Press.

Gottmann, J. (1976) 'Megalopolitan systems around the world', *Ekistics*, 243, 109–13.

Gough, J. (1992) 'Workers' competition, class relations, and space', *Environment and Planning D* 10: 265–86.

Grabher, G. (ed.) (1993) *The Embedded Firm: On the Socioeconomics of Industrial Networks*. London: Routledge.

Graham, S. (2004) 'Constructing premium network spaces: reflections on infrastructure networks and contemporary urban development', in R. E. Hanley (ed.), *Moving People, Goods, and Information in the 21st Century: The Cutting Edge Infrastructures of Networked Cities*. London: Routledge, pp. 225–44.

Graham, S. (2010) *Cities Under Siege: The New Military Urbanism*. London: Verso.

Graham, S. and Marvin, S. (2001) *Splintering Urbanism: Networked Infrastructures, Technological Mobilities and the Urban Condition*. London: Routledge.

Grant J. (2006) 'The ironies of New Urbanism', *Canadian Journal of Urban Research* 15: 158–74.

Gregory, D. (1982) *Regional Transformation and Industrial Revolution: A Geography of the Yorkshire Woollen Industry*. London: Macmillan.

Haas, P. (1992) 'Introduction: epistemic communities and interrnational policy coordination', *International Organization* 46: 1–35.

Haberly, D. (2011) 'Strategic sovereign wealth fund investment and the new alliance capitalism: a network mapping investigation', *Environment & Planning A* 43: 1833–52.

Hakfoort, J., Poot, T., and Rietveld, P. (2001) 'The regional economic impact of an airport: the case of Amsterdam Schiphol airport', *Regional Studies* 35: 595–604.

Hall, P. (2002) *Cities of Tomorrow*. 3rd edn. Oxford: Blackwell.

Hall, P. A. and Soskice, D. (2001) *Varieties of Capitalism*. Chichester: Wiley.

Hampton, M. (2010) 'Enclaves and ethnic ties: the local impacts of Singaporean cross-border tourism in Malaysia and Indonesia', *Singapore Journal of Tropical Geography* 31: 239–53.

Hanes, J. E. (1993) 'From megalopolis to megaroporisu', *Journal of Urban History* 19: 56–94.

Hanlon, B., Vicino, T., and Short, J. R. (2006) 'The new metropolitan reality in the US: rethinking the traditional model', *Urban Studies* 43: 2129–43.

Hannam, K., Sheller, M., and Urry, J. (2006) 'Mobilities, immobilities and moorings', *Mobilities*, 1: 1–22.

Harbison, R. (1989 [1977]) *Eccentric Spaces*. London: Secker & Warburg.

Harding, T. and Javorcik, B. S. (2011) 'Roll out the red carpet and they will come: investment promotion and FDI flows', *The Economic Journal* 121: 1445–76.

Harris, R. (2004) *Creeping Conformity: How Canada became Suburban, 1890–1960*. Toronto: University of Toronto Press.

Harris, R. (2010) 'Meaningful types in a world of suburbs', in M. Clapson and R. Hutchinson (eds), *Suburbanization in Global Society*. Bingham, pp. 15–47.

Harris, R. and Larkham, P. J. (1999) 'Suburban foundation, form and function', in R. Harris and P. J. Larkham (eds), *Changing Suburbs: Foundation, Form and Function*. London: Spon, pp. 1–31.

Harrison, A., Wheeler, P., and Whitehead, C. (2004) *The Distributed Workplace: Sustainable Work Environments*. London: Spon.

Hart, J. F. (1982) 'The highest form of the Geographer's art', *Annals of the Association of American Geographers* 72: 1–29.

Harvey. D. (1985) *The Urbanisation of Capital*. Oxford: Blackwell.

Harvey, D. (1989) 'From managerialism to entrepreneurialism: the transformation in urban governance in late capitalism', *Geografiska Annaler Series B* 71: 3–17.

Harvey, D. (1991) *The Condition of Postmodernity: An Enquiry into the Origins of Cultural Change*. Oxford: Blackwell.

Harvey, D. (2003) *The New Imperialism*. Oxford: Oxford University Press.

Harvey, D. (2005) *A Brief History of Neoliberalism*. New York: Oxford University.

Hassler, M. (2005) 'Global markets, local home-working: governance and inter-firm relations in the Balinese clothing industry', *Geografiska Annaler B* 87: 31–43.

Hatziprokopiou, P. (2009) 'Strangers as neighbours in ten cosmopolis: new migrants in London, diversity and place', in S. H. Donald, E. Kofman, and C. Kevin (eds), *Branding Cities: Cosmopolitanism, Parochialism and Social Change*. London: Routledge, pp. 15–27.

Haughton, G. (1999) 'Environmental justice and the sustainable city', *Journal of Planning Education and Research* 18: 233–43.

Haynes, P. (2010) 'Information and communication technology and international business travel: mobility allies?', *Mobilities* 5: 547–64.

Healey, P. (1986) 'Diffusion of the new town idea in the developing world', in I. Masser and R. Williams (eds), *Learning from Other Countries*. Norwich: GeoBooks, pp. 121–33.

Healey, P. (2006) *Urban Complexity and Spatial Strategies: Towards a Relational Planning for our Times*. London: London.

Healey, R. G. (2015) 'Railroads, factor channelling and increasing returns: Cleveland and the emergence of the America manufacturing belt', *Journal of Economic Geography* 15: 499–538.

Hedlund, G. and Rolander, D. (1990) 'Action in heterarchies: new approaches to managing the MNC', in C. Bartlett, Y. Doz, and G. Hedlund (eds), *Managing the Global Firm*, London: Routledge, pp. 15–46.

Heinrichs, D., Lukas, M., and Nuissl, H. (2011) 'Privatisation of the fringes—a Latin American version of post-suburbia? The case of Santiago de Chile', in Phelps, N. and Wu, F. (eds), *International Perspectives on Suburbanization: A Post-Suburban World?* Basingstoke: Palgrave Macmillan, pp. 101–21.

Heitzman, J. (2004) *Network City: Planning the Information Society in Bangalore*. New Dehli: Oxford University Press.

Held, D. (1995) *Cosmopolitan Democracy*. Cambridge: Polity.

Held, D. and McGrew, A. (2002) *Globalization/Anti-globalization*. Cambridge: Polity.

Henderson, J. (1989) *The Globalization of High Technology Production*. London: Routledge.

Henderson, J., Dicken, P., Hess, M., Coe, N., and Yeung, H. W. C. (2002) 'Global production networks and the analysis of economic development', *Review of International Political Economy* 9: 436–64.

Hennart, J.-F. (2009) 'Down with MNE-centric theories! Market entry and expansion as the bundling of MNE and local assets', *Journal of International Business Studies* 40: 1432–54.

Herbert, C. W. and Murray, M. J. (2015) 'Building from scratch: new cities, privatized urbanism and the spatial restructuring of Johannesburg after apartheid', *International Journal of Urban and Regional Research* 39: 471–94.

Herod, A. (2000) 'Implications of just-in-time production for union strategy: Lessons from the 1998 General Motors-United Auto Workers dispute', *Annals of the Association of American Geographers* 90: 521–47.

Herod, A., Pickren, G., Rainnie, A., and McGrath Champ, S. (2014) 'Global destruction networks, labour and waste', *Journal of Economic Geography* 14: 421–41.

Hess, M. (2004) ' "Spatial" relationships? Towards a reconceptualization of embeddedness' *Progress in Human Geography* 28: 165–86.

Hesse, M. (2010) 'Cities, material flows and the geography of spatial interaction: urban places in the system of chains', *Global Networks* 10: 75–91.

Hidalgo, R., Borsdorf, A., and Sánchez, R. (2007) 'Taller Nacional sobre Migración Interna y desarrollo en Chile: diagnóstico, perspectivas y políticas'. CEPAL—CELADE, División de Población. BID. 1–17.

Hirt, S. (2012) *Iron Curtains: Gates, Suburbs and Privatization of Space in the Post-Socialist City*. Oxford: Wiley-Blackwell.

Hirt, S. (2013) 'Home, sweet home: American residential zoning in comparative perspective', *Journal of Planning Education and Research* 33: 292–309.

Hise, G. (1999) *Magnetic Los Angeles: Planning the Twentieth-century Metropolis*. Baltimore: Johns Hopkins University Press.

Hislop, D. (2012) 'Hanging on the telephone: mobile phone use patterns during UK-based business travellers on work-related journeys', *Transportation Research Part F.* 15: 101–10.

Hislop, D. and Axtell, C. (2015) 'The work-related affordances of business travel: a disaggregated analysis of journey stage and mode of transport', *Work, Employment and Society* 29: 1–19.

Holley, D. Jain, J., and Lyons, G. (2008) 'Understanding business travel time and its place in the working day', *Time and Society* 17: 27–46.

Hood, N. and Young, S. (1976) 'US investment in Scotland: aspects of the branch factory syndrome', *Scottish Journal of Political Economy* 23: 279–94.

Hopkins, A. G. (2002) 'The history of globalization—and the globalization of history', in A. G. Hopkins (ed.), *Globalization in World History*. London: Pimlico, pp. 11–46.

Howells, J. (2006) 'Intermediation and the role of intermediaries in innovation', *Research Policy* 35: 715–28.

Howitt, R. (1998) 'Scale as relation: musical metaphors of geographical scale', *Area* 30: 49–58.

Hubbard, P. and Hall, T. (1998) 'The entrepreneurial city and the new urban politics', in T. Hall and P. Hubbard (eds), *The Entrepreneurial City: Geographies of Politics, Regime and Representation*. Chichester: Wiley, pp. 1–23.

Hudson, A. (2000) 'Offshoreness, globalization and sovereignty: a postmodern geo-political economy?', *Transactions of the Institute of British Geographers*: 25: 269–83.

Hudson, R. (2008) 'Cultural political economy meets global production networks: a productive meeting?', *Journal of Economic Geography* 8: 421–40.

Hughes, A., Buttle, M., and Wrigley, N. (2007) 'Organisational geographies of corporate responsibility: a UK–US comparison of retailers' ethical trading initiatives', *Journal of Economic Geography* 7: 491–513.

Hughes, A., Wrigley, N., and Buttle, M. (2008) 'Global production networks, ethical campaigning, and the embeddedness of responsible governance', Journal of Economic Geography 8: 345–67.

Humphrey, J. and Schmitz, H. (2002) 'How does insertion in global value chains affect upgrading in industrial clusters?', *Regional Studies* 36: 1017–27.

Huws, U. (2014) *Labor in the Global Digital Economy: The Cybertariat Comes of Age*. New York: Monthly Review Press.

Hymer, S. (1979) *The Multinational Corporation: a Radical Approach*. Cambridge: Cambridge University Press.

Iammarino, S. and McCann, P. (2013) *Multinationals and Economic Geography: Location, Technology and Innovation*. Cheltenham: Edward Elgar.

Jacobs, J. (1969) *The Economy of Cities*. London: Jonathan Cape.

Jacobs, W. (2014) 'Rotterdam and Amsterdam as trading places? In search of the economic geographical nexus between global commodity chains and world cities', *Tijdschrift voor Economishe en Sociale Geografie* 105: 483–91.

Jacobsson, B. (2006) 'Regulated regulators: global trends of state transformation', in M. L. Djelic and K. Sahlin-Andersson (eds), *Transnational Governance: Institutional Dynamics of Regulation*. Cambridge: Cambridge University Press, pp. 205–24.

Jensen, P. D. O. and Pedersen, T. (2011) 'Then economic geography of offshoring: the fit between activities and location', *Journal of Management Studies* 48: 352–72.

Jonas, A. (2006) 'Pro scale: further reflections on the "scale debate" in human geography', *Transactions of the Institute of British Geographers* 31: 399–406.

Jones, A. (1999) 'Dialectics and difference: against Harvey's dialectical "post-Marxism"', *Progress in Human Geography* 23: 529–55.

Jones, G. (2005) *Multinationals and Global Capitalism: From the Nineteenth to the Twenty-first Century*. Oxford: Oxford University Press.

Kahn, A. (2002) 'Imagining New York: representations and perceptions of the city', in P. Madsen and R. Plunz (eds), *The Urban Lifeworld: Formation, Perception, Representation*. London: Routledge, pp. 237–51.

Kapelink, D. (2010) 'The repeat appointment factor: exploring decision patterns of elite investment arbitrators', *Cornell Law Review* 96: 47–90.

Kaplinsky, R. (1993) 'Export processing zones in the Dominican Republic: transforming manufactures into commodities', *World Development* 21: 1851–65.

Kaplinsky, R. (2000) 'Globalisation and unequalisation: What can be learned from value chain analysis?', *Journal of Development Studies* 37: 117–46.

Kasarda, J. D. and Lindsay, G. (2011) *Aerotropolis: The Way We'll Live Next*. New York: Farrar, Straws and Giroux.

Katz, B. (2001) 'Welcome to the "exit ramp" economy', *Boston Globe* May 13, p. A19.

Katz, M. L. and Shapiro, C. (1985) 'Network externalities, competition and compatibility', *American Economic Review* 75: 424–40.

Katz, M. L. and Shapiro, C. (1986) 'Technology adoption in the presence of network externalities', *Journal of Political Economy* 94: 822–41.

Katzenstein, P. (2005) *A World of Regions: Asia and Europe in the American Imperium*. Ithaca: Cornell University Press.

Kaufmann, V. (2002) *Re-thinking Mobility: Contemporary Sociology*. Aldershot: Ashgate.

Keane, W. (2001) 'Money is no object: materiality, desire and modernity in an Indonesian society', in F. R. Myers (ed.), *The Empire of Things: Regimes of Value and Material Culture*. Santa Fe: School of American Research Press, pp. 64–90.

Kearns, G. and Philo, C. (1993) 'Culture, history, capital: A critical introduction to the selling of places', in C. Philo and G. Kearns (eds), *Selling Places: The City as Cultural Capital, Past and Present*. Oxford: Pergamon, pp. 1–32.

Keeble, D. and Tyler, P. (1995) 'Enterprising behaviour and the urban-rural shift', *Urban Studies* 32: 975–97.

Kellerman, A. (2010) 'Business travel and leisure tourism: comparative trends in a globalizing world', in J. V. Beaverstock, B. Derudder, J. Faulconbridge, and F. Witlox (eds), *International Business Travel in the Global Economy*. Farnham: Ashgate, pp. 165–75.

Kellerman, A. (2012) *Personal Mobilities*. London: Routledge.

Kelly, P. F. (2001) 'The political economy of local labor control in the Philippines', *Economic Geography* 77: 1–22.

Kelly, P. F. (2002) 'Spaces of labour control: comparative perspectives from Southeast Asia', *Transactions of the Institute of British Geographers* 27: 395–411.

Kenyon, S. and Lyons, G. (2007) 'Introducing multitasking to the study of travel and ICT: examining its extent and assessing its potential importance', *Transportation Research Part A* 41: 161–75.

King, A. D. (1984) *The Bungalow: The Production of a Global Culture*. London: Routledge & Kegan Paul.

King, A. D. (2003) 'Writing transnational planning histories', in Nasr, J. and Volait, M. (eds), *Urbanism: Imported or Exported? Native Aspirations and Foreign Plans*. Chichester: Wiley, pp. 1–14.

Kitchin, R. and Dodge, M. (2011) *Code/Space: Software and Everyday Life*. Cambridge, MA: MIT Press.

Klak, T. and Myers, G. (1997) 'The discursive tactics of neoliberal development in small Third World countries', *Geoforum* 28; 133–49.

Kleibert, J. M. (2014) 'Strategic coupling in "next wave cities": Local institutional actors and the offshore service sector in the Philippines', *Singapore Journal of Tropical Geography* 35: 245–60.

Kleibert, J. M. (2016) 'Global production networks, offshore services and the branch-plant syndrome', *Regional Studies* 50: 1995–2009.

Klingmann, A. (2007) *Brandscapes: Architecture in the Experience Economy*. Cambridge, MA: MIT Press.

Kloosterman, R. C. (2015) 'Forces of agglomeration: Allen Scott's *The Cultural Economy of Cities* revisited', *The Built Environment* 41: 379–89.

Kloosterman, R. C. and Lambregts, B. (2001) 'Clustering of economic activities in polycentric urban regions: the case of the Randstad', *Urban Studies* 38: 717–32.

Knowles S. G. and Leslie, S. W. (2001) '"Industrial Versailles": Eero Saarinen's Corporate Campuses for GM, IBM, and AT&T', *Isis* 92: 1–33.

Knox, P. L. (2008) *Metroburbia USA*. New Brunswick NJ: Rutgers University Press.

Kobrin, S. J. (1987) 'Testing the bargaining hypothesis in the manufacturing sector in developing countries', *International Organization* 41: 609–38.

Kobrin, S. J. (2001) 'Sovereignty@Bay: globalization, multinational enterprise, and the international political system', in A. L. Rugman and T. L. Brewer (eds), *The Oxford Handbook of International Business*. New York: Oxford University Press, pp. 181–205.

Kobrin, S. J. (2009) 'Private political authority and public responsibility: transnational politics, transnational firms, and human rights', *Business Ethics Quarterly* 19: 349–74.

Kolb, D. (2008) *Spralwing Places*. Athens: University of Georgia Press.

Kotkin, J. (2010a) *The Next Hundred Million: America in 2050*. New York: Penguin Books.

Kulcsar, L. J. and Domokos, T. (2005) 'The post-socialist growth machine: the case of Hungary', *International Journal of Urban and Regional Research* 29: 550–63.

Kumar, A. (1997) *Java and Modern Europe: Ambiguous Encounters*. London: Curzon.

Kunstler, J. H. (1993) *The Geography of Nowhere: The Rise and Decline of America's Man Made Landscape*. London: Simon & Schuster.

Lacher, H. (2005) 'International transformation and the persistence of territoriality: towards a new political geography of capitalism', *Review of International Political Economy* 12: 26–52.

Lampel, J. and Meyer, A. D. (2008) 'Guest editors' introduction: field-configuring events as structuring mechanisms: how conferences, ceremonies, and trade shows constitute new technologies, industries, and markets', *Journal of Management Studies* 45: 1025–35.

Lang, R. (2003) *Edgeless Cities: Exploring the Elusive Metropolis*. Washington: Brookings Institution Press.

Lang, R. and Knox, P. (2009) 'The new metropolis: rethinking megalopolis', *Regional Studies* 43: 789–802.

Lang, R. and LeFurgy, J. (2007) *Boomburbs: The Rise of America's Accidental Cities*. Washington DC: Brookings Institution.

Lang, R. and Nelson, A. C. (2011) *Megapolitan America: A New Vision for Understanding America's Metropolitan Geography.* Chicago: American Planning Association.

Lanz, R. and Miroudot, S. (2011) 'Intra-firm trade: patterns, determinants and policy implications', *OECD Trade Policy Papers* 114. Paris: OECD.

Larner, W. (2003) 'Neoliberalism?', *Environment & Planning D, Society & Space* 21: 509–12.

Lash, S. (1999) *Another Modernity: A Different Rationality.* Oxford: Blackwell.

Lash, S. and Urry, J. (1991) *The End of Organized Capitalism.* Cambridge: Polity.

Lash, S. and Urry, J. (1994) *Economy of Signs and Space.* London: Sage.

Lassen, C. (2009) 'A life in corridors: social perspectives on aeromobility at work in knowledge organizations', in S. Cwerner, S. Kesselring, and J. Urry (eds), *Aeromobities.* London: Routledge, pp. 17–193.

Lassen, C. (2010) 'Individual rationalities of global business travel', in J. V. Beaverstock, B. Derudder, J. Faulconbridge,and F. Witlox (eds), *International Business Travel in the Global Economy.* Farnham: Ashgate, pp. 177–94.

Latham, R. (2001) 'Identifying the contours of transboundary political life', in R. Latham, R. Kassimir, and T. M. Callaghy (eds), *Interventions and Transnationalism in Africa: Global-Local Networks of Power.* Cambridge: Cambridge University Press, pp. 69–92.

Latham, R., Kassimir, R., and Callaghy, T. (2001) 'Introduction: transboundary formations, intervention, order, and authority', in R. Latham, R. Kassimir, T. M.and Callaghy (eds), *Interventions and Transnationalism in Africa: Global-Local Networks of Power.* Cambridge: Cambridge University Press, pp. 1–22.

Latour, B. (1993) *We Have Never Been Modern.* Cambridge, MA: Harvard University Press.

Laurier, E. (2002) 'The region as accomplishment of mobile workers', in B. Brown, N. Green, and R. Harper (eds), *Wireless World: Social and Interactional Aspects of the Mobile Age, Computer Supported Cooperative Work.* Berlin: Springer, pp. 46–61.

Laurier, E. (2004) 'Doing office work on the motorway', *Theory, Culture and Society* 21: 261–77.

Leadbeatter, C. (2000) *Living on Thin Air: The New Economy.* Harmondsworth: Penguin.

Leaf, M. (1996) 'Building the road for the BMW: culture, vision, and the extended metropolitan region of Jakarta', *Environment & Planning A* 28: 1617–35.

Lee, M. (1993) *Consumer Culture Reborn: The Cultural Politics of Consumption.* London: Routledge.

Lee, R. (2006) 'The ordinary economy: tangled up in values and geography', *Transactions of the Institute of British Geographers* 31: 413–32.

Lefebvre, H. (1991[1974]) *The Production of Space.* Oxford: Blackwell.

Lefebvre, H. (2003 [1970]) *The Urban Revolution.* Minneapolis: University of Minnesota Press.

Lefevre, C. (1998) 'Metropolitan government and governance in western countries; a critical review', *International Journal of Urban and Regional Research* 22: 9–25.

Leisch, H. (2002) 'Gated communities in Indonesia', *Cities* 19: 341–50.

Leitner, H. and Sheppard, E. (1998) 'Economic uncertainty, inter-urban competition and the efficacy of entrpreneurialism', in T. Hall and P. Hubbard (eds), *The Entrepreneurial City: Geographies of Politics, Regime and Representation.* Chichester: Wiley, pp. 285–307.

Leitner, H., Peck, J., and Sheppard, E. (2007a) 'Contesting urban futures: decentring neoliberalism', in H. Leitner, J. Peck,and E. Sheppard (eds), *Contesting Neoliberalism*. New York: Guilford Press, pp. 1–25.

Leitner, H., Peck, J., and Sheppard, E. (2007b) 'Squaring up to neoliberalism', in H. Leitner, J. Peck,and E. Sheppard(eds), *Contesting Neoliberalism*. New York: Guilford Press, pp. 311–27.

Leonard, D. K. and Strauss, S. (2003) *Africa's Stalled Development: International Causes and Cures*. Boulder CO: Lynn Reinner.

Lepawsky, J. (2009) 'Clustering as anti-politics machine? Situating the politics of regional economic development and Malaysia's Multimedia Super Corridor', *Regional Studies* 43: 463–78.

Lerup, L. (2005) 'American speed, American distance', in Fishman, R. (ed.), *New Urbanism: Peter Calthorpe vs. Lars Lerup. Michigan Debates on Urbanism Vol. II*. New York: Distributed Arts Press, pp. 40–52.

Levi-Faur, D. (2005) 'The global diffusion of regulatory capitalism', *The Annals of the American Academy of Political and Social Science* 598: 12–32.

Levi-Faur, D. (2008) 'Foreword', in J. Braithwaite, *Regulatory Capitalism: How It Works, Ideas for Making It Work Better*. Cheltenham: Edward Elgar.

Leving, Y. (2012) *Anatomy of a Short Story: Nabokov's Puzzles, Codes, "Signs and Symbols"*. London: Continuum.

Lewis, R. (1999) 'Running rings around the city: North American industrial suburbs, 1850–1950', in T. Harris and P. Larkham (eds), *Changing Suburbs: Foundation, Form and Function*. London: Spon, pp. 146–67.

Lewis, R. (2004a) 'Industry and the suburbs', in R. Lewis (ed.), *Manufacturing Suburbs; Building Work and Home on the Metropolitan Fringe*. Philadelphia: Temple University Press, pp. 1–15.

Lewis, R. (2004b) 'A city transformed: manufacturing districts and suburban growth in Montreal, 1850–1929', in R. Lewis (ed.), *Manufacturing Suburbs; Building Work and Home on the Metropolitan Fringe*. Philadelphia: Temple University Press, pp. 76–91.

Li, Wei (1998) 'Anatomy of a new ethnic settlement: The Chinese ethnoburb in Los Angeles', *Urban Studies* 35: 479–501.

Li, Y. and Phelps, N. A. (forthcoming) 'Megalopolis unbound: knowledge collaboration and functional polycentricity within and beyond the Yangtze River Delta Region in China', *Urban Studies*.

Light, D. and Young, C. (2015) 'Toponymy as commodity: exploring the economic dimensions of urban place names', *International Journal of Urban and Regional Research* 39: 435–50.

Line, T., Jain, J., and Lyons, G. (2011) 'The role of ICTs in everyday mobile lives', *Journal of Transport Geography* 19: 1490–9.

Linnros, H. D. and Hallin, P. O. (2001) 'The discursive nature of environmental conflicts: the case of the Öresund link', *Area* 33: 391–403.

Lister, K. and Harnish, T. (2011) 'The state of telework on the U.S.: how individuals, business and government benefit', *Telework Research Network*. Available from http://www.workshifting.com/downloads/downloads/Telework-Trends-US.pdf (last accessed, 1 February 2017).

References

Loveridge, R. (2009) 'The multinational firms as a locus of learning along networks', in S. Collinson and G. Morgan (eds), *Images of the Multinational Firm*. Chichester: Wiley, pp. 217–45.

Lovering, J. (1993) 'MNEs and wannabes', in N. A. Phelps and P. Raines (eds), *The New Competition for Inward Investment*. Cheltenham: Edward Elgar, pp. 39–60.

Lowe, M. S. (2000) 'Britain's regional shopping centres: new urban forms?', *Urban Studies* 337: 261–74.

Lury, C. (2011) *Consumer Culture*. 2nd edn. New Brunswick NJ: Rutgers University Press.

Lyons, G. (2013) 'Business travel—the social practices surrounding meetings', *Research in Transportation Business and Management* 9: 50–7.

McCann, E. (2011) 'Urban policy mobilities and global circuits of knowledge', *Annals of the Association of American Geographers* 101: 107–30.

McCann, P. and Mudambi, R. (2005) 'Analytical differences in the economics of geography: the case of the multinational firm', *Environment and Planning A* 37: 1857.

McDowell, L. (1988) *Capital Culture: Gender at Work in the City*. Oxford: Blackwell.

McFall, L. (2014) 'The problem of cultural intermediaries in the economy of qualities', in J. Smith-Maguire and J. Matthews (eds), *The Cultural Intermediaries Reader*. London: Sage, pp. 42–63.

MacFarlane, C. (2011) 'The city as a machine for learning', *Transactions of the Institute of British Geographers* 36: 360–76.

McGee, T. (1991) 'The emergence of *desakota* regions in Asia: expanding a hypothesis', in N. Ginsburg, B. Koppel, and T. McGee (eds), *The Extended Metropolis: Settlement Transition in Asia*. Honolulu: University of Hawaii Press, pp. 3–25.

McKeever, R. (1970) 'Business parks, office parks, plazas and centers: a study of development practices and procedures', *Urban Land Institute Technical Bulletin* 65: 1–125.

MacKinnon, D. (2012) 'Beyond strategic coupling: reassessing the firm-region nexus in global production networks', *Journal of Economic Geography* 12: 227–45.

McManus, R. and Ethington, P. J. (2007) 'Suburbs in transition: new approaches to suburban history', *Urban History* 34: 317–37.

Magalhaes, C. (2012) 'Business improvement districts and the recession: implications for public realm governance and management in England', *Progress in Planning* 77: 143–77.

Magee, G. B. and Thompson, A. S. (2010) *Empire and Globalisation: Networks of People, Goods and Capital in the British World, c. 1850–1914*. Cambridge: Cambridge University Press.

Mair, A. (1993) 'New growth poles? just-in-time manufacturing and local economic development strategy', *Regional Studies* 27: 207–21.

Mair, A., Florida, R., and Kenney, M. (1988) 'The new geography of automobile production: Japanese transplants in North America', *Economic Geography*: 64: 352–73.

Majone, G. (1989) *Evidence, Argument, and Persuasion in the Policy Process*. New Haven: Yale University Press.

Malpas, J. (2009) 'Cosmopolitanism, branding and the public realm', in S. H. Donald, E. Kofman, and C. Kevin (eds), *Branding Cities: Cosmopolitanism, Parochialism and Social Change*. London: Routledge, pp. 189–97.

Mansfield, E. and Romeo, A. (1980) 'Technology transfer to overseas subsidiaries by US-based firms', *The Quarterly Journal of Economics* 95: 737–50.

Marginson, S. (2010) 'Space, mobility and synchrony in the knowledge economy', in S. Marginson, P. Murphy, and M. A. Peters (eds), *Global Creation: Space, Mobility, and Synchrony in the Age of the Knowledge Economy*. Oxford: Peter Lang, pp. 117–49.

Markusen, A. (1996) 'Sticky places in slippery space: a typology of industrial districts', *Economic Geography* 72: 293–313.

Marshall, A. (1932) Edition. *Economics of Industry*. London: Macmillan.

Marston, S. (2000) 'The social construction of scale', *Progress in Human Geography* 24: 219–42.

Marston, S., Jones, J. P., and Woodward, K. (2005) 'Human geography without scale', *Transactions of the Institute of British Geographers* 30: 416–32.

Martin, R. and Sunley, P. (2001) 'Rethinking the "economic" in economic geography: broadening our vision or losing our focus?', *Antipode* 33: 148–61.

Maskell, P., Bathelt, H., and Malmberg, A. (2006) 'Building global knowledge pipelines: the role of temporary clusters', *European Planning Studies* 14: 997–1013.

Mason, C., Carter, S., and Tagg, S. (2011) 'Invisible businesses: the characteristics of home-based businesses on the United Kingdom', *Regional Studies* 45: 625–39.

Masotti, L. H. (1973) 'Prologue: suburbia reconsidered—myth and counter-myth', in L. H. Masotti and J. K. Hadden (eds), *The Urbanization of the Suburbs*. London: Sage, pp. 115–22.

Massey, D. B. (1984) *Spatial Divisions of Labour*. Basingstoke: Macmillan.

Massey, D. B. (1994) 'A global sense of place', in D. B. Massey, *Space, Place and Gender*. Cambridge: Polity, pp. 146–56.

Matiza, T. and Oni, O. A. (2014) 'The case for nation branding as an investment promotion methodology for African nations: a literature-based perspective', *Mediterranean Journal of Social Sciences* 5: 262–71.

Matthews, J. and Smith-Maguire, J. (2014) 'Introduction: thinking with cultural intermediaries', in Smith-Maguire, J. and Matthews, J. (eds), *The Cultural Intermediaries Reader*. London: Sage, pp. 1–11.

May, J., Wills, J., Datta, K., Evans, Y., Herbert, J., and McIlwane, C. (2007) 'Keeping London working: global cities the British state and London's new migrant division of labour', *Transactions of the Institute of British Geographers* 32: 151–67.

Mbaiwa, J. E. (2005) 'Enclave tourism and its socio-economic impacts in the Okovango Delta, Botswana', *Tourism Management* 26: 157–72.

Meijers E. and Burger, M. (2015) 'Stretching the concept of borrowed size', *Urban Studies* 54: 269–91.

Merrifield, A. (2010) *Magical Marxism*. London: Pluto Press.

Merrifield, A. (2013) 'The urban question under planetary urbanization', *International Journal of Urban and Regional Research* 37: 909–22.

Meyer, J. W., Boli, J., Thomas, G. M., and Ramirez, F. O. (1997) 'World society and the nation-state', *American Journal of Sociology*, 103: 144–81.

Miao, T. and Hall, P. (2014) 'Optical illusion? The growth and development of the Optics Valley of China', *Environment and Planning C: Government and Policy* 32: 863–79.

MIGA (2000) *Investment Promotion Toolkit: Strengthening the Location's Image*. Washington DC: Multilateral Investment Guarantee Agency.

Miles, K. (2013) *The Origins of International Investment Law: Empire, Environment and the Safeguarding of Capital*. Cambridge: Cambridge University Press.

Millar, J. and Salt, J. (2001) 'Portfolios of mobility: the movement of expertise in transnational corporations in two sectors—aerospace and extractive industries', *Global Networks* 8: 25–50.

Miller, D. (2001) 'Alienable gifts and inalienable commodities', in F. R. Myers (ed.), *The Empire of Things: Regimes of Value and, Material Culture*. Santa Fe: School of American Research Press, pp. 91–115.

Miller, D. (2010) *Stuff*. Cambridge: Polity.

Miller, P. and O'Leary, T. (1993) 'Accounting expertise and the politics of the product: economic citizenship and modes of corporate governance', *Accounting, Organizations and Society* 18: 187–206.

Mills, A. (2011) 'Antinomies of public and private at the foundations of international investment law and arbitration', *Journal of International Economic Law* 14: 469–503.

Ministry of Housing and Urbanism—MINVU (1998) 'Memoria explicativa. Modificación del Plan Regulador de Santiago'. Incorporación de las comunas de Colina, Lampa y Til Til. MINVU, Santiago Piedra Roja: http://piedraroja.cl/#Historia (last accessed, 14 January 2017).

Mir, R. and Sharpe, D. R. (2009) 'The multinational firm as an institution of exploitation and domination', in R. Colinson and G. Morgan (eds), *Images of the Multinational Firm*. Chichester: Wiley, pp. 247–66.

Molloy, M. and Larner, W. (2010) 'Who needs cultural intermediaries indeed? Gendered networks in then designer fashion industry', *Journal of Cultural Economy* 3: 361–77.

Molotch, H. (1976) 'The city as a growth machine: Toward a political economy of place', *American Journal of Sociology* 82: 309–32.

Molotch, H. (2004) *Where Stuff Comes From: How Toasters, Toilets, Cars, Computers and Many Other Things Come to Be as They Are*. London: Routledge.

Moore, J. W. (2002) 'Capital, territory, and hegemony over the long dureée', *Science and Society* 65: 476–4.

Moreno-Monroy, A. (2012) 'Informality in space: understanding agglomeration economies during economic development', *Urban Studies* 49: 2019–30.

Morgan, G. (2001) 'The development of transnational standards and regulations and their impacts on firms', in G. Morgan, P. H. Kristensen, and R. Whitley (eds), *The Multinational Firm: Organizing across Institutional and National Divides*. Oxford: Oxford University Press, pp. 225–52.

Morgan, G. (2009) 'Globalization, multinationals and institutional diversity', *Economy & Society* 38: 580–605.

Morgan, G. and Kristensen, P. H. (2009) 'Multinational firms as societies', in R. Colinson and G. Morgan (eds), *The Image of the Multinational Firm*. Chichester: Wiley, pp. 167–91.

Morgan, K. and Sayer, A. (1988) *Microcircuits of Capital: 'Sunrise' Industry and Uneven Development*. Cambridge: Polity.

Morisset, J. (2003) 'Does a country need a promotion agency to attract foreign direct investment? A small analytical model applied to 58 countries', *World Bank Policy Research Working Paper, No. 3028*, Washington, DC: World Bank.

Morisset, J. and Andrews-Johnson, K. (2004) *The Effectiveness of Promotion Agencies in Attracting Foreign Direct Investment.* Occasional Paper No.16. Washington, DC: Foreign Investment Advisory Service.

Morrill, R. (2008) 'Classic map revisited: the growth of megalopolis', *Professional Geographer* 58: 155–60.

Mozingo, L. (2011) *Pastoral Capitalism: A History of Suburban Corporate Landscapes.* Cambridge, MA: MIT Press.

Muller, E. K. (2004) 'Industrial suburbs and the growth of metropolitan Pittsburgh, 1870–1920', in Lewis, R. (ed.), *Manufacturing Suburbs; Building Work and Home on the Metropolitan Fringe.* Philadelphia: Temple University Press, pp. 124–42.

Muniesa, F., Millo, Y., and Callon, M. (2007) 'An introduction to market devices', in M. Callon, Y. Millo, and F. Muniesa (eds), *Market Devices.* Oxford: Blackwell, pp. 1–12.

Murdoch, J. (1997) 'Inhuman/nonhuman/human: actor network theory and the prospects for a nondualistic and symmetrical perspective on nature and society', *Environment & Planning D* 15: 731–56.

Murphy, P. (2010a) 'The enigma of distance', in S. Marginson, P. Murphy, and M. A. Peters (eds), *Global Creation: Space, Mobility and Synchrony in the Age of the Knowledge Economy.* Oxford: Peter Lang, pp. 18–50.

Murray, M. J. (2011) *City of Extremes: The Spatial Politics of Johannesburg.* Durham: Duke University Press.

MVRDV (1999) *Metacity, Datatown.* Rotterdam: 010 Publishers.

Myers, F. (2001) 'Introduction', in F. R. Myers (ed.), *The Empire of Things: Regimes of Value and Material Culture.* Santa Fe: School of American Research Press, pp. 3–64.

NACE (2008) Nomenclature statistique des activités économiques dans la Communauté Européenne. Available at:http://ec.europa.eu/eurostat/ramon/nomenclatures/index. cfm?TargetUrl=LST_NOM_DTL&StrNom=NACE_REV2&StrLanguageCode=EN&In tPcKey=&StrLayoutCode=HIERARCHIC (last accessed, 1 February 2017).

NAICS (2012) North American Industrial Classification System. Available at: http:// www.census.gov/eos/www/naics/ (last accessed, 1 February 2017).

Nadvi, K. (1999) 'Collective efficiency and collective failure: the response of the Sialkot surgical instrument cluster to global quality pressures', *World Development* 27: 1605–26.

Nasr, J. and Volait, M. (2003) 'Introduction: transporting planning', in J. Nasr and M. Volait(eds), *Urbanism: Imported or Exported? Native Aspirations and Foreign Plans.* Chichester: Wiley, pp. xi–xxxviii.

Neilson, J. and Pritchard, B. (2011) *Value Chain Struggles: Institutions and Governance in the Plantation Districts of South India.* Chichester: Wiley.

Neuman, M. (2005) 'The compact city fallacy', *Journal of Planning Education and Research* 25: 11–26.

Ngai, P. and Chan, J. (2012) 'Global capital, the state and Chinese workers: the Foxconn experience', *Modern China* 38: 383–410.

Niedzielski, M. A. and Malecki, E. J. (2012) 'Making tracks: rail networks in world cities', *Annals of the Association of American Geographers* 102: 1409–31.

Nixon, S. and Du Gay, P. (2002) 'Who needs cultural intermediaries?', *Cultural Studies* 16: 495–500.

North, D. and Smallbone, D. (2000) 'The innovativeness and growth of rural SMEs in the 1990s', *Regional Studies* 34: 145–57.

Nuissl, H. and Rink, D. (2005) 'The "production" of sprawl in Eastern Germany as a phenomenon of post-socialist transformation', *Cities* 22: 123–34.

Nye, J. S. (1990) 'Soft power', *Foreign Policy* 80: 153–71.

O'Connell, J. C. (2013) *The Hub's Metropolis: Greater Boston's Development from Railroad Suburbs to Smart Growth*. Cambridge, MA: MIT Press.

O'Connor, K. and Scott, A. (1992) 'Airline services and metropolitan areas in the Asia-Pacific region, 1970-1990', *Review of Urban and Regional Development Studies* 4: 240–53.

O'Mara, M. P. (2005) *Cities of Knowledge: Cold War Science and the Search for the Next Silicon Valley*. Princeton, NJ: Princeton University Press.

O'Riain, S. (2005) *The Politics of High-Tech Growth: Developmental Network Stats in the Global Economy*. Cambridge: Cambridge University Press.

Oakey, R. P. and Cooper, S. Y. (1989) 'High technology industry, agglomeration, and the potential for peripherally sited small firms', *Regional Studies* 23: 347–60.

OECD (2013) *Territorial Reviews: Antofagasta, Chile*. Paris: Organisation for Economic Cooperation and Development.

Ohmae, K. (1999) *The Borderless World: Power and Strategy in the Interlinked Economy, Management Lessons in the New Logic of the Global Marketplace*. New York: Harper Business.

Olds, K. (2002) *Globalization and Urban Change: Capital, Culture, and Pacific Rim Mega-projects*, Oxford: Oxford University Press.

Oliver, N. and Wilkinson, B. (1992) *The Japanization of British Industry: New Developments in the 1990s*. Oxford: Blackwell.

Ong. A. (1999) *Flexible Citizenship: The Cultural Logics of Transnationality*. Durham: Duke University Press.

Osterhammel, J. (2014) *The Transformation of the World: A Global History of the Nineteenth Century*. Princeton, NJ: Princeton University Press.

Pain, K. and Hall, P. (2008) 'Informational quantity versus informational quality: the perils of navigating te space of flows', *Regional Studies* 42: 1065–77.

Palan, R. (1998) 'Trying to have your cake and eating it: how and why the state system has created offshore', *International Studies Quarterly* 42: 625–43.

Palan, R., Murphy, R., and Chavagneux, C. (2010) *Tax Havens: How Globalization Really Works*. Ithaca: Cornell University Press.

Parr, J. B. (2002) 'Agglomeration economies: ambiguities and confusions', *Environment and Planning A* 34: 717–32.

Pascoe, D. (2001) *Airspaces*. London: Reaktion.

Pasotti, E. (2010) *Political Branding in Cities: The Decline of Machine Politics in Bogota, Naples and Chicago*. Cambridge: Cambridge University Press.

Passell, A. (2013) *Building the New Urbanism: Places, Professions, and Profits in the American Metropolitan Landscape*. London: Routledge.

Patiblanda, M. and Petersen, B. (2002) 'The role of transnational corporations in the evolution of a high-tech industry: the case of India's software industry', *World Development* 30: 1561–77.

Paul, D. E. (2002) 'Re-scaling IPE: subnational states and the regulation of the global political economy', *Review of International Political Economy* 9: 465–89.

Pavlínek, P. (2016) 'Whose success? The state-foreign capital nexus and the development of the automotive industry in Slovakia', *European Urban and Regional Studies* 23: 571–93.

Pavlínek, P. and Žížalová, P. (2016) 'Linkages and spillovers in global production networks: firm-level analysis of the Czech automotive industry', *Journal of Economic Geography* 16: 331–63.

Pearce, R. and Papanastassiou, M. (2009) *The Strategic Development of Multinationals: Subsidiaries and Innovation*. Basingstoke: Palgrave-Macmillan.

Peck, F. W. (1996) 'Regional development and the production of space: the role of infrastructure in the attraction of new inward investment', *Environment and Planning A* 28: 327–39.

Peck, F. W. and Stone, I. (1993) 'Japanese inward investment in the northeast of England: reassessing Japanisation', *Environment and Planning C* 11: 55–67.

Peck, J. (2002) 'Political economies of scale: fast policy, interscalar relations, and neoliberal workfare', *Economic Geography* 78: 331–60.

Peck, J. (2011) 'Neoliberal suburbanism: frontier space', *Urban Geography* 32: 884–919.

Peck, J. (2015) 'Navigating economic geographies', unpublished mimeograph, Department of Geography, University of British Columbia (copy available from the author).

Peck, J. and Theodore, N. (2001) 'Contingent Chicago: restructuring the spaces of temporary labour', *International Journal of Urban and Regional Research* 25: 471–96.

Peck, J. and Theodore, N. (2015) *Fast Policy: Experimental Statecraft at the Thresholds of Neoliberalism*. Minneapolis: University of Minnesota Press.

Peck, J. and Tickell, A. (1992) 'Local modes of social regulation? Regulation theory, Thatcherism and uneven development', *Geoforum* 23: 347–63.

Peck, J. and Tickell, A. (2002) 'Neoliberalizing space', *Antipode* 34: 380–404.

Peck, J., Theodore, N., and Ward, K. (2005) 'Constructing markets for temporary labour: employment liberalization and the internationalization of the staffing industry', *Global Networks* 5: 3–26.

Peet, R. (2003) *Unholy Trinity: the IMF, World Bank and WTO*. London: Zed Books.

Perlin, F. (1983) 'Proto-industrialization and pre-colonial South Asia', *Past and Present*: 30–95.

Perlmutter, H. V. (1972) 'The multinational firm and the future', *Annals of the American Academy of Political and Social Science* 403: 139–52.

Petri, P. A. (1994) 'The regional clustering of foreign direct investment and trade', *Transnational Corporations* 3: 1–24.

Peyroux, E., Pütz, R., and Glasze, G. (2012) 'Business improvement districts: the internationalizaton and contextualization of a "travelling concept"', *European Urban and Regional Studies* 19: 111–20.

References

Phelps, N. A. (1992) 'External economies, agglomeration and flexible accumulation', *Transactions of the Institute of British Geographers* 17: 35–46.

Phelps, N. A. (1993) 'Branch plants and the evolving spatial division of labour: a study of material linkage change in the Northern Region of England', *Regional Studies* 27: 87–101.

Phelps, N. A. (1998) 'On the edge of something big: Edge-city economic development in Croydon, South London', *Town Planning Review* 69: 441–65.

Phelps, N. A. (2000) 'The locally embedded multinational and institutional capture', *Area*: 32: 169–78.

Phelps, N. A. (2004a) 'Clusters, dispersion and the spaces in between: for an economic geography of the banal', *Urban Studies* 41: 971–89.

Phelps, N. A. (2004b) 'Archetype for an archipelago? Batam as anti-model and model of industrialization in reformasi Indonesia', *Progress in Development Studies* 4: 206–29.

Phelps, N. A. (2007) 'Gaining from globalisation? State extra-territoriality and domestic economic impacts—the case of Singapore', *Economic Geography* 83: 371–93.

Phelps, N. A. (2010) 'Suburbs for Nations: Some interdisciplinary connections on the suburban economy', *Cities* 27: 68–76.

Phelps, N. A. (2012a) *An Anatomy of Sprawl: Planning and Politics in Britain*. London: Routledge.

Phelps, N. A (2012b) 'The sub-creative economy of the suburbs in question', *International Journal of Cultural Studies* 15: 259–71.

Phelps, N. A. (2012c) 'The growth machine stops? Urban politics and the making and remaking of an edge city', *Urban Affairs Review* 48: 670–700.

Phelps, N. A. (2016) *Sequel to Suburbia: Glimpses of America's Post-Suburban Future*. Cambridge, MA: MIT Press.

Phelps, N. A. and Dawood, S. R. S. (2014) 'Untangling the spaces of high technology in Malaysia', *Environment and Planning C: Government and Policy* 32: 896–915.

Phelps, N. A. and Fuller, C. (2000) 'Multinationals, intracorporate competition and regional development', *Economic Geography* 76: 224–43.

Phelps, N. A. and Fuller, C. (2016) 'Inertia and change in multinational enterprise subsidiary capabilities: an evolutionary economic geography framework', *Journal of Economic Geography* 16: 109–30.

Phelps, N. A. and Ozawa, T. (2003) 'Contrasts in agglomeration: proto-industrial, industrial and post-industrial forms compared', *Progress in Human Geography* 27: 583–604.

Phelps, N. A. and Parsons, N. (2003) 'Edge urban geographies: notes from the margins of Europe's capital cities', *Urban Studies* 40: 1725–49.

Phelps, N. A. and Tewdwr-Jones, M. (1998) 'Institutional capacity building in a strategic policy vacuum: the case of the Korean firm LG in South Wales', *Environment & Planning C, Government & Policy* 16: 735–55.

Phelps, N. A. and Tewdwr-Jones, M. (2001) 'Globalisation, regions and the state: exploring the limitations of economic modernisation through inward investment', *Urban Studies* 38: 1253–72.

Phelps, N. A. and Tewdwr-Jones, M. (2008) 'If geography is anything maybe it's planning's alter ego: reflections on policy relevance in two disciplines concerned with place and space', *Transactions of the Institute of British Geographers* 33: 566–84.

Phelps, N. A. and Valler, D. (2017) 'Urban development and the politics of dissonance', *Territory, Politics and Governance*.

Phelps, N. A. and Waley, P. (2004) 'Capital versus the districts: A tale of one multi-national company's attempt to disembed itself', *Economic Geography* 80: 191–215.

Phelps, N. A. and Wijaya, H. (2016) 'Joint action in action: local economic development forums and industry cluster development in Central Java, Indonesia', *International Development Planning Review* 38: 425–48.

Phelps, N. A. and Wood, A. M. (2011) 'The new post-suburban politics?' *Urban Studies* 48: 2591–2610.

Phelps, N. A. and Wood, A. M. (forthcoming) 'The business of location: site selection consultants and the mobilisation of knowledge in the location decision', *Journal of Economic Geography*.

Phelps, N. A. and Wu, F. (2009) 'Capital's search for order: foreign direct investment and modes of social order in East and Southeast Asia', *Political Geography* 28: 44–54.

Phelps, N. A., Fallon, R., and Williams, C. (2001) 'Small firms, borrowed size and the urban rural shift', *Regional Studies* 35: 613–24.

Phelps, N. A., McNeill, D., and Parsons, N. (2002) 'In search of a European edge urban identity: trans-European networking among edge urban municipalities', *European Urban and Regional Studies* 9: 112–24.

Phelps, N. A., MacKinnon, D., Stone, I., and Braidford, P. (2003) 'Embedding the multinationals? Institutions and the development of overseas manufacturing affiliates in Wales and North East England', *Regional Studies* 37: 27–40.

Phelps, N. A., Parsons, N., Ballas, D., and Dowling, A. (2006) *Post-Suburban Europe: Planning and Politics at the Margins of Europe's Capital Cities*. Basingstoke: Palgrave-Macmillan.

Phelps, N.A., Power, M., and Wanjiru, R. (2007) 'Learning to compete: the investment promotion community and the spread of neoliberalism', in K. England and K. Ward (eds), *Neo-liberalization: States, Networks, Peoples*. Oxford: Blackwell, pp. 83–109.

Phelps, N. A., Stillwell, J. C. H., and Wanjiru, R. (2009) 'Broken chain? AGOA and foreign direct investment in the Kenyan clothing industry', *World Development* 37: 314–25.

Phelps, N. A., Parsons, N., Ballas, D., and Dowling, A. (2010) *Post-suburban Europe: Planning and Politics at the Margins of Europe's Capital Cities*. Basingstoke: Palgrave-Macmillan.

Phelps, N. A., Wood, A. M., and Valler, D. C. (2010) 'A post-suburban world? An outline of a research agenda', *Environment & Planning A* 42: 366–83.

Phelps, N. A., Bunnell, T., and Miller, M. A. (2011) 'Post-disaster economic development in Aceh: neoliberalization and other economic-geographical imaginaries', *Geoforum* 42: 418–26.

Phelps, N. A. Bunnell, T., Miller, M., and Taylor, J. (2014) 'Urban inter-referencing within and beyond Indonesia', *Cities* 39: 37–49.

Phelps, N. A., Atienza, M., and Arias, M. (2015) 'Encore for the enclave: the changing nature of the industry enclave with illustrations from the mining industry in Chile', *Economic Geography* 91: 119–46.

Phelps, N. A., Vento, A. T., and Roitman, S. (2015) 'The suburban question: grassroots politics and place making in Spanish suburbs', *Environment & Planning* C 33: 512–32.

Pierre, J. (2005) 'Comparative Urban Governance Uncovering Complex Causalities', *Urban Affairs Review* 40: 446–62.

Pike, A. (2013) 'Economic geographies of brands and branding', *Economic Geography* 89: 317–39.

Pike, A. and Pollard, J. (2010) 'Economic geographies of financialization', *Economic Geography* 86: 29–51.

Pla-Barber, J. and Camp, J. (2011) 'Springboarding: a new geographical landscape for European foreign investment in Latin America', *Journal of Economic Geography* 12: 519–38.

PLADECO (2009–2012) 'Ilustre Municipalidad de Colina'. Available at: http://reportescomunales.bcn.cl/2012/index.php/Colina#Indicadores_demogr.C3.A1ficos (last accessed 18 January 2017).

Popp. A. (2000) '"Swamped in information but starved of data": information and intermediaries in clothing supply chains', *Supply Chain Management* 5: 151–61.

Potter, A. and Watts, D. H. (2011) 'Evolutionary agglomeration theory: increasing returns, diminishing returns, and the industry life cycle', *Journal of Economic Geography* 11: 417–55.

Poulsen, L. N. S. (2014) 'Bounded rationality and the diffusion of modern investment treaties', *International Studies Quarterly* 58: 1–14.

Powell, W. W. (1990) 'Neither market nor hierarchy: network forms of organization', *Research in Organizational Behaviour* 12: 295–336.

Power, D. and Jansson, J. (2008) 'Cyclical clusters in global circuits: overlapping spaces in furniture trade shows', *Economic Geography* 84: 423–48.

Prince, R. (2015) 'The spaces in between: mobile policy and the topographies and topologies of the technocracy', *Environment & Planning D* 34: 420–37.

Princen, T., Maniates, M., and Conca, K. (2002) 'Confronting consumption', in T. Princen, M. Maniates, and K. Conca (eds), *Confronting Consumption*. Cambridge, MA: MIT Press, pp. 1–20.

Pritchett, L., Woolcock, M., and Andrews, M. (2013) 'Looking like a state: techniques of persistent failure in state capability for implementation', *Journal of Development Studies* 49: 1–18.

Rabinow, P. (1986) 'Representations are social facts: modernity and post-modernity in anthropology', in S. Clifford and G. E. Marcus (eds), *Writing Culture: The Poetics and Politics of Ethnography*. Berkeley, CA: University of California Press, pp. 234–61.

Rainie, L. and Wellman, B. (2012) *Networked: The New Social Operating System*. Cambridge, MA: MIT Press.

Ramamurti, R. (2001) 'The obsolescing "bargaining model"? MNC-host developing country relations revisited', *Journal of International Business Studies* 32: 23–39.

Ramírez-Pasillas, M. (2008) 'Resituating proximity and knowledge cross-fertilization in clusters by means of international trade fairs', *European Planning Studies* 16: 643–62.

Ramsay, A. (1986) 'International exchange of ideas about new towns', in I. Masser and R. Williams (eds), *Learning from Other Countries*. Norwich: GeoBooks, pp. 91–9.

Rankin, W. J. (2010) 'The epistemology of the suburbs: knowledge, production and corporate laboratory design', *Critical Inquiry* 36: 771–806.

Rantisi, N. (2014) 'Exploring the role of industry intermediaries in the construction of "local pipelines": the case of the Montreal fur garment cluster and the rise of fur-fashion connections', *Journal of Economic Geography* 14: 955–71.

Rapaport. E. (2015) 'Sustainable urbanism in the age of Photoshop: images, experiences and the role of learning through inhabiting the international travels of a planning model', *Global Networks* 15: 307–24.

Reade, E. (1983) 'If planning is anything, maybe it can be identified', *Urban Studies* 20: 159–171.

Reich, R. (1990) 'Who is us?', *Harvard Business Review* 61: 53–64.

Relph, E. (1976) *Place and Placelessness*. London: Pion.

Renard, M.-C. (1999) 'The interstices of globalization: the example of fair coffee', *Sociologia Ruralis* 39: 484–500.

Renski, H. (2008) 'New firm entry, survival, and growth in the United States: a comparison of urban, suburban and rural area', *Journal of the American Planning Association* 75: 60–77.

Reuschke, D. (2010) 'Job-induced commuting between two residences: characteristics of a multilocational living arrangement in the late modernity', *Comparative Population Studies* 35: 107–34.

Riddle, L., Brinkerhoff, J. M., and Nielsen, T. M. (2008) 'Partnering to beckon them home: public-sector innovation for diaspora foreign investment promotion', *Public Administration and Development* 28: 54–66.

Riles, A. (2001) 'The view from the international plane: perspective and scale in the architecture of colonial international law', in N. Blomley, D. Delaney, and R. T. Ford (eds), *The Legal Geographies Reader*. Oxford: Blackwell, pp. 276–84.

Rimmer, P. J. and Dick, H. W. (2009) *The City in Southeast Asia: Patterns, Processes and Policy*. Singapore: NUS Press.

Robinson, E. A. G. (1953 [1931]) *The Structure of Competitive Industry*. Cambridge: Cambridge University Press.

Robinson, J. (2006) *Ordinary Cities: Between Modernity and Development*. London: Routledge.

Rodgers, D. T. (1998) *Atlantic Crossings*. Cambridge, MA: Harvard University Press.

Roitman, S. and Phelps, N. A. (2011) 'Do gates negate the city? Gated communities' contribution to the urbanisation of suburbia in Pilar, Argentina', *Urban Studies* 48: 3481–3503.

Roy, A. (2009) 'The 21st-century metropolis: new geographies of theory', *Regional Studies* 43: 819–30.

Rudolph, R. and Brade, I. (2005) 'Moscow: processes of restructuring in the post-Soviet metropolitan periphery', *Cities* 22: 135–50.

Ruggie, J. G. (1993) 'Territoriality and beyond: problematizing modernity in international relations', *International Organization* 47: 139–74.

Rugman, A. Verbeke, A., and Yuan, W. (2010) 'Re-conceptualising Bartlett and Ghoshal's classification of national subsidiary roles in the multinational enterprise'. *Journal of Management Studies*, 48: 253–77.

Rycroft, R. and Kash, D. (1999) *The Complexity Challenge*. London: Pinter Publishers.

Sack, R. D. (1980) *Conceptions of Space in Social Thought: A Geographic Perspective*. Minneapolis: University of Minnesota Press.

Sack, R. D. (1992) *Place, Modernity and the Consumer's World: A Relational Framework for Geographical Analysis*. Baltimore: Johns Hopkins University Press.

Sack, R. D. (2003) *A Geographical Guide to the Real and the Good*. London: Routledge.

Salt, J. (2010) 'Business travel and portfolios of mobility within global companies', in J. V. Beaverstock, B. Derudder, J. Faulconbridge, and F. Witlox (eds), *International Business Travel in the Global Economy*. Farnham: Ashgate, pp. 107–24.

Sassen, S. (2013) 'When territory deborders territoriality', *Territory, Politics, Governance* 1: 21–45.

Saunders, P. (1981) *Urban Politics: A Sociological Interpretation*. London: Hutchinson.

Saunier, P. -Y. (2001) 'Sketches from the urban international, 1910–50: voluntary associations, international institutions and US philanthropic foundations', *International Journal of Urban and Regional Research* 25: 380–403.

Saunier, P. -Y. (2002) 'Taking up the bet on connections: a municipal contribution', *Contemporary European History* 11: 507–27.

Sauvant, K. P. and Alvarez, J. E. (2011) 'Introduction: international investment in transition', in J. E. Alvarez and K. P. Sauvant (eds), *The Evolving International Investment Regime: Expectations, Realities and Options*. Oxford: Oxford University Press, pp. xxxi–xlii.

Saxenian, A. (2007) *The New Argonauts: Regional Advantage in a Global Economy*. Cambridge, MA: Harvard University Press.

Sayer, A. (1984) *Method in Social Science. A Realist Approach*. London: Hutchinson.

Sayer, A. (1999) 'Valuing culture and economy', in L. Ray and A. Sayer (eds), *Culture and Economy after the Cultural Turn*. London: Sage, pp. 53–76.

Schafran, A. (2014) 'Rethinking mega-regions: sub-regional politics in a fragmented metropolis', *Regional Studies* 48: 587–602.

Schmitz, H. (1995a) 'Small shoemakers and Fordist giants: tale of a supercluster', *World Development* 23: 9–28.

Schmitz, H. (1995b) 'Collective efficiency: growth path for small scale industry', *Journal of Development Studies* 31: 529–66.

Schmitz, H. (1999a) 'Global competition and local cooperation: success and failure in the Sinos Valley, Brazil', *World Development* 27: 1627–50.

Schmitz, H. (1999b) 'Collective efficiency and increasing returns', *Cambridge Journal of Economics* 23: 465–83.

Schueth, S. (2011) 'Assembling international competitiveness: the Republic of Georgia, USAID, and the doing business project', *Economic Geography* 81: 51–77.

Scott, A. J. (1982) 'Locational patterns and dynamics of industrial activity in the modern metropolis', *Urban Studies* 19: 111–42.

Scott, A. J. (1983) 'Industrial organization and the logic of intra-metropolitan location, 1: theoretical considerations', *Economic Geography* 59: 233–50.

Scott, A. J. (1986) 'Industrial organization and location: division of labor, the firm and spatial process', *Economic Geography* 62: 215–31.

Scott, A. J. (1988) 'Flexible production systems and regional development: the rise of new industrial spaces in North America and Western Europe', *International Journal of Urban and Regional Research* 12: 171–86.

Scott, A. J. (2008) *The Social Economy of the Metropolis: Cognitive-Cultural Capitalism and the Global Resurgence of Cities*. Oxford: Oxford University Press.

Scott, A. J. (2011) 'Emerging cities of the third wave', *City* 15: 289–321.

Scott, A. J. (2012) *A World in Emergence. Cities and Regions in the 21st Century*. Cheltenham: Edward Elgar.

Scott, A. J. and Roweis, S. T. (1977) 'Urban planning in theory and practice: a reappraisal', *Environment and Planning A* 9: 1097–1119.

Scott, A. J. and Storper, M. (1987) 'High technology industry and regional development: a theoretical critique and reconstruction', *International Social Science Journal* 112: 215–32.

Scott, A. J. and Storper, M. (2015) 'The nature of cities: the scope and limits of urban theory', *International Journal of Urban and Regional Research* 39: 1–15.

Scully, V. (1994) 'The architecture of community', in P. Katz (ed.), *The New Urbanism: Toward an Architecture of Community*. New York: McGraw-Hill, pp. 221–30.

Selwyn, B. (2015) 'Commodity chains, creative destruction and global inequality', *Journal of Economic Geography* 15: 253–74.

Sell, S. K. (2003) *Private Power, Public Law: The Globalization of Intellectual Property Rights*. Cambridge: Cambridge University Press.

Senn, L. and Gorla, G. (1999) 'Networking strategies as a factor in urban decentralization', in A. Summers, P. C. Cheshire, and L. Senn (eds), *Urban Change in the United States and Western Europe: Comparative Analysis and Policy*. Washington, DC: Urban Institute Press, pp. 243–62.

Sharma, S. (2014) *In the Meantime: Temporality and Cultural Politics*. Durham: Duke University Press.

Sheard, P. (1983) 'Auto production systems in Japan: organizational and locational features', *Australian Geographical Studies* 21: 49–68.

Shearmur, R., Coffey, W., Dubé, C., and Barbonne (2007) 'Intrametropolitan employment structure: polycentricity, scatteration, dispersal and chaos in Toronto, Montreal and Vancouver', 1996–2001, *Urban Studies* 44: 1713–38.

Sheller, M. and Urry, J. (2000) 'The city and the car', *International Journal of Urban and Regional Research* 24: 737–57.

Sheller, M. and Urry, J. (2006) 'Introduction: mobile cities, urban mobilities', in Sheller, M. and Urry, J. Eds. *Mobile Technologies of the City*. London: Routledge.

Sheppard, E. (2002) 'The spaces and times of globalization: place, scale, networks and positionality', *Economic Geography* 78: 307–30.

Sheppard, E. (2003) 'Competition in space and between places', in E. Sheppard and T. J. Barnes (eds), *A Companion to Economic Geography*. Oxford: Blackwell, pp. 169–87.

Sheppard, E. (2008) 'Geographic dialectics?', *Environment & Planning A* 40: 2603–12.

Sheppard, E., Barnes, T. J., and Peck, J. (2012) 'The long decade: economic geography, unbound', in T. J. Barnes, J. Peck, and E. Sheppard(eds), *The Wiley-Blackwell Companion to Economic Geography*, Oxford: Wiley-Blackwell, pp. 1–24.

Sidaway, J. D. (2007) 'Enclave space: a new metageography of development?', *Area* 39: 331–9.

Sieverts, T. (2003) *Cities without Cities: An Interpretation of the Zwischenstadt*. London: Routledge.

Sieverts, T. (2011) 'The in-between city as an image of society: from the impossible order towards a possible disorder in the urban landscape', in D. Young, R. Keil, and P. Wood (eds), *In-Between Infrastructure: Urban Connectivity in an Age of Vulnerability.* Kelowna: Praxis(e) Press, pp. 19–27.

Simmie, J. (2000) *Innovative Cities.* London: Spon.

Sinclair, T. J. (1994) 'Passing judgement: credit rating processes as regulatory mechanisms or governance in the emerging world order', *Review of International Political Economy* 1: 133–59.

Singer, H. W. (1950) 'The distribution of gains between investing and borrowing countries', *American Economic Review* 40: 473–85.

Sklair, L. (2001) *The Transnational Capitalist Class.* Oxford: Blackwell.

Sklair, L. (2005) 'The transnational capitalist class and contemporary architecture in globalizing cities', *International Journal of Urban and Regional Research* 29: 485–500.

Sklair, L. (2011) *Assembling for Development: The Maquila Industry in Mexico and the United States.* London: Routledge.

Smith, N. (1984) *Uneven Development.* Oxford: Blackwell.

Smith, N. (2007) Nature as accumulation strategy', *Socialist Register* 16: 19–41.

Smith-Maguire, J. (2014) 'Bourdieu on cultural intermediaries', in J. Smith-Maguire and J. Matthews (eds), *The Cultural Intermediaries Reader.* London: Sage, pp. 15–24.

Soja, E. (2000) *Postmetropolis.* Oxford: Blackwell.

Sorensen, A. (2011) 'Post-suburban Tokyo? Urbanization, suburbanization and reurbanization', in N. A. Phelps and F. Wu (eds), *International Perspectives on Suburbanization: A Post Suburban World?* Basingstoke: Palgrave-Macmillan, pp. 210–24.

Sornarajah, M. (2010) *The International Law on Foreign Investment.* 3rd edn. Cambridge: Cambridge University Press.

Sornarajah, M. (2015) *Resistance and Change in the Law on International Investment.* Cambridge: Cambridge University Press.

Stilgoe, J. R. (1983) *Metropolitan Corridor: Railroads and the American Scene.* New Haven: Yale University Press.

Stone, D. (2004) 'Transfer agents and global networks in the "transnationalization" of policy', *Journal of European Public Policy* 11: 545–66.

Storper, M. (1995) 'The resurgence of regional economies, ten years later: the region as a nexus iof untraded interdependencies', *European Urban and Regional Studies* 2: 191–221.

Storper, M. and Scott, A. J. (2016) 'Current debates in urban theory: a critical assessment', *Urban Studies.*53: 1114–36.

Suarez-Villa, L. (1989) 'Polycentric restructuring, metropolitan evolution, and the decentralization of manufacturing', *Tijdschrift voor Economische en Sociale Geografie* 80: 194–205.

Sutcliffe, A. (1986) 'The historian's perspective', in I. Masser and R. Williams (eds), *Learning from Other Countries.* Norwich: GeoBooks, pp. 3–10.

Swyngedouw, E. (1997) 'Excluding the other: the production of scale and scaled politics', in R. Lee and J. Wills (eds), *Geographies of Economies.* London: Arnold, pp. 167–76.

Tachieva, G. (2010) *Sprawl Repair Manual.* New York: Island Press.

Tait, M. and Jensen, O. (2007) 'Travelling ideas, power and place: the cases of urban villages and business improvement districts', *International Planning Studies* 12: 107–27.

Taylor, G. R. (1970 [1915]) *Satellite Cities: A Study of Industrial Suburbs.* New York: Arno Press and The New York Times.

Taylor, J. E. (2002) 'The bund: littoral space of empire in the treaty ports of East Asia', *Social History* 27: 125–42.

Taylor, P. J. (1995) 'Beyond containers: internationality, interstateness, interterritoriality', *Progress in Human Geography* 19: 1–15.

Taylor, P. J., Catalano, G., and Walker, D. R. F. (2002) 'Exploratory analysis of the world city network', *Urban Studies* 39: 2377–94.

Teaford, J. C. (1997) *Post-suburbia: Government and Politics in the Edge Cities.* Baltimore: Johns Hopkins University Press.

Teece, D. J. (1977) 'Technology transfer by multinational firms: the resource cost of transferring technological know-how', *Economic Journal* 87: 242–61.

Terranova, T. (2004) *Network Culture: Politics for the Information Age.* London: Pluto Press.

Tétreault, M. A. (1999) 'Out-of-body experiences: migrating firms and altered states', *Review of International Political Economy* 6: 55–78.

Thomas, K. P. (2000) *Competing for Capital: Europe and North America in a Global Era.* Washington DC: Georgetown University Press.

Thomas, K. P. (2011) *Investment Incentives and the Global Competition for Capital.* Basingstoke: Palgrave-Macmillan.

Thompson. G. F. (2004) 'Is all the world a complex network?', *Economy & Society* 33: 411–24.

Thorngren, B. (1970) 'How do contact systems affect regional development?', *Environment and Planning* 2: 409–27.

Thrift, N. (1996) 'The rise of soft capitalism', in A. Herod, G. O'Tuathail, and J. Roberts (eds), *An Unruly World? Globalization, Governance and Geography.* London: Routledge, pp. 25–71.

Thrift, N. (2006) 'Reinventing invention: new tendencies in capitalist commodification', *Economy and Society* 35: 279–306.

Thrift, N. and Glennie, P. (1993) 'Historical geographies of urban life and urban consumption', in G. Kearns and C. Philo (eds), *Selling Places the City as Cultural Capital, Past and Present.* Oxford: Pergamon, pp. 33–48.

Thrift, N. and Olds, K. (1996) 'Refiguring the economic in economic geography', *Progress in Human Geography* 20: 311–37.

Thrift, N., Leyshon, A., and Daniels, P. W. (1987) *'Sexy Greedy': The New International Financial System, the City of London and the South East of England.* Liverpool: Department of Geography, University of Liverpool.

Tiebout, C. (1956) 'A pure theory of local expenditures', *Journal of Political Economy* 64: 416–24.

Tracey, P. and Clark, G. L. (2003) 'Alliances, networks and competitive strategy: rethinking clusters of innovation', *Growth and Change* 34: 1–16.

Trudeau, D. and Malloy, P. (2011) 'Suburbs in disguise? Examining the geographies of the new urbanism', *Urban Geography* 32: 424–47.

UN Habitat (2009) *Global Report on Human Settlements 2009: Planning Sustainable Cities*. Geneva: United Nations.

UNCTAD (1985) *The History of UNCTAD, 1964–1984*. Geneva: United Nations.

UNCTAD (1993) *World Investment Report, 1993: Transnational Corporations and Integrated International Production*. Geneva: United Nations.

UNCTAD (1997) *Survey of Investment Promotion Best Practices*. Geneva: United Nations.

UNCTAD (2001) *The World of Investment Promotion at a Glance: A Survey of Investment Promotion Practices*. Geneva: United Nations.

UNCTAD (2013) *World Investment Report, 2013: Global Value Chains—Investment and Trade for Development*. Geneva: United Nations.

United Nations (1995). *Reviving Investment in Africa: Constraints and Policies*. Addis Ababa: Economic Commission for Africa.

Urry, J. (1995) *Consuming Places*. London: Routledge.

Urry, J. (2003) *Global Complexity*. Cambridge: Polity.

Urry, J. (2008) 'Governance, flows, and the end of the car system?', *Global Environmental Change* 18: 343–9.

Urry, J. (2009) 'Aeromobilities and the global', in Cwerner, S., Kesselring, S., and Urry, J. (eds), *Aeromobilities*. London: Routledge, pp. 25–38.

Urry, J. (2014) *Offshoring*. Cambridge: Polity.

Valler, D. C., Phelps, N. A., and Radford, J. (2014) 'Soft space, hard bargaining: planning for high-tech growth in "Science Vale"', *Environment and Planning C* 32: 824–42.

Van Meeteren, M., Neal, Z., and Derudder, B. (2016) 'Disentangling agglomeration and network externalities: a conceptual typology', *Papers in Regional Science* 95: 61–80.

Van Wijk, M., Brattinga, K., and Bontje, M. (2011) 'Exploit or protect airport regions from urbanization? Assessment of land-use restrictions in Amsterdam-Schiphol', *European Planning Studies* 19: 261–77.

Vento, A. T. (2016) 'Megaproject meltdown: post-politics, neoliberal urban regeneration and Valencia's fiscal crisis', *Urban Studies* 54: 68–84.

Vernon, R. (1966) 'International investment and international trade in the product cycle', *The Quarterly Journal of Economics* 80: 190–207.

Vernon, R. (1979) 'The product cycle hypothesis in a new international environment', *Oxford Bulletin of Economics and Statistics* 41: 255–67.

Vogel, S. K. (1996) *Freer Markets, More Rules: Regulatory Reform in Advanced Industrial Countries*. Ithaca: Cornell University Press.

Von Luebke, C., McCulloch, N., and Pantunru, A. A. (2009) 'Heterodox reform symbioses: the political economy of investment climate reforms in Solo, Indonesia', *Asian Economic Journal* 23: 269–96.

Wainwright, J. (2007) 'Spaces of resistance in Seattle and Cancun', in H. Leitner, J. Peck, and E. Sheppard (eds), *Contesting Neoliberalism*. New York: Guilford Press, pp. 179–203.

Wakeham, R. (2003) 'Dreaming the new Atlantis: science and the planning of technopolis, 1955–1985', *Osiris* 18: 255–70.

Walker, R. A. (1981) 'A theory of suburbanization: capitalism and the construction of the urban space in the United States', in M. Dear and A. J. Scott (eds), *Urbanization and Urban Planning in Capitalist Societies*. London: Methuen, pp. 383–429.

Walker, R. A. (1985) 'Is there a service economy? The changing capitalist division of labor', *Science & Society* 49: 42–83.

Walker, R. A. (1989) 'A requiem for corporate geography: New directions in industrial organization, the production of place and the uneven development', *Geografiska Annaler B* 71: 43–68.

Walker, R. A. (2004) 'Industry builds out the city: the suburbanization of manufacturing in the San Francisco Bay Area, 1850–1940', in R. Lewis (ed.), *Manufacturing Suburbs: Building Work and Home on the Metropolitan Fringe*. Philadelphia: Temple University Press, pp. 92–123.

Walker, R. A. (2016) 'Why cities? A response', *International Journal of Urban and Regional Research* 40: 164–80.

Walker, R. A. and Lewis, R. D. (2001) 'Beyond the crabgrass frontier: industry and the spread of North American cities, 1850–1950', *Journal of Historical Geography* 27: 3–19.

Walton, W. and Dixon, P. (2000) 'The deregulation of the provision of motorway service areas in the United Kingdom and the consequent dilemmas for planning', *Town Planning Review* 71: 333–59.

Wang, J. J. and Olivier, D. (2006) 'Port-FEZ bundles as spaces of global articulation: the case of Tianjin, China', *Environment and Planning A* 38: 1487.

Ward, K. (2006) '"Policies in motion", urban management and state restructuring: trans-local expansion of business improvement districts', *International Journal of Urban and Regional Research* 30: 54–75.

Ward, S. V. (1998) *Selling Places: The Marketing and Promotion of Towns and Cities, 1850–2000*. Abingdon: Taylor & Francis.

Ward, S. V. (2003) 'Learning from the U.S.: the Americanization of Western Urban Planning', in J. Nasr and M. Volait(eds), *Urbanism: Imported or Exported? Native Aspirations and Foreign Plans*. Chichester: Wiley, pp. 83–106.

Ward, S. V. (2005) 'A pioneer "global intelligence corps"? The internationalization of planning practice, 1890–1939', *Town Planning Review* 76: 119–41.

Warner, S. B. (1978) *Streetcar Suburbs: the Process of Growth in Boston (1870–1900)*. Cambridge, MA: Harvard University Press.

Watts, H. D. (1981) *The Branch Plant Economy*. London: Longman.

Watts, M. (2004) 'Petroleum conflict and the political ecology of rule in the Niger Delta, Nigeria', in R. Peet and M. Watts, *Liberation Ecologies: Environment, Development and Social Movements*, 2nd edn. London: Routledge, pp. 250–72.

Watts, M. and Peet, R. (2004) 'Liberating political ecology', in R. Peet and M. Watts, *Liberation Ecologies: Environment, Development and Social Movements*, 2nd edn. London: Routledge, pp. 3–43.

Webber, M. M. (1964) 'The urban place and the nonplace urban realm', in M. M. Webber (ed.), *Explorations into Urban Structure*. Philadelphia: University of Pennsylvania Press, pp. 79–153.

Webster, C. (2002) 'Property rights and the public realm: gates, green belts, and Gemeinschaft', *Environment and Planning B: Planning and Design* 29: 397–412.

Weijland, H. (1999) 'Microenterprise clusters in rural Indonesia: Industrial seedbed and policy target', *World Development* 27: 1515–30.

Weisskoff, R. and Wolff, E. (1977) 'Linkages and leakages: industrial tracking in an enclave economy', *Economic Development and Cultural Change* 25: 607–28.

Wells, L. T. and Wint, A. (2000) *Marketing a Country: Promotion as a Tool for Attracting Foreign Investment (revised edition)*. Occasional Paper 13. Washington DC: Foreign Investment Advisory Service.

Westenholz, A. (2006) 'Identity, Times and Work', *Time & Society* 15: 33–55.

Whebell, C. F. J. (1969) 'Corridors: a theory of urban systems', *Annals of the Association of American Geographers* 59: 1–26.

White, P. and Hurdley, L. (2003) 'International migration and the housing market: Japanese corporate movers in London', *Urban Studies* 40: 687–706.

Whitley, R. (ed.) (1992) *European Business Systems: Firms and Markets in Their National Contexts*. London: Spon.

Whitley, R. (2009) 'The multinational firm as a distinct organizational form', in R. Colinson and G. Morgan (eds), *The Image of the Multinational Firm*. Chichester: Wiley, pp. 145–66.

Whyte, R. E. and Poynter, T. A. (1984) 'Strategies for foreign-owned subsidiaries in Canada', *Business Quarterly* 49: 59–69.

Whyte, W. H. (1967 [1956]) *The Organization Man*. Harmondsworth: Penguin.

Wildavsky, A. (1973) 'If planning is everything, maybe it's nothing', *Policy Science* 4: 127–53.

Wilkins, M. (1974) *The Maturing of Multinational Enterprise: American Business Abroad from 1914 to 1970*. Cambridge, MA: Harvard University Press.

Wilson, K. L. and Portes, A. (1980) 'Immigrant enclaves: an analysis of labor market experiences of Cubans in Miami', *American Journal of Sociology* 86: 295–319.

Winter, S. G. and Szulanski, G. (2001) 'Replication as strategy', *Organization Science* 12: 730–43.

Witt, P., Van Oort, F., Wiegmans, B., and Spit, T. (2014) 'European corridors as carriers of dynamic agglomeration externalities', *European Planning Studies* 22: 2326–50.

Wolman, H. (2008) 'Comparing local government systems across countries: conceptual and methodological challenges to building a field of comparative local government studies', *Environment & Planning C* 26: 87–103.

Wood, A. (2004) 'The scalar transformation of the US commercial property-development industry: a cautionary note on the limits of globalization', *Economic Geography*: 80: 119–40.

World Bank (2012) *Global Investment Promotion Best Practices 2012*. Washington DC: World Bank.

Wrigley, N., Coe, N., and Currah, A. (2005) 'Globalizing retail: conceptualizing the distribution-based transnational corporation (TNC)', *Progress in Human Geography* 29: 437–57.

Wu, F. (2004) 'Transplanting cityscapes: the use of imagined globalization in housing commodification in Beijing', *Area* 36: 227–34.

Wu, F. (2005) 'Rediscovering the "gate" under market transition: from work-unit compounds to commodity housing enclaves', *Housing Studies* 20: 235–54.

Wu, F. (2014) *Planning for Growth: Urban and Regional Planning in China*. London: Routledge.

Wu, F. and Phelps, N. A. (2011) '(Post) suburban development and state entrepreneurialism in Beijing's outer suburbs', *Environment and Planning A* 43: 410–30.

Yanarella, E. J. and Green, W. C. (eds) (1990) *The Politics of Industrial Recruitment: Japanese Automobile Investment and Economic Development in the American States*. New York: Praeger.

Yeung, H. W. C. (1994) 'Critical reviews of geographical perspectives on business organizations and the organization of production: towards a network approach', *Progress in Human Geography* 18: 460–90.

Yeung, H. W. C. (1998) 'Capital, state and space: contesting the borderless world', *Transactions of the Institute of British Geographers* 23: 291–309.

Yeung, H. W. C. (2000) 'China's transitional economy: The political economy of Singaporean investments in China', *Political Geography* 19: 809–40.

Yeung, H. W. C. (2003) 'Practicing new economic geographies: a methodological examination', *Annals of the Association of American Geographers* 93: 442–62.

Yeung, H. W. C. (2004) *Chinese Capitalism in a Global Era: Towards a Hybrid Capitalism*. London: Routledge.

Yeung, H. W. C. (2005) 'Rethinking relational economic geography', *Transactions of the Institute of British Geographers* 30: 37–51.

Yeung, H. W. C. (2016) *Strategic Coupling: East Asian Industrial Transformation in the New Global Economy*. Ithaca: Cornell University Press.

Yeung, H. W. C and Coe, N. M. (2015) 'Toward a dynamic theory of global production networks', *Economic Geography* 91: 29–58.

Yeung, H. W. C., Weidong, L., and Dicken, P. (2006) 'Transnational corporations and network effects of a local manufacturing cluster in mobile telecommunications equipment in China', *World Development* 34: 520–40.

Young, A. (1928) 'Increasing returns and economic progress', *The Economic Journal* 38: 527–42.

Young, C., Diep, M., and Drabble, S. (2006) 'Living with difference? The "cosmopolitan" and urban reimaging in Manchester, UK', *Urban Studies* 43: 1678–714.

Young, D. and Keil, R. (2010) 'Reconnecting the disconnected: the politics of infrastructure in the in-between city', *Cities* 27: 87–95.

Young, S., Hood, N., and Dunlop, S. (1988) 'Global strategies, multinational subsidiary roles and economic impact in Scotland', *Regional Studies* 22: 487–97.

Zukin, S. (1998) 'Urban lifestyles: diversity and standardization in spaces of consumption', *Urban Studies* 35: 825–39.

General Index

absenting processes 35
actor network theory (ANT) 30, 37, 60, 205
actors
  and relational geometry 27–8
advertising
  and the cognitive-cultural economy 242
aeromobility 128
aesthetics
  in the cognitive-cultural economy 240–1
Africa
  enclaves and economic development 24
  EPZs 228–9
  investment promotion 244, 246, 272
  IPAs 269
  Nigeria 215, 216, 217
  and policy mobility 170
  and the second global economy 181
ageing populations 101, 106
agglomerations 3, 8, 9–10, 12, 16, 29, 35, 40,
    64–6, 67, 285, 287, 293–5, 296
  airports as 134
  and arenas 63
  and the cognitive-cultural economy 232,
    238–9, 247, 248
  conceptual development of 32, 33
  defining agglomeration 51
  economic corridors 103
  and enclaves 57, 58, 64, 67
  exurbia 125–6
  and GPNs 203, 218–20
  and inter-urban competition 158
  and intermediaries 50
  and the international economy 256, 274
  and the logic of concentration 51–5, 64, 66
  MNEs as 178, 181, 185, 201
  and networks 64, 66
  and policy mobility 151, 161, 162, 163–4,
    165, 170, 174
  post-suburban enclaves 118, 119
  and the production of space 36–7
  scope and delimitation of 65
  in second modernity 23, 24, 25
  suburban 75, 76, 96
  see also industry agglomerations

airports 59, 128, 129, 130, 131–4, 136
  the airport as flow 132–3, 146–7
  fly-in/fly-out modes of working 131
  Gatwick 111
  rail links to 136
  Schiphol 133–4
  Shannon 225
  United States 116, 133, 134, 138
  as workplaces 87
  see also planes
alternative markets 164
American Dream 80
ANT (actor network theory) 30, 37, 60, 205
Apple 120–1, 192
architectural practices
  and policy mobility 154
arenas 3, 8, 9–10, 12, 16, 35, 40, 67, 285, 287,
    291–2, 295–6
  of the cognitive-cultural economy
    234–6, 247
  conceptual development of 32, 33
  deployments, networks and arenas 55–6
  dictionary definition of 61
  and intermediaries 41, 42, 50
  of the international economy 67, 256–8,
    262–5, 272–80, 281
  lifespan of 66
  logic of convocation 61–4, 256–7, 264
  as part-places 292
  and the production of space 36–7
  scope and delimitation of 65
  in second modernity 24–5
  trade shows 279–80
art and geography 26
Asia
  East Asia 54, 103–6, 215
  enclaves 59
Australia
  Darwin suburbs 88
automobiles see cars

BANANA attitudes 81
Beijing 108
BHP Billiton 216

BIDs (Business Improvement Districts)
159, 162
bilateral investment treaties (BITs) 261
Bintin Beach International Resort 250
BITs (bilateral investment treaties) 261
Bombay 102
boomburbs 97, 116–17, 139
borrowed size 53–4
BPO (business process outsourcing) 266
branding
  city branding 250–4
  and policy mobility 161
  and the symbolic economy of
      consumption 241–6
  territories 294
Brazil
  GPNs and agglomeration 218–19
  Porto Alegre 167–8, 274
BRIC countries
  and MNEs 186
Britain
  MNEs 197–8
  railways and train travellers 135, 147–8
  road infrastructure 139–40
  science parks 121–2
  shopping malls 124
  suburban housing 81
British Empire 43–4, 170
bungalows 78–9
business conventions 264
Business Improvement Districts (BIDs)
159, 163

Canada
  house-building 78
  industrial suburbs 74, 78
capital
  spatial immobilization of 35
capital accumulation
  and in-between cities 101–2
capital transmission
  and networks 60
capitalism
  and Chinese business networks 187
  and city marketing 252
  and consumption 247–8
  disorganized 87, 89, 144
  global capitalism and MNEs 180–1
  human geography and interplaces 17,
      20–1, 22
  and inter-urban competition 156–9
  and the international economy 256
  and nation states 55
  pastoral 118
  and the production of space 36
  and second modernity 23
  and suburbia 72, 74–95

TCC (transnational capitalist class) 153–5, 264
  see also regulatory capitalism
cars 25, 129
  automobility 87, 89
  and the exit ramp economy 137–40
  motorway service station car parks 139–40
  parking structures 129
  and work on the move 130, 141–2, 143, 148–9
Castro, Pedro 112
Chamberlinian competition
  and the cognitive-cultural economy
      234, 239
Chicago
  O'Hare airport 133
  rail corridor 136–7
Chile
  CiudadEmpresarial 114
  former mining town enclaves 222–3
  Santiago de Chile 82–4
China
  business networks 66, 187
  danwei 118
  Foxconn in 198
  investment promotion 271–2
  megapolitan regions 98
  post-suburban development 108, 109
  railways 147
  science parks 122
  suburban development 85–6
  trade shows 280
  urbanization and policy mobility 172
circular migration 91–2
cities
  as agglomerations 51, 52, 53–4, 64–5, 293
  and airports 132, 136
  as arenas 36
  city marketing 250–4
  and the cognitive-cultural economy 247
  edgeless 116
  European regional scale cities 100–3
  and housing developments in China 85
  human geography and interplaces 20
  and inter-urban/international economies 3,
      6, 10, 11, 12
  and intermediaries 41
  and policy mobility 156, 160–1, 163, 170–1
  post-suburbia and city development 112–17
  and rail corridors 136–7
  satellite cities 75, 76
  and second modernity 24
  smart cities 200
  and suburbia 71, 72, 73, 94
  urban agglomeration and the cognitive-
      cultural economy 238–9
  and urban policy intermediaries 152–3
  see also edge cities; inter-urban competition;
      inter-urban economies; world cities

civil society
  and ethical consumption 207
  and the international economy 257, 264
  and MNE networks 185
classification and comparison 38–9
clusters
  temporary clusters of the international
    economy 258, 279–80, 295–6
co-dependence, tragedy of 58
co-ethnic business networks 43–4
cognitive-cultural economy 5, 230–55, 285
  arenas of 234–6, 247
  brands and the symbolic economy of
    consumption 241–6
  city marketing 250–4
  cognition and aesthetics 238–41
  enclaves as a place of consumption 247–50
  intermediaries 230, 231, 232–8, 288–9
  and the international economy 256,
    261, 265
  interstitial spaces 126
  and policy mobility 161, 173
  and suburbia 88, 94–5
  urban agglomerations 294
Colina (Santiago de Chile) 83–4
colonial trading companies 56–7, 177, 180
commodities
  social life of 230, 232, 236–8
communities
  epistemic communities 61
  and inter-urban competition 156
  and the mid-urban realm 97
  and suburbia 73
comparison and classification 38–9
concentration
  agglomeration and the logic of 51–5, 66
conferences 258
consumption
  and the cognitive-cultural economy 230–1,
    241–6
  ethical consumption 207–8, 235
  and GPNs 204, 207, 210
  and in-between cities 101–2
  and MNEs 192
  and policy mobility 161–2
  retail malls 122–4
  in the suburbs 74, 77, 78, 79–80, 92–5
  and virtual mobility 146
conventions 63
convocation
  arenas and the logic of 61–4, 256–7, 264
corporate campuses 11
corporate contract systems
  dissolution of 86–8, 88–9
  and work on the move 148
Corporate Europe Observatory 278
corporate head offices 59

corporate offices 118–21
corporate social responsibility (CSR) 208
cosmopolitan democracy
  arenas of 63, 292
cosmopolitanism
  and global capitalism 180
creative industries 88
credit rating agencies 212
critical realism 34
Croydon 110–12
CSR (corporate social responsibility) 208
cultural capital 90–1, 250
cultural fields
  and investment arbitration 276
cultural intermediaries 45–7, 49–50
  and the cognitive-cultural economy
    232–4, 241

Dadeland Mall 123–4
democracy
  arenas of cosmopolitan democracy 63
democratic governance
  and the international economy 257
  and regulatory capitalism 48
deployments
  dictionary definitions of deployment 57
  networks and arenas 55–6
  see also enclaves
desakota in East Asia 54, 103–6
dialectical method
  and the production of space 33–7
diasporas
  and investment promotion 271
  and trading company MNEs 180
digiports 199–200
disorganized capitalism 87, 89, 144
distancing processes 35
divisions of labour
  and regulatory capitalism 48
DLC (Dubai Logistics City) 172
Dominican Republic 226–8
dormitory suburbs 94, 107
Dubai Logistics City (DLC) 172
Dulles Airport 116

e-commerce and MNEs 193
East Asia
  desakota 54, 103–6
  labour and GPNs 215
East India Companies 177–8, 180
economic agglomerations 157
economic capital
  and network capital 90–1
economic corridors 98–9, 103
  East Asian desakota 105–6
  internet alley 116
economic dependency 59

economic enclaves 117–24
edge cities 4, 108, 110
    and the exit ramp economy 138–9
    as post-suburban communities 112–14, 116
    and rail corridors 136
edgeless cities 116
Edwardian Britain
    consumption in 92–3
emails, work-related 140, 141
empirical study
    and theoretical abstraction 29–33
employment change
    Croydon 110–11
    in the mid-urban realm 97
    post-suburban development 107, 108, 110
    urban-rural shift 125–6
enclaves 3, 6, 8–9, 9–10, 11, 12, 16, 35, 40, 285,
        287, 290–1, 295, 296
    and agglomerations 57, 58, 64, 67
    airports as 134
    and the cognitive-cultural economy 247–50
    conceptual development of 32, 33
    economic enclaves of post-suburbia
        117–24
    ethnic 57
    GPNs as 203, 204, 220–9
    and intermediaries 41, 42, 58
    as intermediate locations 223–5
    and the international economy 57, 59, 256,
        259–62
    lifespan of 66
    and the logic of deployment 56–9, 64, 66–7
    mid-urban realm 97, 98, 117–24
    MNEs as 56–7, 58, 184, 185, 193–200, 201,
        290–1
    and networks 64
    as part-places 292
    and policy mobility 151, 161
    and the production of space 36–7
    scope and delimitation of 65
    in second modernity 23, 24, 25, 84–5
    suburban 59, 80–1, 86, 291
    tourism 161, 249–50, 255
energy corridors 113
Engels Law 239
England
    industrial coffin 100–1
enterprise resource planning (ERP) 210
enterprise zones (EZs) 159
environmental protection 278
    and GPNs 215–18
epistemic communities 61
EPZs (Export Processing Zones) 58, 66, 159,
        203, 225–9, 260
ERP (enterprise resource planning) 210
ethical consumption 207–8, 235
ethnic enclaves 57

ethnicity
    and suburbia 73, 92
ethnoburbs 92
EU (European Union) 182
Europe
    offshoring by MNEs 198
    trade shows 280
European cities
    post-suburban 108, 112
    regional-scale 100–3
European Commission 173
Eurostar 147
exhibitions 258
exit ramp economy 137–40
Export Processing Zones (EPZs) 58, 66, 159,
        203, 225–9, 260
expressive symbolism
    and the cognitive-cultural economy 240
external economies and agglomeration 51,
        53–4, 55
externalities
    economic corridors 103
    and new housing 81
exurbia
    interstitial spaces of 124–6
exurbs 77, 97, 99
EZs (enterprise zones) 159

Fantus Factory Locating Service 267–8
fast subjects of globalization 141–4
FDI (foreign direct investment) 58
    and the international economy 259, 260,
        263, 265
    and investment arbitration 275, 276, 278
    and investment promotion 243, 244–6, 271
    and MNEs 182, 196, 197, 198, 199–200
    regulatory meetings 264
    and site selection consultants 266
financial centres, offshore 159
financial intermediaries 285
    and GPNs 211–12
first global economy
    urban policy mobility 152–3
flat ontologies 19, 21, 26, 40, 61, 229
flows 8, 26
    the airport as flow 132–3, 146–7
    enclaves and distortion of finance flows 24
    intelligent corridors 99
    and the international economy 264
    mid-urban realm 98
fluidity 15
Fordism 87
foreign direct investment see FDI (foreign direct
        investment)
formal institutional strategies
    and relational geometry 28
Foxconn 192, 198

France
  technopolis 112
franchising 183
Free Ports 159, 260
FTZs (free trade zones) 58, 225

garden cities 166–7
garden suburbs 121–2
gated residential communities 59, 81, 82–4, 86
  and economic corridors 99
  as enclaves 291
  and network capital 91
GATT (General Agreement on Tariffs and
    Trade) 182, 273
GCCs (global commodity chains) 202, 204–5
gender and the interplace economy 286
Geneva Freeport 261
gentrification 93
geometries of power 33
Germany
  regional-scale cities 101–2
  suburban sprawl 108
Getafe 112
GIC (global intelligence corps) 153, 154
GINs (globally integrated networks) 185
global commodity chains (GCCs) 202, 204–8
global governance
  arenas of 25, 63, 256, 257
  and site selection consultants 267–8
global intelligence corps (GIC) 153, 154
global North
  circular migration 91–2
  home working 87
  housing and corporate contract systems 87
global production networks see GPNs (global
    production networks)
global South
  circular migration 91–2
  and the cognitive-cultural economy 239
  world cities 155
global supply chains 204
global value chains (GVCs) 33, 202, 204–5, 219
globalization
  and airports 132
  and the cognitive-cultural economy 242
  and ethical consumption 207–8
  fast and slow subjects of 140–6
  and human geography 15
  and the international economy 260
  and interstateness 56
  and MNEs 181
glocal/glocalization 7, 8
governance see global governance
GPNs (global production networks) 6, 12, 22,
    37, 57, 60, 61, 65, 66, 67, 202–29, 286,
    289, 290
  and agglomeration 203, 218–20

and brands 242
and city marketing 253
and the cognitive-cultural economy 255
and cultural intermediaries 46
dark side of 203, 213, 219, 220
as enclaves 203, 204, 220–9
and GCCs/GVCs 33, 202, 204–5, 219, 220
intermediation in 203, 206–18, 289
and the international economy 256
and the mid-urban realm 122, 127
and MNEs 185, 192, 199, 201, 203, 204, 206,
    208, 215, 219
and policy mobility 165
power geometries of 206
relational approach to 27–8
and theory-building 30–1
three competitive dynamics of 206
GVCs (global value chains) 33, 202, 204–5, 219

heritage industry 101, 126
hierarchies
  and MNEs 178, 179–82, 194
  and networks 60
hinges
  megapolitan regions as 98–117
the home
  home ownership 80
  and suburban consumption 92, 94–5
  and work life balance 5
home working 87, 145
housing
  suburban 73–4, 75
    production networks 77–9
  Tysons Corner 114
human capital
  and airports 132
  and MNEs 199
human geography 15–40
  idiographic-nomothetic duality of 17–25,
      26, 32–3
  and inter-disciplinary relations 37–9
  theory, method, and interplaces 25–37
human rights violations
  and enclaves 58
  and MNEs 195

ICSID (International Center for the Settlement
    of Investment Disputes) 265, 277
ICTs (information and communications
    technologies) 25, 34, 128, 129
  and MNEs 182
  and mobile work 142, 144–5, 149
  and topologies of power 28–9
  and virtual mobility 89, 90, 130, 144
  see also internet
idiographic perspectives
  on human geography 17–25, 26, 32–3

ILO (International Labour Organization) 272
IMF (International Monetary Fund) 265, 273
in-between times 295–6
income inequality 144
India
  Bhopal disaster 58, 195
  investment promotion 271
  MNEs 199–200
  post-suburban development 108
  smart cities 200
  urbanization and policy mobility 172
individualism, networked 90
Indonesia 108
  desakota 54, 103–6
  GPNs 219–20
  investment promotion 246, 271
  Jakatra 84–5, 118
  selling of suburbia 84–5
  Solo/Surakarta 168, 169
Indonesia-Malaysia-Singapore-Growth
    Triangle (IMS-GT) 260
industrial capitalism
  and MNEs 183
industrial coffin (England) 100–1
industrial suburbs 74–7, 78, 107, 112
industrialization
  and East Asian *desakota* 104
industries
  intermediaries 42
industry agglomerations 52–3, 54, 55, 65
  and East Asia *desakotas* 104–5
  and enclaves 58
  and GPNs 203, 219, 221–2
informal institutional strategies
  and relational geometry 28
information costs 44, 45
informational barriers 44–5
infrastructures
  of mobility 11, 129, 130–40
  networks and the mid-urban realm 98
  and policy mobility 160
  and suburban development 84
INGOs (international non-governmental
    organizations) 48, 256, 264
innovation
  and GPNs 209
  in urban policy 166–8
inquisitive activities 263–4
intangible assets
  and relational geometry 28
intellectual property
  law 277
  rights negotiations 3, 6, 62, 264
  trade related intellectual property
    (TRIPS) 274
intelligent corridors 98–9

inter-disciplinary relations 37–9
inter-urban competition
  ordinariness of strong forms of 163–73
  strong 156–9
  weak 156–9
inter-urban economies 3–7, 11, 37, 66, 281
  and airports 133–4
  arenas 64
  enclaves 57, 59
  European regional scale cities 100–3
interaction
  networks and the logic of 59–61
intermediaries 12, 41, 42–50, 66, 288–9, 295
  and the cognitive-cultural economy 230,
    231, 232–8, 288–9
  and GPNs 203, 206–18, 289
  and informational barriers 44–5
  and intermediate places 49–50
  international investment arbitration
    275–8
  and MNEs 192
  and networks 60
  and the production of space 37
  in regulatory capitalism 47–9
  rise of urban policy intermediaries 151–5
  and the selling of suburbia 79–86
  site selection consultants as 265–8
  the state as intermediary in
    competition 159–61
  see also cultural intermediaries
intermediate locations, enclaves as 223–5
intermediate places 49–50
internalization and MNEs 183
international arenas 62–4
international business travel
  and work-related activities 141–4
International Center for the Settlement of
    Investment Disputes (ICSID) 265, 277
international economy 3–7, 11–12, 256–81
  agglomerations 256, 274
  arenas 67, 256–8, 262–5, 272–80, 281
  enclaves 57, 59, 256, 259–62
  and human geography 15–16
  intermediaries 66, 265–8
  international investment arbitration
    275–8
  and investment promotion communities of
    interest 265–72
  and the mid-urban realm 97
  networks 256, 258, 262–5, 281
  non-territorial realm 257, 258–65
  and regulatory capitalism 48, 256–7, 281
  temporary clusters 258, 279–80, 295–6
international law
  and arenas 62
International Monetary Fund (IMF) 265, 273

international non-governmental organizations (INGOs) 48, 256, 264
International Observatory on Participatory Democracy (IOPD) 165
international trade fairs 63, 258, 264, 279–80
internet 140
  and the cognitive-cultural economy 249
  global use 128–9
  and GPNs 203
  shopping 94, 146
internet alley 116
interplaces 41–67
  betweenness of 33–7
  deployments, networks and arenas 55–6
  as the economy in between 3, 4
  emergence of 'soft' planning spaces 48
  enclaves and arenas as 65
  and human geography 15–40
  studying 7–10
  subjective experiences of 285
  see also intermediaries
interstitial spaces of exurbia 124–6
intervening in-between 287–95
investment arbitration 275–8, 291, 292
investment flows
  enclaves and distortion of 24
investment negotiations
  and international economies 3, 6
investment promotion 265–72
  and the cognitive-cultural economy 242–6
  geoeconomics of 268–72
  site selection consultants 265–8
investment promotion agencies (IPAs) 243–5, 265, 267, 269
IOPD (International Observatory on Participatory Democracy) 165
IOs (international organizations) 256, 264–5
IPAs (investment promotion agencies) 243–5, 265, 267, 269
Ireland 54, 191
  Industrial Development Authority (IDA) 243, 269–70, 271
  Shannon Airport 225
island states 260–1, 268–9
ITT 184

Jakatra 84–5, 118
Japan
  core business cities 114–16
  desakota 104, 106
  megalopolis 106
Japanese MNEs 186–7
Johannesburg
  post-suburban development 117

Khimki 109–10, 133
KIBS (knowledge intensive business services) 209

labour
  personal networks of autonomous labour 88–92
labour market intermediaries
  and GPNs 212–15
labour organizations
  and MNE networks 185
land ownership
  and policy mobility 166
language
  and human geography 26
latent strong competition
  of ordinary cities 171–3
Latin America
  gated residential communities 82–4
  MNEs 196
  and the second global economy 181
  urban policy mobility 167–8
  see also Chile
law
  and the international economy 257, 258
  international investment law 275–8
lawyer compradors 275
LG site in South Wales 197–8
liminal spaces 11
  see also cars; planes; trains
liquidity 15
local actors
  and relational geometry 27–8
local governments
  and consumption in the suburbs 93
  and MNEs 197–9
  and post-suburban development 111
local politics
  and inter-urban competition 156
logistics and GPNs 210–11
London
  and Croydon 110
  policy mobility 163
lumping 29

Malaysia
  Multimedia Supercorridor 98
manufacturing industries 74–7
marketing
  city marketing 250–4
markets
  and the cognitive-cultural economy 230
  and networks 60
  Type 1 and Type 2 157
matrix organizational structures 183
Mauritius 269

mediating processes 35
  see also intermediaries
megapolitan regions 97–8, 296
  as hinges 98–118
meta-clustering 53
meta-theories
  in economic geography 29–33, 33–4, 37
Mexico City 102
Mexico, US offshoring to 198
mid-urban realm 37, 97–127
  desakota in East Asia 103–6
  megapolitan regions 97–8
  and rail corridors 135–7
  suburb to post-suburbia 94, 108–12
  see also post-suburbia
Middle East
  enclaves for European expatriates 194
migration
  circular 91–2
  of skilled labour from cities 125
mining camps/towns 65, 66, 296
mining towns 221–3
MNEs (multinational enterprises) 3–4, 5–6,
      11–12, 25, 177–201
  as agglomerations 178, 181, 185, 201
  as container and contained 182–4
  early trading companies 56–7, 177, 196
  enclaves/deployments 56–7, 58, 184, 185,
      193–200, 201, 290–1
  environmental concerns 215, 218
  and GPNs 185, 192, 199, 201, 203, 204, 206,
      208, 215, 219
  and hierarchies 178, 179–82, 194
  and history 178–82
  and the international economy 256, 259,
      262, 265
  and investment arbitration 275
  and investment promotion 269–70
  Japanese 186–7
  matrix organizational structures 188
  networks 60, 61, 179–82, 184–93, 289
  and non-capitalist competition 164
  offshoring 198, 198–200
  retail and service sector 192–3
  securitized producer services
      198–200
  and site selection consultants 266, 267
  subsidiaries 184, 187–91, 194–8, 258
  and transnational corporations (TNCs) 178–9
mobile communications 89, 128, 129, 140,
      149, 294
  work-related 140, 141
mobility 4, 128–49
  and agglomeration 294
  and human geography 15
  hypermobilities 21
  infrastructures of 11, 129, 130–40

of labour and GPNs 213–14
  and the mid-urban realm 127
  mobile work 87–8, 140–9
  personal 4, 20–1, 89
  personal networks of autonomous
      labour 88–92
  in second modernity 25
  and suburbia 11, 71–2
  see also cars; planes; policy mobility; trains
modernity
  and arenas 63, 64
  and the cognitive-cultural economy 232
  human geography and interplaces 20, 21,
      22, 37
  and the mid-urban realm 98
  and networks 60
  and policy mobility 171, 174
  and rail corridors 135–7
  and suburbia 74
  see also second modernity
Mokia 219
Moscow
  Khimki 109–10, 133
Motorola 120
Motorway Service Areas (MSAs) 139–40, 148
multimedia supercorridors 171
multinational enterprises *see* MNEs
      (multinational enterprises)
multitasking 142

NAFTA (North American Free Trade
      Agreement) 182
Nanjing
  post-suburban development 108, 109
nation states
  and arenas 63
  human geography and interplaces 22
  and the international economy 257, 259,
      260, 262
  and MNEs 182, 191
  and the network society 8
  and the production of space 36
  in second modernity 24–5
  territoriality of 39
  and urban policy intermediaries 152–3
national economies
  and enclaves 57
  and intermediaries 41
nations
  and airports 132
  and economic activity 55
  human geography and interplaces 20
  and the international economy 12
  and interurban/international economies 3,
      6, 10
  and second modernity 24
  and urban corridors 99

nature
  environmental concerns and GPNs 215–18
neoliberalism 31, 37
  and investment promotion 246
  and New Urbanism 81
  and policy mobility 155, 159, 163, 168
  and regulatory capitalism 47–8
neoliberalization 31, 37, 173
  and investment promotion 246
Netherlands
  polycentric economy 100
  Schiphol airport 133–4
  suburbs 93, 94
network externalities 54–5
network society 8, 140–1
networks 3, 8, 9–10, 12, 16, 26, 35, 40, 67, 285,
    287, 289–90, 296
  and agglomerations 64, 66, 294–5
  co-ethnic business networks 43–4
  and the cognitive-cultural economy
    232, 247
  conceptual development of 32, 33
  deployments, networks and arenas 55–6
  dictionary definition of 60
  economic corridors 103
  and enclaves 64
  and inter-urban competition 172–3
  of intermediaries 50
  and the international economy 256, 258,
    262–5, 281
  and interplaces 41
  and the logic of interaction 59–61, 64
  and methodology 30–1, 32
  mid-urban realm 97, 98
  MNEs 60, 61, 179–82, 183–93, 289
  personal networks of autonomous
    labour 88–92
  and policy mobility 151, 174
  and the production of space 36–7
  and relational geography 27
  scope and delimitation of 65
  in second modernity 23, 24, 25
  technological 129
  and topologies of power 28
  transnational 48, 165
  see also GPNs (global production networks)
new towns
  China 85–6, 108–9
  and policy mobility 166–7
New Urbanism 80–1
New World Order
  and MNEs 189
NGOs (non-governmental organizations)
  and arenas 292
  and GPNs 207
  and the international economy 6, 256,
    257, 264

and investment arbitration 278
and MNE networks 185
and policy mobility 173
and regulatory capitalism 48, 49
Nigeria
  environmental concerns and GPNs 215,
    216, 217
NIMBY attitudes 81
nomadic workers 87
nomothetic perspectives
  on human geography 17–25, 26, 32–3
non-capitalist competition
  and policy mobility 164–6
non-local actors
  and relational geometry 28
non-markets 164

OECD (Organization for Economic
    Cooperation and Development) 265
OFCs (offshore finance centres) 159, 203
office development
  Croydon 111
office parks 59, 107
offshore finance centres (OFCs) 159, 203
offshoring 182, 185
  and GPNs 210
  MNEs 198, 198–200
  offshore economy 50
  and site selection consultants 266
online shopping 94
outsourcing 87–8, 182, 185
  and site selection consultants 266
Oxfordshire
  Science Vale 121–2

Pakistan
  GPNs and agglomeration 218–19
part-places 292, 294–5
participatory budgeting 167–8
pastoral capitalism 118
Pedro de Valdivia, Chile 222–3
periphery
  and in-between cities 101–2
personal networks
  and the mid-urban realm 98
Pittsburgh
  industrial suburbs 76
place
  and agglomerations 55, 294–5
  and human geography 15, 17–18
  intermediate places 49–50
  and interplaces 26
  and mobility 129–30
  non-places 107, 108, 122
  part-places 292, 295–6
  places and networks 61
  and policy mobility 165–6

place (*cont.*)
  scaled places 36
  and second modernity 23
  and space 7–8, 9, 16, 18, 23, 40,
    64–5
  substitutability of places 158–9
  and suburbia 71–2
planes 25, 128, 129
  nomadic workers on 87
  and work on the move 130, 141–2, 143
  see also airports
planetary urbanism
  as a suburban revolution 72–4
planning
  edge cities 108
  policy arenas of the international
    economy 273–4
policy intermediaries
  in regulatory capitalism 47–9
policy mobility 150–74
  innovation in urban policy 166–8
  non-capitalist competition 164–6
  and the power of seduction 152, 168–71
  rise of urban policy intermediaries
    151–5
  the state as intermediary in
    competition 159–61
  see also inter-urban competition
political intermediaries
  in regulatory capitalism 47–9
politics
  and city marketing 253–4
polycentric economies 100–1, 108
polycentricity 52–3
population change
  and East Asia *desakotas* 105–6
  edge cities 108
  post-suburban development 108, 113–14,
    114–15
population growth
  and suburban development 83–4
Porto Alegre
  participatory budgeting 167–8
  and the World Social Forum 274
post-modernity 15
  and capitalism 20–1
  and economic geography 38
post-socialist nations 108–9
post-structuralism 19
post-suburbia 93, 106–17
  and cars 129
  and city development 112–17
  Croydon 110–12
  economic enclaves of 117–24
  and mobility 129
poverty
  and suburban development 83–4

power, topologies of 28–9
private/shadow governments 64
product differentiation 233
production
  and GPNs 204, 207, 210
  and in-between cities 101–2
professional networks 258
prosumption 94
  in the cognitive-cultural economy
    232–4, 235
protectorates 260–1
public service employment 93

rail corridors 135–7
railways 128, 129, 130
  and suburbia 75
  see also trains
recycling goods and services 95
regional integration agreements 261–2
regional shopping malls 122–3
regionalization 53
regulatory capitalism
  and the arena 292
  and the international economy 48,
    256–7, 281
  political and policy intermediaries in 47–9
relational geography 18–19, 20, 27
  and networks 290
relational geometries 27–8
representation
  and the cognitive-cultural economy 240
research campuses 59, 107, 118–21
residential suburbs 71, 72, 73, 77–95
  China 85–6
  and circular migration 91–2
  and consumption 77, 78, 79–80, 92–5
  Croydon 111–12
  dormitory suburbs 94, 107
  Indonesia 84–5
  Latin America 82–4
  post-suburbia 107, 118, 119
  transformation of 86–95
resistance
  and policy mobility 172
retail malls 11, 59, 97, 122–4
  in-between cities 102
  Latin America 82
  Mall of Africa 117
  Mall of America 124
  symbolic economy of 249
retail sector MNEs 192–3
rhizomes 8, 26
ribbon development
  and East Asia *desakotas* 105–6
roads 130
Ruhrbism 101
rural economy 125–6

rural hinterland 97
Russia
    Khimki 109–10, 133

San Francisco
    industrial suburbs 76
Santiago de Chile 82–4
Sao Paulo 102
satellite cities 75, 76
scatteration 53
Schumpeterian model
    and policy mobility 155, 156
science
    and geography 26
science parks 59, 97, 121–2
second global economy
    and IPAs 244
    and MNEs 180–1, 182
    urban policy mobility 152–3, 173–4
second modernity 20, 21, 37
    arenas in 24–5, 64
    and the cognitive-cultural economy 232
    and the international economy 256, 281
    and networks 60
    production of space in 22, 23–5
    and suburbia 74
seduction, power of 152, 168–71
sendentarist perspectives 15
    and policy mobility 150
    and suburbia 71
service sector MNEs 192–3, 198–9
service workers 286
SEZs (special economic zones) 203,
    226, 227
shopping
    online 94, 146
shopping malls see retail malls
signification
    and the cognitive-cultural economy 240
simultaneity 8
Singapore 54, 170–1, 191, 199, 200
    Economic Development Board (EDB) 243,
        269, 270–1
single-company suburban towns 75
site selection consultants 265–8
slow lane, labour in the 144–6
small states
    and investment promotion 268–72
SMEs (small and medium sized firms) 209
social actors
    and relational geography 27
social class
    and suburbia 73, 75, 77
sociology
    and the interplace economy 37
software code
    importance of in economic relations 43

Solo/Surakarta 168, 169
sovereign territories
    and the international economy 260
sovereignty
    and MNEs 183
space
    and agglomerations 55
    and interplaces 26–7
    interstitial spaces of exurbia 124–6
    liminal spaces 11, 129
    and the mid-urban realm 97–8
    and place 7–8, 9, 16, 18, 23, 40, 64–5
    production of 22, 23–5, 33–7, 287
    and relational geography 18–19
    social construction of 287
    space/time compression 90, 129
    and time 286
Spain
    Getafe 112
    policy mobility 160
spatial fix 178
spatial mobility 4
spatial switching 158
special economic zones (SEZs) 203, 226
splitting 29
springboarding strategies of MNEs 191
states see nation states
strategic coupling 194
strong inter-urban competition 156–9, 174
    ordinariness of 163–73
structuration theory 15, 34
subcontracting 183
'Subdivisions' (song) 71
subjective experiences of interplaces 285
suburbia 71–96
    boomburbs 97, 116–17, 139
    and cars 129
    and consumption 74, 77, 78, 79–80,
        92–5
    definition of 73
    and economic activity 4, 5, 11, 72–3, 92
    economic diversity of 37
    enclaves 59, 80–1, 86, 291
    industrial suburbs 74–7, 78, 107
    megapolitan regions 97–8
    and the mid-urban realm 97
    and mobility 71–2, 129
    and planetary urbanism 72–4
    see also mid-urban realm; post-suburbia;
        residential suburbs
sunk costs 157, 192, 197
supply chains 44–5
    global 204
sustainability
    and policy mobility 167
symbolic analysts 233
symbolic economy of consumption 241–6

tangible assets
and relational geometry 28
tax havens 260
taxation
and regulatory capitalism 49
TCC (transnational capitalist class) 153–5, 264
technoburbs 97, 107, 112, 119
technological networks
and mobility 129
telephones 78, 128
teleworking 145
temporary clusters
of the international economy 258, 279–80,
295–6
territorality
of agglomeration 65, 293–4
deterritorialized approach to place 15
of enclaves 58, 65
and GPNs 203
and human geography 21–2
and interplaces 28, 29
of MNEs 58, 178
of the nation state 39
and the non-territorial realm of the
international economy 259–60
theoretical abstraction
and empirical study 29–33
time
and the cognitive-cultural economy 236
space/time compression 90, 129, 249
temporalities of economic geography 286
and work on the move 144–5
TNCs (transnational corporations) 12, 178–9
Tokyo 102, 114
topologies of power 28–9
toponymy (place names)
and city marketing 253
tourism enclaves 161, 249–50, 255
tourist industry 101, 126
tournaments of value
and the cognitive-cultural economy 232,
234, 237, 255
trade
flows 24
and global production 6
meetings/negotiations 3, 6, 62
trade fairs/shows 63, 258, 264, 279–80
trade related intellectual property (TRIPS) 274
trade related investment measures
(TRIMS) 274
trade unions
and the global economy 6
trading companies 56–7, 177, 196, 259
trains 128, 129
rail corridors 135–7
stations 129
working on 87, 130, 141–2, 143, 147–8

transnational capitalist class (TCC) 153–5, 264
transnational corporations (TNCs) 12,
178–9
transnational governance
and the international economy 262–3
transport
and intermediate places 224
and mobility 128–49
see also cars; planes; trains
TRIMS (trade related investment
measures) 274
Trinidad and Tobago 269
TRIPS (trade related intellectual property) 274
Tysons Corner, USA 4, 5, 113–14, 116, 136
exit ramp economy of 138–9

UCLG (United Cities and Local
Governments) 165
underdevelopment 59
uneven development 40, 57
United Kingdom see Britain
United Nations (UN) 265
Conference on Trade and Development
(UNCTAD) 178–9, 267, 269, 273
Industrial Development Organization
(UNIDO) 267, 273
UN Habitat 273–4
United States
airports 116, 133, 134, 138
boomburbs 116–17
exit ramp economy 137–9
internet alley 116
megapolitans 100
offshoring by MNEs 198
rail corridors 135–7
residential suburbs 118
retail malls 122–4
Site Selectors Guild 267
suburbia 59, 71–2, 73–4, 74–5,
79–80, 95
suburbs to post-suburbia 106–7, 112
trade shows 280
Tysons Corner 4, 5, 113–14, 116
see also edge cities
urban agglomeration
and the cognitive-cultural economy
238–9, 294
urban policy intermediaries
rise of 151–5
urban-rural fringes
and economic corridors 99
urbanization 97
counter-urbanization 125
East Asian desakota 104
and the economic corridor 99–100
in-between cities 101–2
of suburbia 107–8

Victorian Britain
  consumption in 92–3
Vietnam 271
virtuality 8, 26
voters
  and consumption in the suburbs 93

WAIPA (World Association of Investment
    Promotion Agencies) 267
Washington D.C.
  Dulles airport 116, 133, 134, 138
  and policy mobility 163
weak inter-urban competition 156–9, 174
weakness of contemporary policy
    mobility 161–3
WEF (World Economic Forum) 264, 274
welfare states
  and policy mobility 173
Westphalia, Treaty of 55, 259
Westphalian economies
  and MNEs 179
work on the move 87–8, 140–9
  fast and slow subjects of globalization 140–6
work-life balance 4–5, 89, 90, 91
workfare
  and policy mobility 155, 163

working class
  and industrial suburbs 75, 77
workplace restructuring 87–8,
    89–90
World Association of Investment Promotion
    Agencies (WAIPA) 267
World Bank 265, 273
  Doing Business Index 268
World Business Council for Sustainable
    Development 264
world cities 153–5
  and the cognitive-cultural economy
    232, 246
  and GPNs 213
  and the international economy 256
World Economic Forum (WEF) 264, 274
World Social Forum (WSF) 264, 274
World Trade Organization (WTO) 265,
    277, 292
WSF (World Social Forum) 264, 274
WTO (World Trade Organization) 182, 265,
    277, 292

ZODUCs (zones of conditional
    development) 83–4
Zones of Economic Integration 260

Name Index

Adey, P. 131
Agnew, J. 7, 36, 54, 178, 183, 259
Aguilar, A. 146, 149
Akince, G. 225–6
Allen, F. 211
Allen, J. 21, 27, 28, 33, 42, 57, 151–2, 169, 240, 241
Allmendinger, P. 48, 162, 293
Alonso, W. 53–4
Alvarez, J. E. 259, 278
Amin, A. 196, 208, 235, 293
Anan, N. 235
Andersson, U. 188, 190
Andrews, M. 171
Andrews-Johnson, K. 243
Angotti, T. 118
Anholt, S. 161, 171, 212, 242, 244–5, 252
Anttiroiko, A.-V. 31, 251, 252, 254, 294
Appadurai, A. 33, 151, 171, 207, 231, 232, 233, 234, 235, 236, 237, 271
Appold, S. J. 133
Arias, M. 33, 57, 58, 65, 201, 203, 221, 223, 295
Ashworth, G. J. 161, 170, 253
Atheye, S. S. 199
Atienza, M. 33, 57, 58, 65, 201, 203, 221, 222, 295
Atkinson, R. 91
Augé, M. 107, 122, 129
Axtell, C. 134, 140, 147, 148

Badcock, B. 77
Baigent, E. 99
Bair, J. 218
Baldacchino, G. 33, 194, 259, 260–1, 268
Banham, R. 137
Barff, R. 192
Barnes, T. J. 26, 38
Barnet, R. J. 177, 192, 193, 201, 215, 216, 233, 257, 259
Barnett, C. 208, 235
Bartlett, C. A. 188, 189
Bartolo, E. 138
Basten, L. 101

Bathelt, H. 18–19, 33, 45, 51, 55, 63, 225, 258, 264, 279, 280
Baudrillard, J. 248
Bauman, Z. 248
Bayly, C. A. 20, 152, 153, 181, 194, 259
Beauregard, R. 95
Beaverstock, J. 140
Beaverstock, J. V. 140, 141, 147
Beck, U. 20, 23, 48
Beer, A. 77
Bennett, R. J. 101
Bergsten, C. F. 201, 290
Beugelsdijk, S. 5, 177
Beunza, D. 212
Bhan, G. 171, 172
Bhaskar, R. 35
Birkinshaw, J. 188, 189, 258
Birtchnell, T. 210
Blomley, N. 276, 277
Blunt, A. 77, 86, 92, 296
Bock, R. 132
Boddewyn, J. J. 195
Bogart, W. 126
Boli, J. 25, 33, 48, 262
Bond, D. W. 35
Bonnett, A. 129, 137, 261
Bonss, W. 23, 48
Bontje, M. 108, 133, 134
Borden, A. 132, 133
Bornschier, V. 269
Borsdorf, A. 114
Bourdieu, P. 45–6, 50, 232, 241, 276
Bowen, J. T. Jnr 144
Boyang, G. 108
Boyenge, J. P. S. 225
Brade, I. 109
Braidford, P. 196
Braithwaite, J. 48–9, 61, 63, 151, 195, 272
Brattinga, K. 134
Brautigam, D. 271, 272
Breheny, M. 81
Brennan-Horley, C. 88
Brenner, N. 36
Bridge, G. 202

Brinkerhoff, J. M. 245, 271
Bristow, G. 158
Britton, S. G. 162, 249, 250
Brown, C. 278
Buckley, P. J. 202
Budd, L. 131, 141
Buliung, R. N. 89, 90, 144, 146
Bunnell, T. 27, 151, 168, 171, 246, 250
Burdack, J. 108, 133
Burgand, J.-M. 226, 228
Burger, M. J. 54
Burgess, A. 203, 229
Burzelius, N. 160
Buttle, N. 207, 208
Buzzelli, N. 78

Cademartori, J. 223
Cairncross, F. 3, 181
Caliskan, K. 42, 43
Callon, M. 42, 43, 231, 233–4, 238
Cameron, J. 164, 165, 291, 292
Cantwell, J. 188
Cardoso, F. H. 33, 167, 195, 196
Carr, C. M. H. 71
Carrión, F. 114
Carroll, W. K. 20, 155, 173, 256, 264, 290
Casey, E. 3, 7–8, 17, 19, 35, 51, 59, 62, 66, 149,
    203, 285, 286
Cassirer, E. 240
Casson, M. 44, 45, 202, 204
Castells, M. 121
Castree, N. 31
Cavusgil, S. T. 192
Ceruzzi, P. E. 138
Chan, J. 198
Charles, D. C. 121
Chavagneux, C. 260
Chong, A. 270
Cidell, J. 133–4, 136–7, 294
Clapson, M. 71
Clark, G. L. 51, 157
Clarke, D. B. 247, 248
Cobb, J. C. 246
Cochoy, F. 122–3, 208
Coe, N. M. 27, 30, 33, 53, 193, 194, 201, 203,
    204, 205, 206–7, 212, 213
Contractor, F. 185, 189
Cooley, A. 263
Cooley, C. H. 135
Cooper, A. F. 268, 269
Cooper, F. 56–7
Cooper, S. Y. 125
Corey, K. E. 99
Coupland, D. 131
Cowen, D. 34, 172, 181, 203, 210, 213, 214,
    217, 224, 290
Cowling, K. 183

Cox, K. R. 33, 48, 53, 156, 157, 158, 159, 254
Coyle, D. 240
Cresswell, T. 15, 25, 129, 130, 131, 144, 149
Crewe, K. 121
Crowther, L. 93
Currah, A. 193
Cwerner, S. 89–90, 131

Dahmann, N. 24
Daniels, P. W. 3
Das, D. 171, 172, 200
Datta, D. 200
Davis, K. E. 263, 267
Dawood, S. R. S. 98, 171
De Grazia, V. Ed. 92
De Jong, J. K. 102
Dear, M. 24, 116
Delaney, D. 276
Dematteis, G. 174
den Hertog, P. 209
Dennis, R. 78
Derudder, B. 51, 55
Dezalay, Y. 49, 275, 276, 277, 292
Dick, A. W. 117
Dick, E. 91
Dicken, P. 177, 179, 185, 186, 200, 204, 205,
    206, 219, 220
Dietz, J. L. 33
Dixon, D. 35
Dixon, P. 139
Djelic, M. L. 259, 262, 263
Dodge, M. 43, 94, 131, 132, 210
Dodgshon, R. 17, 19, 20, 21, 22, 93
Domokos, T. 109
Donaghu, M. T. 192
Donald, S. H. 251
Dorow, S. 131
Dossani, R. 199
Dowding, K. 111
Dowling, R. 77, 86, 92, 296
Drahos, P. 61, 63, 151, 195, 272
Drori, G. S. 262
DuGay, P. 47
Duncan, S. 34
Dunford, M. 108
Dunham-Jones, E. 24, 107
Dunlop, S. 188
Dunning, J. 186
Dunning, J. H. 182, 187, 195
Duranton, G. 90
Dutton, J. A. 72

Easterling, K. 130, 137
Edensor, T. 249, 250
Eggert, R. G. 215
Elden, S. 20, 21
Elkins, Z. 261

Elliott, A. 21, 90–1
Entrikin, J. N. 8, 10, 15, 16, 17–18, 19, 23, 33, 285
Erikson, R. A. 76
Escobar, A. 218, 255
Ethington, P. J. 72

Faletto, E. 33, 167, 195, 196
Fallon, R. 125
Farole, T. 220, 225–6, 228
Faulconbridge, J. 140, 141, 147, 213
Feagin, J. R. 113
Felker, G. B. 219
Ferguson, J. 56, 170, 216, 217
Firn, J. 196
Fishman, R. 71, 97, 107, 119
Fleming, D. K. 135, 224
Florida, R. 88, 132, 186
Flyvbjerg, B. 160
Folmer, E. 93–4
Ford, R. T. 276
Forsyth, A. 116, 121
Freestone, R. 131, 132, 133
French, S. 211
Friedmann, J. 154, 239
Fröbel, F. 187, 204
Fuentes, C. 114
Fuller, C. 189, 190, 191
Fuller, G. 131

Garreau, J. 108, 110, 112–13
Garth, B. G. 49, 275, 276, 277, 292
Garud, R. 212
Gereffi, G. 30, 33, 178, 192, 202, 204, 205, 218
Gershuny, J. 89, 94–5, 144, 236
Ghoshal, S. 188, 189
Gibbon, P. 220
Gibson-Graham, J. K. 31, 145, 158, 164, 165, 216, 286, 291, 292
Giddens, A. 15
Ginsburg, N. 106
Glaeser, E. 87, 127
Glasmeier, A. 119
Glasze, G. 163
Glennie, P. 232, 293
Glückler, J. 18–19, 45, 51, 63, 191, 264, 279
Goddard, J. B. 86–7
Golfetto, F. 63, 279, 280
Golubchikov, O. 109, 133
Goodwin, M. 160, 161
Gordon, I. R. 53, 160, 172, 173, 219
Gorla, G. 54
Gospodini, A. 93
Goss, J. 248, 249
Gottdiener, M. 79, 118, 131, 230, 248, 251
Gottmann, J. 97–8, 99–100, 136, 296
Gough, J. 33, 157

Grabner, G. 55
Graham, S. 98, 129, 199, 223
Grant, J. 80
Green, W. C. 198
Gregory, D. 34
Gruen, V. 123
Guzman, A. T. 261

Haas, P. 61
Haberly, D. 196
Hakfoot, J. 134
Hall, P. 121, 122, 159, 166
Hall, P. A. 186
Hall, T. 155
Hallin, P. O. 264
Hampton, M. 250
Hanes, J. E. 107
Hanlon, B. 77
Hannam, K. 15
Harbison, R. 130, 137–8
Harding, T. 244
Harnish, T. 143, 145
Harris, R. 72, 73, 78, 129
Harrison, A. 87, 89
Hart, J. F. 26
Harvey, D. 11, 33, 49, 77, 93, 118, 119, 157, 161, 168, 171, 178, 249, 287
Hassler, M. 220
Hatziprokopiou, P. 252
Haughton, G. 48, 167, 293
Haynes, P. 141
Hayuth, Y. 135, 224
Healey, P. 135, 166, 291, 292, 293
Healy, S. 164, 165
Hedlund, G. 187
Hegel, G. 241
Hegel, G. W. F. 34
Heinrichs, D. 84
Heitzman, J. 200
Held, D. 25, 33, 62, 63, 155, 257, 258, 292
Henderson, J. 33, 67, 187, 205
Hennart, J.–F. 188
Herbert, C. W. 117
Herod, A. 214, 218, 290
Hess, M. 26, 33, 60, 61, 194, 201, 203, 205, 206, 213, 225
Hesse, M. 203, 224
Hidalgo, R. 114
Hirt, S. 86, 95
Hise, G. 73
Hislop, D. 134, 140, 147, 148, 149
Holley, D. 144, 145, 147, 148
Hood, N. 188, 189, 196, 258
Hopkins, A. G. 180
Howard, E. 166
Howells, J. 209
Howitt, R. 19

Hubbard, P. 131, 141, 155
Hudson, R. 242, 260
Hughes, A. 207, 208
Humphrey, J. 33, 220
Hurdley, L. 154
Huws, U. 90, 145, 146, 199, 213, 214, 289
Hymer, S. 183, 187, 204

Iammarino, S. 21, 61, 64, 185, 190, 218

Jacobs, J. 6, 33
Jacobs, W. 211
Jacobsson, B. 263
Jain, J. 140
Jansson, J. 279, 280
Javorcik, B. S. 244
Jensen, O. 162
Jensen, P. D. O. 199
Jonas, A. 20, 22, 26, 29
Jones, A. 34
Jones, G. 20, 44, 153, 177, 180–1, 182,
    188, 259
Jones, J. P. 26, 35, 40

Kahn, A. 162
Kapelink, D. 276
Kaplinsky, R. 202, 228
Kasarda, J. D. 128, 132, 136, 146
Kash, D. 42
Katz, Bruce 138
Katz, M. L. 54
Katzenstein, P. 30, 44, 184, 186–7, 195,
    246, 262
Keane, W. 231
Kearns, G. 160, 161, 253
Keeble, D. 125
Keil, R. 101, 102–3
Kellerman, A. 4, 113, 128, 138, 178, 213,
    252, 294
Kelly, P. 200
Kelly, P. F. 215
Kenney, M. 186, 199
Kenyon, S. 142
Kevin, C. 251
King, A. D. 78, 79, 152
Kingsbury, B. 263, 267
Kitchen, R. 43, 94, 131, 132, 210
Klak, T. 245, 246
Kleibert, J. M. 199, 201, 221, 229
Klingmann, A. 177
Kloosterman, R. C. 100, 231
Knight, G. 192
Knowles, S. G. 121
Knox, P. 11, 100, 127
Knox, P. L. 79–80, 86, 95
Kobrin, S. J. 5, 25, 58, 63, 178, 179, 183, 274
Kofman, E. 251

Kolb, D. 26, 80, 95, 254, 291
Kolb, D. L. 157
Korzeniewicz, M. 33, 204
Kotkin, J. 5
Kristensen, P. H. 185–6
Kulcsar, L. J. 109
Kumar, A. 168, 180
Kunstler, J. H. 72

Lacher, H. 55, 259
Lagopoulos, A. 230
Lai, K. 204, 212
Lambregts, B. 100
Lampel, J. 33, 235
Lang, R. 11, 97, 100, 116, 127, 139
Lanz, R. 177
Larkham, P. J. 72, 73
Larner, W. 31, 47
Lash, S. 8, 20, 23, 87, 89, 130, 231, 232, 236,
    237, 238, 240, 241, 252
Lassen, C. 90, 99, 141, 146
Latham, R. 8, 10, 33, 56, 58, 59, 61–2, 63, 64,
    194–5, 196, 216, 225, 247, 257, 263, 279,
    281, 290
Lau, C. 23, 48
Laurier, E. 87, 88, 144, 148–9
LeFurgy, J. 97, 116, 139
Leadbeatter, C. 240
Leaf, M. 85
Lee, R. 31
Lefebvre, H. 22, 27, 35, 36, 38–9, 40, 41,
    42, 72, 77, 99, 156, 158, 159, 213, 218,
    233, 241, 287
Leisch, H. 84, 85
Leitner, H. 155, 159, 163, 164, 166, 173
Leonard, D. K. 24, 56, 58, 216
Lerup, L. 81
Leslie, S. W. 121
Levi-Faur, D. 33, 36, 47–8, 50,
    257, 292
Leving, Y. 230
Lewis, R. 73, 74, 75
Lewis, R. D. 53, 76
Leyshon, A. 3
Li, Wei 92
Li, Y. 98
Light, D. 253
Lindsay, G. 128, 132, 136, 146
Line, T. 140
Linnros, H. D. 264
Lister, K. 143, 145
Loveridge, R. 209
Lovering, J. 4
Lowe, M. J. 123, 124
Lukas, M. 84
Lury, C. 94, 231, 237
Lyons, G. 140, 142

McCann, E. 15, 150, 165, 166, 273
McCann, P. 21, 61, 64, 185, 188, 190, 218, 219
McDowell, L. 3
McFall, L. 47, 49, 241
MacFarlane, C. 150, 164
McGee, T. 54, 103, 104
McGrew, A. 62, 155, 257
MacKay, Benton 137
McKeever, R. 119
Mackinnon, D. 196, 201, 229, 289
McManus, R. 72
McNeill, D. 173
Magalhaes, C. 163
Magee, G. B. 22, 43–4, 180, 279–80
Mair, A. 33, 48, 53, 156, 157, 186
Majone, G. 48, 152
Malecki, E. J. 136
Malloy, P. 80
Malmberg, A. 33, 55, 185, 225, 258
Malpas, J. 247
Mansfield, E. 184
Marginson, S. 142
Markusen, A. 21, 49, 55, 61
Marshall, A. 33, 51
Marston, S. 19, 26, 40, 92
Martin, R. 37
Marvin, S. 129
Marx, K. 241
Maskell, P. 33, 55, 225, 258
Mason, C. 87
Masotti, L. H. 107
Massey, D. B. 9, 10, 18, 27, 174, 190, 196, 214, 288
Matiza, T. 244
Matthews, J. 46
May, J. 145, 286
Mbaiwa, J. E. 249
Meijers, E. 54
Merrifield, A. 90, 165, 169
Merriman, P. 149
Merry, S. E. 263, 267
Meyer, A. D. 33, 235
Meyer, J. W. 262
Miao, T. 122
Miles, K. 215–16, 277–8
Millar, J. 141
Miller, D. 5, 17, 18, 29–30, 34, 93, 169, 170, 212, 231, 241, 250, 288
Miller, M. 168
Miller, M. A. 246
Miller, P. 207, 231, 234
Millo, Y. 42–3
Mills, A. 63, 276, 277
Mir, R. 200
Miroudot, S. 177
Miyamachi, Y. 186
Molloy, M. 47

Molotch, H. 5, 66, 154, 157, 202, 203, 218, 241, 253
Moore, J. W. 20
Moreno-Monroy, A. 104
Morgan, G. 34, 185–6, 259, 262
Morisset, J. 243, 244, 245
Morrill, R. 99
Mozingo, L. 118–19, 291
Mudambi, R. 5, 177, 188
Muller, E. K. 76
Muller, R. E. 177, 192, 193, 201, 215, 216, 233, 257, 259
Muniesa, F. 42–3
Murakami, H. 4
Murdoch, J. 30, 206
Murphy, P. 170, 172, 269
Murphy, R. 260
Murray, M. J. 117
Muzaini, H. 250
Myers, F. 230
Myers, G. 245, 246

Nabokov, V. 230, 241, 255
Nadvi, K. 219
Nast, J. 153
Neal, Z. 51, 55
Neilsen, J. 202, 207
Nelson, A. C. 99, 100
Neuman, M. 167
Ngai, P. 198
Niedzielski, M. A. 136
Nielsen, T. M. 245, 271
Nixon, S. 47
North, D. 125
Nuissl, H. 84, 108, 109
Nye, J. S. 171

Oakey, R. P. 125
O'Connell, J. C. 139
O'Connor, K. 131
Ohmae, K. 3
Olds, K. 8, 26, 27, 32, 59, 67, 142, 153, 200, 287
O'Leary, T. 207, 231, 234
Oliver, N. 186
Olivier, D. 260
O'Mara, M. P. 107–8, 119
O'Neill, P. 216
Ong, A. 33, 59
Oni, O. A. 244
O'Riain, S. 191, 269, 270
Osterhammel, J. 21, 22, 32, 39, 44, 97, 101, 103, 135, 153, 170, 174, 180, 181
Ozawa, T. 53, 231

Pain, K. 159
Palan, R. 225, 260
Papanastassiou, M. 190

Parsons, N. 108, 173
Pascoe, D. 131
Pasotti, E. 253–4
Passell, A. 80, 81
Patiblanda, M. 199
Paul, D. E. 269
Pavlínek, P. 198
Pearce, R. 190
Peck, F. W. 197
Peck, J. 19, 26, 29, 113, 150, 155, 157, 163, 164, 165, 166, 167–8, 173, 214, 274
Peck, P. 179
Pedersen, T. 199
Peet, R. 216, 265, 292
Perlin, F. 220, 231
Perlmutter, H. V. 181
Petersen, B. 199
Petri, P. A. 179
Peyroux, E. 163
Phelps, N. A. 31, 33, 39, 51, 53, 57, 58, 65, 81, 82, 98, 106, 107, 108, 109, 111, 112, 113, 121, 123, 125, 133, 168, 169, 171, 173, 189, 190, 191, 195, 196, 197, 201, 203, 206, 220, 221, 223, 229, 231, 246, 267, 270, 271, 291, 293, 295
Philo, C. 160, 161, 253
Pierre, J. 38
Pike, A. 211, 242, 247
Pla-Barber, J. 191
Pollard, J. 211
Ponte, S. 220
Poot, T. 134
Portes, A. 57
Potter, A. 53
Poulsen, L. N. S. 261
Powell, W. W. 33, 60
Power, D. 279, 280
Power, M. 246
Poynter, T. A. 184, 188, 196
Prince, R. 150
Princen, T. 204, 207, 220, 290
Pritchard, B. 202, 207
Pritchett, L. 171
Pütz, R. 163

Rabinow, P. 16
Radford, J. 121
Rainie, L. 90, 128–9
Ramamurti, R. 262
Ramírez-Pasillas, M. 279, 280
Ramsay, A. 166
Rantisi, N. 209
Rapaport, E. 167
Reade, E. 31
Reich, R. 5, 185, 202, 209, 212, 233, 240, 288
Relph, E. 72, 130, 294
Renard, M.–C. 208

Renski, H. 126
Reuschke, D. 91
Richardson, H. W. 53
Riddle, L. 245, 271
Rietveld, P. 134
Riles, A. 277, 278
Rimmer, P. J. 117
Rinallo, D. 63, 279
Rink, R. 108, 109
Risselada, A. 93–4
Robins, K. 196
Robinson, E. A. G. 52, 54
Robinson, J. 164, 239
Rodgers, D. T. 150, 153, 163
Roitman, S. 82, 108, 112
Rolander, D. 187
Romeo, A. 184
Roseman, S. 131
Rothengatter, W. 160
Roweis, S. T. 23
Roy, A. 170, 171, 172, 173
Rudolph, R. 109
Ruggie, J. G. 25, 33, 235, 257, 258, 262
Rugman, A. 189, 190
Ryecroft, R. 42

Sack, R. 122
Sack, R. D. 15, 26, 39, 287, 294–5
Sahlin-Andersson, K. 259, 262, 263
Salt, J. 141
Sánchez, R. 114
Santomero, A. M. 211
Sassen, S. 145, 210
Saunders, P. 30
Saunier, P.-Y. 56, 150, 153
Sauvant, K. P. 259, 278
Saxenian, A. 55, 271
Sayer, A. 15, 34, 288–9, 289–90
Schmidt, H. 33
Schmitz, H. 219, 220
Schrafran, A. 100
Schueth, S. 264, 268
Scott, A. 131
Scott, A. J. 23, 32, 33, 52, 74, 88, 92, 94, 104, 125, 126, 173, 222, 238–9, 242, 247, 250, 294
Scully, V. 80
Sell, S. K. 274
Selwyn, B. 61, 229, 295
Senn, L. 54
Shapiro, C. 54
Sharma, S. 34, 132, 133, 143, 145, 214, 286, 289
Sharpe, D. R. 200
Shaw, T. M. 268, 269
Sheamur, R. 127
Sheard, P. 186
Sheller, M. 15, 89

Sheppard, E. 19, 26, 35, 61, 155, 159, 160, 163, 164, 166, 173, 200, 224
Short, J. R. 77
Sidaway, J. D. 57, 223, 250
Sierralta, C. 114
Sieverts, T. 102, 103
Simmie, J. 54
Simmons, B. 261
Sinclair, T. J. 212
Singer, H. W. 57
Sklair, L. 153, 154, 198, 258
Smallbone, D. 125
Smith, A. 231
Smith, Adam 54
Smith, N. 9, 27, 32, 35, 36, 40, 158, 217
Smith-Maguire, J. 46, 47
Soja, E. 24
Sorensen, A. 106
Sornarajah, M. 25, 277, 278
Soskice, D. 186
Stilgoe, J. R. 75, 135–6
Stillwell, J. C. H. 229
Stone, D. 150
Stone, I. 196
Storper, M. 32, 33, 52
Strauss, S. 24, 56, 58, 216
Sturgeon, T. 33
Suarez-Villa, L. 52, 53
Sugden, R. 183
Sunley, P. 37
Sutcliffe, A. 20
Swyndedouw, E. 36
Szulanski, G. 193

Tachieva, G. 24
Tait, M. 162
Tang, X. 271, 272
Tarazona Vento, A. 108, 112
Taylor, G. R. 55, 75
Taylor, J. 168
Taylor, J. E. 194, 260
Taylor, P. J. 155
Teaford, J. C. 97, 107
Teece, D. J. 184
Terranova, T. 94
Tétreault, M. A. 195, 281
Tewdwr-Jones, M. 31, 39, 197
Theodore, N. 165, 167–8, 214, 274
Thomas, G. M. 25, 33, 48, 262
Thomas, K. P. 246, 269
Thompson, A. S. 22, 43–4, 180, 279–80
Thompson, G. F. 30–1, 32, 61, 190–1, 287
Thorngren, B. 86, 87, 147
Thrift, N. 3, 8, 15, 26, 27, 32, 59, 67, 142, 200, 205, 217, 232, 234, 238, 252, 287, 293
Thrift, N. J. 235, 293
Tickell, A. 179

Tiebout, C. 93
Townsend, A. R. 53
Tracey, P. 51
Trezzini, B. 269
Trudeau, D. 80
Tyler, P. 125

Urry, J. 15, 20, 21, 29, 32, 34, 42, 49, 50, 67, 87, 89, 90–1, 130, 131, 133, 162, 170, 171, 185, 210, 231, 232, 236, 238, 240, 241, 249, 252, 272, 291

Valler, D. 107, 122, 293
Van Meeteren, M. 51, 55
Van Wijk, M. 134
Vento, A. T. 160
Vernon, R. 182, 184, 187
Vicino, T. 77
Vogel, S. K. 47
Volait, M. 153
Von Luebke, C. 106
Voogd, H. 161, 170, 253

Wainwright, J. 292
Wakeham, R. 112
Waley, P. 206
Walker, R. A. 52, 53, 73, 76, 119, 157, 240, 293
Walton, W. 139
Wang, J. J. 260
Wanjiru, R. 229, 246
Ward, K. 214
Ward, S. V. 152, 153–4, 162, 163, 273
Watson, M. R. 235
Watts, D. H. 53
Watts, H. D. 220
Watts, M. 215, 216, 217
Webber, M. M. 29, 141
Webster, C. 291
Weidong, L. 108, 219
Weijland, H. 219
Weisskoff, R. 196
Wellman, B. 90, 128–9
Wells, L. T. 243
Westenholtz, A. 145
Whebell, C. F. J. 98, 99
White, P. 154, 184
Whitehand, J. W. R. 71
Whitley, R. 179
Whyte, R. E. 184, 188, 196
Whyte, W. H. 71–2, 80
Wijaya, H. 103, 220
Wildavsky, A. 31
Wilkins, M. 181, 183
Wilkinson, B. 186
Williams, G. 125
Williams, P. 132, 133

Williamson, J. 24, 107
Wilson, K. L. 57
Wint, A. 243
Winter, S. G. 193
Witt, P. 103
Wojcik, D. 204, 212
Wolff, E. 196
Wolff, G. 154, 239
Wolman, H. 38
Wood, A. 78, 107
Wood, A. N. 267
Woodward, K. 26, 35, 40
Woolcock, M. 171

Wrigley, N. 193, 207, 208
Wu, F. 85, 86, 108, 195

Yanarella, E. J. 198
Yeung, H. W. C. 10, 18, 27–8, 30, 33, 39, 60,
    61, 177, 187, 194, 200, 205, 206–7, 219, 271
Young, A. 42
Young, C. 252, 253
Young, D. 101, 102–3
Young, S. 188, 189, 196

Zizalová, P. 198
Zukin, S. 250–1